Becoming Old Stock

Becoming Old Stock

The Paradox
of German-American Identity

Russell A. Kazal

PRINCETON UNIVERSITY PRESS

PRINCETON AND OXFORD

LIBRARY OF CONGRESS CATALOGING-IN-PUBLICATION DATA
Kazal, Russell A. (Russell Andrew)
  Becoming old stock : the paradox of German-American identity / Russell A. Kazal.
    p. cm.
  Includes bibliographical references and index.
  ISBN: 0-691-05015-5 (acid-free paper)
    1. German Americans—Pennsylvania—Philadelphia—Ethnic identity. 2. German
  Americans—Cultural assimilation—Pennsylvania—Philadelphia. 3. Whites—Race
  identity—Pennsylvania—Philadelphia. 4. German Americans—Pennsylvania—
  Philadelphia—Social conditions—20th century. 5. Immigrants—Pennsylvania—
  Philadelphia—Social conditions—20th century. 6. Social classes—Pennsylvania—
  Philadelphia—History—20th century. 7. Philadelphia (Pa.)—Race relations.
  8. Philadelphia (Pa.)—Social conditions—20th century. 9. Ethnicity—United
  States—Case studies. 10. Pluralism (Social sciences)—United States—Case studies.
  I. Title.
  F158.9.G3K39 2004
  305.83′1074811—dc21   2003056331

British Library Cataloging-in-Publication Data is available

This book has been composed in Sabon

Printed on acid-free paper. ∞

www.pupress.princeton.edu

Printed in the United States of America

1 3 5 7 9 10 8 6 4 2

FOR MY PARENTS AND FOR DEB, EMMA, AND ALICE

Contents

Part Four: *Reshaping Identities in the 1920s*

Illustrations

Tables

Acknowledgments

HISTORIANS, so the commonplace goes, spend a lot of time alone engaged in a collective enterprise. Looking back over the long journey that brought me to this page, I am struck by how a line of work so solitary can be so utterly dependent on the help, advice, and support of others. It is a pleasure, at last, to be able to thank the friends, family, and fellow scholars who made this book possible.

This work reflects, I hope, some of what I have learned about history over the years from a series of remarkable teachers: William Davies, Richard Challener, James McPherson, John Murrin, Natalie Davis, David Abraham, Michael Zuckerman, Richard Dunn, Drew Faust, Tom Childers, Marc Trachtenberg, and Wayne Bodle, among others. Particular thanks go to three scholars who guided this project through its first incarnation as a dissertation at the University of Pennsylvania. Michael Katz, my dissertation advisor, set high standards and then followed through with a level of support that can only be described as phenomenal. He gave generously of his time and his considerable experience and insight as a social historian and was the project's constant advocate. The example he sets as a historian is one I can only hope to follow. Ewa Morawska, perhaps my toughest critic, pushed me to think more systematically about assimilation and the role of gender in that process. Gary Gerstle asked the question that led me to this topic, and his influence shows throughout the study. This book began, in a sense, in his spring 1993 seminar at Penn on American nationalism; that the project has made it this far owes much to Gary's boundless generosity as a critic and advocate.

When it became apparent that the project would involve a substantial quantitative component, I found an indispensable guide in Mark Stern. Mark became my main source of advice for working out the design of the neighborhood census samples, and he then arranged to have one of them serve as the coding project for his class in statistical analysis for historians. Michael Guilfoyle served as my statistical consultant; he himself drew the samples, using a computer program, and he also devised and executed the resampling program used to judge the reliability of the study's P* results. A number of other scholars generously offered advice on the sample design and analysis as it evolved, including Olivier Zunz, Michael White, Samuel Preston, Douglas Massey, Herbert Smith, Ram Cnaan, Steven Ruggles, and William Yancey. My thanks go as well to the staff members at the Free Library of Philadelphia's Map Collection and the Geography and Map Division of the Library of Congress, which hold the fire insurance atlases used to prepare the neighborhood sampling frames. My fellow graduate students in Mark's statistics class uncomplainingly coded much of the 1900 Girard Avenue district sample. Coders I subsequently hired to complete the remaining samples included Allison Miller, Katherine Minarik, Erika Piola, Norm Roessler, Rachel Rothman, Kevin Schmiesing, Elizabeth Tung, and Rachel Volkman; I thank them all for carrying out what is without question a tedious job. Walter Licht greatly aided my analysis of the 1900 samples by making available lists of occupational titles organized by class level that he had used in his own work on turn-of-the-century Philadelphia. Christopher Brest worked as my cartographer, transforming a mass of data into elegant maps of the city and the neighborhoods.

Perhaps the most rewarding aspect of my research was exploring the rich archival holdings available on Germans in Philadelphia. I have enjoyed the use of Penn's Van Pelt Library, Krauth Memorial Library of the Lutheran Theological Seminary at Philadelphia, and Ryan Memorial Library of St. Charles Borromeo Seminary in Wynnewood, Pennsylvania, and I thank their staffs for their assistance. Gail Farr, Eric Pumroy, and other staff members at the Balch Institute for Ethnic Studies introduced me to that archive's extensive collection of German associational records. (These and other Balch holdings have since been transferred to the Historical Society of Pennsylvania, as part of the Balch Institute's merger with that organization). The Joseph Horner Memorial Library at the German Society of Pennsylvania holds a remarkable collection of German-American publications, much of which was undergoing conservation during the project's research phase. My thanks go to Elliott Shore and the staff members engaged in this conservation effort for their assistance in making use of the library's available materials, especially its microfilmed holdings of the *Philadelphia Tageblatt*. John Peterson at the Lutheran Archives Center at Philadelphia aided me in locating German Lutheran church records, while Shawn Weldon and Joseph Casino guided me through the extensive collections of the Philadelphia Archdiocesan Historical Research Center. I especially wish to thank the Archdiocese of Philadelphia for granting me permission to examine the center's holdings of parish annual reports and baptismal and marriage records, as well as the Dennis Cardinal Dougherty Papers. The priests of St. Peter the Apostle Church likewise allowed me access to that parish's marriage and baptismal registers.

The archivists at the Mid Atlantic Regional Office of the National Archives in Philadelphia, especially Kellee Blake and Robert Plowman, first assisted me as I photocopied manuscript census returns for my census samples and then proved enormously helpful in exploring records relating to the experience of German Philadelphians during the First World War. Margaret Jerrido and the staff of Temple University's Urban Archives aided me in reviewing its rich holdings of associational records, while Barbara Silberman and the librarians of the Germantown Historical Society Library and Archives proved to me that Germantown is Philadelphia's best-documented neighborhood. I thank as well the staffs of the Free Library's Government Publications Department, the Historical Society of Pennsylvania, the National Archives Building in Washington, and the New York Public Library. Finally, I want to express my appreciation to those Philadelphians of German background who shared with me their recollections of growing up in the city. They may or may not agree with my conclusions, but this book would not have been possible without them.

This research and the writing that followed were made possible by the generous financial support of a number of organizations. I was very fortunate to receive a five-year Benjamin Franklin Graduate Fellowship from the University of Pennsylvania—funded in part by the Andrew W. Mellon Foundation—which supported me through the first two years of dissertation research. The Pew Program in Religion and American History at Yale University funded an additional year of work through a dissertation fellowship, while other research and writing was aided by a dissertation scholarship from the German Historical Institute in Washington, a George E. Pozzetta Dissertation Research Award from the Immigration and Ethnic History Society, grants from the Annenberg Fund of Penn's History Department, and Faculty Development Awards from Arcadia University. The Center for Ethnicities, Communities, and Social Policy at Bryn Mawr College awarded me a Rockefeller Foundation Resident Fellowship in the Humanities for a new research project and then graciously let me spend some time on final manuscript preparation for this book. Center co-director Rick Davis lent his technical expertise by reproducing the photograph of Schützen Park.

As the manuscript took shape, particular chapters benefited greatly from the perceptive comments of a bevy of readers: Gabi Arredondo, Stephanie Camp, Deborah Gesensway, Jon Gjerde, David Goldston, Maria Hoehn, Matt Jacobson, Rebecca Kobrin, and David Roediger. Tom Sugrue and two anonymous readers for Princeton University Press waded through drafts of the entire work, and their incisive suggestions helped make the final version shorter and stronger. My thanks as well to the audiences and commentators who gave parts of the work a careful and critical hearing at meetings of the American Historical Association, the American Studies Association, the Social Science History Association, and the Pennsylvania Historical Association. I am likewise grateful to participants in lively discussions at the Balch Institute's Balch Faculty Associates Forum and the 1997 Pew Fellows Conference at Yale University. The German Historical Institute provided not one but three very enjoyable and illuminating venues for this work in progress, at its seminar for Dissertation Scholars in Washington and at conferences it sponsored in conjunction with Texas A&M University in College Station, Texas, and with the American Studies Institute of the University of Leipzig in Leipzig, Germany. A special thanks to Andreas Daum and Christof Mauch at the GHI, and to Vera Lind, Hartmut Keil, and the other participants in Leipzig for sharing their knowledge about matters of race and color in modern Germany. At Arcadia University, Geoff Haywood, Norah Peters-Davis, Jeff Shultz, Jonathan Church, Warren Haffar, Ana Maria Garcia, Michael Berger, and my other colleagues buoyed me with their support and enthusiasm. At Princeton University Press, Brigitta van Rheinberg provided a keen critical eye and excellent editorial guidance combined with extraordinary patience. Others at Princeton helped shepherd the final manuscript into and through production, including production editor Gail Schmitt, copy editor Molan Goldstein, and editorial assistant Alison Kalett. Jim O'Brien prepared the index.

Sections of the book first reached publication in other forms. I worked through my initial thoughts on assimilation in "Revisiting Assimilation: The Rise, Fall, and Reappraisal of a Concept in American Ethnic History," *American Historical Review* 100 (April 1995): 437–471. To some extent, the book grew out of this essay, the argument of which forms part of the introduction; I thank the *Review* for granting permission for the essay's use. Parts of chapters 1 and 5 appeared as "Irish 'Race' and German 'Nationality': Catholic Languages of Ethnic Difference in Turn-of-the-Century Philadelphia," copyright 1999 from *Race and the Production of Modern American Nationalism,* edited by Reynolds J. Scott-Childress. This material is reproduced by permission of Routledge, Inc., part of the Taylor & Francis Group.

I owe a different kind of debt to friends, within and outside the academy, who kept this project from becoming more all-consuming than it was: Ed Baptist, Nell Booth, Beth Clement, Frank Gavin, David Goldston, Stan and Claudia Green (along with Harrison, Devin, and Sophie Green), Maria Hoehn, Hannah Joyner, Mike Kahan, Ann Little, Max Page, Andrew and Rebecca Reumann-Moore (and their daughters, Kyra and Maia), Liam Riordan, Alan Sipress, Julie Sneeringer, and fellow former reporter Bob Zecker.

Lastly, I never could have gotten through the nine years it took to produce this book without the support and love of my two families, the Kazals and the Gesensways. The Kazal family has no German background whatsoever. For a long time, this fact kept me from realizing that I was, to some extent, using the project to reflect on the experience of my father, Henry Lawrence Kazal, a second-generation Polish immigrant, and my mother, Eleanore Anderson Kazal, whose ancestors came from Sweden, Denmark, and Ireland. As children in the 1920s and 1930s, they, like the second-generation Germans studied here, felt the impact of conformist nationalism. To be "American" was both a virtue and a goal in my Polish grandmother's household, and my father and his siblings inherited that sense. I and my brother and three sisters felt it in our family growing up; in some ways, I have been wrestling ever since with the question of what, exactly, being "American" means. My parents may reach different answers than the ones I have arrived at, but they have everything to do with my pursuit of the question, and in that sense this book is particularly for them and for my siblings.

I could not work for long on or in Philadelphia without getting tangled up with my Gesensway in-laws, who have their own extended history in the Quaker City. My mother-in-law, Eleanor Gesensway, took an active interest in this project from the start. Not a few of the books cited here came from her shelves, and her wide circle of contacts in the city led me to a number of key sources. Ellie demanded frequent progress reports, and she continued to do so even after our lives were engulfed by two personal tragedies that made this study assuredly the least important thing in them. This book, then, is for her, too. Like all good Gesensways, my late father-in-law, Daniel, wanted to see me finish this project. It is one of my regrets that I was not able to complete it before his untimely death. I do so now with his memory and that of my late sister-in-law, Ellen Gesensway, in mind.

Emma Gesensway Kazal entered this world a month after I turned in my dissertation. This means she and her younger sister, Alice, have waited their entire lives for a positive answer to Emma's not-infrequent question, "Have you finished your book, Dad?" To be able to answer yes now is one small gift I can give in return for the many extraordinary ones they have given me. Deborah Gesensway feels like she has been waiting her whole life, too. That I finished my book at all, however, is a tribute to Deb's determination, her considerable skills as an editor and as a historian, and the emotional and financial backing she has given me over the past nine years. Her affection and support have meant more to me than I can say. As I dedicate this book to my parents in honor of their past, so I dedicate it to her, Emma, and Alice, with love, in anticipation of our future.

Becoming Old Stock

Introduction

MORE Americans trace their ancestry to Germany than to any other country, according to the federal census.[1] Arguably, by this measure, people of German descent form the nation's largest ethnic group. Yet that fact could easily elude the casual observer of American life. Today, comparatively few signs remain of the once formidable political clout, organizational life, and ethnic consciousness of German Americans. Over the twentieth century, the ethnicity that went by that label underwent what the historian Kathleen Conzen calls a "thorough submergence."[2]

This ethnic eclipse is reflected publicly in the calendar of American holidays and, more privately, in survey research. There is no nationally recognized tribute to German ethnicity to compete with St. Patrick's Day or Columbus Day. On a regional level, the Midwest, which drew the greatest concentrations of nineteenth-century German immigrants, does seem more willing to display its German ethnic roots, as a visitor to Cincinnati's annual Downtown Oktoberfest might note. Yet in the mid-Atlantic—the focus of eighteenth-century German settlement and a close second to the Midwest as a destination for nineteenth-century German newcomers—German ethnicity has a remarkably low profile. In the popular imagination, the descendants of eighteenth-century Rhenish immigrants who populated the Pennsylvania backcountry are known as "Pennsylvania Dutch," a usage that evokes the Netherlands. The region's cities yield barely a sign that they once hosted some of the nation's largest populations of German immigrants.

Such ethnic quiescence is brought into sharp focus when one compares it with local manifestations of Irish identity. The bulk of Irish and German immigrants to the United States arrived at roughly the same time, in waves running from the 1830s to the 1890s. Survey research carried out in the mid-1980s in the Albany, New York, area, however, found that while Irish and German ancestries were each claimed by roughly one-third of native-born whites, only some 20 percent of respondents saw *themselves* as "German," compared with 31 percent who asserted an "Irish" identity.[3] One can see a similar contrast in how Philadelphia celebrates these two ethnicities. The city's annual Steuben Day parade in September draws scattered onlookers to the Benjamin Franklin Parkway, but a visitor strolling through other downtown sections might never know that the day was dedicated to a German immigrant who became a Revolutionary

War hero. On March 17, that same pedestrian would find it impossible to miss the fact that Philadelphia was honoring St. Patrick. At the most prosaic level, she or he could not walk down Center City's Walnut Street for more than two blocks without having to maneuver around a line of people snaking out of a bar with green plastic hats on their heads.

The eclipse of German-American identity today is all the more startling, given its condition at the beginning of the twentieth century. Then, German Americans were perhaps the best-organized, most visible, and most respected group of newcomers in the United States. Germans, whose migration to America peaked in the 1880s, made up the largest single nationality among the foreign-born during the 1910s, greater in number than the Poles, Italians, and other southern and eastern Europeans of the "new immigration." The National German-American Alliance, a federation of ethnic associations, laid claim by 1914 to more than two million members. Before the First World War, the Germans were widely esteemed as "one of the most assimilable and reputable of immigrant groups"; a group of professional people surveyed in 1908 ranked German immigrants ahead of English ones and, in some respects, above native-born whites.[4]

German Americans, in other words, present an unsettling paradox. If ours is an age of multiculturalism—as many Americans like to think— then how is it that the nation's largest ethnic group has gone missing from the national scene and in regions like the mid-Atlantic? How do scholars square this awkward fact with the depictions of an enduring American pluralism that have dominated the historical literature on immigration and ethnicity since the 1960s? The German-American case thus forces us to confront the much larger question of assimilation.

Assimilation as a topic was largely neglected by historians in the 1970s and early 1980s, as I have argued elsewhere,[5] and it remains controversial. By the early 1960s, notions of assimilation and Americanization cast ethnic Americans as remaking themselves to fit an Anglo-American core culture. Such ideas did not survive the decade; their underlying assumptions were torpedoed by cultural and political upheaval. The Vietnam War discredited "the Anglo-American establishment," antiwar and civil rights protests cast doubt on the virtue of a uniform American national culture, and a resurgent black separatism fueled more general affirmations of pluralism and group identities. For many immigration historians, mindful of the very real, coercive side of early twentieth-century Americanization efforts, assimilation and Americanization became "myths" to be "vanquished."[6] Those scholars instead stressed ethnic persistence within a pluralistic society.

Historians in the 1970s and 1980s produced many intriguing and sophisticated studies of particular ethnic and racial groups. Yet rejecting assimilation hindered, rather than aided, their understanding of pluralism, for those two phenomena are deeply intertwined.[7] The study of pluralism requires examining not just ethnic groups but also the relations among them, and those relations can have an assimilative effect in drawing groups or their members closer to one another. Postwar theorists such as Will Herberg and Milton Gordon understood this; they depicted many European Americans as submerging their specific ethnic identities in the broader religious ones of Protestant, Catholic, and Jew.[8]

Since the early 1980s, an interest in pluralism has helped lead a number of historians toward a cautious reexamination of assimilation. They have revisited the topic without resurrecting the idea of an Anglo-American core. Some immigration historians now view assimilation, in essence, as one of a number of processes operating historically *within* a pluralist order that itself has evolved.[9] They and other historians have come to understand that process as one by which European ethnics of different national backgrounds found common ground with one another or with longer-settled Americans. These scholars have described assimilation along class lines, via an industrial unionism that united an ethnically split working class in the 1930s; along lines of race, with European immigrants learning to adopt a common "white" racial identity; and, relatedly, through an emerging mass culture and a brand of American nationalism that allowed those newcomers to join an "imagined community" of specifically white Americans.[10]

These works have shaped my own understanding of assimilation and ethnic identity. I use "assimilation" to refer to processes that result in greater homogeneity within a society. Such processes may operate at different levels: among individuals, between groups, or between groups and a dominant group in the society. They may operate within different arenas, with individuals or groups drawn together in terms of culture or intermarriage or shared institutions or shared elements of identity, such as "whiteness." And they may operate to varying degrees within and across different arenas. In the immigrant context, I find it most useful to see assimilation as referring to processes that generate homogeneity beyond the level of the ethnic group.[11] "Ethnic group" itself refers, in Milton Gordon's sense, to a group with "a shared feeling of peoplehood" tied to a specific Old World ancestry.[12] "Identity" in its most basic sense refers to an individual's sense of self,[13] a construct to some extent both volitional and ascribed. In the words of one historian, identity "concerns how individuals understand their place in the social world as well as how others view them." Key to the concept is the insight that individuals hold multiple identities in the form of socially recognized categories: a particular person can see herself at one and the same time as, for example, a middle-class professional, a woman, a white, an American, and someone of German descent.[14] Such an individual may partake of various collective or group identities, each of which, on its own terms, seems singular. Collective identity "tends to appear homogeneous and based on clear boundaries for the sake of expression beyond the group."[15] But for the individual, changes in how one views oneself can be accomplished by emphasizing one collective identity over another, by introducing new elements to the mix of identities one holds, or by holding a collective identity that itself is changing internally. The different identities of any one person ebb, flow, and interact in complex ways that can result, over time, in a significantly different self-image.

Like other historians revisiting assimilation, I seek to understand its operation within particular historical contexts and its long-term social and political consequences. Here, the German-American experience cries out for study. As John Higham noted, that experience represents the most "spectacular case of collective assimilation" in the last century.[16] Historians of German America certainly never neglected assimilation, and they have long offered explanations for why the group's ethnic profile fell so dramatically. The most obvious relates to the contingencies of twentieth-century history. That century saw the United States fight two world wars against Germany and witnessed the genocide perpetrated by the Third Reich; it therefore left Americans with few incentives to identify with a German ancestry. Even before those events, institutional German America—which encompassed everything from secular gymnastic and singing societies to German Lutheran congregations and German Catholic national parishes—was unraveling. Historians such as John Hawgood once pointed to the intense nativist backlash that accompanied American intervention in World War I as the key to the destruction of this ethnic world.[17] More recently, Guido Andre Dobbert, James Bergquist, and other scholars have portrayed German ethnic institutions as suffering a long-term decline beginning in the 1890s.[18]

Yet, while we know much about the erosion of German America, we know little of the fate of those who left it. If many Americans of German background were leaving German ethnic circles at the beginning of the twentieth century, where did they then go? What kind of Americans did most German Americans become once their ethnic identity was so strikingly submerged? Did they reshape their multiple identities in ways that reflect or that go beyond the findings of assimilation's reappraisers? Specifically, what role did class, gender, religion, mass culture, nation, and race play in their redefinitions? Did German Americans, for example, find refuge in the "monolithic whiteness" that Matthew Jacobson sees as flattening "racial" distinctions among European immigrants after the 1920s? Did they take to the powerful and often exclusive American nationalism that Gary Gerstle depicts as dominating much of American life between the First World War and the 1960s?[19] Or did they find other routes away from German America?

Such questions lead to broader ones. German Americans, who belonged to so large an ethnic group, could not redefine themselves without affecting others. What impact did their choices have on other groups and on American pluralism as such? How, in light of the German case, has that pluralist order itself been reshaped over the twentieth century? Pluralism, in turn, has had a long and complicated relationship with American nationalism, for diversity raises the question of how to reconcile *pluribus* and *unum,* the many and the one—the group constituents of society and the aspiration to unity inherent in the idea of the nation. How, then, has American nationalism changed in relation to a changing pluralism? Similarly, race has long operated as an organizing principle of American pluralism and, to some extent, American nationalism. But if European ethnics, including Germans, in part assimilated to a white racial identity, what has the nature of that whiteness been, and how has it changed over time?

When looking for answers to large questions, it sometimes helps to dig in small places. I address the issues of assimilation, pluralism, nationalism, and race that the German-American paradox raises by reconstructing the fate of that group in one such place: Philadelphia from the turn of the twentieth century to the 1930s. This work is, in great measure, a study of identity change—of how some Germans moved away from ethnic affiliations and toward new formulations of multiple identity. I feel that such changes are best traced within the tight geographic focus of a case study. That focus allows one to connect shifts in identity to specific social and demographic changes—local as well as regional and national—including changing relations with non-Germans, which form an essential part of this story.

At first glance, the choice of Philadelphia might seem questionable. That city could appear less representative of the German-American experience than the heavily German cities of the Midwest, which have formed the focus of much historical writing on German America. Yet Philadelphia offers key advantages for a study of assimilation. It allows one to examine that process in a region, the mid-Atlantic, that took the waning of German-American identity further than appears to be the case in the urban Midwest and that nonetheless had a substantial urban German population. Philadelphia itself is a case in point. Only 5.5 percent of its inhabitants were German immigrants in 1900, but its rank as the nation's third-largest city meant that it had more German-born residents than Buffalo, Cincinnati, Milwaukee, or St. Louis.[20] Philadelphia, moreover, held a strategically important position within German America. The National German-American Alliance, which rallied German associations across the country to resist assimilation, was founded in the city in 1901 under the leadership of a coterie of local middle-class activists. One of them, Charles J. Hexamer, served as the organization's president and guiding spirit until 1917. Finally, while German Philadelphia's story differs in certain respects from the German experience in Midwestern cities, there are, nonetheless, striking and important parallels between them, as we shall see.

This book argues that in the first third of the twentieth century, many German Philadelphians, especially the children of immigrants, retreated from a "German-American" identity and instead crafted new multiple identities keyed to particular understandings of race, religion, mass culture, and the American nation. Today's marked submergence of German-American ethnicity owes a great deal to the anti-German backlash of the First World War, yet that was just one of several developments that came together during the 1910s and 1920s to reshape German Philadelphians' sense of self. Those developments also included the rise of a narrower, more conformist American nationalism that discredited older, pluralist views of the nation; a related tide of racialized nativism; and the first Great Migration of black Southerners to the North, which transformed Philadelphia's racial geography during and after the war.

The convergence of these events both pushed and enticed many Philadelphians of German background to rework their identities, but their response was hardly uniform. Rather, it varied along lines of class, religion, and, to some extent, gender that had long divided German Philadelphia. Some middle-class and Lutheran Germans embraced an "American" identity cast in opposition to Italians, Poles, and other southern and eastern European "new immigrants." At its extreme, this stance employed the language of racialized nativism to recast German Philadelphians as "old-stock" or "Nordic" Americans. They were deemed superior to new immigrants because their racial "stock" was better and because it was older—German settlers having brought it to the mid-Atlantic before the Revolution. In contrast, many working-class and Catholic Philadelphians of German background had by the 1920s begun to mix, in their associations and parishes, with Irish and new immigrant neighbors. These workers and Catholics increasingly saw themselves as sharing a common white identity with such neighbors, an identity that gained in salience with the increased presence of African Americans near working-class European-American neighborhoods. Here, the interwar period saw a foretaste of a type that would emerge, decades later, as the "white ethnic." Women as well as men partook of such identities, but the different social contexts and expectations women faced meant they could understand those identities somewhat differently. Moreover, German women took particular advantage of a separate development that predated the war: the rise of a mass consumer culture, which offered women new kinds of identity grounded in their emerging role as consumers.

Like all historical arguments, this one has limitations. First, it describes a number of important ways in which Philadelphians of German descent distanced themselves from their ethnic origins; it does not, however, attempt to account for all such redefinitions or for every multiple identity cast anew in the 1920s and 1930s. There were many paths out of German America, and this study claims only to have identified some of the more significant routes. Indeed, some Philadelphians of German background never left: a scattering of German voluntary associations, including some examined in this study, still exist today. Second, the book traces the fate of German Philadelphia in part by following four of its most important subcultures: those created by middle-class residents active in secular ethnic associations, working-class socialists, Catholics, and Lutherans. Missing from this list, of course, is the city's German Jewish community. This latter subculture, though smaller than the other four, played a not insignificant role in German Philadelphia; leaving it unaddressed creates a gap in the narrative. However, to explore the German Jewish experience in any depth would have entailed engagement with a massive historiography and an additional set of historical problems. In the interests of finishing this study—and, not incidentally, containing the size of an already lengthy manuscript—I felt it best to let that omission stand.

This story of how German-American identity waned in the early twentieth century and what some German Americans found to replace it, is told in four parts. Part 1 examines German Philadelphia at the turn of the twentieth century. That entity, like German America in general, was remarkably diverse. It encompassed, as chapter 1 describes, a plethora of voluntary associations, or *Vereine,* that reflected the different worlds of middle-class secular club members, working-class socialists, German Catholics, and German Lutherans, to name only the largest such groupings. Yet these subcultures were held together, to some extent, by a common sense of "Germanness," expressed in the use of the German language and mobilized when values common to the group, such as the moderate social consumption of alcohol, came under attack by non-Germans. Chapter 2 focuses on two turn-of-the-century neighborhoods to examine the degree to which assimilatory processes already had made inroads into German Philadelphia: the heavily German, heavily working-class Girard Avenue district; and Germantown, a suburb that was more middle-class and, ironically, far less German. This chapter uses samples drawn from the 1900 federal manuscript census to show that first- and second-generation German immigrants experienced their streets in the Girard Avenue district as a majority, while Germantown's German-stock minority had as their immediate neighbors a mix of residents of northwest European background. These demographic realities were reflected in local institutions, from the German Lutheran and Catholic churches of Girard Avenue's German neighborhood to such Germantown fixtures as the Business Men's

Association, whose founders included first- and second-generation English, German, and Irish immigrants, as well as descendants of colonial settlers. Germantown here provided a hint of the future. The Business Men's Association did not evince a common, northwest European consciousness, but its composition indicated the potential for such an identity.

Philadelphia's German associational world—what German residents referred to as the city's *Vereinswesen*—began a slow decline in the 1890s, as German immigration passed its peak and the children of immigrants turned away from the affiliations of their parents. Part 2 addresses this crisis of assimilation in the years before World War I and the steps some middle-class activists took to stem it. Chapter 3 examines the crisis itself. It was a curiously uneven, indeed, a gendered phenomenon. While many male associations lost members, female organizations grew, as women carved out a larger place for themselves in the city's German-American public sphere.

Still, the membership losses raised the question of where the second generation had gone. The next two chapters consider some of the alternative identities available to such children of German Philadelphia— among them, emerging forms of collective identity. As chapter 4 describes, these included a range of new affiliations grounded in the new mass culture, which itself had an ambiguous impact on German ethnic identity. Because mass commercial culture drew heavily on German-American models of sociability, it could be appropriated to serve the *Vereinswesen* as a source of renewal, as one German association discovered. Nonetheless, many working-class as well as middle-class Germans seem to have succumbed to the lure of commercialized leisure and consumer culture in ways that tended to pull them away from traditional *Verein* pursuits and to de-emphasize the ethnic element of their multiple identities. Consumer culture in particular fostered alternative identities that were especially open to women.

The years before 1914, however, also saw the emergence of new kinds of collective identity that fused racial and national feeling, as chapter 5 argues. German Philadelphians had long known that they were white, although that identification was less salient at the turn of the century than it would later become. Now, within Anglo-America and under the impress of an increasingly racialized nativism, there arose terms denoting a common northwest European consciousness, such as "American race stock" and "old stock." These represented invitations to join a common northwest European group defined as "American" in opposition to southern and eastern European immigrants—although German Philadelphians would, for the time being, leave such invitations unanswered.

In the meantime, activists from Philadelphia's leading middle-class associations moved to shore up the *Vereinswesen* by creating a nationwide organization of German associations—the National German-American Alliance. As chapter 6 describes, this revitalization effort attempted to make German America more attractive to second-generation immigrants by writing it into the center of American history through, among other things, a series of monuments to Germans involved in the nation's founding. The chapter examines the alliance's campaign to raise one such monument in the center of Germantown in commemoration of the neighborhood's colonial German settlers. The effort's high point came in 1908, when the alliance sponsored a massive cornerstone-laying ceremony, timed to coincide with the 225th anniversary of Germantown's founding. The event emphasized the long history of German settlement and thereby inadvertently underscored German Americans' qualifications for a northwest European group seen as superior due not only to its racial characteristics but also to its long residence in America. Yet the commemoration reflected as well the alliance's inability to foster a German-American identity across class and religious divides that was more than episodic. While many unionized workers took part in the event, their participation two years later in a citywide general strike demonstrated their willingness to put class above ethnic solidarity to the extent of cooperating with new immigrant workers.

The slow hemorrhaging of membership in the *Vereinswesen*, while it suggested a degree of ethnic flight, did not entail the massive submergence of German-American ethnicity nor an attendant large-scale recasting of identities. The event that precipitated those developments was, rather, the First World War—the subject of part 3. Initially, the European war actually heightened the ethnic consciousness and unity of those Philadelphians of German background who remained within the *Vereinswesen*, as chapter 7 describes. Many middle-class activists, socialist workers, Catholics, and Lutherans rallied to Germany's defense between 1914 and 1916. Yet the neutrality period also saw a reaction among Anglo-Americans and other non-Germans against such ethnic activism, a backlash expressed in attacks on the national loyalty of "hyphenated Americans" and, eventually, demands that they be "100 percent American." Chapter 8 examines how, with America's entry into the war, this "antihyphen" movement metamorphosed into an anti-German panic. What began as a suspicion of German Philadelphians as potential spies and saboteurs mushroomed into a general assault on German ethnic expression itself and on the very legitimacy of views of the nation—like the National Alliance's—that allowed for a degree of ethnic separatism and, hence, cultural pluralism. Fed in part by the federal government's effort to mobilize support for the war, the panic led to the destruction of the National Alliance, the ending of German instruction in the city's public schools, and the hounding of ordinary German Philadelphians, at times by mobs. As a result, the public expression of German ethnicity became virtually impossible during and immediately after the war and remained problematic thereafter.

The fall of public Germanness had consequences that extended into the 1920s and beyond, consequences explored in part 4. While some German organizations took tentative steps to reassert a public presence, they never again acted with the aggressiveness of the prewar years. Those ethnic institutions that survived the panic manifested a strikingly subdued ethnicity in the 1920s. Chapter 9 examines how the postwar *Vereinswesen* not only remained reticent but also changed internally. German institutions continued to shrink, in part because mass culture competed ever more strongly for the attention of German Philadelphians, generating such new collective identities as radio fan. Many of those institutions, moreover, acquired more and more non-German members during and after the 1920s. Some working-class *Vereine* took on the character of ethnically mixed neighborhood social centers, while German Catholic parishes increasingly took in Irish, Slavic, and Italian members. Chapter 10 revisits the Girard Avenue district and Germantown to illustrate how these shifts occurred within a context of ethnic and racial succession. By the 1920s, the working-class area around Girard Avenue had become less German and less Protestant as southern and eastern European immigrants streamed in. The district's dwindling number of German-stock residents increasingly found themselves mixing with these new neighbors in their streets and Catholic parishes. Germantown's first- and second-generation German immigrants were ensconced more than ever in northwest European worlds, but their neighborhood had become home to Italian and African-American "colonies."

In the altered climate of the 1920s, many Philadelphians who were descended from nineteenth-century German immigrants reached for new definitions of self that downplayed their German ethnic heritage. These new identities were shaped by a number of forces, including mass culture, the more conformist, "100 percent American" nationalism ushered in by the war, the war-related migration of thousands of black Southerners to Philadelphia, and the rise of a racialized nativism that pitted allegedly superior northwest Europeans against southern and eastern European newcomers. The children and grandchildren of immigrants growing up during the decade strongly felt the impulse to define themselves as American first and as German only secondarily, if at all. But the meaning of such "American" affiliations tended to vary along the historic divisions of German Philadelphia. Chapter 11 explores how some middle-class and Lutheran Philadelphians of German descent shaped their American identities in opposition to Italians, Poles, and other southern and eastern European immigrants. At one end of this range stood second-generation German immigrants who belonged to nativist groups intent on excluding new immigrants or who joined Americanization efforts aimed at reforming them. Groups such as the Americanization Committee of Germantown drew on the language of racialized nativism to cast their members—including those of German background—as northwest Europeans who shared the common racial "stock" of "our forefathers." This stock was valued in part because it was old; here, German Philadelphians qualified for admission because German settlement had a history that stretched back to colonial Pennsylvania. Lutherans of German descent who proselytized Italians for the Inner Mission Society eschewed such racialist language but nevertheless betrayed a sense of being American in contrast to their Italian clients.

Working-class and Catholic Philadelphians of German descent were less likely to voice American identities of this kind, in part because they were mixing with Irish and new immigrant neighbors in their associations and parishes. Rather, as chapter 12 describes, these workers and Catholics increasingly felt they had whiteness in common with those neighbors, a sense encouraged by the appearance of African Americans at the edges of their neighborhoods. Racial succession in one German Catholic parish, St. Ignatius', for example, helped foster a sense among its members that they counted less as Germans than as "white Catholics." The rising salience of white identity for such German Philadelphians foreshadowed the emergence, years later, of another working-class patriotic, often Catholic figure—the "white ethnic."

The book's conclusion briefly sketches German Philadelphia's history after the early 1930s and considers the larger significance of its story. That story was, in some ways, a singular tale. Compared to the urban Midwest, Philadelphia and other mid-Atlantic cities had smaller concentrations of German immigrants; that fact likely contributed to a German ethnic profile lower than one would find, even today, in Cincinnati or Milwaukee. The German-American experience itself, moreover, was somewhat idiosyncratic. No other large immigrant group in the twentieth century saw its country of origin twice go to war with the United States; none, correspondingly, faced such sustained pressure to forgo its ethnic identity for an "American" one; and none appeared to mute its ethnic identity to so great an extent.

Nevertheless, as the conclusion relates, the experience of German Philadelphia speaks to larger developments within and beyond German America. First, it underscores the importance of space, especially regional differences, in shaping assimilation. The historically higher concentrations of Germans in Midwestern cities have made public displays of German ethnicity more possible there than in the mid-Atlantic in the years since the First World War, even though many German Midwesterners, too, left the ethnic fold. The mid-Atlantic, on the other hand, had a history of colonial German immigration that made it particularly fertile ground for old-stock identities open to later German arrivals and their children. Midwestern Germans also could claim such identities, but since their region lacked a German presence in the colonial period, they may have given their "American" self-definitions a somewhat different spin. The process of assimilation, in other words, can vary significantly over space; those studying it should be attuned to its local and regional inflections.

Second, the German-American case presents an extreme example of assimilatory pressures that other ethnic groups also faced, if to a lesser extent. The rise of a mass commercial and consumer culture challenged the autonomy of nearly every ethnic community in this period, and women of many ethnic backgrounds, not just Germans, embraced the specifically female, consumption-oriented identities that culture fostered. If German workers and Catholics in interwar Philadelphia reshaped their identities in ways that anticipated the "white ethnic," so, too, did their counterparts in Chicago and Detroit during the 1940s. In Chicago, for example, Germans participated with Irish and eastern European residents in heavily Catholic and working-class mobs that fought to keep blacks from moving into their "white" neighborhoods and parishes. Chicago's working-class and Catholic Germans thereby helped to create a common ground that necessarily influenced the identities of their Irish and new immigrant collaborators. Similarly, when middle-class Germans took refuge in a racial nationalism, they cooperated with other northwest Europeans and echoed the behavior of such other "Nordic" groups as Norwegian Americans. German involvement in nativist groups, moreover, reinforced the message that old-stock or Nordic Americans made the best kind of Americans—a message with which members of every ethnic group, "old immigrant" or not, had to grapple.

Finally, and relatedly, the German-American ordeal during and after World War I played a crucial role in shaping both twentieth-century American pluralism and American nationalism. The constricted "100 percent American" nationalism that arose in the 1910s represented an all-out attack on ethnic pluralism—both the idea of it and the de facto pluralist order that had emerged in the United States before the First World War. That conformist nationalism, with its demand for undivided national loyalty and its corresponding denigration of "hyphenated" ethnic allegiances, would last, in one form or another, until the 1960s. Its long reign, in a very real sense, was made possible by the forcible submergence of German-American identity in the 1910s. For German America, and the National Alliance in particular, was the strongest bearer of what today would be called multicultural concepts of the nation—including the notion that an evolving United States was continually shaped by the contributions of its different ethnic groups. Advocates of conformist nationalism could not succeed unless they first disabled such rival, pluralist visions of the nation. The war allowed them to do so; among other things, it enabled them to destroy the alliance.

At the same time, the pluralist order of today's United States bears traces of the effort German Americans made to recast their identities. That order is fundamentally structured by lines of color, but the European Americans who go by the common designation of "white" retain a measure of internal ethnic differentiation—despite depictions, like Jacobson's, of the ultimate victory of a monolithic whiteness. Such depictions run up against recent sociological research that finds a continuing, if faint, divide between white ethnics on one side and "unhyphenated Americans" of old-stock European background on the other. German Americans, who straddle this division, helped construct it between the world wars. Some took initial steps toward the creation of the "white ethnic;" others joined nativist groups that promoted a deep racial divide between "unhyphenated" northwest European "Americans" and southeast European immigrants. Even within the same ethnic group, that is, class and religious differences spawned different conceptions of whiteness. Although that status as such confers significant privileges on both ethnic and unhyphenated white Americans today, each group understands it differently. White ethnics turn ethnic identity itself into a vehicle for claiming Americanness, invoking a heroic immigrant saga that allows many to overlook the deep structures of discrimination still faced by nonwhites. In this and other ways, German Americans, inadvertently or not, have helped to structure American pluralism in a way that has continuing political consequences for Americans of all racial backgrounds.[21]

What happened to German America, in other words, was both singular in its intensity and consequential for the United States in general. The German-American ordeal of the early twentieth century, and the way German Americans responded to it, did a great deal to shape the landscape that other Americans had to cross. If we today scarcely recognize the impact German Americans made, that merely testifies to the depth of their transformation.

PART ONE

1900

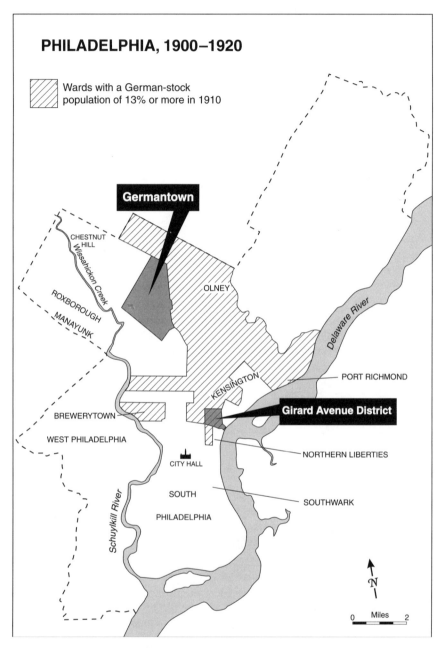

PHILADELPHIA, 1900–1920

Wards with a German-stock
population of 13% or more in 1910

Germantown

CHESTNUT
HILL

Wissahickon Creek

ROXBOROUGH

MANAYUNK

OLNEY

Delaware River

PORT RICHMOND

KENSINGTON

BREWERYTOWN

Girard Avenue District

WEST PHILADELPHIA

NORTHERN LIBERTIES

CITY HALL

SOUTH

SOUTHWARK

PHILADELPHIA

Schuylkill River

N

0   Miles   2

Map 1.1. Philadelphia, 1900–1920. Sources: John Daly and Allen Weinberg,
Genealogy of Philadelphia County Subdivisions, 2d ed. (Philadelphia, 1966),
83; U.S. Department of Commerce, Bureau of the Census, *Thirteenth Census of
the United States, Taken in the Year 1910*, vol. 3, *Population, 1910: Reports by
States . . . Nebraska-Wyoming* (Washington, 1913), 605–608.

CHAPTER ONE

German Philadelphia: A Social Portrait

ON a November evening in 1901, Charles John Hexamer looked out over a mass of people gathered at the German Society of Pennsylvania and told them they had reason to be proud. His audience had crowded into the society's Philadelphia headquarters on Spring Garden Street for the opening of a charity fair that was organized to pay for renovations to the building. Hexamer, the society's president, described the "all-German bazaar" as a success of ideals, a "coming-together of the Germans of the city, at this place dedicated to brotherly love and beneficence." He capped his speech with the words of Franz Daniel Pastorius, whose 1683 journey to Philadelphia German Americans honored as the beginning of their people's immigration to the New World: "Hail to you, German posterity! Hail, German brothers!"[1]

The bazaar proved an undoubted financial success, netting $7,000 for the society. But the success Hexamer lauded—his depiction of the Germans of Philadelphia as drawn together in a common cause—is open to question. To be sure, the German Society, the city's oldest German voluntary association, could claim the role of leader of German Philadelphia in these years. In its first week, moreover, the fair drew visitors from an impressive array of German social clubs and singing societies, some of the scores of groups, or *Vereine*, that made up Philadelphia's German associational life (*Vereinswesen*).[2]

Yet a significant segment of the city's German working class seems to have stayed away. Seventeen singing societies appeared, or were scheduled to appear, at the bazaar. None belonged to the United Workers' Singing Societies, an organization affiliated with the umbrella group for German labor unions in Philadelphia, the United German Trades (UGT). The UGT's official newspaper, the *Philadelphia Tageblatt*, also did not appear to overflow with enthusiasm for the German Society's fair. It managed to schedule a celebration of its own anniversary for the very evening Hexamer was to open the bazaar.[3]

Hexamer's image of a unified German Philadelphia was threatened by divisions not just of class but also of religion and region. His opening speech touched on these other fault lines that ran through the city's "Germandom," or *Deutschtum*. The German Society's hall, he asserted, was "neutral ground." From it, every impulse for the welfare of "the whole of

Germandom" could radiate out, "without running up against particularistic jealousy . . . or religious differences."[4] His mention of "particularistic
jealousy" may have been a veiled reference to differences among immigrants from various regions of Germany. Hexamer could see those differences on display as associations built around regional identities made their
way to the event, from the Cannstatter Volksfest-Verein, with its Swabian
roots, to the Plattdeutscher Verein, representing immigrants from an area
far to the German north. More serious were the religious differences. As
Hexamer well knew, the potential for conflict among German Protestants,
Catholics, Jews, and freethinkers required that a group seeking to speak
for all Germans avoid religious controversy. Society policy required that
its hall not be used for meetings of a religious or political nature.[5] The
building on Spring Garden Street was, quite literally, and of necessity, "neutral ground."

When middle-class German Americans such as Hexamer sought to speak
for Philadelphia's *Deutschtum,* they took on a daunting task. Like German
America in general,[6] the German Philadelphia of 1900 was distinguished
by its heterogeneity. It was in actuality a collection of largely separate
worlds loosely linked by a sense of common Germanness. Hexamer's
sphere of secular, middle-class leaders was far removed from that of Philadelphia's working-class German socialists, the Catholics who centered
their lives around the city's German national parishes, and the congregants who worshipped in its German Lutheran churches.

This chapter sketches the nature of German Philadelphia at the turn of
the twentieth century by exploring its diversity, its relationship to the rest
of the city, and the bonds that held it together. Philadelphia itself was not
so heavily immigrant a city as New York or Chicago, but neither was it
simply an Anglo-American enclave. Rather, it was dominated by a mix of
residents of northwest European descent and shaped by more than two
centuries of German immigration. The *Deutschtum* created by nineteenth-
century immigrants was itself riven by divisions of class, religion, space,
and gender. These divides were reflected most clearly in the associational
subcultures forged by middle-class ethnic activists, working-class unionists, Catholics, Lutherans, and others.

Despite their differences, members of those subcultures could and did
see themselves, at least occasionally, as sharing an identification as German
or German-American. All recognized some common interests, including
the defense of German-language institutions and shared cultural values
against attacks by outsiders. Middle-class activists such as Hexamer invoked those interests to promote an overarching "German-American"
identity that, however tenuously, still tied German Philadelphia's separate
worlds together as of 1900.

GERMANS IN AN "OLD IMMIGRANT" CITY

"Philadelphia . . . is the most American of our greater cities," Lincoln Steffens wrote in 1903. If one defined "American" as native-born, Steffens was right. Between 1870 and 1920, Philadelphia had a smaller proportion of foreign-born inhabitants than any other large city in the North. First- and second-generation immigrants together—the category termed "foreign stock" in the census—made up only 55 percent of the city's population in 1900. In comparison, more than three-quarters of the residents of New York and Chicago that year were foreign stock.[7]

Of Philadelphia's foreign-stock residents in 1900, four-fifths were of "old immigrant"—that is, northwest European—origin.[8] Irish newcomers and their offspring made up the city's largest immigrant ethnic group, at 21 percent of the population. First- and second-generation immigrants from Germany (15 percent) and Britain (8 percent), formed the second- and third-largest such groups. Philadelphia had attracted some Italians, Poles, Russian Jews, and other "new immigrants" from southern and eastern Europe by then, but their presence remained relatively small;[9] not until 1920 would they appear in the census as a majority of the city's foreign-born. Smaller still was the city's non-European immigrant population. The single largest such group appears to have been residents of Chinese origin, who made up less than one-tenth of one percent of all Philadelphians in 1900.[10]

In contrast, Philadelphia's proportion of black residents (4.8 percent) was markedly higher than that of most Northern cities in 1900. Philadelphia had long had a significant black presence; by the early nineteenth century, one could speak of a self-consciously black community in the city, with its own independent institutions, middle-class leaders, and "intricate systems of self-support." That community was continually remade by migration, especially from Philadelphia's southern hinterland. Surveying the city's Seventh Ward in the late 1890s, W.E.B. Du Bois found that more than half of its black residents were born in the South, particularly Virginia and Maryland.[11]

At the turn of the twentieth century, then, Philadelphia's Germans and their children were only the second-largest immigrant ethnic group in a population dominated by residents of northwest European background, whether native- or foreign-born. Yet the city's sheer size meant that its German population was enormous. In 1900, Philadelphia had 71,319 inhabitants born in Germany, a German-born population larger in absolute terms than those of such heavily German cities as Milwaukee, Cincinnati, St. Louis, and Buffalo. Philadelphia's first- and second-generation German immigrants together numbered 159,238.[12]

In 1900, however, this population had just begun a demographic de-

cline induced by the tailing-off of two centuries of mass German immigration. That migration stream effectively had commenced with the
founding of Germantown. Under Pastorius's leadership, a party of thirteen Rhineland families took up property in 1683 in what would become
Philadelphia County's "German Township." This settlement initiated the
first of several phases of German migration to British North America.
The largest ran from roughly 1717 to 1775, when more than 80,000 German speakers arrived. Most were Protestants of the Lutheran or Reformed faiths, and most entered through Philadelphia.[13] By 1760, German-
speaking settlers in the city's rural hinterland had created "a clearly
defined 'Pennsylvania German' landscape." This "German crescent" swept
west and south around Philadelphia, in an arc centered on the outlying
counties of Northampton, Berks, Lancaster, and York. In 1790, much of
the state's German population lived here in "rural, ethnic enclaves," and
in concentrations great enough to make Pennsylvanians of German background the state's largest European ethnic group.[14]

The Revolutionary War and the subsequent upheavals in Europe halted
large-scale German immigration for nearly half a century. The influx of
Germans resumed in a small way in the late 1810s, became noticeably
large in the 1830s, and then grew to staggering proportions. Between
1820 and 1970, more than 6.9 million immigrants entered the United
States from Germany—that is, from the territories incorporated in the
new German Empire in 1871—a greater number than came from any
other country. The flow peaked in 1854 and again in 1882, before drop-
ping off sharply in the 1890s. German immigration to Philadelphia
roughly tracked these trends. Beginning in 1850, when the federal census
first indicated individuals' place of birth, the number of German-born residents recorded in the decennial count both nationally and in Philadelphia
climbed steadily, reaching a high point in 1890. That number declined
slightly by 1900 and then evidenced a marked downward trend by 1910,
which accelerated in the following decade.[15]

The nineteenth-century German immigration differed in significant
ways from that of the previous century. Although it began in the German
southwest, the home of almost all of the eighteenth-century immigrants,
the impulse to emigrate soon spread north and east within Germany. An
initial stream of small farmers, artisans, and shopkeepers, not unlike the
peasant villagers of the eighteenth-century migration, increasingly was
joined by displaced agricultural laborers; these, in turn, would be super-
seded by industrial workers after the mid-1890s.[16] These immigrants
also had a greater degree of religious diversity. While Catholics in mid-
eighteenth-century Pennsylvania made up a tiny proportion of all German
immigrants, the overall stream of nineteenth-century German newcomers
may have been one-third Catholic. That stream likewise included a sig-

nificant number of Jews fleeing discrimination in the German south and east.[17]

More diverse than their colonial-era forerunners and more inclined to settle in cities, nineteenth-century German immigrants created a markedly different social world. Their German Philadelphia stood at an uneasy remove from the descendants of colonial German immigrants. Many of the latter had spent the decades after the Revolution out in the German crescent, crafting their own "Pennsylvania German" culture. An amalgam created by settlers from different German regions, this culture was expressed through the spoken language of Pennsylvania German, a tongue based primarily on the dialect of the Rhenish Palatinate but incorporating Swiss-German and English features. Religious differences among Pennsylvania Germans remained, with Lutheran and Reformed "church people" on one side and a minority of Moravians and members of "plain people" sects, such as the Amish, on the other. But by the nineteenth century, most "could speak in ethnic terms of *unser Satt Leit*—'our kind of people.'"[18]

Pennsylvania German culture flourished through most of the nineteenth century; only in the twentieth century did it contract to the shrunken form we know as "Pennsylvania Dutch." The best barometer of this change is language. The Pennsylvania German dialect, or *Deitsch,* is still spoken by some German crescent residents today. Its usage, in fact, peaked fairly late, between 1870 and 1880, when it served as the everyday language of some 600,000 Pennsylvanians. Although the use of written High German declined in the German crescent in the late nineteenth and early twentieth centuries, *Deitsch* began to emerge as a written language in the 1860s through what the folklorist Don Yoder terms "a full-fledged dialect literary movement."[19]

Even as Pennsylvania Germans became more self-conscious about their dialect, they declined to see themselves as having much in common with nineteenth-century German immigrants. In fact, as Yoder argues, that encounter helped crystallize a Pennsylvania German identity. This sense of a separate peoplehood found expression in the terms nineteenth-century Pennsylvania Germans used to describe German immigrants: *Deitschlenner* (literally, "people from Germany"), or "Europeans," or "Germany-Germans." Most Pennsylvania Germans also declined to call themselves "German American," the label employed by nineteenth-century immigrants and their children. The lack of fellow-feeling carried over to social relations and institutions. As a Reformed church journal declared in 1895, "[t]he Pennsylvanians now do not readily associate with the European German, and where not sufficiently numerous to form societies of their own, they prefer the society of Americans of English descent to that of their German cousins." At the founding convention of the Pennsylvania

German Society in 1891, delegates voted to restrict regular membership to direct descendants "of early German or Swiss emigrants to Pennsylvania"—much to the chagrin of two German-born visitors from the German Society of Pennsylvania.[20]

The presence of a separate Pennsylvania German element in the German crescent and in Philadelphia at the turn of the twentieth century is important to keep in mind. Ultimately, Pennsylvania Germans' portrayals of themselves as old-line Americans made it easier for some descendants of nineteenth-century German immigrants to reshape themselves as such Americans after the First World War. These redefinitions were greatly aided by the fact that an undeniable portion of southeastern Pennsylvania's "old stock" was composed of people of colonial German as well as colonial English ancestry. In 1800, 1850, and 1880, the proportion of household heads in Berks County bearing German surnames remained at nearly 80 percent. Since German-born residents amounted to just 2.6 percent of this German crescent county's total population in 1880, it seems likely that most of the county's "German" majority that year was of colonial descent.[21] Philadelphia, too, had its Pennsylvania Germans. Some of the German families that settled in the city in the eighteenth century remained there—notably the Peppers, who anglicized their last name from Pfeffer, amassed a large fortune, and eventually entered the upper class that sociologist E. Digby Baltzell termed "Proper Philadelphia." If the Peppers remade themselves in an Anglo-American mold, other prominent Philadelphians retained an identification as Pennsylvania Germans. They included Samuel Whitaker Pennypacker, one of the Pennsylvania German Society's architects and, later, governor of the state; and department store magnate John Wanamaker, who served as the society's president in 1908. Pennypacker was born in Chester County, west of Philadelphia, and moved to the city with his family as a child.[22] His experience suggests that Philadelphia's hinterland supplied the city with a stream of Pennsylvania German migrants during the nineteenth century—and reinforced the Pennsylvania German contingent among those residents the census counted as "native whites of native parentage."

CITY OF SKILLED WORKERS

By popular stereotype, German workers in nineteenth-century America were skilled workers: bakers, carpenters, brewers, and practitioners of other traditional crafts. Behind this image lay a good deal of truth—especially in Philadelphia, for reasons having to do with the nature of the city's manufacturing economy. In the century after 1850, that economy was characterized by a diversity of products and work settings, by specialized rather than vertically integrated firms, by a stress on the making of high-quality specialty items, and by an abundance of small to medium-sized enterprises that were family owned and operated. No one industry dominated. The largest—textile and clothing manufacture—shared the stage before the First World War with three other major industries: metal products; printing and publishing; and the production of leather and leather goods.[23]

Such an economy had a particular bent for workers—usually male—with specialized skills. The leading industries drew machinists, pressmen, printers, and skilled workers in leather and textiles. Philadelphia textiles, for example, had a reputation as " 'the paradise of the skilled workman' after the Civil War." Conditions were less rosy for female operatives, who made up 46 percent of the textile workforce in 1900 and who lagged behind "workmen" in skill and pay.[24]

Philadelphia's high demand for skilled labor made it a magnet for German artisans. Consequently, German Philadelphia's class structure was dominated by skilled workers. They accounted for more than two-thirds of the city's immigrant German male workforce in 1850 and still made up a majority (53 percent) of immigrant and second-generation German household heads in 1900, as an analysis of manuscript census data shows (see table 1.1). Compared with all working household heads in 1900, these German-stock heads were overrepresented in skilled labor and underrepresented in both unskilled and white-collar work, although nearly one-quarter had white-collar occupations. The German-stock heads continued another nineteenth-century pattern: they retained a "middle-rung" position between Irish-stock household heads, who were more likely to hold unskilled jobs, and native-born whites of native parentage, who avoided unskilled work and held the highest proportion of white-collar positions.[25]

If Philadelphia's German workers in 1900 still had an artisanal cast, so too did they conform, though decreasingly, to popular expectations of what a German artisan was. Nineteenth-century German newcomers were strongly identified with a set of crafts oriented mostly toward the production of consumer goods, particularly food and drink.[26] Philadelphia's Germans were strongly entrenched in such consumer crafts in 1900, according to aggregate occupational data published by the U.S. Census Bureau.[27] Although immigrant German men and their sons composed only 16.5 percent of the city's male workforce that year, they made up a majority in three trades, forming 56 percent of all male cabinetmakers, 69 percent of male bakers and 88 percent of male brewers and maltsters (see table 1.2). These occupations were the most concentrated of a set of German "ethnic niches," defined as occupations where the percentage of workers belonging to a given ethnic group is at least one and one-half

TABLE 1.1
Class/Skill Levels of Working Household Heads, by Ethnicity:
Philadelphia, 1900 (Percent)

	All Household Heads	German Stock	NWNP*	Irish Stock	British Stock**	Black
1. High white-collar	4.6	3.6	9.0	1.7	4.1	1.0
2. Low white-collar	21.2	20.6	27.4	18.4	22.3	5.0
3. Blue-collar skilled	41.7	53.1	41.2	33.2	54.4	10.8
4. Blue-collar semi/ unskilled	32.5	22.7	22.4	46.7	19.1	83.1
Total (N)	6,357	1,170	1,972	1,343	627	397

Source: U.S. manuscript census schedules, Philadelphia sample, 1900 (see note 25).

Note: This table shows all household heads, male and female, for whom a class level could be discerned from an available occupational title; excluded are household heads who had no occupation listed, were retired, or were otherwise out of the labor market, and heads whose occupational titles could not be classified.

"Stock" includes immigrants and their second-generation children, with the second generation defined as native born with both parents or father born in specified country or, if father is native, with mother born in specified country. If parents are born in different foreign countries, birthplace of father determines parentage of native born.

This contingency table was analyzed to determine the degree of association between class level and ethnicity. This Pearson chi-square analysis produced a result of $\chi^2 = 905.43$, $p = .000$. The result clearly indicates marked differences by class level for household heads according to ethnic background. An analysis of the category of all household heads by class level produced a result of $\chi^2 = 926.36$, $p = .000$.

*Native-born whites of native parentage.

**Immigrants from England, Scotland, and Wales and their children.

times greater than the group's percentage in the entire workforce.[28] Thus, occupations with a proportion of first- and second-generation German immigrant men equal to at least 24.7 percent qualify as male German niches in 1900. There were thirty such occupations out of 145 described by the Census Bureau. Of these, somewhat more than half counted as traditional crafts, while at least half involved the production of goods for direct sale to consumers, and a third involved the processing of food or drink.

Yet, though these trades qualified as particularly "German," most German men did not work in them. The thirty niche occupations employed only a quarter of the 69,310 German-stock males—those of German birth or parentage—in Philadelphia's workforce. These niches, in fact, tended to differ from the occupations that claimed the greatest shares of the over-

TABLE 1.2
German-Stock Occupational Niches in Philadelphia's Male Workforce, 10+, 1900 (Rank Order)

Occupation	% German1&2	N German1&2
All workers	16.5	69,310
1. Brewers and maltsters	88.4	751
2. Bakers	69.0	3,287
3. Cabinetmakers	55.5	883
4. Buttonmakers	47.2	108
5. Trunk and leather-case makers, etc.	46.6	193
6. Bottlers and soda-water makers, etc.	46.5	297
7. Confectioners	46.3	620
8. Butchers	44.3	1,999
9. Copper workers	42.9	84
10. Sugar makers and refiners	42.5	94
11. Wheelwrights	42.2	201
12. Piano and organ makers	39.7	73
13. Gunsmiths, locksmiths, and bell hangers	38.4	121
14. Leather curriers and tanners	33.3	1,426
15. Barbers and hairdressers	31.7	1,314
16. Saloon keepers	31.4	376
17. Musicians and teachers of music	31.4	552
18. Boxmakers (wood)	29.9	43
19. Coopers	29.8	322
20. Furniture manufactory employees	29.7	94
21. Boot- and shoemakers and repairers	29.1	1,505
22. Tobacco- and cigar-factory operatives	27.3	1,024
23. Clock- and watchmakers and repairers	26.6	195
24. Silk-mill operatives	26.5	113
25. Bartenders	25.7	796

continued

TABLE 1.2
Continued

Occupation	% German1&2	N German1&2
26. Engravers	25.7	217
27. Gold and silver workers	25.6	123
28. Hotel keepers	25.2	115
29. Newspaper carriers and newsboys	25.2	81
30. Broom and brush makers	25.1	133

Source: U.S. Department of Commerce and Labor, Bureau of the Census, *Special Reports: Occupations at the Twelfth Census* (Washington, D.C., 1904), 672–677.

Note: German 1&2 refers to all male workers age 10 or older, whether born in or outside the United States, having either both parents born in Germany or one parent born in Germany and one parent born in the United States; ibid., 427, 672–677.

all German-stock workforce. In 1900, fifteen occupations each had a share of at least 2 percent of that workforce; together they employed 50.2 percent of all German-stock males. Of these fifteen lines of work, only four—baking, butchering, boot- and shoemaking, and leather tanning— were also German niches, and only five were in consumer industries, the same five that counted as traditional crafts. Four white-collar occupations drew substantial numbers of German-stock males, including their leading line of work, retailing. Four occupations in producer industries also put in strong showings: machining, textiles, iron and steel work, and leather tanning.

In other words, by 1900, what German-born men and their sons did for a living corresponded less and less to the image of a skilled workman pursuing a traditional, consumer-oriented craft. In fact, a segment of the German workforce appears to have been in the process of shifting out of consumer crafts where skills had suffered a devaluation and into better-paying skilled jobs in producer and some consumer industries. Historians of Philadelphia's nineteenth-century workforce have argued that between 1850 and 1880, the native-born sons of German and Irish immigrants began to leave traditional consumer trades such as tailoring, cabinet-making, baking, shoemaking, and blacksmithing. By 1880, these immigrant sons increasingly took jobs in such high-wage sectors of the consumer crafts as printing and the building trades, and in the well-paying new metal industries. They claimed the rewards, in terms of pay and prestige, of "labor aristocrats" in their new fields.[29]

The aggregate census data suggests that this trend continued among

German-stock men at the turn of the century. For example, 6.5 percent of German immigrants and 2.2 percent of second-generation German men were shoemakers in 1880; in 1900, only 2.2 percent of German-stock men worked in the larger field of shoe- and bootmakers and repairers. In contrast, the producer industries of textiles and metals and the building trades of carpentry and plumbing continued to increase their share of the German-stock workforce. The gains were particularly dramatic in the new metal industries. Machinists had made up 2 percent of the immigrant German workforce and 1.8 percent of the second-generation German workforce in 1880; by 1900, 4.3 percent of all male German-stock workers practiced that trade.[30]

The shift toward jobs in a "labor aristocracy" of machinists, steelworkers, skilled textile operatives, and construction workers had a particular ethnic cast. As German-stock males abandoned consumer crafts, their places were taken by immigrants from southern and eastern Europe. The better-paying jobs to which these Philadelphia Germans fled tended, in contrast, to be dominated by workers of northwest European background. New immigrants rarely could predominate in particular occupations at the turn of the century: of the city's male workforce in 1900, Russians made up only 3.1 percent, Italians 2.4 percent, and Poles 1.0 percent. Yet Russian Jews and Italians had begun to make their presence felt in particular crafts, some of which were also German niches. Russians, already a majority in shirtmaking, were overrepresented in the butcher's trade; they and Italians both were overrepresented in cabinetmaking and had carved out ethnic niches in tailoring and boot- and shoemaking. By contrast, men of northwest European origin—who made up 83 percent of the overall male workforce—accounted for more than 90 percent of the city's male machinists; steam-boiler makers; printers, lithographers, and pressmen; carpenters and joiners; plasterers; plumbers and pipefitters; and textile workers. Significantly, in none of these trades did Germans establish ethnic niches. Rather, German-stock males tended to hover around their proportion in the workforce as a whole, sharing such occupations with workers of Irish and British background and with those of native parentage, almost all of them descended from northwest European immigrants.

Philadelphia's labor aristocracy thus provided potential common ground for the integration of some German-stock residents into a common "old stock" or "old immigrant" world. As we shall see, however, much of the city's German working class ultimately would not take that path. At the turn of the century, moreover, many German workers appear to have preferred specifically German labor organizations. By 1900, German-speaking workers had organized a score of their own unions, grouped under the umbrella of the United German Trades. The city's "English" unions belonged to the United Labor League, which, while it incorporated some of the UGT unions in the 1890s, was seen as both a citywide trade federation and as the central body for the English unions. German workers had UGT representation, predictably, in such niche occupations as brewing, baking, and shoemaking. But UGT unions also existed in the metal, textile, and construction industries.[31] Philadelphia's German workers retained sufficient ethnic consciousness to maintain separate working-class organizations, even in industries where they formed one part of a northwest European whole.

Dispersed in the City of Homes

The turn of the twentieth century found German Philadelphians spread out across much of the city. Philadelphia seems to have fallen short of the high German residential concentrations evident in nineteenth-century Midwestern cities such as Milwaukee, which in 1860 had four wards that were at least 75 percent German. Philadelphia's German population, like that of other eastern cities, was more diffuse, due in part to such factors as a preexisting housing stock and the city's large expanse, which made job location more important in housing choice. Certainly, German immigrants dispersed across the city increasingly in the late nineteenth century, as the geographer Alan Burstein documented in his work with the Philadelphia Social History Project. The project's researchers divided Philadelphia into grid squares measuring roughly one and one-quarter blocks square. Burstein found German-born residents in 57 percent of the city's inhabited grid squares in 1850, a proportion that climbed to 71 percent by 1880.[32]

Nevertheless, Burstein determined that Philadelphia Germans did cluster together. Two clusters of German-born residents appeared in 1850. The larger ran from the old colonial city north through the industrial suburbs of Northern Liberties and Kensington. A smaller German cluster appeared in Southwark, south of the old city. As Philadelphia grew between 1850 and 1880, the northeastern cluster expanded, pushing further north through Kensington. A third, small concentration of German immigrants also appeared in the near northwest, close to the Schuylkill River. This northwest cluster may have reflected a westward shift of the city's German brewing industry.[33] The neighborhood around the new breweries eventually would bear the name "Brewerytown."

Whether these German clusters in turn represented neighborhoods inhabited mainly by Germans is an open question. Historians have long debated whether European ethnic groups in nineteenth-century American cities were clustered in neighborhoods dominated by one group or shared such territories with others. Burstein argued that German-born Philadelphians tended not to dominate their grid squares. Using an "index of dominance," he calculated that the average German immigrant in 1880 lived in a grid square that was just 12 percent German-born.[34] This citywide measure, however, could overlook the existence of greater ethnic concentrations within German clusters specifically. As chapter 2 describes, even in 1900, two wards in the northeastern cluster had a majority of household heads who were either born in Germany or the children of German immigrants.

Whether or not German immigrants dominated their northeastern cluster, they were quite visible there. James Bergquist has labeled the several square miles extending north and northeast from the city's old commercial core as Philadelphia's late-nineteenth century "German district." In the 1870s and after, the area was home to a German theater, a German shooting club, two German gymnastics societies, and the headquarters of most of the city's twenty-four German singing societies.[35] The district, however, did not remain static. In the thirty years after 1880, German immigrants and their children remained entrenched in Northern Liberties, Kensington, and Brewerytown, but they also established new concentrations to the north and northeast. This pattern emerges from a ward-by-ward ethnic breakdown derived from the published 1910 federal census. German immigrants and their children made up 9.7 percent of Philadelphia's population that year.[36] Not surprisingly, the city's northern sector—the area north of Vine Street and east of the Schuylkill River—remained its German stronghold in 1910. Nearly 80 percent of Philadelphia's first- and second-generation German immigrants lived in that sector, which contained every ward in which they were overrepresented. In none of the city's forty-seven wards, however, did such German-stock residents have anything close to a dominant position. The most "German" ward was the Twenty-ninth, which encompassed Brewerytown, but only 26 percent of that ward's population was of German stock. In only six wards did the proportion of German-stock residents exceed 20 percent.

A map of the most overrepresented wards in 1910 does show, however, that the old northeastern German cluster now extended all the way north to the city's border (map 1.1). That year, slightly more than half of all German-stock Philadelphians resided in thirteen wards where they made up 13 percent or more of the population. These wards included the Twenty-ninth and Twenty-eighth, in the city's near northwestern section, and several wards in Northern Liberties and Kensington that traced the outlines of the northeastern German cluster of 1880. Most strikingly, however, by 1910, German immigrants and their children had fanned out from the top of that cluster. The main extension of their settlement ran north from the Nineteenth Ward, following a corridor roughly bounded by Kensington

Avenue on the east and Broad Street and Germantown Avenue on the west. This German corridor peaked in the Forty-second Ward, which included the Olney neighborhood.

The German shift northward was reflected in contemporary accounts and institutional growth. Olney, for example, was still relatively undeveloped at the turn of the century. Maps show that most of the street grid pattern that would grow over the neighborhood by 1920 was not yet in place as of 1899. Yet enough German speakers lived in the area to justify the founding, in 1898, of a German Lutheran church. Tabor Lutheran, with 165 members in 1900, was a sign of the deluge of German-stock residents to come. By 1915, Olney would count, in the words of one reporter, as "one of the most German suburbs that Philadelphia has."[37]

CLUB AND CHURCH: PHILADELPHIA'S *VEREINSWESEN*

When, in 1900, a professor of German at the University of Pennsylvania wanted to characterize German America, he chose to describe it in terms of culture embodied in voluntary associations. Marion Dexter Learned named "the three different phases of German-American life" as "music, physical training, and popular education," represented, in turn, by "the singing societies, the alliance of gymnastics clubs, and the alliance of [German] teachers."[38] Learned's equation of German America with its voluntary associations has been echoed since then by observers and historians. Kathleen Conzen, for example, argues that nineteenth-century German Americans defined their ethnicity in cultural terms, within a set of essentially cultural community institutions: singing societies, gymnastics clubs, fraternal lodges and church sodalities, parochial schools and secular academies, picnics and beer gardens. Here was molded "the sense of what it means to be ethnically German-American."[39]

The complex of voluntary associations created by nineteenth-century German Philadelphians did serve to define and sustain their public ethnic identity. Yet this *Vereinswesen* also reflected the extreme heterogeneity of German Philadelphia. To describe it is to describe the different subcultures forged by middle-class notables, working-class radicals, Catholic parishioners, and Lutheran congregants.

A reader who opened one of the city's secular German-language newspapers at the turn of the twentieth century could hardly doubt the central role voluntary associations played in German life. Inside, he or she would find a set of columns, sometimes running to a page of small print, of "Verein Reports" or news "From the Verein-life," detailing the meetings, excursions, balls, concerts, fairs, festivals, and anniversary celebrations of a multitude of groups. Philadelphia had no fewer than 642 *Vereine,* according to one 1892 list. These included 5 charitable associations, 36 singing societies (among them the United Singers of Philadelphia, an umbrella organization for 29 singing groups), 3 *Vereine* dedicated to running regional festivals, 4 gymnastics clubs, 99 building societies, 285 mutual benefit associations, 14 veterans associations, 15 professional societies, and 160 German lodges.[40]

This mass of secular *Vereine* reflected divisions of space and gender. All three festival associations had Old World regional orientations: the Bavarian Volksfest Verein, the Swiss National-fest Verein, and the Canstatter Volksfest-Verein, which harked back to a festival celebrated in the Württemberg town of Cannstatt.[41] In the leading middle-class associations, such as the German Society, formal membership was open to men only. German-American women, however, created women's affiliates of male societies and their own, independent voluntary associations. In the three decades before the Civil War, German Philadelphians founded at least fifteen female lodges, some female benevolent societies, and at least one women's singing society. From the 1860s through the 1880s, at a minimum, another thirteen female associations emerged. Women's affiliates proliferated as well, so that by the turn of the twentieth century, nearly every large male *Verein* in the city had one.[42]

The most visible division within the secular *Vereinswesen,* however, pertained to class. Class differences had emerged among different kinds of German associations in the antebellum period. By the 1880s, as Lesley Ann Kawaguchi argues, the city's *Vereinswesen* had come to operate on two levels. On one, beneficial societies, lodges, burial funds, and building and savings and loan associations drew skilled workers; on another level, "a new group of German elites and leaders emerged" that tended to affiliate with the German Society of Pennsylvania and the German Hospital Society.[43]

At the turn of the twentieth century, the German Society remained both a middle-class institution and perhaps the leading association within the secular *Vereinswesen.* By that time, however, radicalized immigrants had created a self-consciously socialist working-class subculture in German Philadelphia. Its backbone was the United German Trades. The labor federation not only had the *Tageblatt* as its official daily newspaper, with a circulation of 41,000 in 1900, but also had founded the Labor Lyceum Association in 1889 to provide a hall for its member unions. The association purchased its own building in Northern Liberties in 1893; in the same decade, German-speaking unionists established sister lyceums in Southwark and Kensington. At the Northern Liberties hall, known simply as the Labor Lyceum, the UGT held its meetings and workers could enjoy evening entertainments with music provided by the sixty-singer

Arbeiter Männerchor. This choir, along with thirteen others in the Philadelphia area, belonged to the citywide UGT-affiliated United Workers' Singing Societies.[44] Politically, these institutions had an explicit commitment to Marxist socialism of the kind pursued in the homeland by the Social Democratic Party of Germany. For the UGT, this meant supporting first the Socialist Labor Party and then, after 1901, the Socialist Party of America. The federation's ties to these parties were extremely close; the *Tageblatt,* for example, accepted campaign contributions for the Socialist Party at its offices.[45]

The web of institutions around the UGT gave Philadelphia's German workers the opportunity to live their lives almost entirely within a German socialist milieu. Whether many German-speaking workers opted for this self-contained world is difficult to say, but some did. One was Friedrich Bertram, who imbibed "the Marxist gospel" as an apprentice tailor in Hamburg. Bertram emigrated to the United States in 1887 and settled in Philadelphia, where he joined the Socialist Labor Party and helped found the German Custom Tailors Union. He served as an officer in both organizations before his death in 1899.[46]

The distance between Bertram's world and that of Charles Hexamer, the civil engineer who led the German Society, measured the diversity of the secular *Vereinswesen.* Yet nineteenth-century German immigrants found the greatest division within German America to be between such secular "club" Germans and "church" Germans. Church Germans, in turn, reflected the deep religious divides of nineteenth-century Germany. To the split between Jews and Christians in the German lands, the Reformation had added divisions among Catholics, Lutherans, and Calvinists. The German unification of 1871 was quickly followed by a state campaign, labeled the *Kulturkampf,* against the new Empire's Catholic minority. Laws passed in the 1870s did away with church supervision of schools, expelled Jesuits from Germany, and gave state bodies disciplinary power over the church. Religious Germans who came to America replicated homeland divisions. By one 1892 count, Philadelphia contained ten German Catholic parishes, sixteen German Lutheran congregations, ten German Reformed churches, four German Presbyterian churches, three congregations of German Baptists and two of German Methodists, six churches belonging to the German Evangelical Association, a German Mennonite church, and four German-Jewish synagogues.[47]

At the turn of the century, Catholics outnumbered Protestants of any one denomination within German Philadelphia, and both groups appear to have overshadowed the city's German Jewish population. In 1900, the city had eleven Catholic national parishes reserved for German speakers and their children. These "pure-German Catholic parishes" embraced an estimated total of 23,395 men, women, and children.[48] In contrast, that year, the nineteen city congregations of the Philadelphia German Conference of the Evangelical Lutheran Ministerium of Pennsylvania had a communing membership that totaled 6,429.[49] The combined memberships of three additional German Lutheran churches—an independent congregation in Northern Liberties and two Missouri Synod churches—likely would not greatly increase the total for all German Lutherans.[50] Among Protestants, German Lutherans appeared more numerous than the German Reformed, who had only ten congregations in the city in 1900.[51]

Women appear to have dominated the active membership of the city's German Catholic and Lutheran churches. Women congregants, of course, had long played a leading if not primary role in Christian devotional life. In western Europe and the United States, among Protestants and Catholics alike, female churchgoers routinely outnumbered men during the nineteenth century. That they did so in German Philadelphia is suggested by the surprise shown by Lutheran and Catholic residents of German background whenever a church service drew a significant number of men. An account of a forty-hour devotion at the German national parish of St. Peter's in May 1900 pointed out "the great number of men and youths" who attended. Adolph Spaeth, the pastor of the German Lutheran church of St. Johannis', reacted similarly when preaching in Germany in 1904: "It was an inspiration to look down upon this mass of humanity, so quiet, devout and attentive, and so many men among them."[52]

If German Catholics outnumbered German Lutherans, Germans themselves were outnumbered within the Catholic Church. They made up only 17 percent of the city's Catholic population, according to an 1892 estimate, and ran a distant second to the Irish, who dominated Philadelphia Catholicism. Most of the city's seventy-three parishes in 1900 were, in effect, Irish parishes. Technically, these territorial parishes ministered to all English-speaking Catholics within a relatively small area. Since most such Catholics were of Irish background, however, the territorial parish was almost always predominantly Irish. This parish system supported an Irish-dominated hierarchy. Of the six bishops—or, after 1875, archbishops—of Philadelphia consecrated in the nineteenth century, four were born in Ireland.[53] The English-language newspaper of the Archdiocese of Philadelphia, *The Catholic Standard and Times*, reflected this ethnic bent, catering to immigrants with a column headlined, "Doings in Ireland."[54]

Within this largely Irish church, the city's German-speaking Catholics carved out a place for themselves through the device of the national parish. Structurally, the national parish took in all Catholics of a particular ethnic background within a relatively large area. For German speakers, the national parish provided a place to have confession heard in one's own language, to practice a devotional life with a distinct German style, to create a social life based in German parish societies, and to educate one's children at least partly in the mother tongue in parish schools.[55]

Each German parish thus served as a neighborhood-level enclave for German Catholics, providing those who wished it with a social world parallel to but separate from the secular *Vereinswesen*. And, not unlike German socialists, Philadelphia's German Catholics created citywide institutions that linked them together within the larger church. German Catholics were instrumental in the founding in the 1860s of St. Mary's Hospital. German parish mutual aid societies were tied together by the city's Volksverein, organized in 1876 as a unit of a national federation of such associations, the German Roman Catholic Central-Verein of North America. The most important such institution, however, was St. Vincent's Orphan Asylum, a home for German Catholic orphans founded in 1855. In the 1870s, St. Vincent's launched an annual Orphan Festival and two German Catholic newspapers: the daily *Volksblatt* and the weekly *Nord Amerika*. The festivals functioned as "the only celebration of the year, at which all [German] parishes met." The newspapers likewise fostered a sense of German Catholic distinctiveness. While the *Volksblatt* succumbed to financial troubles in 1898, *Nord Amerika* reached a circulation of 6,000 in 1905.[56]

The pages of *Nord Amerika* in 1900 provide a window on German Catholic identity and on attitudes toward non-Catholic Germans and non-German Catholics. The newspaper cultivated a certain distance toward other Germans in America and the common umbrella term of "German American." *Nord Amerika* most frequently spoke of its ethnic constituency simply as "German Catholic(s)."[57] Less frequently, it referred to "German-American Catholics."[58] The use of "German American" as a noun—that is, as a name for an individual German in America, or for all such people—seems to have been relatively rare.[59] *Nord Amerika* could reflect a common feeling of Germanness in a homeland sense, taking pride, for example, in Germany's industrial achievements. The newspaper even had kind words on occasion for "our Lutheran fellow-countrymen," particularly when discussing the common interest of protecting parochial schools from state interference.[60]

Overall, however, *Nord Amerika* betrayed a continued ambivalence toward German Lutherans and the German nation-state. One frequent contributor ridiculed Martin Luther as "fat Martin" and denounced German Lutheran newspapers as "enemies of the Catholic Church." Above all, the newspaper could not forget the *Kulturkampf*. The weekly referred to it frequently in 1900 and worked to sustain its memory by, among other things, promoting a church-basement lecture titled "Bismarck and the Kulturkampf." Indeed, *Nord Amerika* used that memory as a weapon against what it saw as anti-Catholic movements in American politics, at one point invoking a verb to describe such behavior: *kulturkämpferlt* ("to wage a *Kulturkampf*").[61] Given such a stance, German Catholics in Philadelphia seemed unlikely to have smooth relations with German Lutherans, not to mention anticlerical elements among working-class and middle-class Germans. In fact, church strictures discouraged observant Catholics from too deep an involvement with non-Catholic Germans. Priests warned parishioners against joining secular gymnastics clubs or marrying outside the faith.[62]

If German Catholics seemed wary of other German Philadelphians, however, they appeared even more hostile to fellow Catholics of Irish background. Some chimed in on national debates within the church that took on ethnic overtones, in particular the Cahensly controversy. In 1891, Peter Paul Cahensly, a layman from Germany, presented a memorial to the Pope recommending that the hierarchy in the Americas include bishops of the same nationality as Catholics then arriving there. This document sparked an uproar in the United States. Many American Catholics saw it as calling for a reorganization of their hierarchy, with the Germans and other immigrant groups to be governed by their own national bishops. The controversy was only one of several debates during the late nineteenth century that pitted "liberals" against "conservatives" within the church. Germans tended to fall into the conservative camp and to paint their liberal opponents as advocates of an "Americanism" that sought a perilous adjustment of the church to the modern world. Since all of the leading liberal "Americanizers" were Irish, these disputes took on the character of Irish-German fights, while also linking the Irish with Americanism. Through the 1890s, *Nord Amerika* consistently took the German side, denouncing Americanism and defending Cahensly.[63]

By 1900, these battles were memories. But animosity toward the Irish lived on in *Nord Amerika*. The newspaper heaped a startling amount of abuse on Irish priests, the Irish-dominated *Catholic Standard and Times*, and the Irish in general.[64] Such vitriol was never more apparent than on St. Patrick's Day. Fed up with holiday claims regarding the achievements of pagan Irish civilization and the saint's feats of conversion, *Nord Amerika* printed a long column under a headline roughly translatable as "The Brag of the Irish." In the author's judgment, when St. Patrick converted the Irish to Catholicism, he converted a relatively small population. A long line of missionaries had done as much, or more, in other countries; no one could claim that Patrick's work overshadowed the apostolic activity of, say, St. Boniface in Germany. In fact, *England* had accepted Catholicism long before the Irish ever did. The author's closing blast betrayed all the resentment German Catholics had built up toward their Irish co-religionists:

When the Irish then say to us: Irish is Catholic, and further: Irish is American, and the Americans are Christian and about to jump into the Catholic Church, this is all the same incomprehensible drivel: but it lies at the bottom of all the absurd patriotic speeches and prattle made by Irish Americans and their ilk not only on St. Patrick's [Day], but the whole year through.[65]

In columns such as this, *Nord Amerika* showed greater hostility toward the Irish in 1900 than toward non-Catholic Germans. The column also demonstrated how the newspaper could conflate suspicions of the Irish and America, as when its author attacked Irish claims that "all political happiness flows from the American Constitution."[66] As separate as many German Catholics might have felt from other German Philadelphians, they were not ready to give up on a specifically German Catholic identity.

German Lutherans in Philadelphia faced a situation in some ways analogous to that of German Catholics. As first- and second-generation immigrants, self-identified German Lutherans held to their own congregations within a church structure shared with English speakers, built their own set of separate, citywide institutions, and quarreled with their English-speaking compatriots. However, German Lutherans appeared less heated in their disputes with "English Lutherans" and created congregations less institutionally complete than Catholic national parishes. Moreover, they seemed more inclined than German Catholics to participate with secular Germans in institutions that promoted a German-American identity.

Almost all Philadelphians who saw themselves as German Lutheran in 1900 worshipped in churches belonging to the Evangelical Lutheran Ministerium of Pennsylvania. Formed in Philadelphia in 1748 under the guidance of the immigrant pastor Heinrich Melchior Muhlenberg, the Pennsylvania Ministerium became the organizational taproot of eastern Lutheranism and of much of the Lutheran church in the United States. Immigration and a series of schisms in the nineteenth century spawned a welter of Lutheran synods. Six of these had congregations in Philadelphia at the turn of the twentieth century, with three synods representing small numbers of Scandinavian and Slovak Lutherans, and a fourth incorporating the two Missouri Synod churches. By far the largest number of Lutherans in the city, however—nearly 17,000 in 43 congregations—came under the purview of the Pennsylvania Ministerium and the larger synod to which it belonged, the General Council of the Evangelical Lutheran Church in North America. A smaller number—3,872 in 1906—attended ten churches adhering to the Evangelical Lutheran Synod of East Pennsylvania and its parent body, the General Synod of the Evangelical Lutheran Church in the United States of America.[67]

German Lutheran congregations in Philadelphia shared the Ministerium with a larger number of "English" churches—those that made exclusive use of English. German Lutherans and English Lutherans in the Ministerium and General Council stressed Lutheranism's identity as a faith grounded in specific confessional texts, above all the Augsburg Confession of 1530 in its unaltered form. Their insistence on this position had contributed to the Ministerium's secession from the General Synod and its formation with several other synods of the General Council in 1867. That schism reflected the nineteenth-century collision between advocates of an "American Lutheranism" and those who sought to put the faith in America on a more solidly confessional basis. "American Lutheran" theologians wished to accommodate Lutheranism to what they saw as a doctrinal consensus among other American Protestants. While some of their positions contradicted articles of the Augsburg Confession, they felt belief in those articles could be left to individual choice, allowing Lutheranism to move toward closer relations with other Protestant denominations.[68]

While American Lutheran tendencies were dominant in the General Synod for two decades following its creation in 1820, they encountered rising opposition thereafter. A Lutheran "confessional revival" in Germany, the renewed German immigration, and a new interest among American pastors in specifically Lutheran theological works all contributed to the development of a party in the General Synod that stressed Lutheranism's distinctiveness. The conflict came to a head in the 1850s and 1860s. Confessionally minded Lutherans, led by such clergymen as Charles Porterfield Krauth, took the Pennsylvania Ministerium out of the General Synod in 1866 and formed the General Council the following year, hewing to "the unaltered Augsburg Confession" and other Lutheran confessions as "pure and scriptural statements of doctrine." The move amounted to an assertion of a Lutheran identity distinct from that of other American Protestants.[69]

The schism of the 1860s did not overtly follow lines of ethnicity or language. American Lutherans, however, tended to embrace features of American evangelicalism that German immigrants found distasteful, such as temperance. Moreover, the Pennsylvania Ministerium appeared to have a greater commitment to the use of German than the synod it left behind. An 1882 report found that most of its congregations used both German and English, whereas few employed either language exclusively.[70]

At the turn of the twentieth century, language and a commitment to Lutheran distinctiveness still distinguished Philadelphia's Ministerium congregations from those attached to the General Synod's East Pennsylvania Synod. The city's ten East Pennsylvania congregations used English exclusively. Their synod, in fact, was created in 1842 by English-speaking Lutherans who had withdrawn from the Ministerium out of resentment over its use of German in synodical meetings. The East Pennsylvania synod also had American Lutheran leanings, although its parent body, the General Synod, did become more confessionally minded over time. This movement permitted the beginnings of a rapprochement in eastern Lutheranism. Yet General Synod Lutherans in 1900 remained much more open than those in the General Council to cooperation with other Protestant denominations, especially in such common evangelical causes as temperance and Sabbatarianism.[71]

In contrast, Ministerium Lutherans, and German Lutherans in particular, remained protective of Lutheranism's theological distinctiveness, suspicious of Protestant ecumenicism, and hostile to evangelical reform. German Lutherans in 1900 expressed these views in the *Lutherisches Kirchenblatt,* a weekly published by "a number of pastors" of the General Council and based in Reading and Philadelphia, and, less vehemently, in the Philadelphia German Conference's own bimonthly newspaper, *Der Kirchenbote.* Both newspapers were explicitly anti-Catholic, but they also took a dim view of other Protestant denominations and of pan-Protestant efforts generally.[72] The *Kirchenbote,* for example, dismissed the interdenominational Christian Endeavor Society with a warning that "German Lutherans keep away from such societies." The *Kirchenblatt* evinced as well a distate for the temperance movement, deriding a preacher whose sermons "dealt in temperance."[73]

German Lutherans also quarreled, however, with the Pennsylvania Ministerium's English Lutherans. This conflict revolved around the fading use of German within the Ministerium, and specifically within its seminary, which had moved to the suburban Philadelphia neighborhood of Mount Airy in 1889. Immigration in the last third of the nineteenth century strengthened what one historian characterizes as "a vocal German nationalistic group which resisted the growing use of English" in the Ministerium. What the *Kirchenblatt* saw as the curtailment of instruction in German at the Mt. Airy seminary became a matter of open conflict in the 1890s. During that decade, two professors who lectured in German departed from the seminary. The *Kirchenblatt* alleged that they were forced out by elements unfriendly to the German Lutheran side and engaged in a running battle in 1900 with the Ministerium's English-language newspaper, *The Lutheran,* over the matter.[74] The issue appears to have touched a chord with ordinary German Lutherans. A number of Philadelphia women, invited to a seminary open house, complained to the *Kirchenblatt* that no one had provided for a German speech at the event. "We don't understand the English sermon, it leaves us cold, and we gain nothing from English song and prayer," they wrote. "[W]e Germans—do we have no rights at all?"[75]

Relations between German-speaking and English-speaking Lutherans within the Ministerium do not appear to have become as hostile as those between German Catholics and Irish Catholics. The *Kirchenblatt* readers' complaint, however, does betray a sense of being specifically *German* Lutheran. The *Kirchenblatt* and *Kirchenbote* fostered this sense with invocations to "stay German!" and cultivate the German tongue and by focusing on the figure of Luther.[76] But the base of a separate German Lutheran identity lay in the city's German Lutheran congregations. Like the Catholic national parishes, the German Lutheran churches maintained ethnic identity by creating neighborhood-level enclaves where congregants could hear sermons and sing familiar hymns in German, participate in church societies, and, in some cases, educate their children in a German Lutheran parochial school. German Lutherans also created citywide and regional institutions that brought them together as a separate group within the Ministerium. They had their own mission society for the metropolitan area, a Sunday School society made up of the schools of all but one of the area's German Lutheran congregations, and an area conference for German Lutheran teachers. Pastors from the city and the surrounding region belonged to the Ministerium's Philadelphia German Conference. They began publication of the *Kirchenbote* in 1900 with the hope that its readers would "take joy in the great number of German congregations of our faith and become conscious that you belong to them and they belong to you."[77]

Overall, however, German Lutherans did not succeed in building enclaves as complete, in an institutional sense, as the Catholic national parishes. Most notably, they lacked the latter's extensive educational system. Of the city's nineteen German Lutheran congregations, only nine had parochial schools in 1900. In contrast, each of the eleven German Catholic parishes had a parochial school. According to pastors' estimates, 90 percent of the Catholic children within those parishes attended their parish school.[78] German Lutheran congregations simply could not build as strong an enclave when it came to shielding the next generation from influences outside the church.

A Tenuous Balance: Philadelphia's German America in 1900

To speak of a German Philadelphia at the turn of the twentieth century may seem presumptuous, given the deep divides among the city's German-speaking immigrants and their children. Yet leaders such as Charles Hexamer did presume to speak on behalf of Philadelphia's *Deutschtum*. In fact, their claims of a unified Germandom were not illusory. Running against the fault lines of German Philadelphia were a set of interests and values common to the great majority of those who made up the city's secular and religious *Vereinswesen.* Middle-class spokesmen played on these interests as they sought to unify the disparate elements of German Philadelphia under a German-American banner.

The project of creating a German-American identity in the city had roots that trailed back to the antebellum years, as Lesley Ann Kawaguchi described. As she pointed out, because German immigrants were so diverse and, before 1871, lacked a nation-state of origin, they had to create first a German identity and then a German-American one. The latter identity, forged between 1830 and 1880, complemented rather than replaced religious and provincial allegiances. The prime movers in its creation, Kawaguchi argued, were the leaders of middle-class voluntary associations, newspaper editors and publishers, and brewery owners, many of whom had an occupational stake in a community that saw itself as German. As she noted, a massive 1883 celebration of the 200th anniversary of Germantown's founding was planned by men overwhelmingly white-collar in occupation. Most belonged to voluntary associations; three-quarters of those had membership in the German Society, and half belonged to the German Hospital Society. Together they—including a very young Charles Hexamer—brought together scores of *Vereine* in a large-scale demonstration of a manifestly German-American identity.[79]

Kawaguchi stressed the role of an elite in forging a German-American identity. Yet other forces also pushed together the subcultures of German Philadelphia. First, while those subcultures could eye each other warily, they faced conflicts with their non-German analogues that reminded them of their Germanness. Such disputes could also betray a larger discomfort with America that might buttress a German identity, as with Catholic attacks on Americanism and the confessional reaction against American Lutheranism.

Second, German Philadelphia's subcultures shared certain interests that kept them aware of their common ties. German-language maintenance was one. All elements of the city's *Vereinswesen* had a stake in keeping German alive, especially among the younger generation, and this concern in turn generated common support for German-language instruction: *Nord Amerika* could speak kindly of German Lutherans when it came to fending off state meddling in parochial schools. Perhaps the issue with the greatest power to unify German Philadelphia, however, was that of alcohol use. The moderate consumption of alcohol played a key role in the social life of most German ethnic associations. From the 1840s on, however, German immigrants who saw "a convivial glass of beer or wine" as central to proper sociability clashed with Anglo-Americans bent on reducing or prohibiting alcohol consumption. These conflicts carried potentially severe consequences for *Vereine.* The passage of a state law raising liquor license fees prohibitively, for example, led the Cannstatter Volksfest-

Verein to cancel its annual festival in 1888. The society blamed the law for a 21 percent drop in its membership.[80] The antialcohol movement, in turn, drew opposition from all corners of the *Vereinswesen;* it was the Lutheran *Kirchenblatt* that attacked a "temperance" preacher.

The alcohol issue shows how middle-class activists could exploit common interests to promote a broader German-American identity. The middle-class leadership Kawaguchi described itself succeeded in crossing religious lines. The German Society's members included Lutheran ministers and at least one prominent Catholic: Joseph Bernt, who served as an editor of *Nord Amerika* from 1873 to 1896 and again from 1903 to 1908.[81] When these middle-class leaders sought to unify German Americans as a whole, they found the fight against prohibition essential to their success. As chapter 6 describes, the coterie of Philadelphians who founded the National German-American Alliance in 1901 discovered that the best way to build grass-roots support for the organization was to take on the "drys."

These leaders, then, could reasonably hope to make successful appeals to the city's "Germandom" that could even cross class lines. The German Society's 1901 bazaar may not have garnered much support from the city's organized German workers. Yet when the National Alliance was born the same year, the *Tageblatt* announced the event at the top of its front page with the celebratory headline, "The Founding Accomplished."[82] At least on occasion, even adherents of German Philadelphia's socialist subculture could see themselves as holding a German-American identity in common with others, including their presumed class enemies.

The German and German-American identities that leaders like Hexamer worked so hard to evoke did, then, have reality for some within each of the city's German subcultures. The sense of belonging to a common ethnic group surfaced, or was mobilized, at least occasionally among members of these subcultures, and it had concrete underpinnings in an awareness of interests common to the entire ethnic group. At the turn of the century, this sense held together the entity Kawaguchi called Philadelphia's German-America. Yet the common bonds of identity were always somewhat tenuous, and their strength likely differed from one subculture to another. German Catholics, for example, with their elaborate network of parallel institutions and their experience of discrimination, seem to have had a comparatively weak sense of pan-German ethnic identity. German Lutherans, who had established less complete enclaves, appeared more involved in the common life fostered by the middle-class societies.[83] They likely had a stronger sense than Catholics of German and German-American identity.

Moreover, the same non-German analogues that pushed German Philadelphia's subcultures together could also pry them apart. Working-class

Germans cultivated separate unions, but many found themselves moving into skilled lines of work shared with others of northwest European background or sharing established niches with new immigrants. German Catholics shared their church, however reluctantly, with the dominant Irish. Immigrant German Lutherans and their offspring worshipped within a synod that included many English Lutherans, some of colonial German ancestry. With time, members of these German subcultures would mix more and more with non-Germans; ultimately, they would do so along lines that echoed the divisions within the *Vereinswesen* itself.

Two Neighborhoods

SPACE, as well as class, religion, and gender, divided Philadelphians of German descent at the turn of the twentieth century. These Philadelphians lived widely scattered across the city, and their experience could vary greatly from one locale to another. This chapter uses that variety to explore the range of German ethnic experience and assimilation around 1900 through the lens of two very different neighborhoods: the Girard Avenue district and Germantown. The Girard Avenue district, comprising two wards close to the old city center, resembled a classic immigrant neighborhood: crowded, heavily industrial, and dominated by a German population that was largely but not exclusively working-class. Germantown, in contrast, was a leafy railroad suburb, distinctly more middle-class and, despite its name, home to only a small minority of first- and second-generation German immigrants.

While Girard Avenue and Germantown reflect only part of the German experience in Philadelphia, they do suggest the *range* of that experience. The two neighborhoods stand at either end of a continuum of assimilation running from ethnic maintenance to large-scale mixing with non-Germans. The Germans of Girard Avenue inhabited a largely ethnic world in 1900, a neighborhood that they experienced as a majority, that had room for Germans of all occupational classes, and that supported a wealth of ethnic institutions that reinforced the German aspect of their identities. Germantown, on the other hand, offered its German inhabitants only a handful of ethnic associations. Rather than turn to them, many of the neighborhood's first- and second-generation Germans found themselves entering social worlds defined by a mix of residents of northwest European origin. In their streets and voluntary associations, these German Philadelphians consorted with first- and second-generation Irish and English immigrants and with descendants of colonial-era settlers from Britain and Germany to the near exclusion of African Americans and "new immigrants" from Italy, Poland, and Russia. Mediated in complex ways by class, religion, and gender, this mixing ensured that those who left a German ethnic fold did not merely "melt" into a larger American universe but entered a crucible in which the common denominator was a northwest European background.

As of 1900, the Girard Avenue experience may have been more representative. The Girard Avenue district had roughly five times as many first- and second-generation German—that is, German-stock—residents as Germantown.[1] Even in 1910, most German immigrants and their children lived in wards with higher German-stock proportions than Germantown had in 1900. At the same time, those proportions were relatively low. By 1910, only one-quarter of German-stock residents lived in a ward as German as the Girard Avenue district was that year—in other words, in a ward more than 20 percent German-stock. Those six wards tended to include the most visible German neighborhoods, such as Brewerytown and a swath of the old German cluster in Northern Liberties and Kensington.[2] Hence, an appreciable number of German Philadelphians appear to have lived away from such German neighborhoods by the early twentieth century, dispersed in a manner that may have resembled Germantown more than Girard Avenue.

Neighborhood and Ethnic Identity

This chapter presumes that life in different city neighborhoods with different concentrations of German residents could reflect and shape different degrees and kinds of ethnic attachment. Such assumptions have a long scholarly history. Early in the twentieth century, sociologists at the University of Chicago framed assimilation in such spatial terms through the concept of ecological succession. Immigrant groups were portrayed as moving from "colonies" near the city center through a series of outlying districts. As it moved, a group became less concentrated physically, less united culturally, and more accepting of "American standards of living." The group's residential dispersion marked "the absorption of [individual members] into the general American population."[3]

Ecological succession, however, came under increasing attack after the mid-1960s. Historians and geographers questioned whether long-term ethnic residential concentrations could have existed before the late nineteenth century, given appreciable rates of upward and geographic mobility in American cities. Even in the twentieth century, they argued, immigrant "ghettos" tended to contain a number of different ethnic groups while holding comparatively few of a given group's members. Scholars with the Philadelphia Social History Project, for example, held that Philadelphia's urban form corresponded to the Chicago School model in 1930 but not during the nineteenth century. Mid-nineteenth-century Irish and German immigrants dispersed across the city, locating more on the basis of what industry employed them than what their ethnic background was. As Kathleen Conzen noted, such arguments implied that ethnic residential behavior could hardly serve as an indicator of either assimilation or ethnic maintenance.[4] The concept of neighborhood itself likewise came in for criticism. Kenneth Scherzer, for example, depicted the idea of "neighborhoods"—bounded geographic units that reflected the character of their inhabitants—as one that only emerged during the mid-nineteenth century. He argued that in antebellum New York, social networks operated less within particular localities than over distances, tying individuals together in "aspatial communities."[5]

Such arguments have not gone uncontested, however. First, Scherzer's "aspatial communities" may have had less salience in later periods and other cities. Alexander von Hoffman argued for the importance of neighborhoods to urban organization in the late nineteenth and early twentieth centuries. "[F]ar-flung forms of community" in fact reinforced a close-knit neighborhood life, fostering a local sense of place through a heightened awareness of the larger city "outside." Second, if most members of an ethnic group did not at any given time reside in ethnic "ghettos," that finding, as Conzen pointed out, can be read as *supporting* the Chicago School interpretation of such "colonies" as "way-station[s] on the path toward assimilation." Finally, neighborhoods may have been "ethnic" without being the exclusive turf of one ethnic group. Olivier Zunz found that in late nineteenth-century Detroit, a given ethnic group usually dominated an area or several small areas within a larger region of the city, while sharing this space with a scattering of members of other groups. Frequently, in the sample of small subsections Zunz analyzed, 60 percent or more of the household heads living in a given subsection were of the same ethnicity. Detroit in 1880 and 1900 was made up "largely of cross-class ethnic communities"—ethnic neighborhoods where members of the dominant group came from all social classes.[6]

This chapter defines "neighborhood" along von Hoffman's lines, as "an urban spatial unit with generally recognized geographic boundaries, a name, and some sense of psychological unity among its inhabitants." Within one neighborhood, separate ethnic and religious groups could foster their own social networks. These might have spatial boundaries that sometimes coincided with and sometimes overlapped the neighborhood's boundaries, or they might extend aspatially beyond the neighborhood.[7] Moreover, neighborhood boundaries themselves were subject to change and contestation. I use the term "ethnic neighborhood" in Zunz's sense: as a geographic area of the city—here, the Girard Avenue district—dominated by one ethnic group. The chapter employs an analysis of census data modeled on that of Zunz to show that a cross-class contingent of German-stock residents dominated the district in 1900, a finding that suggests the Philadelphia Social History Project generalized too broadly in describing nineteenth-century German immigrants as a residentially integrated group.

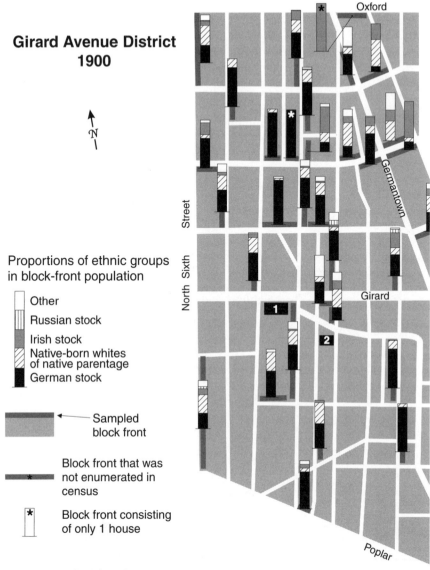

Girard Avenue District
1900

N

**Proportions of ethnic groups
in block-front population**

☐ Other

▥ Russian stock

▨ Irish stock

◩ Native-born whites
of native parentage

■ German stock

◄── Sampled
block front

★ Block front that was
not enumerated in
census

★ Block front consisting
of only 1 house

Landmarks

1 St. Peter the Apostle Roman Catholic Church
2 St. Paul's Independent Evangelical Lutheran Church
3 Christian Schmidt & Sons Brewing Co.
4 St. Michael's Roman Catholic Church
5 Immaculate Conception Roman Catholic Church

Map 2.1. Girard Avenue District, 1900. The area north of Girard Avenue corresponds to the Seventeenth Ward; the area south of Girard Avenue is the Sixteenth Ward. Sources: Author's census sample; George W. Bromley and Walter S. Bromley, *Atlas of the City of Philadelphia* (Philadelphia, 1895); Ernest Hexamer, *In-*

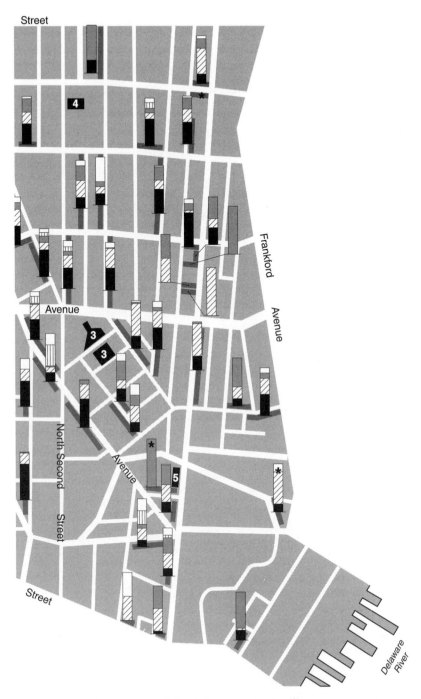

surance Maps of the City of Philadelphia (Philadelphia, 1873–1906), vols. 4, 8; and Ernest Hexamer and Son, *Insurance Maps of the City of Philadelphia* (Philadelphia, 1879–1920), vols. 4, 8 (for more specific publication information, see appendix, note 3).

A WALK DOWN GIRARD AVENUE

Just north of Philadelphia's old city center stand the brick row houses and narrow streets of what, in 1900, were the Sixteenth and Seventeenth wards. Jammed into this half-square-mile area that year were some 33,000 residents.[8] The wards were bounded on the east by Frankford Avenue and a small stretch of the Delaware River, on the south by Poplar Street, on the west by Sixth Street, and on the north by Oxford Street (see maps 1.1 and 2.1). Separating the wards was an east-west line defined by the area's main commercial thoroughfare, Girard Avenue.

Strictly speaking, the Sixteenth and Seventeenth wards by themselves did not constitute a neighborhood. Rather, they included parts of two larger neighborhoods: Northern Liberties and Kensington. The wards, in fact, reflect neighborhood malleability, for the border between Northern Liberties and Kensington ran through them, and few at the turn of the century could agree on precisely where that border was.[9] I nonetheless treat the wards together as "the Girard Avenue district," for several reasons. First, they were chosen as a unified object of study because together they encompassed the heart of the city's largest cluster of first- and second-generation German immigrants.[10] The two wards, that is, roughly described a recognized German ethnic neighborhood. Second, I describe the wards as the Girard Avenue district for reasons of convenience, but also because the street itself could function as a neighborhood place name. One newspaper referred in 1905 to the "advance of Girard Avenue as a business thoroughfare," exemplified by the "success of the only department store in the locality," an establishment just west of Sixth Street.[11]

To gain a better sense of life in the "locality" of the Sixteenth and Seventeenth wards, let us take a walk westward down Girard Avenue. An observer starting at the corner of Frankford and Girard at the turn of the twentieth century would look down a broad, treeless boulevard teeming with people and traffic and lined with row houses, almost all of them small stores that also functioned as dwellings. Behind Girard Avenue's commercial facade loomed the workshops and factories that betrayed the area's industrial heart. Walking westward, one could glance down side streets and see machine shops, dye works, yarn spinning mills, leather works, furniture manufactories, and a myriad of other industrial concerns interspersed among the ubiquitous row houses. These establishments could be as large as the Peoples Works iron foundry, which took up half a block. But the area was littered as well with smaller workshops, many of them confined to a single house.[12]

Our pedestrian would soon see signs that he or she was entering a German neighborhood. A third of the way down the boulevard, a smokestack towering behind row houses signaled the presence of Christian Schmidt & Sons, one of Philadelphia's largest breweries. Founded in 1860 by a Württemberg immigrant, the firm may have been the anchor for the many "breweries and German restaurants" around Girard and Second Street recalled by one local resident. Farther along the boulevard, three spires rising in succession marked a cluster of German congregations: St. Paul's Independent Evangelical Lutheran Church, at Fourth Street below Girard; St. Peter the Apostle Roman Catholic Church, the headquarters of the city's largest German national parish, on Girard between Lawrence and Fifth streets; and Zion Reformed Church, on Sixth Street just above Girard.[13]

The Girard Avenue district not only had the look of a German neighborhood; it was consistently recognized as such by contemporaries. "Girard Avenue was the hub of German-speaking Philadelphia" around the turn of the century, one observer recalled. As late as 1937, the *WPA Guide to Philadelphia* identified the vicinity of Fifth and Girard as one of the city's "German neighborhoods." Moreover, this ethnic designation stretched far to the north and south of the avenue itself. A 1907 survey described the length of Sixth Street from Dauphin Street, in the Nineteenth Ward, south along the western edge of the Seventeenth, Sixteenth, and Twelfth wards to Spring Garden Street, as "[i]n the German Section."[14]

These impressions were not illusory. They stemmed, ultimately, from the high concentration of Germans in the Sixteenth and Seventeenth wards, a concentration confirmed by an analysis of the wards' population. This analysis is based on a cluster sample of census households drawn in a manner similar to that used by Zunz in his study of Detroit. As described more fully in the appendix, I took a 15 percent simple random sample of the area's residential block fronts, with a block front defined as one side of a city block. I then located the households belonging to each sampled front in the 1900 federal manuscript census and coded them. The resulting coded sample of sixty-nine block fronts, containing about 4,000 individuals, yielded population estimates for the ethnic and class composition of the two wards and allowed me to examine the ethnic and class composition of each front.

From the sample emerges a picture of the Girard Avenue district as predominantly working-class and heavily German. Three-quarters of the 689 working household heads in the sample were blue-collar workers, most of them skilled (table 2.1). The district had very few "high-white-collar" household heads—professionals, major proprietors, or high-level officials and managers. Yet the area did have a substantial minority (23 percent) of clerks, salesmen, small-business people, and other low-white-collar household heads.

German immigrants and their children made up a plurality of the over-

TABLE 2.1
Class/Skill Levels of Working Household Heads, by Ethnicity: Girard Avenue District, 1900 (Percent)

	All Household Heads	German Stock	NWNP*	Irish Stock	British Stock	Russian Stock
1. High white-collar	2.5 (±2.0)	1.9 (±1.8)	1.5 (±1.9)	2.9 (±2.7)	10.5	4.6
2. Low white-collar	22.9 (±4.7)	20.3 (±4.2)	27.3 (±10.2)	25.5 (±8.8)	27.6	27.7
3. Blue-collar skilled	45.3 (±4.2)	54.4 (±4.6)	41.5 (±7.5)	21.2 (±7.9)	51.3	50.8
4. Blue-collar semi/unskilled	29.3 (±4.8)	23.4 (±4.1)	29.7 (±8.5)	50.3 (±9.4)	10.5	16.9
Total (N)	689	360	112	102	25	22

Source: Author's census sample.
Note: Figures in parentheses are 95 percent confidence intervals for each proportion, corresponding to the 0.05 level of significance. Confidence intervals were not calculated for British-stock or Russian-stock household heads, because of the small size of these groups (see appendix).

"Stock" includes immigrants and their second-generation children, with the second generation defined as native born with both parents or father born in specified country or, if father is native, with mother born in specified country. If parents are born in different foreign countries, birthplace of father determines parentage of native born. For composition of British and Russian stock, see table 2.2.

*Native-born whites of native parentage.

all population and a majority of household heads. German-stock residents—defined here as those either born in Germany, with both parents born in Germany, with a German-born father, or a native-born father and German-born mother—totaled 45 percent of the district's population in 1900 (table 2.2). This percentage was three times greater than the citywide proportion. The German presence was even more dramatic in terms of families, for more than half (52 percent) of the district's household heads were German-stock. Trailing the two wards' German-stock contingent were native whites of native parentage (28 percent of all individuals), and the Irish (13 percent). There was a scattering of residents of other backgrounds, including small numbers of British-stock and Russian-stock individuals, the latter almost all Russian Jews.

The district's German-stock population was distinguished by a heavy concentration in skilled work. Fifty-four percent of German-stock house-

TABLE 2.2

Ethnic Composition of Philadelphia, Girard Avenue District, and Germantown, 1900 (percent of total populations)

	Philadelphia	Wards 16 and 17	Germantown
German stock	15.1	44.6 (±5.8)	8.2 (±1.4)
Native white of native parentage	40.3	27.6 (±3.9)	43.3 (±3.5)
Irish stock	21.2	13.1 (±3.4)	24.6 (±3.6)
British stock*	8.4	2.9 (±0.9)	16.0 (±2.2)
Russian stock**	3.6	3.4 (±2.5)	0.0
East European stock***	—	1.7 (±1.1)	0.1 (±0.2)
South European stock†	—	0.4 (±0.5)	0.6 (±0.5)
Other Northwest European stock	—	3.4 (±1.3)	1.2 (±0.6)
Other††	—	2.8 (±3.8)	6.0 (±1.7)
Total (N)	1,293,697	3,936	6,181

Source: Percentages for Philadelphia are population figures, derived from the published 1900 federal census and presented in Theodore Hershberg, Alan N. Burstein, Eugene P. Ericksen, Stephanie W. Greenberg, and William L. Yancey, "A Tale of Three Cities: Blacks, Immigrants, and Opportunity in Philadelphia, 1850–1880, 1930, 1970," in *Philadelphia: Work, Space, Family, and Group Experience in the Nineteenth Century,* ed. Theodore Hershberg (New York, 1981), 465, table 1. Percentages for the Girard Avenue district and Germantown are derived from the author's census samples.

Note: Figures in parentheses are 95 percent confidence intervals for each proportion, corresponding to the 0.05 level of significance (see appendix).

"Stock" includes immigrants and their second-generation children, with the second generation defined as native born with both parents or father born in specified country or, if father is native, with mother born in specified country. If parents are born in different foreign countries, birthplace of father determines parentage of native born. The final four ethnic categories were created as part of my analysis of the census samples; as they could not be easily calculated from the published census, I have left these categories blank in the Philadelphia column.

*Includes immigrants from England, Scotland, and Wales and their children.

**Includes immigrants from Russia, Lithuania, Estonia, and Latvia and their children.

***Includes immigrants from Poland, Hungary, Bohemia and Romania and their children.

†Includes immigrants from Italy and Portugal and their children.

††Includes African Americans and immigrants from Canada, South America, and China and their children. African Americans made up 4.8 percent of the city's population, 4.8 percent (±1.7 percent) of the Germantown sample, and 2.2 percent of the Girard Avenue sample. However, African Americans composed only 0.7 percent of the actual population of the Sixteenth and Seventeenth wards in 1900; U.S. Census Office, *Census Reports: Twelfth Census of the United States, Taken in the Year 1900,* vol. 1, *Population* (Washington, D.C., 1901–1902), 639.

hold heads held skilled blue-collar positions, the highest percentage among the district's five major ethnic groups (table 2.1). The wards' Germans likewise were largely a product of the most recent wave of German immigration. Of the sample's 407 household heads either born in Germany or native-born of German parents, 72 percent were immigrants. More than three-quarters of the German-born heads had arrived since the Civil War, and half had landed since 1880.

What made the Sixteenth and Seventeenth wards a cross-class German *neighborhood,* in an experiential sense, was the pattern of clustering the German plurality followed. Two-thirds (65 percent) of the sample's 426 German-stock household heads lived on block fronts where more than half of the heads were German-stock. Moreover, just over half (52 percent) of the sample's German-stock heads shared their block front with a German majority that included members who were unskilled, skilled, and low-white-collar workers.

The location of these German-majority fronts, moreover, suggests the outlines of a German-dominated neighborhood *within* the Sixteenth and Seventeenth wards that ran from the middle of the district, roughly around Second Street and Girard, to the northwest, in a curving, widening fan. Of the twenty-seven block fronts with a majority of German-stock household heads, four were between Front and Second streets, four farther west between Second and Third, four between Third and Fourth, and no fewer than fifteen between Fourth and the district's western edge at Sixth Street. The district's more heavily Irish area, in contrast, appeared to lie further east. (See map 2.1. For technical reasons, this map shows the ethnic composition of each sampled front's population of individuals rather than household heads.) In a very real sense, then, to walk west down Girard Avenue was to walk *into* a German neighborhood, one with a gateway marked by the smokestack over Schmidt's.

The district's heavily German streets offered the potential for a local German ethnic community. What gave that community life, however, were the ties that first- and second-generation German immigrants forged among themselves. Here, Philadelphia's *Vereinswesen* provided connecting links, tying Girard Avenue Germans, in a series of overlapping social relations, to each other and to German neighbors in adjoining wards. These relations in part followed the *Vereinswesen*'s own cleavages. Among the *Vereine* that called the Girard Avenue district home in 1900 were singing societies such as the middle-class Mozart Harmonie, a German veterans' group, and a "Bavarian" club. Specifically working-class affiliations in the neighborhood were maintained, for example, by the Girard Avenue Arbeiter Unterstützungs-Verein, No. 1, a workers' beneficial society, and the organized brewery workers at Schmidt's, who belonged to the United German Trades. The UGT connection in turn fostered local ties, for the federation's Brewers Union No. 5 held meetings every other Sunday at the Labor Lyceum on Sixth Street, two blocks south of the Sixteenth Ward.[15] The best-documented of such local spatial German communities, however, are the religious ones embodied in the neighborhood's Lutheran and Catholic churches.

German Lutheranism in the district centered on three congregations: St. Paul's Independent Evangelical Lutheran Church, in the Sixteenth Ward; St. Paul's German Lutheran Church, one block below the Sixteenth Ward; and St. Jacobus' German Lutheran Church, one block above the Seventeenth Ward. In 1900, St. Jacobus' was the Pennsylvania Ministerium's largest German Lutheran congregation in Philadelphia, with 962 communing members. St. Paul's was the fifth-largest, with 500 communing members. St. Paul's Independent appeared roughly as robust as St. Paul's, confirming seventy-eight members on Palm Sunday 1900 to the latter's sixty-eight.[16] Of the three churches, St. Paul's German Lutheran left behind the fullest historical record, including a memoir by one of its pastors, Georg von Bosse. With him as our guide, we will examine local German Lutheran life through a closer focus on St. Paul's.

Von Bosse came to Philadelphia from Germany in 1889 to serve as an assistant to St. Paul's then-pastor, Friedrich Wischau. He stayed until called to a congregation of his own in 1891. On Wischau's death in 1905, von Bosse returned to St. Paul's as pastor.[17] The church was strongly rooted in its neighborhood. An 1895 membership list indicates that many of St. Paul's 513 congregants came from the larger vicinity of Northern Liberties, defined as the Eleventh, Twelfth, and Sixteenth wards. A quarter of all members (26 percent) lived in the Sixteenth Ward alone. The membership tailed off with distance, however; the Seventeenth Ward accounted for only 6 percent of church members.[18] The congregants also appear to have been fairly evenly divided in terms of gender. Of the members on the 1895 list, 234, or 46 percent, had an identifiably female first name or bore the title of "Frau." Significantly more women than men, however, participated in the church's societies. In 1895, three male associations in the church—the Männlicher Armenverein, the Jungmännerchor, and the Kranken-Unterstützungs-Verein—had 41, 50, and 72 members, respectively. In contrast, the church's female-only Frauen-Verein had 114 members that year, and its Jungfrauen-Verein had more than 200.[19]

Von Bosse's recollections suggest that a significant number of St. Paul's immigrant members in 1889 came from the same locality in Swabia, a region of southwest Germany. The congregation's origins shifted east over time, however. On his return in 1905, von Bosse observed that many members he had known as an assistant pastor had died or moved away to "newly created suburbs," their places filled by German Hungarians and Russian Germans.[20]

For all their regional diversity, the members of St. Paul's were encouraged to think of themselves as Germans in a larger sense. Both Wischau and von Bosse had strong ethnic commitments. They were active in the German Society of Pennsylvania and the National German-American Alliance, and they did not hesitate to carry their convictions into church. Wischau, in von Bosse's view, maintained St. Paul's during his thirty-five-year tenure as "a nursery of German faith, German character, and the German language." Sunday school instruction under Wischau was entirely in German. The church's parochial school used both German and English, but the first hour of instruction was in German and pupils in the upper classes learned German history and geography.[21]

Von Bosse portrayed these efforts as successful. Yet his own account of the congregation in 1889 suggests that English language use had made great inroads with the second generation. Among themselves, the Sunday school students spoke English almost exclusively. This reluctance to use German in everyday settings became quite clear when von Bosse made the expected visits to congregants' families in the neighborhood. At one stop, the German-speaking lady of the house, an immigrant, invited him into "den Parlor" and had him sit in "diesen Rockingchair."[22] From there, things went downhill:

> All at once, an urchin, about five years old, stormed into the room and screamed, "Mam, I want a piece of cake." "Well, Georgie, *du mußt deutsch sprechen* [you must speak German]." [The boy, in English:] "No I wont." "*Komm, Georgie, das ist unser neuer Pfarrer,* shake *mal* hands *mit ihm* [Come, Georgie, this is our new pastor, shake hands with him]." "No, I wont," the whippersnapper replied. . . . Somewhat astonished at this kind of child rearing, I excused myself. To my farewell, the woman said [in English] "Good bye" and urged her offspring to say the same, but instead came back, again, "No I wont."[23]

In this five-year-old's obstinate use of English, von Bosse might have seen an ominous portent. St. Paul's, with its societies and schools, provided its children with something of an ethnic enclave. But if the Sunday school's experience is any indication, their common language, at least with each other, was English.

Like St. Paul's, St. Peter's Roman Catholic Church represented, in many ways, an ethnic bastion. St. Peter's at the turn of the century took in between 7,000 and 7,500 Catholics. The territory of the parish included part of Kensington and almost all of Northern Liberties, and contained the Sixteenth and Seventeenth wards.[24] With its church, convent, school, and church hall, St. Peter's offered local German-speaking Catholics a nearly complete spiritual and social world. Parishioners could hear sermons and have confession heard in German, participate in any of nine fraternal and beneficial societies, send their children to join the 1,100 pupils at the parish school, and bury their dead at St. Peter's cemetery. The parish, in fact, was well on its way to having its own saint, the Bohemian-born German-speaking fourth bishop of Philadelphia, John Neumann. Neumann, whose remains were interred in St. Peter's basement chapel, had been declared Venerable, and the process of his beatification was under way by the turn of the century.[25] The life of so vibrant a parish seems to have attracted men as well as women. Female parishioners appeared to predominate among those who attended mass, but the parish societies may have counted more male than female members.[26]

Yet this German-speaking parish was not monolithically German, in an ethnic sense. Its diversity becomes clear when one looks at St. Peter's baptismal register for 1900, which listed the father's and mother's birthplace for almost all of the 391 people baptized that year. The register suggests that St. Peter's remained predominantly an immigrant parish; 60 percent of those baptized had fathers born outside the United States. Of these 235 children, the great majority (69 percent) had fathers born within the bounds of the German Empire, mostly in southern Germany. Just under a third, however, had fathers born outside Germany, and not all of those fathers were ethnically German. A few hailed from other countries in northwest Europe, including England, Ireland, Holland, and Sweden. The register even notes one baptized child with an Italian father. But by far the largest contingent of foreign fathers born outside Germany came from eastern Europe, from Hungary above all. Here, the ethnic picture becomes quite complicated. There are signs that ethnic Germans from Hungary had found their way to St. Peter's, for fifteen of the thirty-three children of Hungarian-born fathers had surnames that were clearly or possibly German. Most of the remaining eighteen children, however, had clearly Slavic surnames. Similarly, of the twelve children with fathers listed as either from Austria or Austria-Hungary, nine had clearly or possibly German surnames, but the remaining three surnames were of Slavic, Magyar, and either Slavic or Magyar derivation, respectively.[27]

A somewhat different pattern emerges when one considers the 148 children with American-born fathers baptized at St. Peter's in 1900. The vast majority of these children (82 percent) had fathers with clearly or possibly German surnames. However, of the twenty-seven children with clearly non-German surnames, two-thirds had names that were clearly Irish (six individuals), clearly British (four individuals), or of either Irish or British derivation (eight individuals). Of the fourteen fathers with clearly or possibly Irish surnames, moreover, eleven were paired with mothers who had clearly German maiden names. For its American-born fathers, then, St. Peter's remained a predominantly German church that nonetheless saw a small degree of ethnic mixing. This mixing, however, occurred almost entirely along northwest European lines, for only two "new immigrant" surnames—one clearly Slavic and one clearly Italian—appeared among the American-born fathers.[28] The church's marriage register hints at a similar kind of intermixture. Of the sixty-one parish weddings performed in 1900, forty-four (72 percent) involved brides and grooms who both had clearly German surnames. However, thirteen of these parish weddings (21 percent) clearly united German spouses with non-German ones. Five of these thirteen matches were German-Irish, five united Germans and individuals of English or Anglo-American background, and at least one brought a Slavic groom together with a German bride.[29]

German predominance extended to the parish's self-image. The author of a 1901 parish history cast the church as founded "to fill the spiritual needs of the Germans residing in the up-town district." The history nowhere mentioned the east European background of some current parish members. German predominance could not, however, guarantee the predominance of the German language. Where Wischau would never have thought to preach in English, St. Peter's by 1901 offered a low mass with a "short English sermon" on Sunday mornings before the regular high mass. And while St. Paul's 1895 anniversary history was entirely in German, St. Peter's printed its 1901 commemorative volume half in German and half in English.[30]

Still, St. Peter's appears to have kept most local Catholics of German background within its orbit at the turn of the twentieth century. Their obvious alternative would have been one of the two territorial parishes in the Girard Avenue district, St. Michael's and Immaculate Conception. Yet these parishes, whose spatial boundaries overlapped those of St. Peter's, remained predominantly Irish at the time. A closer look at St. Michael's, the larger of the territorial parishes,[31] illustrates the degree of, and limits to, mixing between local German and Irish Catholics.

St. Michael's in 1900 was effectively an Irish parish. The best evidence of this comes from the annual "fall collection," during which the parish priests visited every household in the parish, partly to secure donations.[32] The name of each donor was printed every December in the parish bulletin. The December 1901 list named 1,679 donors; 89 percent of them had clearly or possibly Irish surnames. Of the 178 clearly non-Irish donors, a plurality (sixty-nine, or 39 percent) had clearly German surnames, while nearly a third had surnames clearly of English, Scottish, or Welsh derivation. No Slavic or Italian surnames appeared on the list. The small German presence at St. Michael's—donors with clearly German names made up just 4.1 percent of all individuals on the list—factored hardly at all in the parish's ethnic self-image, to judge by the parish bulletin. The bulletin featured a column titled "Hooley and Finnessy," whose eponymous heroes provided a running commentary on parish life. In the December 1901 column, they scolded those parishioners who skipped mass. Finnessy noted that "many of them came from the Island of Saints," while "[s]ome of them hail from England and Scotland." Neither he nor Hooley even hinted at the existence of German parishioners.[33]

What does emerge from the parish bulletin is a clear sense of the boundary separating the Germans of St. Peter's from the mainly Irish parishioners of St. Michael's. This boundary was not impermeable, but it was generally recognized and was well-policed by the parish priests. During the 1899 fall collection, for example, the priests of St. Michael's discovered that "some persons" were alternately claiming membership in St. Michael's *and* St. Peter's, to avoid making a donation to either. The bulletin warned readers sternly that a Catholic "must select ONE [parish], and, once having selected it, he cannot go back and again claim membership in what he has thought well to leave."[34]

Nevertheless, one can find portents of a future erosion of the barriers between German and Irish Catholics. Of the seventy-five weddings performed at St. Michael's in 1900, no fewer than eighteen (24 percent) clearly involved at least one German partner, according to a surname analysis of the parish marriage register. Six of these eighteen were German-Irish matches, while five united Germans with spouses of English or Anglo-American background. Indeed, clearly Irish-Irish matches accounted for only twenty-three, or 31 percent, of the seventy-five weddings.[35] Such intermarriage suggests that the divide between German and Irish Catholics had weakened among young people by 1900. Over time, more Catholics would follow their lead.

A STREETCAR RIDE TO GERMANTOWN

Four miles northwest of crowded, gritty, treeless Girard Avenue lay Germantown, a city neighborhood the *Philadelphia Press* columnist "Morris" proclaimed the "most beautiful jewel in the crown of Philadelphia's suburbs."[36] (See maps 1.1 and 2.2.) In May 1905, he advised readers to take a streetcar up from the heart of the city for a visit. A rider would pass endless ranks of North Philadelphia row houses and the smoke-shrouded Midvale Steel plant. Then, the trolley would climb up Wayne Avenue to a sudden hilltop view of "a different city":

Look out of the front of the car. You will not gaze far for the perspective is lost in a frame of green as the tree tops bend and seem to meet across the ample avenue. Look to right and left. . . . Macadam pavements give a suburban air. . . . Up and down these streets you may wander for miles and when your tour is ended you will almost be persuaded that you have not seen two houses that are alike.[37]

This was Germantown.

Observers like "Morris" shared a common perception of Germantown as a suburban haven for the middle and upper classes. Germantown was, after all, one of the nation's first railroad suburbs and, by the 1890s, home to a highly visible segment of aristocratic "Proper Philadelphia." But the neighborhood was also an important industrial center. These two Germantowns, in fact, existed side by side, in the form of a distinctly middle-class west side and a heavily immigrant, working-class east side.

Dispersed across both sides of Germantown in 1900 was a small minority of first- and second-generation German immigrants. These German-stock Germantowners, some 2,800 people in a community numbering more than 37,000 residents,[38] did not cluster on their block fronts, but neither did they disappear into a larger "American" sea. Rather, they lived next door to—and, in many cases, shared institutions with—a mix of neighbors of northwest European background.

That only 7.4 percent of Germantown's population was immigrant German or of immigrant German parentage in 1900 is a matter of some irony. The Frankfurt radical pietist Franz Daniel Pastorius founded Germantown in 1683 at the head of a party of Rhineland families. No matter that these families, variously described as Quaker and Mennonite, appear to have been mostly Dutch in origin.[39] By the late nineteenth century, historians and German-American activists had cast the Pastorius party as the first contingent in the large-scale migration of Germans to America. The massive German emigration to Pennsylvania during the eighteenth century contributed to the settlement's growth, with German commonly used there in the colonial period. But the town was ethnically and religiously heterogeneous, and its German residents married out and increasingly anglicized their surnames over the eighteenth century. This Germantown also attracted many water-powered mills and craft workshops, along with an increasing number of wealthy summer visitors from Philadelphia.[40]

These traits—industrial, residential, and assimilatory—were amplified over the nineteenth century. First, Germantown emerged as a major textile center, which drew a heavy stream of English immigrants. By 1899, the neighborhood had eighty-two textile firms employing more than 4,000 workers, mostly in hosiery knitting.[41] Second, commuter rail lines turned the neighborhood into a year-round address for "Proper Philadelphia" families, who made the Germantown Cricket Club an important social center for upper-class Philadelphians.[42] Third, descendants of colonial German settlers remained a visible part of town life, but by the end of the nineteenth century they constituted one part of a local Protestant mainstream[43] that fused some colonial German and English cultural elements. In that respect, those residents could be described as Pennsylvania Germans, albeit ones for whom English had become the sole language.

This last development can be traced institutionally through the history of two churches that had been the town's largest in the eighteenth century: St. Michael's Lutheran Church and the German Reformed Church at Market Square. Both were founded in the 1730s as German-language churches. By the mid-nineteenth century, German services had given way to English ones at St. Michael's, although not before some impatient congregants seceded in 1836 to form an "English Lutheran" congregation, which became Trinity Lutheran Church. The next secession from St. Michael's, in 1855, involved German-speaking, presumably immigrant congregants who still desired German services. They left to create St. Thomas' Evangelical Lutheran Church.[44]

Of Germantown's three Lutheran churches in 1900, then, only the smallest—St. Thomas'—still used German. St. Michael's retained a certain confessional distinctiveness as a Pennsylvania Ministerium congregation. Yet it appeared open enough to Anglo-American ways to feature the Anglo-Protestant hymn "Rock of Ages" at a 1905 anniversary service. Trinity, a General Synod church, appears to have joined wholeheartedly in the larger world of Protestant ecumenism, which was made possible locally by the proliferation of Anglo-Protestant churches over the nineteenth century. German Lutherans, German Reformed, and Quakers had composed the town's largest religious groups in the eighteenth century. By 1811, however, Germantown had a Methodist, a Presbyterian, and an Episcopalian church. In 1900, such Anglo-American congregations far outnumbered Protestant churches with colonial German roots. Within this larger Anglo-Protestant milieu, Trinity Lutheran felt quite at home. Its pastor, for example, "breathed out the true spirit of unity" at a 1902 service commemorating the fiftieth anniversary of Germantown's First Baptist Church. By this point, the town's German Reformed congregation had literally annexed itself to Anglo-American Protestantism: in 1856, it joined the Fourth Presbytery of Philadelphia and became the Market Square Presbyterian Church.[45]

These developments suggest that local residents of colonial German descent, while they shed the German language, did not simply vanish into an Anglo-Protestant sea. Rather, as Germantowners of long lineage—in some cases, as descendants of the town's founders—they could claim

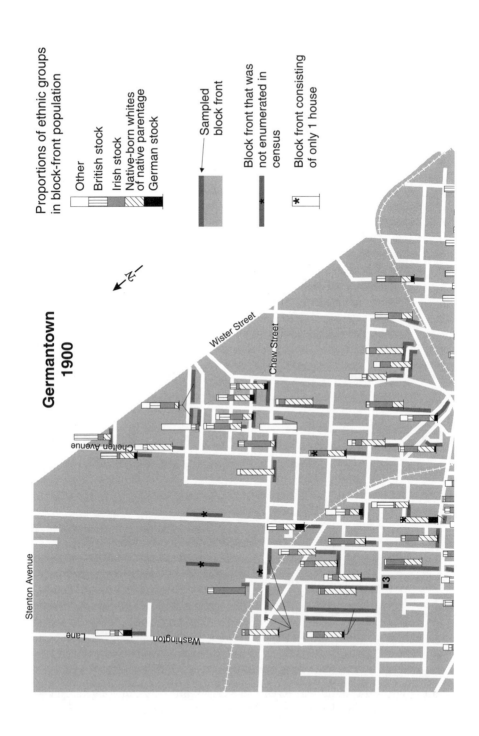

Germantown
1900

Proportions of ethnic groups
in block-front population

Other
British stock
Irish stock
Native-born whites
of native parentage
German stock

Sampled
block front

Block front that was
not enumerated in
census

Block front consisting
of only 1 house

Stenton Avenue

Washington Lane

Chelten Avenue

Wister Street

Chew Street

Landmarks

1 Vernon Park
2 St. Vincent de Paul Roman Catholic Church
3 St. Thomas' Evangelical Lutheran Church
4 Trinity Lutheran Church
5 Germantown Cricket Club
6 YMCA
7 Market Square Presbyterian Church

Map 2.2. **Germantown, 1900.** Sources: Author's census sample; George W. Bromley and Walter S. Bromley, *Atlas of the City of Philadelphia, Twenty-second Ward* (Philadelphia, 1899); Ernest Hexamer and Son, *Insurance Maps of the City of Philadelphia* (Philadelphia, 1890–1914), vols. 16, 21, 28, 29, 33 (for more specific publication information, see appendix, note 3).

a place at the center of the town's history. They, together with Anglo-Protestants of colonial origin and some more recently arrived Protestants, *were* Germantown's mainstream. The sense that the local mainstream was a middle-class amalgam with English and German colonial roots comes across in contemporary descriptions of the area's old families. For when Germantowners referred to the neighborhood's "old" or "prominent" families in 1900, they meant not only the Ashmeads and Bringhursts of colonial English derivation,[46] but also families of colonial German descent—the various lines of the Keyser, Kulp, Pastorius, Rittenhouse, Saur, Shoemaker, Wistar, and Wister clans, among others[47]—as well as the Johnsons and Luckens of colonial Dutch Quaker origin.[48]

Germantown's mainstream Protestants in 1900 lived amid a larger population composed primarily of residents of different northwest European backgrounds. Its nature becomes clearer when we consider Germantown's ethnic and class composition, as shown by an analysis of a 15 percent sample of the neighborhood's block fronts in 1900. This sample of 140 fronts yielded 6,181 individuals and 1,220 household heads (see appendix). The neighborhood here is defined as the territory encompassed by the borough of Germantown before its 1854 incorporation into the city of Philadelphia (see map 2.2).[49]

Germantown in 1900 was distinctly more middle-class than the Sixteenth and Seventeenth wards. Fully 41 percent of working Germantown household heads held white-collar positions (see table 2.3). Where the Girard Avenue district had very few professionals, major proprietors, and other high-white-collar household heads, this stratum made up a third of Germantown's white-collar workers and 15 percent of the overall workforce. The neighborhood's working class was, correspondingly, smaller than that of the Sixteenth and Seventeenth wards but still took in a majority (59 percent) of all employed household heads.

In its ethnic makeup, Germantown differed strikingly from the Girard Avenue district. As in Philadelphia overall, native whites of native parentage made up the largest group, comprising 43 percent of the individuals in the sample (see table 2.2). Given Germantown's history, this group clearly included a perceptible number of residents of colonial German descent. The neighborhood's second- and third-largest ethnic groups were first- and second-generation immigrants from Ireland (24.6 percent) and Britain (16 percent). German immigrants and their children, a plurality in the Sixteenth and Seventeenth wards, finished fourth in Germantown; they made up 8.2 percent of all individuals in the sample. African Americans formed Germantown's fifth-largest group at 4.8 percent, equal to their proportion in the city as a whole. Noticeably absent from the Germantown sample were Russian-stock individuals, who made up the largest

TABLE 2.3

Class/Skill Levels of Working Household Heads, by Ethnicity: Germantown, 1900 (Percent)

	All Heads	German Stock	NWNP*	Irish Stock	British Stock	South European Stock	Black
1. High white-collar	14.8 (±3.6)	12.5 (±7.1)	22.9 (±6.2)	4.1 (±2.6)	14.2 (±5.8)	0.0	0.0
2. Low white-collar	26.1 (±4.3)	21.4 (±6.9)	35.7 (±6.3)	17.5 (±5.5)	22.5 (±6.7)	0.0	7.7
3. Blue-collar skilled	33.7 (±4.6)	54.5 (±9.2)	26.4 (±6.3)	30.9 (±6.0)	43.1 (±8.3)	16.7	17.9
4. Blue-collar semi/unskilled	25.3 (±4.5)	11.6 (±6.0)	15.0 (±4.4)	47.5 (±6.0)	20.2 (±6.2)	83.3	74.4
Total (N)	1,026	112	406	217	218	6	39

Source: Author's census sample.

Note: Figures in parentheses are 95 percent confidence intervals for each proportion, corresponding to the 0.05 level of significance. Confidence intervals were not calculated for South European–stock or African-American household heads, because of the small size of these groups (see appendix). For definition of "stock," see table 2.1. For composition of British and South European stock, see table 2.2.

*Native-born whites of native parentage.

new immigrant group in the Girard Avenue district. In both samples, the proportions for east European and south European (mostly Italian) individuals were so small as to be suggestive at best. However, the Germantown sample had proportionally fewer east European and slightly more south European residents than the Girard Avenue sample.

A Germantowner's place in the local class structure had a great deal to do with his or her ethnic affiliation (see table 2.3). First, most native whites of native parentage led white-collar lives. Fifty-nine percent of the working household heads in this group fell into either the high-white-collar or low-white-collar category. For these people, Germantown functioned as the middle-class suburb its boosters portrayed. Second, British-stock and German-stock residents had substantial minorities in the white-collar sector, but, as along Girard Avenue, they were anchored in skilled blue-collar work. However, to the extent their small sample numbers allow such generalizations, it seems that German-stock household heads in Germantown were better able than those in the Sixteenth and Seventeenth wards to avoid unskilled labor and hold white-collar jobs.

Third, the Germantown Irish, while somewhat more successful in obtaining skilled blue-collar work than the Girard Avenue Irish, remained rooted in semiskilled and unskilled labor. Finally, insofar as their small sample numbers permit conclusions, African Americans and new immigrants appear to have lived on the bottom rungs of Germantown's class ladder.

These class and ethnic differences translated into spatial differences. Essentially, there existed at least two Germantowns in 1900, and the dividing line between them was the neighborhood's main thoroughfare and primary business street: Germantown Avenue, or Main Street. A majority (57 percent) of the 1,026 working household heads in the sample lived east of Main, while 43 percent lived west of that line. Yet an astonishing 72 percent of Germantown's high-white-collar household heads lived on the west side. Low-white-collar household heads straddled Main Street, with almost equal proportions residing on either side. Nearly two-thirds of all skilled household heads, however, lived east of Main, as did 71 percent of semiskilled and unskilled heads. Most immigrant-stock household heads in the sample also lived on the east side. The east side claimed 55 percent of all household heads, but held 62 percent of British-stock, 66 percent of Irish-stock, and 67 percent of African-American household heads.

In their faces, the east and west sides reflected this uneven spatial distribution. The east side, or East Germantown, as it was called, was, in effect, Germantown's immigrant and working-class quarter. Here, 61 percent of household heads were European immigrants or the children of immigrants, and 71 percent of working heads were blue-collar workers. Maps of the area show a host of textile mills, dye works, machine shops, and other manufactories.[50] On the west side, native whites of native parentage composed 48 percent of all household heads, and white-collar workers made up 56 percent of working heads. Factories were scarce in this district outside its far southern end. Instead, one found the institutions sustained by Proper Philadelphia: large estates, Germantown Academy, and the Germantown Cricket Club. East Germantown had its middle-class railroad commuters, but the west side was the section that became fixed as the "suburb of Germantown" in the imagination of middle-class Philadelphians—a place of "spacious, elegant homes with lawns meeting the tree-shaded avenues."[51]

German immigrants and their children experienced Germantown as something of an in-between group. Being relatively few in number, they had to find their place in the interstices of a local social structure dominated by others. Their class position was midway between native whites of native parentage, who were concentrated in white-collar occupations, and the Irish, with their base in semiskilled and unskilled labor. Spatially,

Germantown's German-stock residents were scattered among their neighbors; the vast majority lived on block fronts where they were a distinct minority. In fact, unlike the other major ethnic groups, German-stock household heads were almost exactly split between the east side (49.2 percent) and the west side (50.8 percent).

The residential world into which Germantown's Germans dispersed, moreover, had a distinct ethnic cast: on their block fronts, they lived next door to a mix of northwest Europeans. This mixing is evident on map 2.2, which shows the ethnic composition of each block front, but it is most succinctly illustrated through an index of exposure known as the P^* statistic. The index summarizes the degree to which the "average" German lived on a block front with members of other ethnic groups. (For a more detailed description, see the appendix.) In the Sixteenth and Seventeenth wards, the average German-stock individual lived on a front that was 53 percent German-stock, 25 percent native white of native parentage, and 10 percent Irish-stock, with a scattering of members of other ethnic groups. In contrast, the average German-stock individual in Germantown lived on a front that was 19 percent German-stock, 16 percent British-stock, 20 percent Irish-stock, and 39 percent native white of native parentage. Representatives of other groups were so few as to be negligible. (See table 2.4.)

As a small and scattered minority in Germantown, immigrant Germans had a relatively weak set of local ethnic institutions at the turn of the twentieth century. There was no German Catholic church in the neighborhood. Germantown boasted a mere four German-American secular *Vereine,* three of which would fold before 1917: a lodge of the German Order of the Harugari; the German-American Building and Loan Association of Germantown; the Deutscher Bruderbund Unterstuetzungs Verein, a mutual beneficial society; and the Germantown Maennerchor. The Harugari lodge vanished between 1900 and 1908. The building and loan association was "[f]ounded by prominent German-Americans" in 1872; it appears to have been a first-generation enterprise, for all of its meetings were conducted in German. With the aging of that generation, the association passed on, closing its books in 1905.[52] Organized in the early 1880s, the Bruderbund found in the mid-1910s that "[c]essation of German immigration" had prevented its growth. It disbanded in 1915 or 1916. The Germantown Maennerchor, a male choir founded in 1867, was somewhat more durable. The group had its own building, Maennerchor Hall, and seems to have had an affiliated women's choir. The Maennerchor, however, appeared to be losing some steam by 1915, when a local newspaper termed it "nominally a male singing society, but in reality a social club."[53]

Germantown's only other immigrant German institution at the turn of the century was St. Thomas' Lutheran Church. St. Thomas' was small: it

TABLE 2.4
Ethnic Composition, by Percent, of the "Average" German-Stock Resident's Block Front: Girard Avenue District and Germantown, 1900 (P* Indices)

	Wards 16 and 17	Germantown
German stock	53.3*	18.6*
Native whites of native parentage	25.3*	38.6*
Irish stock	9.8*	20.5*
British stock	2.6*	15.8*
Russian stock	2.4*	0.0
East European stock	1.5	0.4
South European stock	0.3	0.5
Other Northwest European stock	2.9	1.7
Other	1.9	4.0
Total	100.0	100.1

Source: Author's census samples.

Note: For definition of "stock," see table 2.1. For composition of ethnic categories listed here, see table 2.2. The Germantown column totals 100.1 percent, due to rounding of individual results. The P* value for German-stock Germantowners in regard to black residents specifically was 3.2 percent, although this did not fall within the 95 percent confidence interval of the corresponding resampled mean P*. No corresponding P* value for the Girard Avenue district was calculated, given the very small number of African Americans living there in 1900.

Population parameter can be reliably inferred from result, as latter falls within the 95 percent confidence interval of the corresponding resampled mean P (see appendix).

had seventy communicant members in 1900. The congregation appears to have been primarily female, immigrant, and working-class. Although the pastor and church board members were male, more than two-thirds of the forty-three communicants at the church's 1901 Easter service were female.[54] The church's marriage records suggest a heavy immigrant presence. Of the thirty-one weddings recorded in the parish register between 1895 and 1905, fifteen involved a groom born in Germany, while in sixteen the bride was German-born. More than half of the thirty-one grooms, moreover, were skilled blue-collar workers, while nearly one-quarter held unskilled positions; only four grooms were low white-collar workers.[55]

That St. Thomas' was a German-language institution, however, did not preclude ethnic mixing. Seven of the thirty-one weddings (22.6 percent) clearly united German spouses with non-German ones. All but one of these involved a German bride—either born in Germany or with a clearly German maiden name—marrying out. Moreover, these six female out-marriages had a specific class and ethnic tendency. The grooms involved were predominantly working-class: they included a weaver, a machinist, a cook, a tinsmith, an electrician, and a railroad employee. In addition, all six grooms were of northwest European background: two were born in England, another was Belgian-born, and the three American-born grooms had clearly Anglo-American or Irish surnames.[56] For the young German women of St. Thomas', out-marriage took place along northwest European and largely working-class lines.

If Germantown provided a weak set of ethnic institutions for its immigrant German residents and their children, where did they then go? The remainder of this section examines three neighborhood institutions through which some second-generation Germans, in particular, were able to modify their identities and assume roles removed from a specifically German ethnicity. These are the Business Men's Association of Germantown; the Germantown Young Men's Christian Association; and the territorial Catholic parish of St. Vincent de Paul.

The Business Men's Association of Germantown was organized in the late 1890s to encourage "trade to its members and the advancement of the interests of Germantown." By 1902, it had 224 members.[57] In its first decade, it pushed for improvements to local parks and roads and lobbied for the establishment of a high school in Germantown. But the association also pursued the class interests of the retailers, professionals, and small manufacturers who belonged to it, seeking in particular to "encourage on the part of our towns-people a disposition to give precedence to its home industries and trade."[58]

Beyond its stated goals, the Business Men's Association offered its members an arena within which to socialize and work with other middle-class men. Second-generation German residents helped to create this opportunity, for they were instrumental in the association's founding. A look at the twenty members who put their names to the group's 1898 charter reveals an organization that united immigrants from northwest Europe and their children with longer-settled white residents, around the shared interests of a broadly defined middle class of local "business men."

The association's charter members stood on Germantown's economic middle ground, running businesses that oriented them toward the neighborhood.[59] Most were substantial retail merchants, many with shops on Germantown Avenue. Of seventeen whose occupations could be traced in manuscript census and city directory entries, three ran grocery stores, three conducted men's furnishing stores, two had furniture and storage

businesses, one ran a hardware store, one was a coal dealer, and one man-
ufactured and retailed candy.[60] The upper echelon among the charter
members included a real estate agent, Charles J. Schaefer; the association's
paid secretary, John J. Kenney; and the publishers of two of the neighborhood's three weekly newspapers, Walter Bonsall of the *Germantown
Guide* and Horace F. McCann of the *Germantown Independent-Gazette*.
Most charter members thus had an intensely local perspective that differentiated them from the upper-class residents who commuted to downtown offices and the local textile manufacturers who sold to a broader
market. The two exceptions here were the group's sole identifiable textile
manufacturer, Wilson Woods, a partner in a small, east-side quilt factory;
and its sole Proper Philadelphian, Lewis Wynne Wister. Wister, the some-
time treasurer of the Germantown Cricket Club, came from one of Germantown's most prominent families, descended from eighteenth-century
German immigrant John Wister. During his lifetime, Lewis Wister was a
member of a family insurance firm with downtown offices. However, his
primary position in 1900 was as a partner in a local lumber dealership.[61]

These men represented not only Germantown's middle class but also
immigrants and children of immigrants who had entered that class along
with whites of colonial English and German descent. Of fifteen charter
members whose ethnic background could be traced in the census, three
were immigrants and no fewer than seven were American-born children
of immigrant parents.[62] The remaining five members were native whites
of native parentage; three had clearly German surnames, and at least
three—Wister, Jacob C. Bockius, and Levi S. Tull—descended from Germantown families dating to the colonial era.[63] The three immigrant
charter members came from England, Ireland, and Germany. Of the seven
second-generation members, four had at least one English-born parent,
while three—Schaefer, hat store proprietor Frederick W. Kaplan, and gro-
cer Henry W. Pletcher—had German-born mothers and fathers.[64]

This immigrant presence brought religious diversity to the nonsectarian Business Men's Association. Of the seven charter members for whom
I could determine religious affiliations, one was Presbyterian, three were
Episcopalians, and two were Baptists—including the lone immigrant German, John Kyle. The charter had room for at least one Catholic signer in
Henry Pletcher. The group appears to have been open as well to Jewish
members. Whether or not Frederick Kaplan was of German Jewish background is unclear, but an immigrant German Jew, Lehman Hoffman, was
active in the association during its early years.[65]

The Business Men's Association did have limits to its openness, however. The group's constituency was somewhat broader in a class sense than
its charter suggests, for the overall membership appears to have included
a fair number of white-collar professionals and self-employed master ar-

tisans. In January 1901, for example, the association's board of directors approved twelve applicants for membership, including a stone cutter, a horse shoer, a baker, and the proprietors of a plumbing business, as well as a dentist and an insurance agent. Still, to judge by the organization's minutes, its membership remained confined to whites of northwest European origin. For the south and east European immigrants, particularly Italians, then settling in Germantown, this may have reflected the fact that most were in no class position to join an organization of "business men." The association appears to have regarded Germantown's African Americans as, in any case, outsiders. At a February 1906 meeting, the membership discussed a letter to the *Germantown Guide* asking "the white people of this old town" to assist black residents in acquiring a cemetery, "[a]s they are not permitted to bury their dead in our cemeteries." The minutes noted of black Germantowners that "[t]hey had a piece of ground that they could get," indicating that such residents were considered as "they," rather than as potentially part of the association.[66]

For the first- and second-generation immigrants who helped found it, the association provided a forum for sociability that transcended some ethnic lines while remaining firmly ensconced within those of color, gender, and class. Second-generation immigrants played leading roles in the group's formative years: its first two presidents were Hiram T. Parker, whose father was born in England, and Schaefer. Association records, however, contain virtually no indications that members ever expressed a sense of ethnic identity, whether English, Irish, or German, at its gatherings. The sole exception appears to have been a "St. Patrick's Day Smoker" organized for the members in 1910. Rather, the association's all-male meetings, smokers, and banquets allowed participants to socialize self-consciously as solid, middle-class business men. Thus, member McCann's newspaper, the *Independent-Gazette,* told readers that before the 1908 annual banquet, "the members and guests were congregated in the reception room, talking over the affairs of the country, city and local matters that are always interesting and entertaining to business men."[67] Here, members could recast their identities on middle-class lines, within a northwest-European American context, but in an institution far removed from specifically ethnic concerns.

Not all accepted this invitation to tone down or escape the ethnic elements of their identities. Albert Insinger, elected to the association's board of directors in 1900, was at the same time treasurer of the Deutscher Bruderbund Unterstuetzungs Verein. Charles Schaefer likewise served as a director of the German-American Building and Loan Association, although this may have had to do with his real estate interests; Schaefer generally "was very active in building and loan associations, in which he was a great believer." At least some of the association's German Americans, however, appear to have avoided such ethnic attachments. The clearest evidence here comes from the booklet McCann published in 1908 to mark the festivities surrounding the 225th anniversary of Germantown's settlement. As chapter 6 describes, the celebrations combined the city's Founders' Day with the German Day commemorated by the National German-American Alliance. On page 45, the booklet displayed, on one side, the "Officers and Directors of the Business Men's Association" and, on the other, members of the "German Committee of Germantown for the Celebration of German Day." The two lists had no names in common, even though Frederick Kaplan was among the association directors listed. Likewise missing from the "German Committee" was Henry Pletcher, although one could find him four pages later, displayed as a director of the Germantown and Chestnut Hill Improvement Association.[68] For second-generation Germans such as Kaplan and Pletcher, it seems, the role of "business man" meant far more than an affiliation as "German."

The nonsectarian atmosphere of the Business Men's Association made it something of an exception among the neighborhood's major institutions. Religious divisions remained important in Germantown at the turn of the twentieth century, ensuring that at least some first- and second-generation German immigrants would integrate into local society partly along confessional lines. For Protestants, this meant integration into the local Protestant mainstream, symbolized best by Germantown's largest pan-Protestant organization, the Young Men's Christian Association. Founded in the early 1870s, the YMCA aimed "to make men . . . Christian," while also providing them with recreational and educational opportunities. In 1900, it offered its 733 members Bible study classes and Sunday afternoon gospel services, along with a library, a gymnasium, evening classes in such practical subjects as bookkeeping, and a set of association sports teams. This menu came with a heavy dose of Protestant evangelicalism, mixed with exhortations to upward mobility. The first page of the organization's monthly bulletin in 1900 featured a doctor's ruminations on "The Kingdom of Heaven" in February and a minister's tips for "Success in Life" in June.[69]

The message, however, was clearly interdenominational. The YMCA's organizational meetings had been held in the Market Square Presbyterian Church and the First Baptist Church, and the 423 members who declared a religious affiliation in 1900 came from nearly every Protestant church in Germantown. About one-quarter were Presbyterian, a fifth were Episcopalian, another fifth were Methodist, and just over a tenth were Baptist. The membership included smaller proportions of Lutherans (7 percent), Quakers (3 percent), and Congregationalists (2 percent), along with a scattering of Unitarians, Reformed, Mennonites, and members of other denominations. The spirit of unity, however, did not extend to Roman Catholicism, although the YMCA did identify fifteen Catholic and two Jewish members in 1900. A reading room containing the *Converted Catholic* was not calculated to make parishioners of St. Vincent de Paul's feel at home.[70]

This largely Protestant membership was overwhelmingly of northwest European background, as is suggested by a surname analysis of the 733 people on the 1900 membership roll. Eighty-three percent of those members had names clearly derived from one or another national group in northwestern Europe. Almost all of the remaining names were northwest European, although they could not be assigned to a single nationality. Only eight members had surnames that were clearly, or even possibly, of Slavic, Italian, or eastern European Jewish origin. Names clearly of British—that is, English, Scottish, or Welsh—origin accounted for 46 percent of the membership, but the roll included substantial minorities of members with surnames that were German (18 percent), Irish (5 percent), or either German or British (11 percent).[71] Some with German surnames were undoubtedly of colonial descent, but others came from nineteenth-century immigrant families, including members Frederick Kaplan and Charles Schaefer.[72]

While circumscribed by religion and ethnicity, the YMCA did bridge, to some extent, Germantown's class divides. Almost half of the 383 members listed with job titles on the roll followed low-white-collar occupations. Yet the roll had nearly equal proportions of high-white-collar (24 percent) and skilled blue-collar (23 percent) workers, along with a smattering of the blue-collar unskilled (6 percent). Clearly, at least some working-class as well as middle-class Germans were integrating into the neighborhood's northwest European Protestant mainstream. Specifically, the membership roll suggests that some of the same German artisans then joining a "labor aristocracy" of well-paid Irish, British, and Anglo-American workers (as chapter 1 describes) were likewise spending their leisure in such ethnically mixed company. More than half of the YMCA's skilled workers, and most of its twenty German-surnamed skilled workers, were employed in industries that defined that aristocracy: textiles, printing, the metal industries, and the building trades.[73]

What might have attracted these German labor aristocrats to the YMCA? Perhaps they were drawn by the organization's religious ethos, for fourteen of the twenty skilled Germans were Protestants. But the YMCA's message of upward mobility may also have resonated with these workers, as it likely did with the thirty-two German-surnamed members who had low-white-collar jobs. There is some evidence that the YMCA attracted Germans whose families were shifting from artisanal to white-collar worlds. Garfield J. Gonaver, for example, the grandson of a German immigrant and the son of a plasterer, joined the organization in 1897; in 1900, he was sixteen years old and working as a trust company clerk. William J. Gruhler, a son of German immigrants and a member since 1892, appeared to have moved up from craftsman to entrepreneur, for the manuscript census described him as a "carpenter & builder."[74]

Yet young Germans did not have to efface their ethnic background to join the YMCA. In fact, they could use that background to shape the local mainstream. Fred Reith, a twenty-three-year-old glazier and second-generation German immigrant, appears to have done just that. Reith joined the YMCA in 1899 and quickly became a star in its gymnastics drills. He drew his expertise directly from the world of German gymnastics associations, or turner groups *(Turnvereine)*, for he was also a prize-winning member of the Turnerbund, a national federation of those associations. This highly skilled worker thus helped inject a German cultural element into the YMCA. Modern gymnastics had been pioneered by turner groups in Germany, and German turners brought the sport to the United States. As participatory sports rose in popularity in the 1890s, YMCAs helped to popularize this immigrant German pastime among the larger population. When Reith, with the aid of a fellow turner, gave a gymnastics demonstration at the First Baptist Church or took center stage in the association's annual gymnastics exhibition with his work on the "German horse," he formed a direct cultural link between the turners and the larger, northwest European Protestant world of the YMCA.[75]

While Germantown's local mainstream was distinctly Protestant, the neighborhood's growing Catholic population constructed its own, parallel social world, which bore the impress of its Irish-stock majority. Germantown at the turn of the century was undergoing a building boom, and a sizable number of those moving into its new homes were more affluent Irish Philadelphians leaving behind the crowded neighborhoods to the southeast.[76] One sign of that movement was the increase of territorial Catholic parishes covering Germantown from one to three between 1899 and 1901. St. Vincent de Paul's was the first and largest. In 1900, St. Vincent's served almost 5,000 parishioners. They supported a score of parish associations, most segregated by gender, from devotional sodalities to charitable and temperance societies to cycling and dramatic clubs.[77]

St. Vincent's was decidedly Irish, as is suggested by a surname analysis of the parish marriage register for 1900. Of the seventy-five weddings performed in St. Vincent's Church that year, sixty (80 percent) involved at least one partner with a clearly Irish surname. The register records only six weddings that clearly involved at least one German; three of these were German-Irish marriages, and one was a German-German match. Another four weddings united African-American couples.[78] That parishioners of

German background found themselves awash in an Irish sea is suggested as well by a list of 481 contributors to the parochial school fund in 1900: the surnames on the list are overwhelmingly Irish, while clearly German surnames number no more than 34 (7.1 percent). Eighty percent of the contributors were women, suggesting a great degree of female involvement in parish life. The parish's monthly bulletin reflected its Irish demographic tilt, entertaining readers with travelogues such as "The Lakes of Killarney."[79]

The experience of moving into suburban neighborhoods and joining their largely Irish territorial parishes was becoming increasingly common for German Catholics at the turn of the century. The pastor of St. Ignatius', the German national parish for suburban West Philadelphia, complained in 1906 that "[t]here are a good many of our people who have joined the nearest [E]nglish church."[80] With no national parish church in their neighborhood, Germantown's German Catholics likely had a greater incentive to attend predominantly Irish churches like St. Vincent's. Such Catholics consequently found themselves entering Irish Catholic social networks and adopting some elements of Irish Catholic identity.

The clearest example is that of Henry Pletcher. Pletcher was born in Germantown in 1859, the son of immigrants who had arrived in the neighborhood from Baden ten years before. His mother was a German Catholic of some commitment, for, as he later recalled, she would regularly walk the four miles from Germantown to what was then the nearest German national church, none other than St. Peter's at Fifth and Girard. Henry, however, became a parishioner of St. Vincent de Paul's. Exactly when he did so remains unclear, but it may have been by the early 1880s. At that time, Pletcher and his brother launched the grocery business of James J. Pletcher & Brother on Germantown Avenue.[81] In 1880, James Pletcher married Cecilia M. Horan at St. Vincent's, and in the early 1890s, Henry followed suit by wedding Margaret E. Tracey, a daughter of Irish immigrants.[82] Henry also became deeply involved in the parish's social life. With these commitments came entry into a largely Irish Catholic social and cultural world. As a young man, Henry was a leading actor in the parish's Enterprise Dramatic Association; many of its plays, like "Colleen Machree" and "The Love of the Shamrock," had specifically Irish settings and themes. He later served on the boards of managers of two Irish Catholic institutions, the Gonzaga Home and St. Joseph's Orphan Asylum. That the Pletchers were firmly planted in Irish-American networks is evident from a look at the guests who celebrated James and Cecilia Pletcher's twenty-fifth wedding anniversary in 1905. A few of those attending the function, such as Henry and Margaret Pletcher, had German names, but the overwhelming number of guests whose names the *Independent-Gazette* recorded were Irish: Reilly, O'Rourke, McMahon,

Tully, McEvoy, Gallagher, McAnany, Kelly, and so forth.[83] Henry Pletcher had made his departure from ethnic German institutions; his destinations, however, included both the nonsectarian, northwest European world of the Business Men's Association and the culturally Irish-American world of St. Vincent's parish.

PATTERNS OF ASSIMILATION

Between the narrow streets of the Girard Avenue district and the greener avenues of Germantown, one could find German-American assimilation at its two extremes in 1900. The ethnic neighborhood that ran through the Sixteenth and Seventeenth wards represented as much of a German enclave as Philadelphia had to offer. Yet even here, English-language use was making tremendous inroads among the second generation, and younger German Catholics had begun to marry their Irish neighbors. Many among Germantown's small minority of first- and second-generation German residents had moved away from its dwindling number of immigrant German institutions. Their paths pointed toward greater mixing with other northwest Europeans, yet those trajectories were strongly inflected by factors of class, religion, and gender. The contrasts between and within these two neighborhoods suggest larger patterns in the assimilation of German Philadelphians at the turn of the twentieth century.

Most broadly, a higher class standing seems to have translated into a greater likelihood that German Philadelphians would leave their ethnic worlds for larger, northwest European ones. The weak German institutions of Germantown coincided not only with a small concentration of immigrant Germans but also with a population substantially more middle-class than that of the strongly German Girard Avenue district. Within Germantown, the Business Men's Association offers the most striking examples of second-generation immigrants distancing themselves from specific ethnic identities in favor of roles as middle-class "business men." To this extent, Germantown might seem to confirm an old theme of assimilation as a process or byproduct of advancement into the middle class.[84]

Yet Germantown shows that assimilation was hardly a middle-class-only affair. Other venues that mixed northwest Europeans, like the YMCA, proved attractive to the upper echelons of the working class. The YMCA, moreover, also illustrates how important religion was in defining the bounds of such mixing. Protestantism functioned as common ground for the working- and middle-class northwest Europeans who socialized there and for the working-class northwest European grooms and German brides who wed at St. Thomas'. Similarly, German Catholics who stepped away from the ethnic fold tended to associate with other Catholics, especially the Irish—a tendency exhibited even by the middle-class Henry Pletcher.

The question of religion, in turn, suggests the importance of differentiating between male and female experiences of assimilation. The limits placed on women's public activity meant that many institutional venues for ethnic mixing, such as the Business Men's Association, were effectively closed to them.[85] For most German women, such mixing as occurred would take place at the level of the family through intermarriage, among immediate neighbors, or in a limited set of public institutions— above all, churches and church-related organizations. Germantown, for example, lacked any large-scale, secular equivalent of the Business Men's Association for middle-class women, at least until the founding of the Women's Club of Germantown in 1917. But women did participate actively in the neighborhood's churches and institutions with church ties, such as the local branches of the Young Women's Christian Association and the Women's Christian Temperance Union.[86] Hence, religious organizations likely loomed larger for women than for men where ethnic mixing was concerned.

A comparison across neighborhoods, however, reveals a larger, overall pattern: German-stock Germantown residents of either middle-class or Protestant background—whether male or female—had a greater chance of mixing specifically with other northwest Europeans than did Catholics in more heavily working-class and German areas like the Girard Avenue district. German Catholicism was strong in the Sixteenth and Seventeenth wards. At the same time, its bulwark, St. Peter's, took in a small but perceptible number of east Europeans, while the relatively few German Catholics who stepped beyond St. Peter's were associating with Irish Catholics. To the degree German Catholics along Girard Avenue crossed ethnic lines, it was to mix with the Irish and, to some extent, "new immigrants."

The beginnings of such an overall pattern were just barely visible at the turn of the twentieth century. While its outlines had emerged in the residential and institutional behavior of some German Philadelphians, few signs existed as yet of corresponding identities. Even Germantown gave little indication of harboring a common northwest European consciousness. The records of the Business Men's Association were essentially silent regarding the national origins of its members. A more logical place to look for such a consciousness might be Germantown's nativist lodges. The neighborhood had a long history of nativist organizing and, in 1900, branches of such groups as the Junior Order United American Mechanics. Yet, as chapter 5 describes, from the available evidence, even Germantown's Junior Order lodge did not evince any great sense of northwest Europeans as a separate and superior group, at least not before

World War I. A pan-European Catholicism likewise seemed fairly distant along Girard Avenue, given the well-policed "national" boundaries between St. Peter's and St. Michael's.

Moreover, even in Germantown, some residents of immigrant German background combined a high degree of integration into the local mainstream with continuing ties to ethnic German associations. This stance, which remained viable until the First World War, amounted to "a kind of biculturalism in spite of structural assimilation," in Kathleen Conzen's formulation. Such German Americans as Fred Reith and Albert Insinger were "able to function effectively both within and outside the ethnic community, often establishing their contacts in circles defined by religion or class."[87]

American entry into World War I, and the anti-German panic that accompanied it, would destroy public biculturalism as a workable option. At that point, many German Philadelphians would confront the issue faced earlier by people like Henry Pletcher: how could one best order one's multiple identities once the German ethnic component had been deemphasized or subtracted? Pletcher, or certainly his acquaintances, found an answer to which some middle-class German Philadelphians would turn in the 1920s. At his death in 1931, a friend composed a remembrance that translated Pletcher's heritage into a common, northwest European currency. For Pletcher's immigrant parents, this friend recalled, "were of the old stock."[88]

PART TWO

Confronting Assimilation, 1900–1914

CHAPTER THREE

The Gendered Crisis of the *Vereinswesen*

WHEN Georg von Bosse sought, on the eve of World War I, to describe the state of German America, he turned to the tiny North Sea island of Helgoland for a metaphor. "Unabated, for millennia, the waves of the sea broke upon it, one crag after another toppled into the deep, smaller and smaller the island became," von Bosse told a German Day audience in Philadelphia. "My friends, Germandom in the United States resembles that island; many a piece has already crumbled away and vanished into the ocean of the American people, but an imposing portion still stands—what shall become of it?"[1]

This perception of erosion was entirely representative. By 1914, in Philadelphia as elsewhere, German immigrants and their children sensed that institutional German America was collapsing in on itself. Since the 1890s, German-language newspapers had lost readers and secular associations had hemorrhaged members. German Lutherans, Catholics, and secular activists alike looked to the future with foreboding. What they saw in the present was a full-scale crisis of the *Vereinswesen*.

For German Philadelphians, the *Vereinswesen*'s crisis was a crisis of assimilation. How some dealt with that challenge in the years leading up to the First World War is the larger theme of part 2. This chapter takes a close look at the crisis itself and its peculiarly uneven nature. Readership and membership losses reached across the secular and religious *Vereinswesen*, yet not all associations suffered; some, in fact, grew. These successes tell us much about the nature of the general crisis—above all, that it was distinctly gendered. Men were indeed abandoning the *Vereinswesen*. Women, on the other hand, appear to have been joining it. Increasingly, they took the place of German men and, in so doing, carved out a larger place for themselves in the city's German-American public sphere.

"DOWNHILL WITH GIANT STEPS"

Looking back from the summer of 1914, the *Philadelphia Tageblatt* offered a bleak view of German associational life. While Philadelphia's *Vereine* had "played a powerful role" fifteen years before, the newspaper recounted, "today almost all are suffering an accelerated decline." Only the German Hungarian societies were doing at all well, due to strong immigration from Hungary, and they were considering a consolidation to avoid the fate that had overtaken associations for immigrants from Germany proper. Other *Tageblatt* reports that summer were equally dismal. As one festival speaker noted, "our German *Vereinswesen* finds itself in such a crisis, as to make the merger of clubs a necessity,"[2] if they were to avoid financial ruin.

This crisis had not happened overnight. In Philadelphia, as in other American cities, the 1890s marked the moment when institutional decline first made itself apparent, through falling newspaper readerships, failing *Vereine,* and an increasing use of English. In its timing, this erosion clearly echoed two demographic trends. The first was a significant trailing off of immigration from Germany during and after the 1890s; Philadelphia's German-born population, like the nation's as a whole, registered its highest point in the census of 1890.[3] The second trend was the rise of second-generation immigrants to a preponderate position within German America. The census of 1900 revealed that the adult children of German immigrants had come to outnumber the German-born, for within the category of male breadwinners, the second generation was 17 percent more numerous than the first.[4] The *Vereinswesen*'s future hinged on the stance taken toward it by this American-born generation, and that stance seemed increasingly one of indifference.

Perhaps the most sensitive barometer of decline was the city's German-language press. Philadelphia in 1890 supported six daily German-language newspapers. Two of those newspapers folded over the following decade. All four of the surviving dailies posted circulation losses at some point in the years between 1890 and 1915. The city's oldest German-language daily, for example, the middle-class *Demokrat,* which had an estimated 28,000 readers in 1870, claimed only 17,500 in 1895, and that figure dropped to 14,000 in 1915; in 1918, the newspaper merged with the *Philadelphia Morgen-Gazette.*[5] Such losses stood out at a time when American journalism in general was expanding.[6]

The experience of the city's secular *Vereinswesen* was similar. Philadelphia retained an impressive number of secular German associations in the early 1910s, but their condition was significantly weaker than it had been a quarter century before. According to a 1911 directory, the city held sixty-one German singing societies, thirty-three clubs of German Army veterans, thirteen associations tied to specific regions of Germany, eight gymnastics clubs, forty-eight charitable and mutual benefit societies, thirteen organizations described simply as "social clubs," and a smattering of other kinds of German ethnic associations. In all, the directory listed 185 German *Vereine,* without even attempting to count the city's German lodges or building and loan associations.[7] Whether these figures represented a drop in the overall number of *Vereine* since the 1890s is difficult to say, since extant lists from the earlier period may not be comparable. The number of German singing societies actually may have increased: the United Singers of Philadelphia, a federation of German choirs, counted twenty-nine member groups in 1892, thirty in 1910, and forty-one in 1912. Yet some other *Verein* categories did show a distinct falloff; the 1911 count of mutual benefit and charitable societies was strikingly lower than the figure of 285 mutual benefit societies given on an 1892 list.[8]

Institutional histories, internal records, and contemporary accounts, however, confirm that after 1890, a significant number of associations either shut their doors, merged with similar organizations, or suffered severe losses in membership. Few types of *Vereine,* moreover, remained untouched; such cases could be found among singing societies, turner clubs, lodges, building and loan associations, mutual benefit societies, festival clubs, and immigrant aid societies. Some groups, such as the German-American Building and Loan Association of Germantown, simply went out of business, citing the difficulty of attracting younger members.[9] Other organizations found salvation in mergers; a constant theme here, too, was the inconstancy of the American-born generation. In 1889 and 1890, for example, the Sängerbund, one of the city's oldest singing societies, yielded its leadership to its mostly native-born younger members. These, however, "did not possess the proper motivation and the necessary interest, and naturally could not maintain the membership as their elders had, and so the passion for entertainment was more indulged in than the cultivation of singing," the group's historian recounted in 1910. Consequently, "the continued existence of the society became a serious question." The Sängerbund merged with another singing society in 1899.[10]

Membership losses plagued the associations that survived. These ranged from small, plebeian, neighborhood-oriented clubs, such as the Germania Turn Verein von Roxborough und Manayunk, to branches of large, nationally organized lodges, like the German Order of the Harugari, to elite, old-line societies, such as the German Society of Pennsylvania. The Germania Turn Verein, founded in 1873, boasted fifty-two adult male members in 1887 and 145 in 1900; by 1910, however, this figure had fallen to seventy-nine.[11] The Turn Verein's smaller female auxiliary showed somewhat more staying power, averaging twenty-two members annually in the 1890s and nineteen in the first decade of the twentieth century, but its rolls experienced a lasting decline in the 1910s; from 1911 to 1917, female membership never rose above fourteen.[12]

Philadelphia's Harugari lodges suffered a steeper, and earlier, decline. The German Order of the Harugari, a fraternal order founded in New York City in 1847, functioned at once as a secret society and a mutual benefit association. The order had a working-class orientation; its elected head in 1870 described its members as belonging mostly to "the workers' estate." That year, the organization nationally boasted more than 17,000 members, nearly a third of them in Pennsylvania. The early 1870s, however, marked its high point in the state and the city.[13] Philadelphia, which counted twenty-two lodges with 2,188 members in 1876, had only 884 members in fifteen lodges in 1890. By 1908, the city was down to four male lodges, holding all of 287 members.[14] In just over thirty years, the order's male membership in Philadelphia had shrunk by nearly 90 percent.

At the other end of the social scale, the city's flagship secular *Verein*, the German Society of Pennsylvania, also underwent a wrenching fall in membership. Founded in 1764, the German Society served as Philadelphia's preeminent German immigrant aid society. It also played a leading cultural role, sponsoring lectures and maintaining a large library. By the late nineteenth century, the society had become a bastion of the city's German-American elite.[15] Despite this privileged position, the group saw a gradual decline in membership in the 1880s and 1890s, which accelerated alarmingly in the following decade. The number of men belonging to the society (formal membership was male only) reached its late-nineteenth-century peak of 1,040 in 1877. Membership fell below 900 within two years and fluctuated around this reduced level for the remainder of the century. After 1898, however, losses snowballed. Membership dropped below 800, then 700, then 600. In 1911, it bottomed out at 520 members—the pre–World War I low point, and a drop of exactly 50 percent from the 1877 figure.[16]

For a group that saw itself as a leader of German Philadelphia, such losses were particularly disturbing. Recruiting new members, the society's historian wrote in 1917, had been "the chief concern of all presidents and boards of directors" since the 1870s. Like other *Vereine,* the society pinned its hopes for long-term survival on attracting the rising generation of German-American men. "That only 17 new members could be won during the year is a tragic sign, a signal that the Society's future is in the most serious danger," F. H. Harjes, the group's longtime secretary, declared in reviewing the year 1909. "First of all, therefore, we urge those of our members with sons who are of age to induce them to join."[17]

The religious subcultures of German Philadelphia also felt such strains. Philadelphia's German Catholics had fared well organizationally through the early 1890s. The archdiocese created no fewer than eight German national parishes in the three decades following the Civil War, three of them between 1891 and 1894.[18] However, after 1894, only one more German national parish would be established: St. Henry's, in 1916, in a North Philadelphia neighborhood along the northbound path of German settlement.[19] The expansion of the German national parish system thus came to a virtual halt in the mid-1890s. Some of the post–Civil War churches, moreover, faced problems in remaining completely German, or, like St. Ignatius', lost congregants to English-speaking territorial parishes. Due in part to the latter factor, overall German parish membership fell by 9 percent between 1900 and 1921.[20]

The city's German Lutheran churches weathered the years after 1900 better than their Catholic counterparts did. Between 1900 and 1920, the Pennsylvania Ministerium's German Conference added two Philadelphia congregations to its roster. The conference's Philadelphia churches even registered a slight increase in overall communing membership, which reached 7,045 in 1920.[21] Nevertheless, those congregations faced some of the symptoms experienced by the secular associations, especially when it came to the next generation. In 1900, nine city churches in the German Conference had a full-fledged parochial school; by 1920, only two such schools remained. These losses were felt even before World War I. On the eve of that conflict, von Bosse noted that German Lutheran parochial schools in the eastern United States generally were in decline, with the sole exception of that of his own church, St. Paul's.[22] German Lutheran churches likewise suffered some losses to English Lutheran congregations and other Protestant denominations. Elsie Spalde Moore, for example, who was born and grew up in North Philadelphia before the First World War, at first attended a German Lutheran church with her working-class family. After the death of her grandmother, who had "insisted we learn as much of the German language as possible," Moore's German-born mother "decided we could go to the Bethel Lutheran Church nearer home." Bethel "did not use German in the service" and in fact belonged to the East Pennsylvania Synod.[23] Other German Lutherans roamed farther afield. During his turn-of-the-century tenure at a German Lutheran church in Harrisburg, Pennsylvania, von Bosse recalled meeting a woman who had left that congregation and joined a Methodist church. As she told him—in English—"Well, I jumped over the fence."[24]

German Philadelphians with strong ethnic commitments also perceived the erosion of the city's *Deutschtum* in linguistic terms. Many, like von Bosse, could not conceive of Germandom surviving in the United States without the survival of spoken German. Many Lutherans and Catholics, moreover, made German language use an intrinsic part of their religious identities, transforming language maintenance into a spiritual imperative. The German Catholic fear that an immigrant's rejection of German could encourage a rejection of Catholicism itself was expressed in a nineteenth-century watchword, "Language Saves Faith."[25] Immigrant German Lutherans had even more reason to see German as central to their religion.

Lutheranism was, after all, a product of the German Reformation and had itself played a formative role in the development of modern High German, through Martin Luther's translation of the Bible. The intimate tie between this denomination and the German tongue was expressed in frequent references to German as *die Sprache Luthers*—"the language of Luther."[26]

What particularly troubled some German Americans at the turn of the twentieth century was the incursion of English into German secular and religious associational life, a matter they termed *die Sprachenfrage*, "the language question."[27] As we have seen, von Bosse found in 1889 that the children of congregants at St. Paul's routinely spoke among themselves in English and frequently used that language at home with their parents. When the children of such families began to participate in German associations and churches, many such organizations felt pressure to allow greater use of English. Starting in 1891, the German Society included an English summary in its annual reports, for the sake of those members "who do not have a command of the German language." The German national parish of St. Peter's published its 1901 parish history in both English and German. The *Tageblatt,* the voice of Philadelphia's German socialists, advertised its job printing department wholly in German in its 1899 almanac; the 1902 almanac ran the printing department's advertisement primarily in English.[28]

As evidence mounted that German newspapers, German associations, and the German language itself were faltering, a growing sense of crisis enveloped German Philadelphia. Secular and religious Germans alike fretted over the future of German America, at times in apocalyptic tones. "Catholic Germandom is going—we cannot mistake it—downhill with giant steps," *Nord Amerika* declared in 1900. The following year, Charles Hexamer, the German Society's president, felt compelled to denounce what he called "[t]he wailing over the 'decline of Germandom.'"[29] Yet that decline, if widely perceived by the turn of the century, did not encompass every association. Some flourished, in particular some female *Vereine*. Their relative health suggested an expansion of the role of women in maintaining the city's *Deutschtum*.

A GENDERED CRISIS

Immigrant German women and their daughters occupied a position within German-American public life that set them somewhat apart from their Anglo-American sisters. The leading German associations excluded them from formal membership, and female political activism was frowned upon by middle-class spokesmen, who identified it with the temperance movement. At the same time, through the nineteenth century, German-American women actively shared in much of the social life enjoyed by their male counterparts, and they carved out an institutional niche for themselves within the *Vereinswesen* by founding both female voluntary associations and separate women's affiliates of male societies.[30]

Behind the status of German-American women lay conceptions of gender roles and family relations that at times differed sharply from those cultivated by many Anglo-Americans. Historians have described a fundamental shift in the family and women's place within it in the late eighteenth- and early nineteenth-century American North. Earlier, European settler families had functioned as largely self-sufficient economic units with productive roles assigned to wives and children as well as husbands. Within these productive households, fathers exercised a control over wives, children, and servants enshrined in law and informed by ideals of patriarchal authority. An expanding market economy, however, eroded the self-sufficiency of families and induced a new division of domestic labor that cast the middle-class father as a breadwinner, often working outside the home, and the middle-class wife as a housekeeper and raiser of children. This particular configuration of "separate spheres" for men and women emerged together with a new "companionate" ideal that portrayed romantic love and mutual respect, rather than economic pragmatism and wifely deference, as the best foundations of marriage. One of the many consequences of these developments was that husbands ceded a large measure of control over child-rearing and household affairs—that is, over the private, "domestic sphere"—to their wives.[31]

Accounts of the rise of "separate spheres," however, have tended to generalize from the middle-class experience of a particular European ethnic group: Anglo-American Protestants, especially New Englanders and their descendants in the northern United States.[32] Other Americans often disagreed with the views held by these "Yankees"[33] as to proper gender roles. For many European immigrants, including Germans, these disagreements reflected homeland family and gender relations that had evolved along a path similar, but not identical, to that taken in the United States.

Patriarchal ideals had governed mid-eighteenth-century family life in German-speaking central Europe as well as in British North America. Fathers exercised dominion over their families as possessors of *Herrschaft*—literally, "lordship." The term describes a particular kind of authority that combined political, economic, and social power and inhered in the individual *Herr*, the lord and master. This authority was diffused through the social order, linking the Lord God to a series of earthly *Herren*, from prince down to family head—the *Herr im Haus*, or, as he was often called, the *Hausvater* ("house father"). Almost always, the *Hausvater* governed a household engaged in economic (usually agricultural) production. His authority was explicitly tied to his gender, although he lent a share of that authority to his wife: she "managed matters relating to the household's internal economy more or less autonomously" and shared in household production. But the *Hausvater* retained control over all major decisions, and his purview could extend well into what later generations would consider women's domain. Under the Prussian Civil Code of 1794, for example, a husband had the right to decide how long his wife might breast-feed their children.[34]

The *Hausvater*'s rule, however, was rooted in a traditional social order based on productive households. By the late eighteenth century, a new urban middle class had emerged that often found its livelihood outside, rather than inside, the home. Its dominant element was the "educated middle class," or *Bildungsbürgertum*—university-trained professionals, teachers, academics, and civil servants. Among these *Bildungsbürger* in particular, the separation of home and work led to a redefinition of gender roles like that in the American North. "By nature," men were constituted to pursue productive activity in the public world, while women were foreordained to the domestic sphere, where their duty to care lovingly for husband and children now took precedence over their role as managers of the household economy.[35] Over the nineteenth century, mothers within the educated and, later, industrial middle classes increasingly took on the responsibility of educating small children and daughters, as fathers retreated from family life into the working world.[36]

This "bourgeois model" of the family expanded beyond the middle classes during the nineteenth century; as the historian Ute Frevert argued, it "gradually won favor also with clerks and manual workers, and finally even in peasant communities." Yet this process was both prolonged and uneven. The notion that the female sphere excluded productive work flew in the face of reality for the many peasant women who engaged in agricultural labor before and after marriage. Similarly, most working-class wives bolstered their families' income by keeping boarders, taking in washing or other outwork, or working in factories. Among these groups, older concepts of household patriarchy could linger. Indeed, such views gained a new source of support in nineteenth-century Europe, through a renewal of corporatist thinking among Catholics and Lutherans that stressed the value of the hierarchical family.[37]

When German men and women immigrated to the United States, they therefore brought with them ideas about gender that varied according to their class position, religious convictions, and rural or urban origins in the homeland. For some, emigration offered a chance to reconstruct family life along the lines of an older patriarchy. Others subscribed to an ideology that resembled the Yankee notion of separate spheres, although not in all its details.

Many rural Germans who resettled in the Midwestern countryside, for example, followed patterns of gender relations that seemed closer to *Herrschaft* than to separate spheres. As Jon Gjerde argued, such European immigrant families were characterized by a "variant of patriarchy" that was "more powerful and all-encompassing" than that practiced by Yankee settlers. These families demanded productive work of all members, and so women and girls joined the men in fieldwork—shocking Yankee observers, who accused German men of exploiting their wives and children and of lacking affection for their spouses.[38]

Echoes of the older patriarchy could be heard even within the immigrant urban *Bildungsbürgertum*. Lutheran pastors in particular seemed inclined to intervene in their wives' domestic sphere with a *Hausvater*'s authority—perhaps because they continued to work from home, perhaps because rural parsonages had been among the last middle-class households in Germany to lose their productive character. The immigrant Philadelphia pastor Adolph Spaeth both used the term "house-father" and had it applied to him by his second wife, apparently accurately.[39] Neither of Spaeth's two wives was of German birth. Nonetheless, everyday life in the Spaeth parsonage, as his American-born second wife recalled, was "very German, almost patriarchal in its simplicity and order. The father was the Priest of his family, and its supreme head. As far as possible a military precision governed the apportionment of the day, especially for little children."[40] Georg von Bosse, who also undertook to create a German home, similarly viewed a range of domestic matters as falling within his purview. Describing his successful effort to interest his American-born wife in "German manners and customs," von Bosse noted that "we" kept a German kitchen, in which his wife herself baked the bread. Von Bosse's project of maintaining a German household was possible only with his wife's cooperation, but he ultimately understood that effort as a projection of his will as a household master, partaking of a specifically German form of patriarchal authority: "In my house, I am *Herr*, and there does not rule some 'New Woman' or the will of the child."[41]

It seems unlikely, however, that many immigrant German fathers had the time or inclination to exert this degree of control over domestic affairs. Artisans working where they lived had the opportunity to do so, but not workers employed away from home; the latter's wives seem to have taken on the role of household manager, administering the domestic sphere in a fairly autonomous way. A study of the budgets of twenty-three working-class families in Kensington, conducted in the early 1910s, described the "prevailing Kensington custom" whereby "the father and the other wage-earning members of the family ordinarily turn all of their earnings into a common fund, of which the mother has charge, and out of which she provides for the needs of the family." Three of the families were headed by a first- or second-generation German immigrant male; all three men turned over some or all of their pay to their wives to manage on behalf of the household.[42] Similarly, Elsie Spalde Moore recalled her German-born mother as "quite a manager" of the family.[43]

The fact that Moore and other daughters in such working-class families went out to work "to help with family expenses," as she put it,[44] would have struck middle-class observers in both Germany and America as a breach of the conventions of domesticity. Yet the German and Anglo-American versions of middle-class domesticity, though similar, were not exactly the same. While both versions featured separate spheres, each configured that separation somewhat differently, most obviously in the matter of sociability. In nineteenth-century American cities, Anglo-Americans who took their leisure outside the home frequently did so in sex-segregated settings, such as the middle-class, all-male private banquet. In contrast, middle-class and working-class German males scandalized Yankees by socializing, in public, with their wives and children, usually at functions involving the consumption of alcohol. New York City's German beer gardens, for example, formed a major exception to the rule that public drinking places, such as saloons, were male territory, in which respectable women dared not linger.[45] German Philadelphians prided themselves on a mixed-sex sociability they considered family-oriented. The Philadelphia Schützen-Verein's male members, for example, brought their wives and children along to the association's Schützen Park, where they felt "at home and at ease, in a circle of good friends and befriended families." A photograph from the club's 1906 anniversary booklet illustrated this claim (see figure 3.1); it showed mixed groups of men and women relaxing around the park's bandstand on a sunny Sunday afternoon, their beer mugs before them. Women's presence at such events, far from sullying female purity, kept German merriment from descending into immorality, or so the Philadelphia historian Oswald Seidensticker suggested in 1883. "[T]he American" was surprised that such "bright jubilation and unbounded gaiety did not end in a brawl"; he would have difficulty "learning the secret of sociable cheer from the German, as long as woman was kept from wielding the 'moral scepter' outside [as well as within] the house."[46] Seidensticker, in other words, accepted middle-class domesticity's portrayal of women as a source of moral values within the home. For the purposes of leisure, however, middle-class Germans did not define family as lodged exclusively in the private, domestic sphere; rather, with

Figure 3.1. A Sunday Afternoon at Schützen Park. A respectable, mixed crowd of men and women enjoying band music and beer at the park of the Philadelphia Schützen-Verein, around the turn of the twentieth century. German-American gender conventions allowed for and encouraged such public, mixed-sex sociability, which ran counter to nineteenth-century Anglo-American notions of separate spheres. Source: *1846–1906: 60. Stiftungsfest des Philadelphia Schützen-Verein, abgehalten in den Tagen vom 19. bis 21. November 1906* (Philadelphia, [1906]), 63, Joseph Horner Memorial Library, German Society of Pennsylvania. Photograph reproduced by Richard Davis. Reproduced by permission of the German Society of Pennsylvania.

the aid of women's moral influence, some of family life could be led in public.[47]

The range of views on proper gender roles within German America bore directly on its future, for those views shaped women's participation in and support of ethnic maintenance. At one extreme, von Bosse, the would-be *Hausvater,* granted women a comparatively restricted role in maintaining America's *Deutschtum,* even within their own households. While von Bosse acknowledged that too many German mothers as well as fathers were failing in "their holy duty" to uphold a German home, this criticism, given his views, amounted to a condemnation of German patriarchs for failing to play their assigned part. On the other hand, Germans who saw mothers as primarily responsible for family life thought them key to keeping the next generation in the ethnic fold. Like women's organizations of other ethnic groups and 1920s Americanizers who followed the admonition to "Go after the women," these Germans considered mothers to be essential preservers and transmitters of ethnic culture. As one of them wrote just after the Civil War, "[w]herever in a family German ways of thinking . . . , the German language[,] and German customs are given up, it is the mother who is the most to blame for it."[48] Finally, some German women used such gender conventions to step beyond their households and offer more public kinds of support for ethnic maintenance.

Toward the end of the nineteenth century, this last stance helped fuel a striking expansion of women's presence in the German-American public sphere. Women, with the encouragement of some German men, began to step in to make up for the apparent abandonment of German America by many of its sons. Newspaper readership was one indicator of this development. As Monika Blaschke argued, the nation's German-language press began to recruit female readers in the 1890s. English-language newspapers and magazines already had started to court women; they sought to gain advertising income by targeting a group then taking on the role of shoppers in an expanding consumer culture. Middle-class German-language newspapers such as the *New Yorker Staatszeitung* followed suit by introducing women's pages, and their socialist counterparts began to promote their advertisers to female readers.[49] This rising female readership was paralleled by rising female membership in German associations. Women, who had long dominated German religious associational life, began to take a significantly greater role in Philadelphia's secular *Vereinswesen*. Specifically, by the early twentieth century, women's affiliates had become increasingly important to—and, in at least one key instance, larger than—their "main" male organizations.

The Order of the Harugari and the German Society provide examples of this phenomenon at either end of German Philadelphia's social scale. At the Harugari's 1890 national convention, the previously all-male order agreed to charter separate "Hertha-degree" women's lodges. This move came at the urging of delegates from Pennsylvania and New York, two states that had suffered significant membership losses. In Pennsylvania, the Hertha lodges soon proved their worth to the order. Between 1894 and 1908, they grew in number from nine to twenty-one and in membership from 426 to 786. Philadelphia's sole Hertha lodge, founded in 1894, expanded from forty-five members that year to seventy-three in 1908. By the latter year, a fifth of all members of the order in the city were women.[50]

The German Society's experience was even more dramatic, for here women came to outnumber men. Women had been explicitly excluded from formal membership in the society since 1849. In 1900, however, a number of women led by Antonie Ehrlich, the German-born wife of the society's vice president, established a female affiliate. They asked the society's board how they could be helpful and were told that "a large field [of work] . . . offered itself in the area of charity, especially in such cases as are more suitable to women in their character, essence and activity than to men."[51] Such work became the major focus of the new group, which called itself the Frauen Hilfsverein der Deutschen Gesellschaft, or Women's Auxiliary. Founded with roughly one hundred members, the Frauen Hilfsverein took responsibility for charity pertaining to needy women and children, while also instituting coffees and other "entertainments" for the society. The auxiliary likewise contributed to the society's financial well-being, playing a major role in organizing the group's 1901 fund-raising bazaar, for example.[52] The Frauen Hilfsverein apparently reflected a demand for organizational involvement among middle-class German-American women, for its membership grew quickly, climbing above 500 by 1903 and above 600 by 1910. The latter year marked a watershed: as the Women's Auxiliary had been gaining members, the society itself had been losing them, and at some point during 1910, the auxiliary's membership surpassed the society's. On a year-to-year basis, as far as available membership figures indicate, the auxiliary retained its numerical edge over the society until at least 1930. By the beginning of 1916, the society counted only 597 members to the Auxiliary's 795.[53] The disparity was such that the society ultimately found itself searching for members among the husbands of the women of the Frauen Hilfsverein. As the society's president, John B. Mayer, wrote in a 1917 letter to auxiliary members, "[t]he married women should at least be able to induce their men to join our society."[54]

Not all of the new women's organizations enjoyed the Frauen Hilfsverein's long-term success. Toward the end of the 1890s, for example, German-American socialist women in New York stepped beyond the auxiliary role by establishing a Social Democratic Women's Federation, which eventually garnered affiliates in Philadelphia and several Midwestern cities. By 1903, Philadelphia had three such branches of the Sozialdemokratische Frauenvereine. Members devoted at least part of their time to discussions of the "women's movement" and succeeded, despite opposition, in affiliating their branches directly with the United German Trades. By 1910, however, only one of the three branches was still listed in the UGT's directory.[55] In effect, women had carved out a more autonomous position within the German socialist subculture but could not sustain that enclave at its original size.

The rising prominence of women's organizations within the *Vereinswesen* can be seen as part of the larger push for separate female institutions undertaken in the late nineteenth century by both Anglo-American women and the middle-class and Social Democratic women's movements in Germany.[56] Indeed, that the Frauen Hilfsverein found its niche in charitable work "suitable to women" suggests that Ehrlich and her allies justified their expanded public activity in much the same way as those larger movements—as an extension of women's "natural" nurturing role. Activists in Germany pursued this approach under the banner of "spiritual motherhood" (*geistige Mütterlichkeit*); historians have given it the name "maternalism" and seen it as key to the creation of public and political roles for German and American women, especially in the realm of social welfare.[57]

Mütterlichkeit had its limits, however, particularly where German-American women were concerned. On the one hand, their drive for greater organizational involvement succeeded to the point that one must consider the *Vereinswesen*'s crisis as gendered—that is, as a crisis to some extent specifically of the *male Vereinswesen*. On the other hand, concerns specific to German America rendered the pursuit of an overt political voice more than usually difficult for middle-class women. Working-class women could at least count here on the rhetorical support of the Socialist Party, which endorsed and, after 1907, campaigned for women's suffrage, albeit haltingly and unevenly. Indeed, evidence suggests that women close to the labor movement leaned toward voting rights and did not hesitate to say so: women polled at the Kensington Labor Lyceum one evening in 1910 voted 133–60 in favor of women's suffrage.[58] Middle-class women, however, encountered significant opposition from many middle-class men to female political activism. This opposition stemmed not simply from traditional attitudes but also from perceptions of the political consequences of such involvement. In the late nineteenth and early twentieth centuries, male and female German Americans felt that their distinctive brand of sociability had come under attack from the temperance movement, which they associated with Anglo-American women's activism, as expressed in such groups as the Women's Christian Temperance Union. Many German-American spokesmen, moreover, linked antialcohol efforts to the movement for women's suffrage, and not without reason. The WCTU embraced female enfranchisement as central to its mission, while the Prohibition Party endorsed women's suffrage in 1900, just as it opened a particularly militant campaign.[59]

In such a climate, German-American women who wished to take on leading roles in the *Vereinswesen* had to step very carefully. While reaching for a measure of power, they could not afford to be identified with those mainstream women whose own reach for power appeared to threaten the ethnic group's way of life. Thus, some defined themselves *against* such politically active Anglo-American women, even as they made their own forays into politics. When, for example, Fernande Richter, a St. Louis woman active in the new, Philadelphia-based National German-American Alliance, took the unusual step in 1904 of testifying on the alliance's behalf before Congress, she did so as part of an alliance effort to stop two prohibitionist bills before the House. Richter presented the House Judiciary Committee with a petition against the legislation signed "by thousands of American women, many of whom are of German descent." She then proceeded to frame her own public testimony as that of a political naïf defending the integrity of her household and the liberties of the men of her ethnic group against "a spirit of maternalism" emanating from a "minority of American women," the "prohibitionists in petticoats." To ban "light drinks"—beer and wine—would only induce men to seek out alcohol in the more concentrated form of hard liquor and in places hidden from their families, she argued.[60] Against this specter, Richter raised a vision of mixed-sex sociability as she and other German Americans understood it:

> It lies in the interest of mothers and wives to share the diversions of men. The experience of centuries has proved that wherever families jointly frequent public places, where they meet good company and where light drinks are served and good music is rendered, the moral qualities have been highest, and the greatest happiness has prevailed. . . . The presence of the wife refines the ways of men.[61]

Here, Richter managed to represent an emerging national voice of organized German America in the most political public sphere imaginable, all the while portraying herself as an unpolitical defender of her home, her husband, and her right to socialize with him. The feat testifies to her political astuteness but also to the difficulties she and other women faced as they sought to maintain a German associational life whose male members often saw female activism as a threat to that world. Women's active involvement might help to slow the erosion of the *Vereinswesen*. But activists like Richter could make scant use of *Mütterlichkeit* to justify that involvement, as long as they felt compelled to attack Anglo-American "maternalism."

The crisis of the *Vereinswesen* was both very real and markedly uneven. German newspapers lost readership, and German associations, secular and religious, lost membership from the 1890s on, and these trends generated a strong sense of crisis within German Philadelphia. Yet the large-scale demographic shifts behind these losses did not doom every kind of German association. Some German Philadelphians resisted the overall decline by tapping women's increasing interest in building separate female institutions. Others found a surprising ally in the emerging culture of mass consumption—a double-edged ally that could bolster the male *Verein-swesen,* even as it beckoned as a destination for those leaving German Philadelphia.

CHAPTER FOUR

Destinations: The Ambiguous Lure
of Mass Commercial and Consumer Culture

WHILE German-American spokesmen grew increasingly troubled over the shrinking *Vereinswesen* after 1890, they rarely specified the fate of those who departed from German-American circles. Georg von Bosse, we have seen, depicted Germandom as an island crumbling into an encroaching "ocean of the American people."[1] Yet his metaphor cast the American people as an undifferentiated mass and said nothing about the particular kind of Americans that formerly German Americans might become.

Where, then, did those who left German America go? In what manner did such Philadelphians of German birth, or of native birth with German parents or grandparents, rework their identities to replace or tone down the German element? An answer that accounts for the experience of every such Philadelphian, is, of course, impossible. Since any one individual holds a number of identities, that individual could shift away from his or her German identity in any number of ways: by emphasizing another category of identification, such as belonging to a particular race, class, gender, or religion; by assembling a particular combination of such affiliations; or by modifying some of them or adding others. Over thousands of individuals, the potential number of different identity combinations is huge. Limited sources and resources bar tracing them for every individual.

Nonetheless, one can point to evidence of certain broad patterns of affiliation. This evidence, some of it detailed in the preceding chapters, suggests that members of particular subcultures within German Philadelphia were already mixing at the turn of the twentieth century with members of analogous, non-German subcultures. Such mixing most obviously followed lines of religion and class. Catholicism served as a common ground for German and Irish congregants in some territorial parishes, especially suburban ones, and for Germans and a few eastern Europeans at St. Peter's. Some German Lutherans made their way into English Lutheran churches, "jumped the fence" into other Protestant denominations, or entered pan-Protestant organizations such as the Germantown YMCA. Similarly, working-class grievances drew German workers into cooperation with English, Irish, and some new immigrant unionists during the Philadelphia general strike of 1910, as chapter 6 describes. And middle-class Germans who joined the Business Men's Association of Germantown cultivated with other members of northwest European background a sense of themselves as businessmen.

Some individuals, moreover, traveled toward several destinations at once, assembling their own, specific constellations of corresponding collective identities. Henry Pletcher, for example, shared in both the collective identities of "businessman" and "Catholic." Elsie Spalde Moore's mother, Henrietta Neumeister Spalde, seems to have remained "a good Lutheran," even as she moved her children from a German to an English Lutheran church. She likely combined that affiliation with a strong sense of being a mother and working-class—or, at least, poor—for she raised seven children on a small income.[2]

The collective identities that formed the building blocks of multiple identities were themselves far from static, however. The first third of the twentieth century saw significant changes in three categories of identity: race, nation, and mass consumption. These changes in turn would profoundly shape the paths some Philadelphians took away from German America and the multiple identities they ultimately crafted—a topic for part 4. Here, we take a closer look at the changes themselves. The next chapter examines the period's shifting conceptions of racial and national identity. This chapter assesses the prewar impact on German Philadelphia of the new mass culture of consumption that emerged in the late nineteenth and early twentieth centuries.

That culture had many facets. Its historians have charted a larger cultural shift toward valuing consumption, specifically the consumption of the ready-made, standardized consumer goods turned out by an emerging mass-production economy. Mass culture in this sense was consumer culture, its rise marked by a set of new institutions designed to encourage and facilitate shopping: department stores, mail-order catalogs, forms of consumer credit such as installment buying, and professional advertising campaigns, among others. Mass consumption, however, involved services as well as goods—above all, new forms of commercialized leisure provided by such new institutions as professional sports teams, amusement parks, lakeside and seaside vacation resorts, movie theaters, and, ultimately, commercial radio.[3]

For German Philadelphia, mass culture was a two-edged sword. Commercialized entertainment itself owed something to immigrant German traditions of festivity and sociability. This affinity allowed some German Philadelphians to appropriate elements of mass culture in a way that strengthened ethnic identity. At least one association—the Cannstatter Volksfest-Verein—achieved a symbiosis with mass culture that enabled it to buck the crisis of the male *Vereinswesen*.

At the same time, mass culture offered both an alternative to the cultural activities of the *Vereinswesen* and a new range of potential identities grounded in consumption. By the mid-1910s, many German Philadelphians were participating in this consumer and entertainment culture, and some had clearly crafted identities linked to it, from shopper to vacationing "bathing beauty." These identities did not have to replace a sense of German ethnicity, but they could render it less significant to an individual, just as visits to an amusement park could cut into time formerly spent at a *Verein*.

Discovering Mass Culture

Philadelphia paced other major urban centers in the innovations of consumer and commercial culture. By the late nineteenth century, department stores such as Wanamaker's, Strawbridge and Clothier, and Lit Brothers lined downtown Market Street. The city hosted its first professional baseball teams in the 1870s and 1880s, witnessed its first projected motion pictures in 1895, and saw the opening of suburban Willow Grove Amusement Park in 1896 and Woodside Park the following year. The amusement parks themselves reflected other technological advances: they were fed by streetcar lines operating the electric trolleys that replaced horse-drawn cars in the 1890s.[4]

The mass culture represented by these innovations certainly proved attractive to many German Philadelphians, in a way that reached across divisions of class and religion. Consumerism, as a particular set of attitudes toward shopping, made inroads even into the German working class. After the turn of the century, for example, Strawbridge and Clothier found it worthwhile regularly to run large advertisements in the labor-oriented *Philadelphia Tageblatt*.[5] Shopping at such venues was eased by the development of installment buying, which had become widespread among wage earners by the beginning of the twentieth century. At least some working-class German Philadelphians purchased liberally "on time." In the early 1910s, investigators for the Kensington budget study discovered that of twenty-three working-class families, the one with the largest yearly household deficit was headed by Mr. and Mrs. E, the native-born, Catholic children of German immigrants. The study blamed their over-expenditure partly on Mrs. E's "tendency . . . to buy things on the installment plan."[6]

New modes of recreation likewise drew participants from across the spectrum of German Philadelphia. As spectator and participatory sports grew in popularity after 1890, they captured the attention of young people especially. The sons of the immigrant Lutheran pastor Adolph Spaeth enthusiastically pursued football and baseball, much as basketball and baseball captivated members of the Germantown YMCA. Spaeth himself succumbed to the "rage for bicycle riding."[7] So, too, did workers: the *Tageblatt* included a bicycle race organized by the Cycle Dealers Association in a 1903 column of *Verein* announcements, while the Socialist Party advertised that its August 1914 outing to Point Breeze Park would feature bicycle and motorcycle races.[8]

Commercialized recreation, however, may have exerted a more widespread appeal, especially those new forms affordable to workers as well as the middle class. Earlier, working-class German families likely had had relatively little discretionary income; one study of seventeen such families in New York in the 1880s found that for most, "[t]rips to the theater, vacations, or other such extras were clearly out of reach." By the 1910s, however, five of the six German families examined in the Kensington study devoted between 4 and 10 percent of their budgets to "recreation and pocket money."[9] Such expenditures permitted a greater range of leisure. In the late nineteenth century, middle-class German families, like those of Spaeth and of the businessman and politician Rudolph Blankenburg, could afford New Jersey summer homes. By the turn of the twentieth century, some working-class Germans were taking their own, albeit far shorter, vacations. Women in two of the Kensington study's German families undertook trips to visit relatives, while the adult daughter in a third family saved enough pocket money for a week at "a country vacation house for working girls."[10] Workers also made their way to New Jersey shore resorts now catering to a public broader than just the wealthy. *Tageblatt* readers in 1903 could peruse a column of advertisements for hotels in Atlantic City and schedules for the trains to take them there.[11]

Closer to home, German Philadelphians took advantage of such new commercial diversions as movies, vaudeville, and amusement parks, which put cheap entertainment within the reach of virtually anyone. One of the poorest of the German families in the Kensington study spent only $2.25 on recreation from November 1913 to November 1914, but that went "mostly for moving pictures." By 1910, the *Tageblatt*'s standing column of advertisements for "Amusements" could include a notice for Keith's, one of the city's two main vaudeville houses, next to announcements of *Verein* masked balls; the newspaper also provided readers with more detailed reviews of the acts at vaudeville theaters.[12] If *Tageblatt* readers came to enjoy vaudeville, they must have loved amusement parks, for by the summer of 1914, Willow Grove Park had become a staple of the "Amusements" column.[13]

Participation in mass culture as such did not require abandoning ethnic identity and might even strengthen it. As Lizabeth Cohen argued in her study of Chicago workers, ethnic consumers of some early mass cultural products had considerable latitude to receive those products on their own terms: they could buy phonograph records of Italian folk music or talk back to the silent figures on the screen in small neighborhood movie theaters. Similarly, phonograph dealers advertising in the *Tageblatt* during the 1910s offered customers a "complete selection of German and Hungarian records," while the Philadelphia Turngemeinde, the city's leading *Turnverein,* hosted showings of "German patriotic" motion pictures after the outbreak of war in Europe.[14]

Moreover, commercialized recreation drew in part on ethnic as well as working-class cultures,[15] and that relationship could prove less parasitic than symbiotic. In the years before the First World War, one of Philadelphia's leading *Vereine* prospered in just this way. The Cannstatter Volksfest-Verein used mass culture to make itself a major exception to the general decline of the male *Vereinswesen.* The association thrived both because it adopted some of the techniques of commercial culture and because it already possessed elements that culture had learned to prize—in particular, mixed-sex sociability. This should come as no surprise, for German Americans themselves played a major role in shaping the culture of commercial entertainment.

APPROPRIATING MASS CULTURE: THE CANNSTATTER VOLKSFEST-VEREIN

Founded in 1873 by a group of German-American businessmen, the Cannstatter Volksfest-Verein aimed to recreate in Philadelphia an annual harvest festival held in the Württemberg spa of Bad Cannstatt.[16] From the beginning, then, the association had both an orientation toward sociability and a south German, specifically Swabian, identification. That regional affiliation did not, however, preclude a larger ethnic one, for the minutes of the founding meeting contemplated "further entertainments that would disseminate German sociability and honorable German customs." The *Verein* regularly put on a winter ball and sponsored a variety of other festivities.[17] The crowning point of its year, however, was the three-day Cannstatter Folk Festival in September. This lavish affair, held at one of the city's commercial picnic grounds, featured food, drink, games, a forty-five-foot-tall "Column of Plenty" composed of fruit, and an elaborate pageant, often on a theme taken from history or folklore.[18] The festival was open to the general public for a fee and became enormously popular. It attracted Germans and non-Germans alike and remained a draw until the United States entered World War I, at a time when similar regional festivals were faltering.[19]

The Volksfest-Verein's membership rolls reflected its popularity. Like other German associations, it fared well during the peak years of German immigration; membership reached its highest point in 1885 at 1,392, before troubles with a state antialcohol measure sent the *Verein* into a slump. However, after 1895, the association's membership grew again, rising above 1,000 in 1902 and staying at that level until 1917. The peak membership year during this period came surprisingly late—in 1908, when the *Verein* claimed 1,188 members.[20]

A number of factors lay behind the Volksfest-Verein's continuing success. First, its festivals met an ongoing demand for sociability among younger German Americans while making that sociability accessible to non-Germans. Through German Philadelphia's complaints of associational decline echoed a recognition that its children avidly sought out companionable amusement. The prodigal younger members of the Sängerbund who neglected singing in the early 1890s did so because of their "passion for entertainment." The secretary of the German Society fretted at the turn of the century over competition from "[t]he already large and still growing number of associations that offer amusements of a sociable kind."[21] Like the newer forms of recreation, the Cannstatter festival answered this demand from younger German Americans. By its nature, moreover, it allowed non-Germans to join in. The festival pageant's theme, which changed every year, took on predominantly Swabian and German topics but occasionally featured those more familiar to a non-German audience, including "The Landing of Columbus" in 1892 and "Jamestown" in 1907. The latter pageant, a play on that year's Jamestown Exposition, offered "leading events in [American] history . . . pictured in pantomime"; no knowledge of German or German history was required to enjoy the show.[22] That the festivals usually attracted many non-Germans as well as "immense numbers of German-speaking people" is suggested by von Bosse's experience and by English-language press accounts. The Lutheran pastor described the events as drawing thousands of people, "among them many Americans." The *Philadelphia Press* previewed the 1907 festival for its readers, noting that the "famous 'Column of Plenty' . . . will be shown again this year, with all the other well-known Cannstatter attractions." *Press* readers, moreover, could take in the event without feeling lost in a German-speaking crowd; von Bosse complained that he heard little enough German at the festivals.[23]

In both its content and the means used to promote it, moreover, the Cannstatter festival bore a striking resemblance to the new public entertainments proffered by commercial entrepreneurs. This was due, in part, to the organizers' readiness to adopt the same techniques those entrepreneurs had used so successfully. With assets in 1910 exceeding $70,000, the Volksfest-Verein could afford both to stage elaborate spectacles and to use up-to-date methods to advertise them. The pageants themselves echoed the increasingly commercialized civic carnivals, with their historical reenactments, sponsored by city officials in Philadelphia and other urban centers beginning in the late nineteenth century, as well as the "historical pageantry" advocated by some genteel intellectuals. The municipal celebrations frequently called on private carnival producers and professional actors to help put on a show.[24] The Cannstatter productions likewise appear to have used not only professional musicians, but also, at least occasionally, hired actors. The Volksfest-Verein, in search of Indians for its 1906 "America" pageant, undertook negotiations with White Cloud, the owner of an American Indian paraphernalia shop who made a business of supplying historical tableaus with Indian actors.[25] The Volksfest-Verein's entertainment committee, moreover, aggressively promoted the festival in ways that would have been familiar to any amusement park proprietor. The committee advertised the event not only through newspaper notices but also through hundreds of placards and "show-cards"; some of these were mailed out, while the committee arranged for others to be displayed in city streetcars. Indeed, organizers made a point of tying the festival in to the city's trolley network. In August 1898, the entertainment committee detailed its secretary to meet with officials of the Reading Railroad and the Union Traction Company, which ran Philadelphia's streetcar system, to make sure they provided "for sufficient transportation" to and from the festival grounds.[26]

While the Volksfest-Verein appropriated some of the methods of commercial entertainment entrepreneurs, it already possessed elements that were becoming central to commercialized amusement. Indeed, those entrepreneurs themselves appear to have borrowed significantly from nineteenth-century German-American festive culture, even as German Americans, especially the children of immigrants, shaped the emerging mass culture of entertainment. In a fascinating essay, Berndt Ostendorf described the German musical establishment that dominated both high and popular culture between 1870 and 1920 in New York City, the center of the nation's commercial music market. Within this world, second-generation "cultural mixers" played a crucial role, first by fusing a German sentimental tradition with popular song and marketing the results through sheet music sales and then by serving as midwives for the introduction of African-American music to, and its appropriation by, a mass European-American audience. Emblematic of this group were the brothers von Tilzer, the sons of an Irishman named Gumm. Harry, the oldest brother, took his German mother's maiden name of Tilzer to increase his chances of success in the music business, adding a "von" for effect. His brothers followed suit, and Harry and Albert von Tilzer went on to write a series of German-style waltzes that came to be seen as quintessentially American. The most notable such waltz, penned by Albert, became an anthem of the new mass culture: "Take Me Out to the Ball Game."[27] A similar if less centralized process appears to have occurred in the realm of public celebration. As Kathleen Conzen argued, German festive culture played "a significant role, both in enhancing the vocabulary of celebration and in demonstrating its potential respectability and commercial profit." Conzen noted the influence of the German carnival and of secular rituals that indulged in "historical allusion," and the Cannstatter pageants, which dated at least to the mid-1880s, fell squarely within these immigrant traditions.[28]

Equally significant, the mixed-sex sociability that the Cannstatter balls and festivals shared with the rest of Philadelphia's *Vereinswesen* was becoming a distinguishing hallmark of the new mass culture. Kathy Peiss described working-class social life in late-nineteenth-century New York City as divided to a great extent by gender, with a male public culture exemplified by the saloon and married women leading more homebound lives. By the turn of the century, however, younger, single working-class women were exploring the new world of commercial amusement, and doing so in the company of young men. As Peiss noted, at the amusement parks and concert halls of Coney Island, this new "heterosocial culture" to some extent also included married women and men, who came in family groups. To that extent, amusement park proprietors were simply learning to profit from the kind of heterosocial sociability that had long characterized German associations like the Volksfest-Verein, which described its 1900 ball as "as usual . . . a real family festival" and which attracted, to judge by photographs, an obviously mixed crowd to its festivals (see figure 4.1).[29]

In essence, the Cannstatter Volksfest-Verein appears to have succeeded where other German associations failed by evolving into something of a vibrant hybrid, fusing useful elements of the *Vereinswesen* with the approaches and attractions of commercialized amusement.[30] In its leadership, the language of its minutes, many of the themes and symbols it chose to display, and its festive tradition, it was immigrant German, or German-American. Simultaneously, however, the association's festival, with its entry fees and rented grounds, its "pantomime" pageants, food, and fireworks, its large, English-speaking crowds that mixed Germans with non-Germans and men with women, its aggressive advertising campaigns, and not least its efficient trolley connections, resembled nothing so much as a temporary amusement park, albeit one without mechanical rides. The Cannstatter experience showed that a *Verein* in a position to adapt to the new culture of commercialized entertainment could resist the forces eroding the *Vereinswesen*. It would take a world war and Prohibition to remove the Cannstatter festival, at least temporarily, from Philadelphia's public life.

Buying into Mass Culture: Elsie Spalde's New Clothes

Mass culture thus could serve a group like the Volksfest-Verein as a kind of resource. Yet, for German associational life and for ethnic identity more

Figure 4.1. Cannstatter Festival, 1902. Holding court at the annual festival of the Cannstatter Volksfest-Verein. The event fused elements of German-American festive culture, including mixed-sex sociability, with commercialized amusement, which itself drew on German traditions of festivity. Thousands of German and non-German spectators came to eat, drink, and enjoy an elaborate pageant—in 1902, a reenactment of a harvest festival, staged at Philadelphia's Washington Park. Note the mix of men and women and of German and American themes, signified by the American flags atop the hay wagon. Source: The Historical Society of Pennsylvania, "Cannstatter Volksfest—Washington Park, 1902," the Balch Institute Collections, *Cannstatter Volksfest-Verein, Philadelphia: Geschichte des Vereins von der Gründung in 1873 bis zum Goldenen Jubiläum im September 1923* (Philadelphia, [1923]), 38. Reproduced by permission of the Historical Society of Pennsylvania.

generally, mass culture also represented competition. In terms of content and control, much of consumer and commercial culture necessarily involved a departure from familiar ethnic ground. Cultural productions such as amusement parks and film were organized by entrepreneurs interested in profit more than ethnic preservation. Some activities central to mass culture—baseball, for example—lay outside of *Verein* traditions and, in fact, were popularly identified as uniquely American.[31]

To walk into a Market Street department store or Willow Grove Park, then, could mean leaving behind an older ethnic world and entering a space stocked with materials for a new kind of consumption-oriented identity. Put another way, mass culture could both complement ethnic culture *and* compete with it for the attention and leisure time of German Americans, with corrosive effects on their ethnic identity. Gerhard Wiesinger and Peter Conolly-Smith found precisely this latter dynamic at work in their studies of German immigrants in, respectively, Holyoke, Massachusetts, and New York City. Holyoke's two turner clubs, for example, lost members as second- and third-generation immigrants embraced such newer sports as baseball and football. Conolly-Smith argued provocatively that over the 1910s, both working-class and middle-class variants of German-American culture in New York were "translated" into American mass culture. German New Yorkers chose such pleasures as the movies, baseball, and Broadway spectacles over German theater and the traditional offerings of the *Vereine*. Indeed, under wartime pressures, they incorporated mass-cultural rituals like baseball into *Vereine* themselves.[32]

By the early twentieth century, mass culture clearly was competing, in this sense, for the interest of German Philadelphians. To some degree, the second generation that displayed a dwindling interest in the *Vereinswesen* and its traditional pastimes turned to mass culture instead. Harriet Spaeth hinted at this kind of generational shift when she described how her sons' athletic interests differed from her husband's. Adolph Spaeth, she recalled, was fond of the bowling he had learned in Germany, but "the games into which his sons entered with so much zeal and success, baseball and football, tennis, golf and what not—were sealed books to him." *Vereine*, however, also found themselves competing with commercial amusements for the attention of both generations, and on their home ground, to boot—within the "Amusements" column of the *Tageblatt*. At the turn of the century, that standing column advertised *Verein* events—picnics, festivals, pinochle tournaments—as well as German-language theater; the only non-German institution to appear regularly, at the column's foot, was the city's zoological gardens.[33] By 1914, however, *Verein* notices often jostled for space within the column with advertisements for vaudeville houses and Willow Grove Park.[34] Indeed, on certain days, the column had no *Verein* advertising at all and consisted entirely of notices for the amusement park, vaudeville, the zoo, or some combination thereof. Here, in a manner similar to that observed by Conolly-Smith, mass culture literally displaced the festive culture of the *Vereine*.[35] If the "Amusements" column is any indication, *Tageblatt* readers increasingly slighted that older, festive culture for the pleasures of Willow Grove and the vaudeville stage.

Mass culture also wrought change in German Philadelphia by occasioning new forms of collective identity that were open especially to women. These affiliations could be mixed-sex, like that of baseball fan, but some were gender-specific, arising from the central role women played in the emerging economy of mass consumption. Married women who functioned as household managers controlled family shopping and, as in Mrs. E's case, decisions about consumer credit. Their emerging role and identity as consumers was recognized and encouraged by advertisers, department stores, and at times even German men. Socialist union-label campaigns, for example, targeted women as shoppers in an attempt to turn consumption to labor's advantage.[36]

It was the single, wage-earning daughters of such women, however, who seem to have embraced mass culture and its potential for self-invention most fully. As Kathy Peiss argued in her study of young women workers in New York City, shorter workdays and new jobs in factories, offices, and department stores allowed those women to carve out a "distinctive sphere of leisure" largely within mass culture. "It was in leisure that women played with identity, trying on new images and roles, appropriating the cultural forms around them—clothing, music, language—to push at the boundaries of immigrant, working-class life," she wrote.[37]

No daughter of German Philadelphia fit this description better than Elsie Spalde. (Spalde took the name Moore on marrying in 1920. Her Swiss father's surname originally was Spälti, but its spelling was changed to Spalde, possibly by an immigration officer). As she recounted in an unpublished memoir, she went out to work in 1908, just before her twelfth birthday. Spalde found employment at a tannery, a woolen mill, a silk hosiery plant, and, from 1914 to 1918, at the Frankford Arsenal, where she made artillery shell fuses. She gave all of her earnings to her mother until 1914; when she turned eighteen that year, she began to pay room and board and to keep the balance of her wages. Especially after she came into this "extra money," Spalde threw herself enthusiastically into mass culture. A fan of nickel movies and dancing from her early teens, she and her friends graduated to vaudeville shows and trips to Willow Grove Park. Once she retained her wages, she "could afford to dress well" and experiment with such cutting-edge fashions as the slit skirt.[38] Spalde and her closest female friend at the arsenal also made their own bathing suits "and went to Ocean City for our vacations." As the photographs in her memoir confirm, her outings at that New Jersey shore resort and elsewhere took place within the same context of youthful, mixed-sex sociability described by Peiss. "Like many young girls then, we had lots of dates and good times," she recalled. Spalde's work at the arsenal gave her the financial independence to enjoy this whirlwind of mass culture and the friends, both female and male, to enjoy it with. It was only fitting, therefore, that she met her future husband at the arsenal, and that on their first date they went to a baseball game.[39]

Elsie Spalde Moore's recollections reveal how one young woman negotiated the new worlds of work and mass culture in a way that ultimately distanced her from her German ethnic roots. In the North Philadelphia neighborhood where she grew up, "almost everyone was German or German descent," and her parents spoke German with the neighbors as well as with the family. At the arsenal, however, she socialized across ethnic and, ultimately, class lines: her friends there included Mary McGovern and Margaret Cahill, and her future husband, F. J. Leigh Moore, was a middle-class New Englander who left college to become an Army officer. Elsie Spalde did not forgo her German identity during these years. Yet in her memoir, her work and active social life take center stage. Mass culture looms very large here, while the sole mention of the *Vereinswesen* comes in the context of fashion, when she describes the ensemble she wore to a ball at "Turners Hall on Broad Street." Indeed, in the 1910s, Spalde seems to have put her German identity on the back burner and allowed herself to play with the new identities made possible by mass culture, to test different presentations of self, literally to try on new images with the new clothes she made and bought. Her care in composing those images is reflected in one 1918 photograph, where Spalde sits elegantly arrayed in a striped blouse, a light skirt, high lace-up boots, and—as she described it—"a lovely real red fox neck piece" (see figure 4.2). At Ocean City, Spalde donned a bathing suit and, perhaps, named her corresponding identity. Another photograph from 1918 shows her posing in that suit before a beach scene—possibly a painted backdrop in a photo studio at the resort. Beneath, she printed this caption in her memoir: "The Bathing Beauty."[40]

If the caption reflects words remembered from 1918, Elsie Spalde even then may not have taken her self-image as "bathing beauty" all that seriously. Perhaps the phrase represented a fleeting thought, a joke she shared one summer day with her friend Mary McGovern, who posed before the same backdrop in her own bathing suit for a virtually identical photograph.[41] The larger point, however, is that Spalde poured enormous energy into the pursuit of fashion, commercial amusement, and heterosocial fun in a manner that kept her away from German ethnic institutions and let her experiment with a range of identities defined by American mass culture. Such experimentation shows how mass culture facilitated a re-

Figure 4.2. Elsie Lillian Spalde (originally Spälti), 1918. Elsie Spalde donned her most fashionable clothes—including a treasured fox stole—for this studio portrait, taken at the seaside resort of Wildwood, New Jersey. The wages she earned as a young, single factory worker allowed her to try out different presentations of self rooted in mass consumer and commercial culture. Such self-fashionings stood at a far remove from the heavily German neighborhood where Spalde grew up, suggesting that her plunge into mass culture facilitated a de-emphasis of the German component of her identity. Photographer: Hoffman Studio, Wildwood, N.J. Courtesy of Jean M. Husher.

construction of multiple identity that de-emphasized Germanness—confining it to one's family and neighborhood—and instead stressed self-images rooted in consumption and shared across ethnic and, to some extent, class lines, with the likes of the presumably Irish-American McGovern and Anglo-American (and middle-class) Leigh Moore.

Elsie Spalde's embrace of mass culture did not reflect the experience of every German Philadelphian. As corrosive as that culture might have been to ethnic identity, some in the *Vereinswesen* managed to tap its power. The Cannstatter Volksfest-Verein's success in this regard, along with women's increasing interest in associational life, suggest that the fate of German America, though uncertain, was by no means fixed before the First World War—and that the war itself played a central role in determining German America's future. As it was, however, many in German Philadelphia, male as well as female, ultimately would follow a path like Spalde's. Their participation in mass culture would signal a retreat from ethnic concerns and from the German ethnic component of multiple identity. How changing conceptions of race and nation shaped another line of retreat is the topic of the next chapter.

Destinations: Fractured Whiteness, "American" Identity, and the "Old Stock" Opening

"INDEED, I'm just not going to marry that 'Chink,'" snapped Hattie Hanf. "Why, he's too stingy and I can't do anything with him." The sixteen-year-old Hattie had just broken off her engagement to Whol Shoo, a well-off Chinese restaurant owner, as the *Philadelphia Press* explained to its readers in August 1905. Hattie's father, Charles Augustus Hanf, was visibly disappointed. "Die veddin' ist postponed," he told the *Press* reporter who turned up on his doorstep. "Mein daughter she say 'no!'"[1]

Charles Hanf had been "very much elated with the prospect of having a Chinese son-in-law," the *Press* noted. But its reporter, who described Hattie as "a tall, graceful, fair-haired, blue-eyed girl of the pure Saxon type," had another idea. "'The Press' representative suggested that an American husband would be better suited for so fair a girl, and for the first time during the visit Hattie's face wore a look of real pleasure. 'That's just what I say,' came in animated tones from her brother, who hitherto had remained silent. 'She's entirely too good for him.'"[2]

Race was not the only element in this domestic drama at the Hanf home, which lay just west of Northern Liberties and a few blocks north of Philadelphia's Chinatown. Greed played a role, too. As Hattie Hanf described Whol Shoo, "[t]he only thing in his favor is his money . . . and if I can't have all I want of that I just won't marry him."[3] But Hattie's racial slur, the reporter's portrayal of her as an avatar of "Saxon" whiteness, and her and her brother's receptiveness to the idea of "an American husband" for "so fair a girl," hint at the complex ways in which race and nationalism shaped the identities of German Philadelphians in the early twentieth century.

Because he was Chinese, Whol Shoo was not "American"—a distinction that was clear to Hattie and her brother but seemed lost on their father, who, given his name and accent, appeared to be a German immigrant. Hattie, on the other hand, was suited to marry an "American" for racial reasons; she was not simply white, but "of the pure Saxon type," a racial reference that had specifically German overtones. Hattie, that is, could qualify as an American at least in part due to her German "racial" background, even as she eschewed a German accent. Charles Hanf, closer to the family's German origins, was unaware of, or indifferent to, his prospective son-in-law's racial unsuitability.

One could read the tale of the Hanfs as a case where an immigrant failed and his children succeeded in becoming American by "becoming white"— by learning the rules for acceptance into an America defined racially as white. But this reading would only begin the analysis, because it begs the questions of what "white" and "American" meant, and to whom, at specific historical moments. For American nationalism and American racial categorization were undergoing profound shifts during this period, shifts that fostered new and altered forms of collective identity.

Nativist pressures during and after the First World War would render American nationalism far less accepting of ethnic allegiances and give it a more narrowly exclusive racial cast. White identity, and Germans' relation to it, likewise would change. In a general sense, German Philadelphians knew they were white at the turn of the twentieth century, but that identity was less salient for many than it would later become. White identity was also fractured. Within German Philadelphia, some middle-class and Lutheran spokesmen stressed the superiority of certain white "races" over others, with northwest Europeans—including, of course, Germans—at the head of the pack. This thinking paralleled developments in Anglo-America, where an emerging racialized nativism increasingly depicted northwest Europeans as the best kind of Americans, at times, in fact, as belonging to an American "race stock" or "old stock." In these formulations, racial and national identity fused, offering some Germans a new kind of destination: a way of seeing themselves as "American" that also fit their patterns of association with northwest Europeans. They would not, by and large, head for that destination until the 1920s, but it had become available to them by the 1910s.

"White Dutchmen" and Racial Indifference

Historians in recent years have begun to chart the evolution of white racial identity in the United States, paying particular attention to how, when, and in what contexts European immigrants "became white." As Matthew Jacobson argued, Europeans entered the United States as white within the context of formal citizenship. They could become citizens and (male) voters under the Naturalization Act of 1790, which made only "free white persons" eligible for citizenship—an eligibility denied to newcomers "of the African race or of African descent" until 1870 and to Asian immigrants until the mid-twentieth century.[4] Yet, in other contexts, the whiteness of many European immigrant groups was questioned. Perhaps the most-studied such group is the Irish.[5] Before the Civil War, as David Roediger noted, "it was by no means clear that the Irish were white." Native-born Americans described them in terms of stereotypes—"savage," "lazy," "simian," and "sensual"—otherwise reserved for African Americans, and some writers suggested the Irish belonged to "a 'dark' race, possibly originally African." Irish immigrants in the United States had to fight their way to the status of "white," claiming it in part as a weapon in their struggle against blacks and native whites for jobs. At the same time, the large-scale entrance of the Irish and other unfamiliar European peoples into the American republic after 1840 helped to fracture whiteness itself, in Jacobson's reading. In racial "science" and popular culture, the newcomers were slotted into a new hierarchy of "white *races*"—Celts, Slavs, Mediterraneans, and so forth—with some deemed more suited to self-government than others. Jacobson saw this hierarchy as fading by the mid-twentieth-century into a monolithic, "Caucasian" whiteness, where former Celts and Slavs now stood on the white side of a black-white color line.[6] Certainly, by about the same time, as other scholarship suggested, whiteness had been visited on the "new immigrant" groups from southern and eastern Europe. They had moved from the status of "not-yet-white ethnics" or "inbetween peoples" to white in ways that indicated they saw becoming white as a way to become American.[7]

Scholars of white identity have given comparatively little study to the situation of German immigrants, perhaps assuming that the whiteness of Germans was less open to question. Yet newcomers from Germany were not automatically welcomed as whites. Benjamin Franklin, reflecting English apprehension over the massive eighteenth-century German immigration to Pennsylvania, asserted in 1751 that most Europeans, including most Germans, did not number among the "purely white people in the world," being "generally of what we call a swarthy complexion." Lorenz Degenhard, a well-educated German immigrant in St. Louis, noted in 1835 that earlier newcomers, who came almost completely from the "lowest classes of people in Germany," had found themselves standing on the same level as "the blacks," or lower. "More recently, [the Americans] have even, here and there, drawn a distinction between *white dutchman* (white German) and *black dutchman* (black German), whereby they possibly want to compliment the educated." Jacobson noted that one Know-Nothing newspaper, the *Ohio Republican,* charged that "Germans were driving 'white people' out of the labor market."[8]

At the same time, evidence suggests that German immigrants considered themselves white and that this self-perception likely was informed, at least in part, by a consciousness of color present in German-speaking central Europe. That consciousness reflected a very small yet perceptible

African presence in the German lands that dated at least to the time of the Crusades and stemmed in part from rulers' employment of Africans as exotic symbols of status. By the seventeenth century at the latest, German princes commonly featured one or two black African servants or musicians at court; black trumpeters and drummers served in the Prussian king's army from the late 1600s until the collapse of the monarchy in 1918.[9] If ordinary Germans did not see Africans in a noble's retinue, they might catch glimpses of them in representations of legendary figures such as St. Mauritius or, by the eighteenth century, in depictions on porcelain and the popular stage.[10] A sense of difference from these strangers eventually became fixed in color terms. Toward the end of the seventeenth century, the words "white" (*weiß*) and "black" (*schwarz*) emerged in common usage to denote the skin color of Europeans and Africans, respectively. At about the same time, the common word for an African began to shift from "moor" (*Mohr*) to "negro" (*Neger*). As Peter Martin argued, this change was indicative of a larger decline in the image of Africa that accompanied European expansion. Germans commonly came to see Africa no longer as a "seductive paradise of refined [Islamic] civilization" but rather as a land of primitive savages. The popular image of the subhuman African became ever more firmly fixed as entrepreneurs put allegedly "wild" blacks on display at fairs and circuses—a practice begun in the mid-seventeenth century and lasting into the twentieth—and as Imperial Germany made its own colonial ventures into Africa during and after the 1880s.[11]

By the end of the seventeenth century, moreover, European intellectuals had begun to develop systems of classification that distinguished between different "species" or "races" of humans, and Germans joined in this effort. Immanuel Kant, for example, brought the French loanword "race" into German, delineating four *Racen* of humanity, including the *Weißen* (whites) and *Neger* (Negroes). Johann Friedrich Blumenbach, writing in the last quarter of the eighteenth century, offered a fivefold classification, in the process introducing the term "Caucasian" for the Europeans.[12] In the first half of the nineteenth century, such thinking would combine with romantic, nationalistic notions of the German *Volk* (people) and with the findings of German philologists to produce a view of the "Germanic race"—understood to include Germans, Scandinavians, and the English—as the elite group among the Caucasians. Later in the century, this Germanic race would receive the name of "Aryan." These ideas, bolstered by Social Darwinism, formed essential elements of a "Volkish" ideology that gathered strength at the turn of the twentieth century and, with its dichotomy between "Germanic" and "Jewish" races, helped set the intellectual stage for the Third Reich and the Holocaust. The development of German racial thinking made for a good deal of linguistic slippage among the terms *Rasse* (the more Germanized form of *Race*), *Volk,* and *Nation.*[13] These words, especially *Rasse* and *Volk,* might be used interchangeably or might signify quite different concepts.

Thus, nineteenth-century German immigrants potentially had access in their homeland to a broad range of ideas about race. This range would find expression in the United States, as newly arrived Germans found their bearings in the American racial hierarchy. At the most basic level, many Germans in Philadelphia made whiteness part of their identity (though perhaps not all did so, if Charles Hanf is any indication). This much is clear from the city's German-language press—working-class, secular middle-class, and religious—in the years leading up to the First World War. That the middle-class *Philadelphia Sonntags-Journal* considered its German-speaking readership white, for example, comes across clearly in an antinativist poem the newspaper published in 1901. The piece reminded nativists that their ancestors had been "whites" and "Europeans" —"'foreigners,' just like us." Otherwise, nativists would look like Indians: "Their faces wouldn't be white, / But beautifully copper-colored!"[14] Crime coverage provides the most consistent evidence of such color consciousness. Like its English-language competitors, the *Philadelphia Tageblatt* routinely identified African-American criminal suspects as "Negro" (*Neger*), "colored" (*farbig*), or "black" (*Schwarzer*). The practice was as evident in 1914 as it was at the dawn of the century. While only scattered issues of Philadelphia's two middle-class German-language dailies are available from this period, the surviving issues of one for 1915 show the same pattern.[15] *Tageblatt* reports of clashes between blacks and whites would identify the latter as such, and it seems clear that between what one article called "the two races," Germans belonged to the white one.[16]

The city's German-language religious weeklies did not cover crime, but they, too, appear to have seen their readerships as white. Denouncing the trade in alcohol between "Indians and white immigrants to this land," the *Lutherisches Kirchenblatt* in 1900 described an Indian appeal to "[m]y white brothers" against that traffic as resounding "heart-renderingly . . . to us." The same year, a reader wrote to the Catholic *Nord Amerika* asking how "the difference between the races of men" could be explained, "when all humans are descended from one human couple, Adam and Eve." The newspaper assured the reader that the existence of races did not overthrow the authority of scripture and pointed to Blumenbach's classification of five such races, including "the Caucasian"—a category within which *Nord Amerika* presumably saw its constituency as fitting.[17]

Whiteness thus appears to have functioned as an element of identity that cut across the various subcultures of German Philadelphia, coexisting quite easily at the turn of the century with a German identity. This shared quality of white identity likely was reinforced by mass culture, with its broad appeal to Germans of different backgrounds. For mass commercial culture conveyed messages that encouraged audiences to see themselves as white. Nineteenth-century blackface minstrelsy and its descendants on the vaudeville stage and on early movie screens performed this function, as a number of scholars have argued; so, too, did movie westerns, with their depictions of frontier battles against Indians.[18] German Philadelphians encountered both mass cultural traditions. Elsie Spalde regularly took in westerns during her visits to the nickel movies. Germans likewise undoubtedly caught blackface shows at the city's vaudeville houses; the *Tageblatt,* in previewing the acts at Keith's, described "*'Blackface' Komiker*" ("blackface comedians"). In turn, blackface minstrelsy surfaced within the national *Vereinswesen,* while Philadelphia *Vereine* featured their own minstrel-type acts. In September 1901, for example, the Kensington Labor Lyceum sponsored an evening of entertainment that included, along with renditions of traditional *Lieder,* one Harry James's "Negro character imitations."[19]

Yet if white and German identities could coexist, whiteness also may have served as a default identity for Philadelphians who sought to loosen their ethnic German ties. W.E.B. Du Bois suggested as much in his classic 1899 study, *The Philadelphia Negro.* He noted at one point that Jews, Italians, and "even [some] Americans" were, like blacks, "unassimilated" to the city's "larger social group," but observed elsewhere that the same was not necessarily true of other European immigrants. Through the nineteenth century, "[n]o differences of social condition allowed any Negro to escape from the group, although such escape was continually the rule among Irish, Germans, and other whites."[20] Like other forms of mass culture, blackface minstrelsy could offer distance from an immigrant background; within some *Vereine* nationally, it served as the vehicle through which second-generation members broke traditions of staging only German-language productions.[21] Identification with a specifically white America could allow even sharper breaks with immigrant origins, as Hattie Hanf showed in rejecting Whol Shoo over her father's objections and favoring the notion of an "American" husband.

The conflation here of "American" and white serves as a reminder of how closely tied those two identities have been through American history. Naturalization law is only one indicator of the extent to which historically, in Toni Morrison's words, "American means white."[22] American nationalism, as Gary Gerstle argued, has long contained dueling "civic" and "racial" traditions. American civic nationalism has been a matter of belief in "the nation's core political ideals" of equality, liberty, and democratic self-government. German-American intellectuals in the nineteenth century played on and, indeed, fostered this view. They argued that since American nationhood was "essentially political," Germans could become good Americans by believing in the "human rights" declared in the nation's founding documents, while continuing to cultivate their own cultural ways.[23] But this civic tradition has competed with "a racial nationalism that conceives of America in ethnoracial terms, as a people held together by common blood and skin color and by an inherited fitness for self-government." The "yearning to be a white republic"—however that whiteness might be defined—shaped definitions of "American" through the nineteenth and twentieth centuries, as much as, and sometimes more than, civic nationalism.[24]

If American often meant white, however, white did not necessarily mean American. Indeed, for some German Philadelphians at the turn of the century, a white identity likely seemed far less problematic than an American one, given the negative connotations "America" could evoke. "Americanism" carried a pejorative meaning for some German Catholics, just as "American Lutheranism" did for confessionally minded German Lutherans. German socialists likewise were not given to an unqualified identification with America. The *Tageblatt* did continue a long Independence Day tradition among working-class radicals of casting workers as the true heirs of the American Revolution. America's organized workers and socialists would complete that revolution by making "real the ideal of democracy . . . in all areas [of life]," the newspaper declared on July 4, 1914. Yet that ideal remained unfulfilled, not least because capitalist industrialization had subjected propertyless wage-earners to "a new slavery."[25] That middle-class German Philadelphians had to labor so long and hard to construct a collective German-American identity may indicate the ambivalence some in their audience felt about the American side of the hyphen.

Whether or not whiteness implied an American identity, it appears to have been a standard item in the multiple identities crafted by German Philadelphians. Yet what seems most striking about that item at the turn of the twentieth century is its relatively low salience. Simply put, many German Philadelphians, while aware that they were white, seemed not all that invested emotionally in whiteness. Working-class Germans in particular appear to have accorded it less importance before the First World War than some Anglo-Americans did and than they themselves would later do. The low profile of white identity, evident in Charles Hanf's welcome of Whol Shoo, can be seen as well in the *Tageblatt*'s complicated stance toward African Americans, which alternated contempt, sympathy, and a tone of distance. The strain of contempt surfaced on occasion in crime coverage, as when the newspaper gratuitously referred to "niggers" (*Niggern*) in a report on fighting between two groups of blacks in South Carolina. At the same time, however, the *Tageblatt* could condemn what one headline called the "white terror" of lynching in the South and denounce the exploitation of black Southern laborers as "the new slavery." Such reports, and the fact that the *Tageblatt* could also apply the metaphor of a "new slavery" to industrial wage work, suggest that some aspects of a nineteenth-century radicalism on racial matters lingered at the newspaper. German-American radicals of the Civil War era had embraced militant abolitionism and legal equality for black Americans. At times, they and other German newcomers crossed color lines in provocative ways, as in the intimate friendship forged between Frederick Douglass and immigrant journalist Ottilie Assing or in the socializing and political cooperation that took place among some Germans, blacks, and Mexicans in Texas.[26] Even after Reconstruction, German radicals and liberals in the North continued to honor the antislavery cause; in 1885, *Der Sozialist,* a New York newspaper, suggested that the anniversary of the Emancipation Proclamation would make a more appropriate national holiday than July 4. Middle-class intellectuals took particular pride in the written protest against slavery lodged by four Germantown settlers in 1688, publicizing it as the first formal antislavery protest in American history. Oswald Seidensticker in 1883 and Charles Hexamer in 1907 both claimed the Germantown protest as a German achievement.[27] The *Tageblatt*'s intermittent sympathy with the plight of black Southerners may have had roots in this antislavery heritage.

Closer to home, such sympathy was in shorter supply: black Philadelphians appeared in the *Tageblatt* most frequently as criminal suspects. Yet before World War I, the *Tageblatt* seems to have taken a relatively muted tone toward local African Americans, approaching the "indifference" to blacks that James Barrett and David Roediger have found among some new immigrants. The newspaper's coverage of the Philadelphia general strike of March 1910 illustrates this stance. The general strike was a sympathy action waged on behalf of streetcar workers who walked off the job in late February. The city's streetcar monopoly, Philadelphia Rapid Transit (PRT), brought in strikebreakers, some of them rumored to be black. To ward off mounting crowd attacks against PRT streetcars, the city government enrolled temporary "special police," some of whom were African American. Such actions triggered racial resentment among many strike supporters. The black "specials" became particular objects of abuse. After a March 7 strike rally at the Labor Lyceum, for example, members of the crowd outside bombarded passing streetcars. "On the last car stood a colored policeman, who was especially singled out as a target," the *Tageblatt* reported. "Bricks and cobblestones flew at him from all sides." John Golden, the national president of the United Textile Workers of America, told a rally two days later of "[t]he most humiliating sight I ever saw . . . an aged man elbowing his way through the crowd was struck down by a negro policeman. I wondered then whether the Liberty Bell had proclaimed that kind of freedom."[28]

German workers may or may not have cheered Golden's words or thrown stones at African-American police. What is striking about the *Tageblatt*'s coverage of such events, however, is how unheated it was. By and large, when the newspaper reported on black police and possible black strikebreakers at all, it did so matter-of-factly, without racist asides like that made by Golden. The *Tageblatt* noted, for example, that there were thought to be "27 Negroes among [one group of] strikebreakers, but these are supposed not to find employment on the cars, but rather to function as cooks for the strikebreakers and other employees." The newspaper did not entirely forgo racist statements during the period covered by the general strike. The crassest ran in early March: a joke about chicken stealing, complete with a cartoon of two stereotyped blacks. The caricature, however, stands out for its rarity. During all of February and March, such racist cartoons appeared in only two issues of the *Tageblatt,* and never on the newspaper's standing Sunday page of jokes and caricatures, which was laced with German ethnic themes.[29] In contrast, the Sunday comics of even so staid an English-language newspaper as the *Public Ledger* were rife with blatant stereotypes of African Americans.[30]

The *Tageblatt*'s relative indifference may have reflected literal distance. In essence, whiteness may have had a relatively low salience for some German Philadelphians because they worked and lived at something of a remove from African Americans. The predominantly skilled German workforce faced little job competition from the small pool of skilled black workers, who were shut out of their trades by white workers, unions, and employers and who generally could only find skilled work in black-owned businesses.[31] Moreover, German and black residents tended to live in different parts of the city. Germans remained concentrated in North Philadelphia, which held almost 80 percent of the city's first- and second-generation German immigrants in 1910. In the late nineteenth century, most African Americans lived at the other end of the city, in South Philadelphia. After 1890, blacks increasingly moved to North Philadelphia, but they would not become a significant presence there until the First World War and the resulting Great Migration. Of the thirteen North Philadelphia wards with the highest concentrations of German immigrants and their children in 1910—wards that together held just over half of the city's German-stock residents—only one ward had a population more than 3 percent black.[32]

Closer workplace and residential proximity, however, had the potential to raise significantly the salience of white identity. That much is clear from a remarkable editorial the *Tageblatt* ran in August 1903. Titled "A Black Invasion," the piece was prompted by a front-page report of a plan "to colonize a half-million [Southern] Negroes in New England," apparently with the sponsorship of Northern employers seeking "cheap hands." Those employers could portray the plan as philanthropic, because, in fact, "[t]he Negro in the South is oppressed," that is, denied equal rights, having no political rights, and miserably paid. Yet the "Yankee-capitalists" were "completely indifferent" to blacks, the editorial declared; they only cared to bring "the Negro" north because they saw him as more exploitable than European immigrants and native white workers. Such a mass importation, moreover, would lead to "murder and death blows" as soon as "the Negroes took on the roles of sweated laborers and strikebreakers." This judgment led the *Tageblatt* to advocate a radically separatist solution:

> The South is the home of the Negro. There he thrives best, and there he should remain. . . . In the low-lying, coastal regions stretching from the Chesapeake Bay to the Rio Grande there is an excellent field of action for the Negro, where the white cannot prosper. Thereby is the border drawn for the natural separation of the races [*die natürliche Scheidung der Rassen*]. Such a mixture, and no further, is to be desired. Negro states [*Negerstaaten*] are possible along the Gulf of Mexico and the South Atlantic coast. There, the Negroes may govern themselves, under the jurisdiction, of course, of the United States. . . . In this question, too, the interest of the worker coincides with the demands of civilization. Not the diffusion of the Negroes over the entire country, in order to use them as helots, can be the goal of true humanity, but rather their concentration in the subtropical regions that are better suited to them than to the whites.[33]

The editorial laid bare a welter of attitudes: fears of possible job competition from racial outsiders manipulated by capitalists; a desire for geographic separation; a recognition of Southern racial oppression and an endorsement of "Negro states" that verged on a form of black nationalism; and the assumption that blacks did not belong in the North. This last view implied that the *Tageblatt,* and, perhaps, its German readers, could safely ignore Philadelphia's own long-standing black community—as long as it did not continue to grow.

Germans and the "Germanic" Race

If many German Philadelphians learned or modified their notions of whiteness in the United States, some also expressed more elaborate conceptions of a Germanic race or people. Significantly, that category encompassed most Americans of northwest European background and was at times portrayed as central to the American nation. Such "Germanic" expressions stressed the Germans' role as leaders of this race and tended to be confined to those most interested in fostering German-American unity, notably men active in the German Society of Pennsylvania and the

National German-American Alliance. In 1896, for example, German Society member Adolph Spaeth described the United States as bringing together the "Nordic (Scandinavian), German, and Anglo-Saxon branches" of the "originally unified Germanic *Stamm*"—a term translatable as "race," "stock," or "tribe."[34] "[W]e are firmly convinced that the Germanic element—and by that we mean Scandinavians, Anglo-Saxons, and Germans together—will decide the future of America," the Lutheran pastor declared. "Not Latin or Slavic, but Germanic will be and must remain the head and heart of America, if it is to fulfill its world-historical mission."[35] Charles Hexamer likewise alluded to a larger Germanic element when he told a German Society audience in 1902 that they belonged to the "noblest branch, the German," of "that people [*Volk*], who defeated the Romans . . . [and] to whom belonged as well those lower German tribes that conquered England [in] the middle of the fifth century."[36]

Such Germanic evocations were, however, relatively scarce outside of secular middle-class and Lutheran circles before the First World War. German Catholics and, to a lesser degree, German socialists, while quite ready to speak of white and black races, for the most part avoided breaking whites down into separate European "races." A review of the Catholic weekly *Nord Amerika* over the first nine months of 1900 shows that it consistently used the word "nationality" (*Nationalität*) to refer to European ethnic groups in general; it almost never employed the term *Rasse* (race) to denote subgroups of Europeans or European Americans.[37] And never during this period did German Catholics in its pages refer to themselves as a *Rasse* or *Race,* whether "German," "Germanic," "Teutonic," or otherwise—in sharp contrast to the Irish Catholic tendency to invoke an Irish "race." *Nord Amerika*'s sole reference to a German or Germanic *Race* came in a translation of a speech given in English by Bishop John Lancaster Spalding, a descendant of English colonial settlers.[38]

Similarly, when the labor-oriented *Tageblatt* did not refer to European ethnic groups by their national names, it preferred to talk of different European "nationalities" or "peoples" (*Völker*), as an examination of the newspaper's summer issues for 1914 and 1916 indicates.[39] There were exceptions: a July 1914 editorial spoke, for example, of "branches of the Slavic race" and of a "Germanic immigration" that included the English, Scots, Swiss, and Dutch, as well as the Germans. Yet even here, the *Tageblatt*'s editors took care to put their first reference to "races" in quotation marks. They appeared particularly reticent on the subject with the outbreak of war in Europe the following month. Melvin Holli has described how Germans in Chicago greeted Germany's battle with Russia as a "war of the Teutonic race against the Slavic." Despite the *Tageblatt*'s contempt for "the Slavic half-barbarians," however, it made only one reference to a European "race" between August 2 and August 15, when it described speakers at a Swiss festival calling for "the final, decisive victory of the Teutonic race!" In October, in fact, the newspaper reprinted an editorial from the Berlin socialist newspaper *Vorwärts* that ridiculed the notion that the European conflict was a "race war." As the editorial stated in its opening lines: "Race? Hmf!"[40]

Hence, while German Catholics and socialists were aware of the concept of a larger Germanic element, they tended to shy away from such views and particularly to avoid describing that element as a distinct *Rasse*. They had good reasons for this stance. Both Catholics and socialists had transethnic—indeed, internationalist—commitments that worked against the glorification of a particular subgroup of European peoples. For socialists, that commitment was to an international working class; for Catholics, it was to a Church Universal, expressed in Philadelphia through the archdiocese's system of national parishes. Both groups likewise harbored an ambivalence toward German nationalism in the homeland that had no equivalent among middle-class activists such as Hexamer, von Bosse, and Spaeth. This ambivalence was conditioned by conflicts with the new German nation-state: for Catholics, the *Kulturkampf* of the 1870s and 1880s; for socialists, the suppression of the Social Democratic Party of Germany under the empire's Socialist Law from 1878 to 1890.[41] Catholic strictures on intermarriage with Protestants, moreover, cut against the idea that the Germans formed a unified biological entity, so that talk of a German race, let alone a Germanic one, made little sense to German Catholics.[42]

Redefining "American": The "Old Stock" Invitation

Crucially, however, German-American notions of a common Germanic race or people had Anglo-American equivalents, ones that, to some extent, grew out of the same sources but evolved and gained strength in the late nineteenth and early twentieth centuries. This evolution brought about a profound change in attitudes nationally toward northwest European immigrants between the Civil War and the 1910s. It yielded, in essence, an invitation to German Americans to enter American life as members of a larger, northwest European category. That category was portrayed as forming the core of the American nation; it was defined in terms both of race and of time; and it was denoted by phrases such as "American race stock" and "old stock."

By 1850, many Anglo-Americans had come to subscribe to what Reginald Horsman called "American racial Anglo-Saxonism." These Americans saw themselves as members of the American Anglo-Saxon branch of the Caucasian race—a superior breed with an innate gift both for conquest and for republican self-government. This ideology drew on the same trends in philology, ethnology, and Romantic nationalist thought that nourished ideas of a Germanic race in Germany, but it also had roots in English political and historical writings of the sixteenth and seventeenth centuries. Antiquarians delving into the history of Anglo-Saxon England borrowed from Continental thinkers associated with the German Reformation and from the Roman writer Tacitus to portray the Anglo-Saxons as descendants of freedom-loving Germanic tribes that had invaded England in the fifth century and brought their liberties and political institutions with them. This portrait pervaded Anglo-American political discourse in the eighteenth century.[43]

Anglo-Saxonist thinking, however, took on a specifically racial cast in the first half of the nineteenth century. This shift was informed by the emerging depictions in Germany of a Germanic race that had inherited all that was racially best in the larger "Indo-European" race newly identified by German philologists. In England and the United States, writers drew on this new learning to cast the Anglo-Saxons as the truest heirs of Germanic racial superiority, with Americans stressing their role as the most vigorous Anglo-Saxons of all. At the same time, Anglo-Americans borrowed from Germany and England the idea that Scandinavians ("the Norse") also fell within the Germanic orbit. By midcentury, then, all of the elements existed for Anglo-Americans to see northwestern Europeans in general—sometimes including, but usually not, the "Celtic" Irish—as members of the same, racially superior Germanic or Teutonic family, the leader among whites. As George Perkins Marsh wrote in 1843, using "Gothic" as a synonym for Germanic, "[t]he Goths, the common ancestors of the inhabitants of North Western Europe . . . are the noblest branch of the Caucasian race. We are their children." Intellectuals would refine and systematize such ideas after the Civil War. They drew on Darwin to propound a "Teutonic germ theory" that saw American political institutions as the result of an evolutionary process begun by the ancient Germans.[44]

Initially, actual German immigrants derived little if any direct benefit from the fact that many Anglo-American "Yankees" prized Germanic roots. Newcomers from Germany endured a wave of nativism in the 1850s, and conflict with Yankees over alcohol use, Sunday recreation, and German religious schools continued after the Civil War. But the arrival after 1880 of increasing numbers of newcomers from southern and eastern Europe—Italians, Poles, Russian Jews, and others—prompted many Anglo-Americans to take a more accepting stance toward their "Teutonic" cousins from Germany. A key role in this realignment was played by nativist intellectuals from New England Yankee families, in particular the economist Francis Amasa Walker. Walker grew convinced that non-

English immigrants—including Irish and German newcomers—were replacing Americans of his background. He became an advocate of restriction, but he could not hope to succeed in stemming all immigration, especially given the political power of second-generation Irish and German immigrants. In the early 1890s, therefore, Walker came up with a crucial distinction: that between "old" and "new" immigrants. By virtue of their time of arrival, old immigrants were those from northwestern Europe, while new immigrants came from southern and eastern Europe. The difference between them, then, was also racial: the new immigrants were "beaten men from beaten races"; they had no inherited traits conducive to self-government, "such as belong to those who are descended from the tribes that met under the oak-trees of old Germany." Walker and his associates in the Boston-based Immigration Restriction League (IRL), founded in 1894, worked to popularize the idea of a divide between old and new immigrants through a campaign for a literacy test for newcomers.[45]

The invention of the "new immigrant" prompted nativists and other Anglo-Americans to begin seeing Anglo-Saxons and the newly discovered "old immigrants" as more of a piece—united by the "Teutonic" bond of race or, even more broadly, by a common northwest European ancestry. As the IRL's Prescott F. Hall asked in 1897, did Americans "want this country to be peopled by British, German, and Scandinavian stock, historically free, energetic, progressive, or by Slav, Latin, and Asiatic races, historically downtrodden, atavistic, and stagnant?" The "Celtic" Irish held an ambiguous place in such racial hierarchies, but even they could be slotted into the northwest European group, as Henry Cabot Lodge managed to do in an 1896 Senate speech. Yet the new appreciation of "old immigrants" did not signify their immediate admission into the inner circle of American life. They remained immigrants in the minds of the IRL's Yankees, for these aristocrats drew a sharp line between European Americans whose forebears had arrived before the Revolution and those who came after. Hall, for example, differentiated in 1894 between "the native American stock" and "the earlier and better immigrants who came over before 1880."[46]

Americans used a succinct term to express this distinction in the late nineteenth century: "old stock." Like "old immigrant," "old stock" was at once a temporal and a racial designation. The *old* referred to time of arrival: old-stock Americans were those whose European ancestors had settled in America during the eighteenth century or before. *Stock* had connotations of family descent, but as Hall's comparison of "British . . . stock" and "Asiatic races" suggests, the term could function as a synonym for "race;" old-stock Americans were biologically distinct from others. *Stock* originally referred to the trunk or stem of a tree, but figurative uses arose as early as the fourteenth century that signified the source of a line of descent or the descendants of that common ancestor. By the sixteenth century, these figurative meanings included what the *Oxford English Dictionary* describes as "[a] race, [or] ethnical kindred," as in a 1549 reference to the "stocke" of "the whole nacion of Jewes." The word also early carried the meaning of a stem into which a graft is inserted, so that "old stock" came to mean, literally and figuratively, the original onto which was grafted something new.[47] By the seventeenth century, "old Stock" was used metaphorically to describe a "race" of original inhabitants of a place, in contrast to newer arrivals.[48]

In late-nineteenth-century American English, "stock" retained its earlier meanings, including that of "race,"[49] but "old stock" had taken on a more specific sense. Like the Americanisms "old planter" and "old settler,"[50] "old stock" expressed deference to those who could claim precedence in settlement. At the same time, the term's ethnic content seemed to vary somewhat by region. New Englanders, whose region's European population in the colonial period was almost entirely of English origin, tended to equate the "old stock" with the descendants of English Protestant settlers. In this view, as a speaker at an 1897 Boston festival honoring Queen Victoria put it, "'Americans of old British birth' were 'the genuine type of Americans.'"[51] In the mid-Atlantic region, which had seen significant immigration from Germany, Holland, and Sweden before 1790, the "old stock" expanded to account for that diversity. The term could even include Catholics. A New Jersey priest complained in the early 1890s that the church had named bishops from a wide variety of immigrant backgrounds, including "the so-called Irish-American and German-American," yet "the 'plain American' element of old stock seems to many to be seriously neglected."[52]

Philadelphia, with its visible contingent of residents of colonial-era "Pennsylvania German" extraction, harbored similarly elastic definitions. This could hardly be avoided. One of the most prominent Philadelphians to serve as an IRL officer at the turn of the century was, after all, the novelist Owen Wister—of the Germantown Wisters, a leading "Proper Philadelphia" family of colonial German descent. Old-stock status attached to such colonial families, whether of British or German background. In October 1908, for example, the *Germantown Independent-Gazette* described a local politician of colonial Welsh origin as deriving "From Real Old Stock." Two weeks before, the newspaper had mourned the death of a prominent local businessman who also "came from good old stock, his paternal grandmother being a Pastorius." The businessman qualified as old stock precisely because he had colonial German ancestry, which went back to Franz Daniel Pastorius, Germantown's founder.[53]

After the century's first decade, however, the usage of "old stock" became more ambiguous and, hence, potentially more inclusive. Between roughly 1910 and 1930, that term and related terms such as "American stock," "old American stock," and "American race stock," began to be used in ways that suggested they might subsume the descendants of nineteenth-century German immigrants. This shift was apparent relatively early in the writings of the historian Frederick Jackson Turner. Turner grew up in a Wisconsin town inhabited predominantly by a mix of Yankees, Germans, Scandinavians, and other northwest European immigrants, and this experience likely fueled his later depictions of the frontier as melting pot. As early as his 1893 essay, "The Significance of the Frontier in American History," Turner blurred the line between old stock and old immigrant. The frontier "promoted the formation of a composite nationality for the American people," derived in part from English, Scotch-Irish, and Pennsylvania German colonial settlers. "In the crucible of the frontier the immigrants were Americanized, liberated, and fused into a mixed race, English in neither nationality nor characteristics." Moreover, this process "has gone on from the early days to our own" and included the mid-nineteenth-century "German element in Wisconsin." "Such examples," Turner concluded, "teach us to beware of misinterpreting the fact that there is a common English speech in America into a belief that the stock is also English." Turner in 1918 referred to this process as the creation of "a new type, which was neither the sum of all its elements, nor a complete fusion in a melting pot. They were American pioneers, not outlying fragments of New England, of Germany, or of Norway." Hence, when, in the midst of a 1910 discussion of "the American pioneer," Turner described "[t]ides of alien immigrants . . . surging into the country to replace the old American stock in the labor market"—immigrants who were "from southern and eastern Europe"—he implicitly linked that old stock to those pioneers who had absorbed the nineteenth-century "German element."[54]

The note of ambiguity around the term "old stock" sounded by Turner was repeated by later commentators, who were influenced by a nativism that increasingly racialized southern and eastern Europeans. As John Higham long ago described, nativists after 1900 cemented the distinction between "old" and "new" immigrants in biological and, indeed, eugenic terms by elaborating a "scientific" racial typology of Europeans. The economist William Z. Ripley provided a key source for this kind of thinking with his 1899 book, *The Races of Europe.* Ripley described that continent as home to a northern, "Teutonic" race of tall, blond longheads; a central, "Alpine" race of stocky roundheads; and a southern, "Mediterranean" race of slender, dark longheads. Nativists such as Madison Grant turned this typology against the "new" southern and eastern European immigrants, while borrowing from the emerging "science" of eugenics to cast those newcomers as undermining the proper biological makeup of the American population. Grant's *The Passing of the Great Race* (1916) warned that the very existence of America's original, "Nordic" population (his word for "Teutonic") was threatened by hordes of Alpines, Mediterraneans, and Jews. Notably, for Grant, the "Nordic" was "the white man par excellence," and here the intellectual trend in nativism paralleled the popular one. For "older" European Americans were coming to question the whiteness of southern and eastern European immigrants. By 1910, as Higham noted, nationwide, "native-born and northern European laborers called themselves 'white men' to distinguish themselves from the southern Europeans whom they worked beside."[55]

This redefinition of whiteness, and the scientific racism that informed it, helped to blur further the boundary between "old immigrant" and "old stock," as can be seen in Prescott Hall's 1919 reference to "the old Nordic stock in New England." For *Nordic,* as Grant used it, both signified the epitome of whiteness and included the Germans who settled in America.[56] In some contexts, "old immigrant" and "old stock" appeared to merge. The congressional Dillingham Commission's forty-two-volume report on immigration, issued in 1911, promoted the distinction between old and new immigrants[57] in a way that sometimes melded the former with those of colonial descent. Volume 5 of the commission's report, the *Dictionary of Races or Peoples,* provided a lengthy entry on the "CAUCASIAN . . . or WHITE race" that moved directly from Ripley's racial taxonomy of Europeans into this observation:

> The most interesting fact in immigration is the sudden and astounding recent change in the character of immigration. While up to 1890 it was almost entirely from northwestern Europe, or in other words, was composed of races or peoples which now constitute the older American stock, immigration comes mainly at the present time from southern and southeastern Europe; that is, chiefly from Italian, Hebrew, and Slavic stocks that differ widely from the American in language, character, and political institutions.[58]

Here, the "older American stock" could easily be taken to include those representatives of northwest European "races" who came over in the nineteenth century. In similar fashion, the economist Scott Nearing lumped those European Americans whose forebears settled "from the earliest days of colonization down to 1880" into the "American race stock," which was "built around the stock of Great Britain and Germany." Correspondingly, "oldness" could be conferred even on the Irish, as one author implied in a 1922 *Literary Digest* article titled, "Are We Still Anglo-Saxon?" This essayist declared that, "I'm glad to believe that an Anglo-Celtic-Germanic-Scandinavian stock will be as Anglo-Saxon as the oldest-minded of us old settlers can desire."[59]

The ambiguity about the meaning of "old stock" persisted at least into the 1940s. One can find citations for "old stock" from that decade that are synonymous with "Anglo-Saxon" but also uses of "old stocks" or "American stock" that leave open the possibility that the writer means by the term, in the words of one, "the west-European whites." Philadelphia writers, however, could be quite explicit in their inclusion of descendants of nineteenth-century German immigrants. In his 1946 autobiography, Cornelius Weygandt, a Germantown native and descendant of colonial German settlers, looked back to the coming of "southern and eastern Europeans" in the 1880s. Recalling the workmen in Germantown, Weygandt described stone masons who "were still then native Americans or Germans," and "American" carpenters and painters. "The only gang wholly foreign was the floor planers," he remembered. "They were Germans, and quickly assimilated into the old stock."[60]

The metamorphosis of "old stock" between the 1880s and the 1940s represented, in essence, an invitation to German Americans to become old stock—to redefine their identities in a way that would put them at the core of European America and the nation itself, in contrast both to non-white African Americans and Asians and to questionably white southern and eastern Europeans. Whether many first-generation German immigrants ever took this step seems unlikely. Into the 1920s, if not beyond, German-speaking Philadelphians commonly referred to Anglo-Americans of colonial descent as *Stockamerikaner*—a cognate of "old stock American" used by middle-class ethnic activists, working-class socialists, Lutherans and Catholics alike.[61] These German speakers obviously did not consider that term as applying to themselves.

It would fall to the children and grandchildren of some German immigrants to avail themselves of American identities cast in old stock terms—that is, in opposition to new immigrants. In Philadelphia, this process would play out after World War I. Nationally, however, some second-generation German immigrants would take up the old stock invitation even before the war through their participation in a nativist organization that pioneered in racializing southern and eastern European newcomers: the Junior Order United American Mechanics (JOUAM).

The Junior Order was launched in Germantown, with the 1853 founding of Washington Council, No. 1. From its Pennsylvania base, the order spread through much of the country. JOUAM state councils existed in thirty-four states and territories by 1908, and the organization counted 224,000 members in 1914. The order's nativism shifted in emphasis from primarily anti-Catholic before the Civil War to antiradical in the 1880s and 1890s. By 1910, its "primary fear [was] of foreign races," and it gave vent to that fear as it lobbied Congress for immigration restriction.[62] The order's national chaplain, the Reverend M. D. Lichliter, warned the

House Immigration and Naturalization Committee in 1910 of a "tide of oriental scum" from eastern and southern Europe. He compared that tide unfavorably with the immigration stream up to 1877, which came, of course, mostly from "northern Europe," was "of the Anglo-Saxon blood, mixed with the Celtic and Teutonic, which originally came from the Aryan race," and had "assimilated with the native born with marvelous facility."[63]

Lichliter may have stressed the role of "Celtic and Teutonic blood" because he shared that background and may himself have been a third-generation German immigrant. As he told the same committee two years later, "[w]e want the kind to come from which we came. My father, on one side, was a German, my father upon the other was an Englishman. My mother, on the one side, was a Yankee, and on the other side an Irish woman."[64] German ancestry was not unknown among other JOUAM leaders. Lichliter's own 1908 accounting in "Who Is Who in the Order" included J. H. Zimmerman, a "simon-pure Pennsylvanian of German extraction," and William Painter, whose "great-great-grandfather came from Germany prior to the Revolution," as well as officials of New England Puritan, Huguenot, Dutch, English, and Scottish background. Intriguingly, however, second-generation German immigrants had also filtered into the national leadership. At least two can be identified from Lichliter's collection of short biographies: John G. A. Richter of Canton, Ohio, a national councilor in the mid-1890s whose parents came from Bavaria; and John J. Weitzel, a Cincinnati lawyer with a German-born father.[65]

Weitzel, in particular, appears to have made the leap to an American identity defined at least partly in opposition to southeast Europeans seen as racially inferior. For it was he who, as national vice councilor, introduced Lichliter at the 1910 hearing and who explicitly endorsed Lichliter's testimony as the official view of the Junior Order and its female auxiliary, the Daughters of America—a step Weitzel took in forwarding that testimony to the Dillingham Commission. Weitzel, moreover, followed Lichliter with his own statement to the House committee. While declaring that "[o]ur desire for better immigration laws is not founded on any religious or other prejudice, foreign or native," he, too, pointed out how "the quality [of immigration] has changed." Weitzel then quoted from the annual report of the U.S. Immigration Bureau regarding "'this increase in the influx of peoples so different racially from the original settlers of the country—peoples who . . . are quite distinct from the Teutonic and Celtic stocks from which our immigration was for so many years derived. . . . There can be but little homogeneity between the people of southern and eastern Europe and the real American.'"[66] This second-generation German immigrant presumably thought that he too was a "real American," and racially so.

As a national spokesman for restriction within the Junior Order, Weitzel may have traveled further toward this kind of American identity than rank-and-file members of German parentage. While the available evidence is sparse, it suggests that before World War I, racial concerns about new immigrants were not high on the agenda of JOUAM councils in Philadelphia. The topic did make its appearance. In 1904, for example, a minister preached to a Philadelphia audience of order members on the "corruption" of the nation's "blood and sinew" through "the large influx in recent years of ignorant and debased immigrants" from southern and eastern Europe.[67] Yet surviving prewar accounts of Germantown's Washington Council, No. 1, bear little trace of such rhetoric. When the *Germantown Telegraph* covered the council's anniversary celebrations in 1902 and 1903, the newspaper touched on immigration restriction only in passing, as an object in the order's constitution and the council's founding declaration. A 1913 history of the Washington Council likewise barely mentioned the topic. The author, member Thomas E. Clemens, devoted far more space to the 525-member council's neighborhood activities, such as presenting flags to schools, and to the schisms that left the council unaffiliated with the national order after 1910. Clemens did declare that the Washington Council stood for "America for Americans," and the council itself accepted only native-born, white male citizens as members. Yet Clemens nowhere gave "American" a racial spin. To the contrary, he described a patriotic vision that "must exhilarate the spirits of all men, no matter what their nationality or creed may be." Indeed, the history's sole mention of a new immigrant group suggests an almost benign view of such newcomers. That mention concerned a vote of thanks the council made to a local newspaper for publishing extracts from *Our Slavic Fellow Citizens*, Emily Greene Balch's sympathetic 1910 account of eastern European immigrants in America.[68] The Washington Council did have some members of German parentage; of the few member names scattered through newspaper accounts, at least two in 1915 belonged to second-generation German immigrants.[69] In Germantown especially, patterns of association with other northwest Europeans might have made attractive an American identity racially cast in northwest European terms. Given the environment reflected in Clemens's history, however, council members with German-born parents likely did not imbibe there the kind of views espoused by Weitzel.

The early twentieth century offered German Philadelphians an evolving set of collective identities from which they might draw in reshaping their own, multiple identities. Those who retreated from or toned down the ethnic German element in their sense of self could emphasize instead a class, religious, or racial affiliation shared with non-Germans; they could likewise reach for identities tied to the rising mass culture of consumption. Beckoning as well was the invitation represented by an emerging definition of "American" cast racially and temporally against the "new" immigrants from southern and eastern Europe. Not until after World War I, however, would some second-generation immigrants accept that "old stock" invitation. Ironically, they would be unwittingly aided in that effort by a movement that sought to bolster German-American ethnic identity—a movement that took shape in the first decade of the twentieth century as the Philadelphia-based National German-American Alliance.

CHAPTER SIX

Resisting Assimilation: Middle-Class and Working-Class Approaches

As evidence mounted of a crisis in German associational life at the turn of the century, a number of middle-class Philadelphians moved to stem the erosion they saw around them. They began a movement that within a few years spawned a nationwide league of German-American *Vereine,* a league that numbered among the largest ethnic organizations in American history: the National German-American Alliance.[1] The alliance, or *Deutsch-Amerikanischer National-Bund,* sought to save the nation's *Deutschtum* from the forces of assimilation, in particular by striving to keep the younger generation of German Americans within the ethnic fold. It pursued this goal by attempting to foster what today would be called "ethnic pride." Alliance leaders saw the key to this effort in a campaign to reshape popular understanding of the place of German Americans in the nation's history. By encouraging historical research on German immigration, agitating for recognition of "German achievements," and initiating a spate of monuments to notable German Americans, these leaders hoped to solidify a claim that their ethnic group shared with Anglo-Americans a role in the nation's founding.

The foremost symbol of this claim was Germantown. Germantown, of course, was not very German by 1900, but the Philadelphia neighborhood had become fixed in German-American memory as marking, with its settlement in 1683, the beginning of German immigration to the New World. On the 225th anniversary of that event, the alliance staged its most ambitious effort to convince the public of the centrality of Germans to American history: a massive commemoration of Germantown's founding centered around the creation of a monument to "the founder," Franz Daniel Pastorius. This 1908 celebration did win greater recognition among non-German Philadelphians of the German role in local history. Yet it also reinforced the perception of German Americans as an "old," long-settled group. That would prove a more lasting legacy than any gain the city's crumbling *Deutschtum* won from the anniversary; ultimately, it would ease the transition to old-stock status some children of German Philadelphia underwent.

The commemoration likewise revealed some limits to the alliance's strategy for preserving "German-Americandom." That strategy was predicated on securing greater unity among German Americans, yet old divisions dogged even the 1908 celebration. German Catholics remained wary of the National Alliance. Organized workers could cooperate with it, but unlike middle-class alliance activists, they did not make ethnic maintenance their overriding priority. As a goal, it competed with the advancement of class interests, and these had an assimilatory effect: they brought German workers into tentative alliances with both old-immigrant and new-immigrant unionists. This would become very clear two years after the Germantown celebration, as Philadelphia's European-American workers achieved a measure of common ground in the city's general strike of 1910.

THE RISE OF THE NATIONAL GERMAN-AMERICAN ALLIANCE

The National Alliance had its origins in a movement for German-American unity that coalesced in Philadelphia in 1899. Activists meeting in the city that year founded the German-American Central Alliance of Pennsylvania, inviting Charles J. Hexamer to serve as the new group's president. The organization appears to have begun as a venture of existing *Vereine* in eastern Pennsylvania. In short order, it began organizing in other states. From these efforts emerged the National German-American Alliance, which held its constituent convention in Philadelphia in October 1901. Structurally, the new National Alliance was composed of individual *Vereine* grouped together into city alliances or branches, which in turn were federated into state alliances; the state alliances together made up the National Alliance.[2] In a real sense, the National Alliance represented an attempt at a nationwide, rationalized organization of America's *Vereinswesen*.

That the alliance leadership in Philadelphia grew out of the city's middle-class *Vereinswesen* is apparent from the close ties most of the leaders had to the German Society of Pennsylvania. Hexamer, who served as president of the Central Alliance until 1915 and held the same position in the National Alliance from its founding until 1917, was also president of the German Society from 1900 to 1916. Hans Weniger, the German Society's long-time treasurer, held that post in the Central and National Alliances until 1914; and Adolph Timm, who was long secretary of the National Alliance, joined the society in 1900 and chaired one of its committees.[3] These ties suggest the middle-class background of the leadership. Hexamer himself was the Philadelphia-born son of Ernst Hexamer, a veteran of the failed Revolution of 1848 who fled Germany and eventually became a publisher of fire insurance maps; Charles joined his father in the family business.[4]

The National Alliance, like the Central Alliance it grew out of, incorporated a variety of impulses. As the Central Alliance's original constitution—adopted largely unchanged by the National Alliance—described, that organization aimed "to awaken and to promote a feeling of unity in the population of German origin in America" and to use its power, "once centralized," to defend its "legitimate desires and interests." The document also pledged the group to fend off "nativistic encroachments" and to safeguard "good, friendly relations" between the United States and Germany, while demanding "the full, honest recognition" of the contributions made by German immigrants to America.[5]

The National Alliance thus functioned at once as a vehicle to bring together a declining and fractured German America and as an organization tending to that entity's perceived interests. One of those interests was what alliance activists called "personal liberty"—in essence, the right to drink beer and wine. The defense of this "right" against a rising tide of prohibitionist sentiment came to dominate the group's political activity. Indeed, Clifton Child, in an early and influential interpretation, argued that the alliance "rose to power as a defensive organization" battling prohibition. Restricted by its 1907 congressional charter from engaging actively in politics, the National Alliance worked nonetheless through state and local alliances to approve "wet" candidates for office and rally votes against "dry" measures and politicians. Beginning in 1913, the organization drew heavy subsidies from the brewing industry to help finance its antiprohibition campaigns. In the years leading up to the First World War, Child maintained, prohibition was "the sole *raison d'être*" of many local branches.[6]

As important as the fight against prohibition became, however, it did not represent an end in itself, at least not for the organization's Philadelphia-based leadership. Rather, the aim that subsumed all others, including "personal liberty," was the *Erhaltung* (preservation) of Germandom. This theme pervaded Hexamer's addresses to the National Alliance's biennial conventions. His statement at the 1909 convention was representative: "As spontaneous German emigration to the United States has essentially ended, it is our first duty, for the good of the whole American nation, to preserve Germandom through our children."[7] For Hexamer and his associates, the threat to that *Deutschtum* was very real; they could see it at first hand in the plummeting membership of the German Society. Hexamer complained in 1905 that "many" German Americans labored "under the delusion that they do a service to the country of their choice when they 'Americanize' as fast as possible, which in their limited view means allowing German to perish in their families." In the same breath, he blasted "those so-called 'educated' people who, out of petty, personal interests, strip off their Germandom like an old glove."[8]

Alliance leaders rarely specified the exact destination of these apostates, although Timm at one point attacked "individuals" who "travel exclusively in Anglo-American circles and want to be German no more."[9] The leadership did, however, have a distinct idea of how it thought true Americanization should proceed. In the words of H. M. Ferren, an alliance activist from Pittsburgh, real Americanization did not mean, as the average Anglo-American thought, "a Circean form of Anglicizing or Hibernicizing foreigners." Rather, "Americanization is a gradual assimilating process, allowing each constituent part of our heterogeneous population ample time and opportunity to contribute its share of what is typically strong and good." Hexamer, who explicitly endorsed Ferren's definition at the 1911 convention, similarly stated, in 1905, that "[m]embers of all races" had a duty not only to absorb "what is good in their new environment," but also "to impart to us that which is best in the cultural development of their race," since the American nation was "still in a formative period." For Germans, he argued in 1901, this required cultivating ethnic solidarity, so that the gifts to be given could be preserved in the first place.[10] These statements fell within a long line of such arguments; nineteenth-century German Americans had crafted similar, cultural pluralist justifications for the perpetuation of a separate German ethnic group, or even ethnic diversity per se, within a common political framework.[11]

Hexamer's conception of what constituted appropriate gifts, however, showed a distinct preference for German high culture. While alliance members generally agreed that the German language was a treasure worth preserving, Hexamer likewise pointed to the promotion of German literature, art, and drama as aspects of what he called "our noble cultural mission."[12] And here he and the leadership may have begun to part ways with the rank and file. Such a split was evident in his call for spiritual uplift among German Americans themselves, his reference to criticism of many of them as utterly indifferent to "higher strivings," and his acid comments on the chronic financial difficulties of an alliance-sponsored teachers' institute in Milwaukee. "Yes, my friends," Hexamer roared at the 1907 convention, "we must not only create a national German-American teachers' seminary, we must also support it, for children aren't raised at the beer table or in card games."[13] In this sense, the increasing focus on antiprohibition activities represented something of an opportunistic compromise by the leadership with a membership that, after all, had made a commitment to club life and its alcohol-centered sociability. As the group's last president, Georg von Bosse's son Siegmund, admitted later, the alliance saw the fight against prohibition as a way to "gain German-American support for its cultural program." At the same time, a defense of "personal liberty" was not at all inconsistent with the alliance's larger mission, for sociability, so highly valued by German Americans, was also a trait worth imparting to American life, as Hexamer himself noted.[14] Thus, *Erhaltung* as a concept could continue to define the alliance's mission in the eyes of its leaders at the same time as they devoted more and more resources to a political battle with prohibitionists.[15]

The key to maintaining Germandom lay in securing the ethnic loyalty of the rising generation of German Americans. Hexamer, himself a second-generation immigrant, understood this quite well; as he said in 1909, Germandom was to be preserved "through our children." The National Alliance and its state and local branches took a number of approaches to accomplishing this goal. They lobbied for the teaching of German in public schools and advocated the founding of more private schools offering instruction in it. The alliance likewise provided a subsidy to the Milwaukee teachers' institute, which was expected to supply the necessary teachers.[16] But alliance leaders felt as well that younger German Americans would only stay within the ethnic fold, and thereby resolve the crisis of the *Vereinswesen,* if they felt sufficient pride in German America. "[O]ur sons don't join the German associations, because they feel ashamed to be the children of German parents," H.A.C. Anderson, the president of the United German Societies of the City of New York, told the 1903 convention. "[I]f, however, through the unification of all Germans in the country, we succeed in becoming respected and honored, yes, even politically feared, then our children will one day be proud that German blood flows in their veins, then the associations will show an increase in younger members and flourish instead of dying out."[17]

Pride required more than unity, however. "To value something, one must know its history," Hexamer declared in 1901. Correspondingly, the new National Alliance sought "a German American history" that would raise the value of being German to the younger generation.[18] Once German-American children learned of "the glorious deeds" done by Germans in Germany and America, Albert J. W. Kern of New York City stated at the 1907 convention, then they would want to count themselves as descendants of those Germans and would "remain with us." But to achieve this, "American history must be rewritten" to include the contributions Germans had made to American development and to put the exaggerated "English-American" role in the proper perspective.[19]

The alliance strove to revise American history by promoting academic research into the German-American past and by popularizing that past through speeches and a parade of monuments to eminent German Americans. The constitutions of the Central and National Alliances both contained a provision recommending "a systematic investigation of the share Germans have had in the development of their adopted country." The most important step alliance activists took in this direction was the creation in 1901 of the Philadelphia-based German American Historical Society. The Historical Society sponsored *German American Annals,* a journal that also became the organ of the National Alliance.[20] The *Annals*'s scholarly section was under the firm editorial control of Marion Dexter Learned, the chairman of the German department at the University of Pennsylvania. A Delaware native of colonial English descent, Learned had early become interested in the Pennsylvania German dialect and culture, and under his direction the *Annals* became an important forum for scholarship in German-American history.[21]

On the popular level, the National Alliance sponsored a more filiopietistic brand of history. Its press bureau issued a series of books and pamphlets with titles such as *German Achievements in America,* and Hexamer, a frequent and energetic speaker, proclaimed those achievements in English as well as German, reaching a larger public through addresses at such venues as the 1907 Jamestown Exhibition.[22] His Jamestown speech was typical, offering a long catalog of German "firsts," decrying the lack of recognition given German Americans in the nation's history, and contrasting them to the Puritans of New England, whose story loomed so large in popular historical consciousness. Though the address spanned the entire history of Germans in America, the bulk of it was devoted to their role up to and including the Revolution, a role he described as crucial to the nation's founding. Citing a historian's words, Hexamer told the audience that "there would have been no united colonial rebellion, nor any United States of America, but for the patriotism of the Germans of the colonies." Through this and other speeches, he suggested, in effect, that Germans did not simply contribute to the progress of America but counted among its founders—just as much as Anglo-Americans, if not more so.[23]

The National Alliance's history campaign, however, took its most concrete form in a push to provide other Americans with what Hexamer called "public visual instruction"—that is, monuments to German-American heroes.[24] At the founding convention of the National Alliance, delegates decided in favor of a plan to erect a monument to Pastorius in Germantown. By 1903, the National Alliance had successfully lobbied Congress for an appropriation to pay for a statue of Baron von Steuben in Washington, while the Central Alliance had won a state appropriation for a statue in Harrisburg of Michael Hillegas, a second-generation German immigrant who became the first treasurer of the United States. By 1911, Hexamer could boast that the Steuben statue had been dedicated, the cornerstone of the Pastorius monument was in place, and a statue to the Revolutionary War general Peter Muhlenberg had been unveiled at Philadelphia City Hall. Plans likewise were afoot to lobby the federal government to take over the care of Steuben's grave site and purchase the grave site and home of the Revolutionary general Nicholaus Herkimer.[25]

This series of monuments, like Hexamer's speeches, emphasized the role of Germans as founders of the nation. German Americans could boast more recent heroes, including Civil War officers such as Franz Sigel, and a move to memorialize him in stone was under way after 1900.[26] But those the alliance movement chose to honor in this fashion—Pastorius, Hillegas, Steuben, Muhlenberg, and Herkimer—had made their mark as participants in the creation of the republic or, in Pastorius's case, as a key figure in the European colonization of America. The immigrants and children of immigrants who made up the alliance leadership were thereby claiming a place in the United States based on temporal precedence.

CLAIMING OLDNESS: GERMAN DAY AND FOUNDERS' DAY, 1908

Whether other Americans accepted such time-based claims is not easy to determine. But we can sketch out an answer through a closer examination of one of these monuments, the alliance's public presentation of it, and the reaction of non-German observers to both. The monument is that to Pastorius, for which the alliance unveiled a cornerstone in Germantown on October 6, 1908, amid what may have been the most elaborate public ceremony ever organized by the group. Through this event, Hexamer and other alliance leaders invoked Germantown in a bid to convince other Americans of the central importance of Germans in American history. They succeeded, certainly in the view of Germantowners, in linking the origins of the town and, by extension, the nation, to German immigration. Their efforts even succeeded, at least temporarily, in displacing an earlier, local vision of what made the neighborhood historically important.

The 1908 dedication was the center of an alliance-sponsored German Day commemoration of the 225th anniversary of Germantown's founding by Pastorius and a band of settlers from Krefeld, in the Rhineland. German Day itself, as a holiday honoring the Krefelders' arrival, had been celebrated by German Philadelphians since the 200th anniversary in 1883. They claimed to have invented the holiday, which spread to other parts of the country, although the date elsewhere varied from the October 6 adopted by Philadelphians. The origins of German Day can be traced directly to the work of the Philadelphia historian Oswald Seidensticker, one of a number of German-American scholars who turned their attention to their ethnic group's past in the years after the Civil War.[27] Himself an immigrant, Seidensticker wrote and lectured prodigiously on Germans in the colonial and Revolutionary periods and in 1880 founded the Deutscher Pionier-Verein von Philadelphia to encourage German-American historical research.[28] He, as the Pionier-Verein's president, ap-

parently suggested in 1882 that the upcoming bicentennial of the Krefelders' arrival should be celebrated as the 200th anniversary of the first
German immigration to America. Seidensticker and the Pionier-Verein
subsequently instigated the cooperation of Philadelphia's German associations in a massive celebration of the bicentennial in 1883, an event that
would be remembered as the first German Day. Few if any of the activities in the four-day commemoration, however, actually took place in Germantown itself. The primary events, including a huge parade, were all
held in central Philadelphia.[29]

German Day remained a holiday celebrated annually—on a much
smaller scale—within German-American circles only. Germantown's importance as a symbol of the onset of German immigration would grow,
however, outside as well as inside German America. This process was fostered by a series of scholarly works that took Pastorius and Germantown's
founding as their theme and that began with Seidensticker's book, *The
First German Immigration to America and the Founding of Germantown
in 1683*, written in honor of the 1883 commemoration. Originally published in German, the book appeared in an English translation, and
English-language works on the same topic came from the Philadelphian
Samuel W. Pennypacker in 1899 and from Learned in 1908. Pennypacker's writings, like those of Julius F. Sachse dealing with Germantown's
early German settlers, can be seen as part of a wave of interest among
Pennsylvania Germans in their own history that resulted in the founding
of the Pennsylvania German Society in 1891.[30] Thus, at the turn of the
century, Germantown was available to Philadelphians of colonial German
background as a symbol for the onset of a specifically colonial German
immigration. At the same time, the neighborhood retained its symbolic
value for German-American activists. A delegate to the National Alliance's founding convention could state that "no place should be holier
to German-Americandom than Germantown."[31]

That delegate, Rudolph Cronau of New York, proposed that the new
organization erect a monument to Pastorius in Germantown, where
"German-Americandom's . . . first achievements of civilization were at-
tained." Cronau later wrote that he had in mind at the time a monument
that also would honor early German immigrants in general and "constantly remind our children and our children's children, what our forefathers did for us and for this great land."[32] Cronau's suggestion was accepted with applause. As chairman of the alliance's Pastorius monument
committee, however, he ran into difficulty raising funds for the project.
The required sum finally was secured with the help of the federal government; in 1911, Congress granted the effort $25,000, on the condition that
German Americans contribute the same amount.[33] In the meantime, the
National Alliance decided to go ahead with the laying of a cornerstone

for the monument, as a way of marking the 225th anniversary in 1908. By this point, too, Cronau's interpretation of the monument had widened into a claim that the Pastorius party stood on the same level with the Pilgrims—in essence, that German Americans could assert a place in the nation equal to that claimed by Anglo-Americans. "What Plymouth Rock, the landing site of the Puritan Pilgrim Fathers, means to Anglo-Americandom, that is Germantown to Americans of German descent," Cronau explained at the 1907 convention: "a place consecrated through historical memory, to which apply the same words as apply to Plymouth Rock: 'Here, if anywhere in our country, every American should stand with uncovered head.'"[34]

The National Alliance's version of Germantown's significance did not, however, necessarily coincide with what Germantowners themselves thought. The depiction of Germantown as a spot "holy" to German Americans was redolent with ironies because it was at variance with some inconvenient facts. First, Germantown by 1900 had relatively few first- or second-generation German immigrants, and its specifically German-American institutions were few and fading. The neighborhood's perceptible number of residents of colonial German background generally stayed aloof from the city's German-American world. Second, although Pastorius himself was German-born, the settlers who came with him appear to have been mostly of Dutch origin, which may or may not have been clear to local residents at the turn of the twentieth century.[35]

Germantowners, moreover, harbored their own ideas of what mattered in local history. The event taking pride of place in the past for many neighborhood residents was not the town's October 1683 founding, but rather the October 4, 1777 Battle of Germantown, at which Washington's army made a determined but unsuccessful attempt to dislodge British troops occupying Philadelphia. Germantown commemorated the battle's centennial on October 4, 1877 with a full day of festivities, and a battle monument was erected in 1905 in Vernon Park, near the center of the neighborhood.[36] The battle also figured largely in the creation in 1900 of the Site and Relic Society, which became one institutional keeper of historical memory for the neighborhood's upper class. The minutes of the gathering that spawned the group state that its "purpose . . . as first expressed was to consider the desirability of forming an organization having for its objects the more perfect preservation and identification by tablets, of historic points on the Battlefield of Germantown, and the preservation and public exhibition of the relics of the battle."[37]

One historian has interpreted the Site and Relic Society as the bearer of "a local colonial revival movement." The larger turn-of-the-century Colonial Revival movement involved a search by native-born middle- and upper-class European Americans for symbols in a "semisacred past" that could provide comfort in a present rendered disconcerting by labor unrest, mass immigration, and urban growth. This depiction of the society rings true, given its surroundings and composition. Germantowners in 1900 lived in a neighborhood geographically divided along class and ethnic lines, and they faced a residential building boom that had resulted in the destruction of "many of Germantown's historic houses," as the *Germantown Independent-Gazette* observed in 1905. The Site and Relic Society itself was most certainly an upper-class organization; its seven presidents through 1940 were all listed in either the *Philadelphia Blue Book* or the *Social Register.* Most of the group's founders, moreover, had American ancestries dating back to the colonial period.[38]

Significantly, however, many of these officers were specifically of colonial German descent. They included Charles J. Wister, of the Germantown Wisters, the society's first president; Daniel Pastorius Bruner, a descendant of Franz Daniel Pastorius; Cornelius Weygandt, Sr.; and Naaman Keyser.[39] Moreover, at least some of the society's officers appear to have been conscious of having such a "Pennsylvania German" ancestry, for some had ties to the Pennsylvania German Society. Keyser served on that organization's governing board from 1906 until his death in 1922. Edwin C. Jellet, who became a director of the Site and Relic Society in 1904, attended the Pennsylvania German Society's 1908 annual meeting.[40]

The colonial German background of some of the Site and Relic Society's officers may have made the group more open to celebrating Germantown's founding as a "German" event. Jellett and founder Charles F. Jenkins, a Quaker with ethnic Welsh affiliations who nonetheless counted three of the 1683 Krefeld party among his ancestors,[41] appeared to think in such terms even before 1908. In an address at the group's formal organizational meeting in 1900, for example, Jenkins declared that Germantown, "[i]n its settlement by the Germans as early as 1683 . . . marks the landing in this country of a race whose tremendous influence in forming and developing our country can never be accurately measured. Is this not worth commemorating?"[42]

Nevertheless, the Site and Relic Society's conception of the founding was more oriented toward Germantown, and less toward the Germans, than the National Alliance's. While the National Alliance celebrated German Day on October 6, the anniversary of the Krefelders' arrival in Philadelphia, the society considered Germantown's founding date to be October 24 or 25, the day the original settlers drew lots for the sites of their future homes. Moreover, for at least some society officers, the Battle of Germantown remained the more important event. Even at the height of preparations for the 1908 Pastorius celebration, society officers who marked thirty historic sights in Germantown listed nine explicitly linked to the battle and only three tied to Pastorius or the 1683 settlers.[43]

Thus, the 1908 commemoration of the founding would be shaped by differing conceptions of Germantown history, as expressed by the institutional players, within and outside of the neighborhood, who organized the event. The idea of celebrating the founding's 225th anniversary appears to have emerged in Germantown by the fall of 1907, before the National Alliance announced its cornerstone plans. Horace F. McCann, a member of the Site and Relic Society, suggested at its October 1907 annual meeting that the group observe the anniversary "of the foundry [*sic*] of Germantown by especially significant ceremonies." The attendees approved the idea, and McCann subsequently played a key role in promoting the commemoration; as publisher of the *Independent-Gazette* and a founding member of the Business Men's Association of Germantown, he was a well-placed advocate.[44]

In February 1908, the city government helped determine the overall framework of the commemoration by deciding to sponsor a celebration of the 225th anniversary of Philadelphia's founding in 1683. Officials dubbed the week of October 4–10 "Founders' Week," and a set of city-appointed committees organized each day under a particular theme; Tuesday the sixth, for example, would be "Municipal Day."[45] By choosing the week of October 4, the city presented Germantowners with a choice: hold a separate founders' celebration on the traditional date in late October, or coordinate the Germantown event with the city's plans. The Site and Relic Society went with the city, choosing in February to commemorate "Founders Day" on October 6. The Business Men's Association initially voted for October 24, but changed to October 6 after consulting with city organizers. The group may also have been influenced by the entrance of a new player: the National Alliance. By late March, both the association and the Site and Relic Society had learned of the alliance's plan for an October 6 cornerstone-laying.[46]

Over the next few months, representatives from these and other groups sorted out how to organize the celebration of what many Germantowners called Founders' Day and the National Alliance called German Day. The resulting committee structure reflected a division between neighborhood German residents tied to the National Alliance and local residents affiliated with the Site and Relic Society, the Business Men's Association, and the Germantown and Chestnut Hill Improvement Association. Officers of the latter three groups organized the Committee for the Celebration of Founders' Day in Germantown, chaired by Charles Jenkins, the Site and Relic Society's president.[47] The National Alliance had its own executive committee, headed by Hexamer, which oversaw a set of subcommittees detailed to organize the alliance's share of the day. These subcommittees were chaired almost exclusively by figures associated with the alliance, including Learned, Timm, von Bosse, and Antonie Ehrlich; however, Jenkins, McCann, and Naaman Keyser also had positions, which related to aspects of local history. Among the other subcommittee chairmen was J. F. Otterstetter, a German immigrant, Germantown real estate broker, and member of the Germantown Maennerchor. Otterstetter had served early on as a local alliance representative, and he headed a German Citizens of Germantown committee charged with "the proper reception" of visiting *Vereine* on October 6—which he called "German Day."[48]

The Founders' Day committee, the alliance executive committee, and the German citizens committee cooperated to run the Founders' Day celebration, and relations among them seem to have been cordial enough. Yet the creation of committees separated along ethnic lines suggests the degree to which the 225th anniversary was seen differently, even within Germantown, by ethnic loyalists like Otterstetter on one side and non-German residents and more assimilated residents of German background on the other. Tellingly, three second-generation German immigrants with strong ties to the Business Men's Association—Charles J. Schaefer, Frederick W. Kaplan, and Henry W. Pletcher—worked for the Founders' Day committee. Their names do not appear on the subcommittee lists of the German citizens committee.[49]

The varying meanings of Founders' Day were on full display October 6. At midmorning, a contingent of about 10,000 Germans—National Alliance members, delegates from Philadelphia *Vereine*, and German-American representatives from other states—arrived at the outskirts of Germantown. There, it linked up with two divisions of Germantowners, and the entire body marched past some 200,000 onlookers to Vernon Park. The first Germantown division represented a broad swath of the neighborhood's fraternal societies. The second featured more than a dozen historical floats, with participants representing, among others and in order: Indian chiefs; Pastorius and the Krefelders; the early German religious "Hermits of the Wissahickon;" Germantown's oldest fire engine, along with its oldest fireman, ninety-four-year-old Joseph Murter; American artillery of the Battle of Germantown; "Ye Olde Academie," presumably a rendition of Germantown Academy, which dated to the colonial period; and Washington and his cabinet, a reminder of the federal government's sojourn in Germantown during the Philadelphia yellow-fever epidemic of 1793.[50]

At Vernon Park, some 50,000 spectators craned to hear orations by National Alliance speakers, delivered from a grandstand opposite the veiled cornerstone. The grandstand bore Philadelphia Mayor John E. Reyburn, the German chargé d'affaires in Washington, and eight descendants of Pastorius. Georg von Bosse spoke in German, and in familiar alliance terms, of German Day as bearing "witness concerning that which Germans have wrought on behalf of our country" and describing Germantown as "the fountain-head of the multitudinously ramifying stream of

German culture." Hexamer then gave a speech, the first half of which was in German, describing the cornerstone "not as part of a local, but of a national monument of the Germans of America." His daughter pulled a rope to release the German and American flags that covered the cornerstone, and Reyburn accepted the unveiled monument for the city, "not only as a tribute to the man Pastorius, but as a tribute from our German citizens to this man who did much to make our country possible." The revealed stone, an eight-foot-tall block of granite, displayed a bas-relief of Pastorius and his followers disembarking. An inscription at the stone's center read: "Cornerstone to Mark the Site of the Monument to be Erected in honor of the Founders of the First Permanent German Settlement in our Land, who arrived at Philadelphia, Oct. 6, 1683." Below ran the words, "Gegründet auf deutsche Mut und auf deutschen Geist" ("Founded on German courage and German spirit") and below that were carved the names of the thirteen men "who, with their families, were the founders," as the *Germantown Guide* explained. Following the ceremony, the more distinguished guests proceeded to a luncheon at the Germantown Cricket Club. It must have pleased Hexamer to no end that here, in the very citadel of Proper Philadelphia, this banquet closed with 200 worthies on their feet, singing both "The Star-Spangled Banner" and the German patriotic air "Die Wacht am Rhein."[51]

The massive celebration on October 6 altered the way local residents viewed their history by significantly raising the profile of the town's founding in public memory. The day's events were hard to ignore; as Jane Campbell, the Site and Relic Society's historian, put it, "Did not all Germantown that was not parading see the cornerstone laying . . . ?" In particular, the Founders' Day festivities completely overshadowed the 131st anniversary of the Battle of Germantown two days before. On October 4 itself, the evening was given over to services "to commemorate the founding of Germantown," as part of the "Religious Day" on the city's Founders' Week calendar.[52] In fact, in the wake of Founders' Day, some called for a literal displacement of the battle by the founding. The *Independent-Gazette* reported a move afoot among Founders' Day committee as well as National Alliance members to shift the Battle of Germantown monument in Vernon Park to one side and put the new Pastorius monument in its place. The newspaper endorsed this idea under the headline, "Give It the Place of Honor," arguing that "the Pastorius monument should occupy the most prominent site in the park."[53]

At the same time, however, the 1908 celebration's impact had its limits. The National Alliance campaign sought to identify Germantown completely with the Germans and to broadcast it nationally as a symbol of the ethnic group's founding role in American history. This was a message that was difficult to miss, even if much of it was delivered in German, for the local weeklies provided English translations of most of what von Bosse and Hexamer had said. As the Philadelphia *Public Ledger* acknowledged, the cornerstone unveiling "will go far to spread a new interest" in "the German stock as a primal and pervading element in the development" of Pennsylvania.[54] Yet the roles Germantowners played in those festivities suggest that for many, the day was more an occasion to celebrate the origin and subsequent history of their neighborhood than solely a tribute to its Germanness. That its origins were German, no one could ignore; indeed, the idea was celebrated. Yet, as the Germantown divisions of the parade indicate, those German beginnings were also seen as the start of a commonly recognized local history that continued down to the present and that included Germantown Academy, and the battle, and Washington's stay, and even the neighborhood's oldest fireman.

Correspondingly, Germantowners insisted on viewing their founding as important apart from its German significance. This insistence is most apparent in the fact that "German Day" as a name never really caught on in Germantown. Otterstetter used the term, and McCann could run an editorial in the *Independent-Gazette* headlined, "Hail to German Day!" But the preferred term among those on the Founders' Day committee, in the Site and Relic Society, and in the Business Men's Association, was "Founders' Day." That was the designation used in the day's *Official Programme* and consistently in the records of the Site and Relic Society and the Business Men's Association; through 1908, the minutes of those groups never employed the term "German Day." Jane Campbell, in fact, may have indulged in some gentle tweaking of the National Alliance for its insistence on "German Day," when she referred to October 6, 1908, as "Germantown Day."[55]

The Limits of *Erhaltung:* German Workers and the 1910 General Strike

The National Alliance had another message to deliver on October 6, 1908, that was, perhaps, less evident to outsiders. As always, the organization wanted to present a united front and to rally Germans of all backgrounds under the German-American banner, for uniting "German-Americandom" was a precondition for preserving it. The German section of the German Day parade itself was supposed to proclaim such unity. Alliance organizers planned a procession that would feature not only singing societies and *Turnvereine,* but also delegations from member unions of the United German Trades and from almost every German Catholic parish in the city.[56]

Yet even at this massive celebration, German America's cracks would show. Parishioners from All Saints' and St. Ignatius' marched, but the *Tageblatt* reported that "the Catholic associations were represented only in limited numbers." Organized workers made a much stronger showing. The newspaper estimated that approximately 1,500 union members appeared in the United German Trades's division, with brewery workers at the head and coopers, textile workers, and typographers following behind. The *Tageblatt* itself displayed a great deal of enthusiasm for the celebration, hailing the "German-American jubilee" editorially.[57]

Not all workers, however, shared in this jubilation. The United German Trades urged all of its affiliated unions to parade, but the German Machinists Lodge 670 refused. "The members stood by the old view, that it is not appropriate for fighting workers to take part in such parades," the union's secretary declared. "[W]e march only with our comrades. Lodge 670 . . . is and remains simply socialist."[58] The Socialist Party likewise declined to take part. Moreover, those German workers who did march likely did so on their own ideological terms. At the pinnacle of the *Tageblatt*'s list of German contributions to America, for example, stood "the naturalization of socialism"—not an achievement of the kind hailed by Hexamer.[59]

Many German workers, it seems, could muster some kind of enthusiasm for a larger, German-American identification. Yet ethnic maintenance was not, for them, the overriding concern it was for middle-class activists like Hexamer. Rather, it competed with other concerns that could prove equally and, at times, more pressing—above all, the need to cooperate with other workers in labor actions. Such class interests did not necessarily cut against ethnic ones and at times could reinforce them. The UGT and the *Tageblatt* themselves were expressions of the commonality of interests felt by many Philadelphians who shared working-class and German backgrounds. Indeed, the same Machinists Lodge 670 that spurned the German Day parade strove to organize specifically German machinists. Nonetheless, working-class German activists knew they were part of a larger labor movement, one that potentially could induce them to cross ethnic lines in a common cause. That potential was institutionalized in the city's multiethnic Socialist Party, which invited German participation not only through its German branch but also, for those comfortable in English, through the overarching Philadelphia local and through two ward-level branches in West Philadelphia. Within such networks, German activists could find themselves agitating among workers of different ethnic backgrounds. In the century's first decade, for example, Louis Werner, a socialist and *Tageblatt* editor, helped to organize weavers in Kensington, including some of Scottish and English background, as his daughter Minna recalled.[60]

At certain moments, in fact, the logic of labor solidarity brought even rank-and-file UGT members into tentative coalitions with workers of other ethnic backgrounds. One of the clearest examples of this phenomenon occurred less than two years after the Germantown commemoration, when tens of thousands of Philadelphia workers staged a three-week general strike. For a time, some German unionists found themselves cooperating with new immigrant as well as old immigrant workers, while the UGT's ethnic bonds themselves threatened to unravel amid the strike's pressures.

The general strike erupted in March 1910 as a sympathy action on behalf of workers who had struck the city's widely hated streetcar monopoly, Philadelphia Rapid Transit. Spontaneous sympathy strikes in textiles, garment work, and the building trades in late February were followed by a general strike in the first week of March, called by a coalition of unions, including the city's Central Labor Union (CLU). At its peak, more than 100,000 workers may have joined the walkout. They included many of the 9,500 workers in the UGT, which voted on March 3 to authorize participation in the action.[61]

The *Tageblatt* at first took a cautious stance toward these developments. It advised German workers at the outset of the general strike to "neither take the lead nor lag behind. As a minority, they must fall in with the actions of the majority of the Anglo-Americans." Within days, however, the newspaper's editors had grown considerably more enthusiastic, as the city's workers joined the action in numbers "beyond expectations." The strike was having "a revolutionizing effect," bringing out thousands of unorganized workers and leading many to join unions. "[T]he workers of Philadelphia have shown a solidarity that one could hardly have expected here," the *Tageblatt* declared on March 15. "Not since 1886 has the local working class been so stirred up."[62]

That reference to the heyday of the Knights of Labor was telling, for 1886 marked a moment when union membership in the city reached new heights and when a dispute over the *Tageblatt* itself shattered cooperation among German, Irish, and Anglo-American unionists. Now, to some extent, such cooperation surfaced again. The UGT set the tone for these efforts on March 6, when it decided to print and distribute an appeal in German *and* English imploring "all class-conscious workers" to join the strike, whether they were "organized or not, regardless of their nationality or religion." Many UGT-affiliated unions responded enthusiastically to the strike call, including Machinists Lodge 670 and Textile Workers' Union No. 8, which resolved on March 5 that its members would "join in the general strike with their English colleagues, wherever possible."[63]

Significantly, the Labor Lyceum in Northern Liberties and the Kensington Labor Lyceum, two pillars of the working-class *Vereinswesen*, emerged as centers of strike activity, where unions of different ethnic backgrounds held their meetings. On the morning of March 7 alone, the Kensington Labor Lyceum played host to no fewer than six union meetings that drew an estimated 6,000 people. Among those using the building that day were separate assemblies of weavers and of "English" and German hosiery workers. At the Labor Lyceum the same day, an overflow crowd heard streetcar union leader Clarence Pratt speak from a platform he shared with CLU president John J. Murphy. This assembly likely held workers of different ethnic backgrounds; it certainly crossed gender lines, for "many women" were present. Such a presence came with the participation of textile workers in particular, given the large number of women among them. Many women attended the weavers' meeting at the Kensington Labor Lyceum, and young women made up the majority of an Upholstery Weavers' Union gathering that day aimed at organizing winders and spoolers.[64]

The general strike thus turned two of the city's main halls for German workers into literal common ground. The textile workers who shared that space most likely were of northwest European background, given the predominance of British-stock, Irish-stock, and Anglo-American workers in textiles. Yet German unionists appear as well to have ventured toward cooperation with new immigrants who populated traditional German niche occupations. Italian and Russian Jewish immigrants had already established their own niches in tailoring at the turn of the century. In December 1909, Italian clothing workers joined German and Jewish tailors in a strike that shut down the city's garment shops. Three months later, Italian, Lithuanian, and "Hebrew" tailors' locals were likewise listed as joining in the general strike, although the *Tageblatt* reported on March 8 that only a small proportion of the Jewish and Italian tailors had gone out.[65] More dramatically, German and Polish bakers appear to have made common cause, at least for a time. The UGT-affiliated local No. 6 of the Bakery Workers International Union already had close relations with that union's local No. 201, which lay outside the UGT and had an indeterminate ethnic composition. A joint committee of the two locals worked to encourage employees at the city's large bakeries to join the general strike. Such efforts enjoyed some fleeting success. On March 12, eighty-two workers at Freihofer's, one of the largest bakeries, walked out. Roughly half were German; the rest were Polish. That afternoon, more than a thousand people attended a bakery workers' rally at the Labor Lyceum, where Germans and Poles were "almost equally strongly represented." Two Polish speakers addressed the crowd, as did organizers who spoke in English and German. "The enthusiasm was great," the *Tageblatt* reported. Such enthusiasm may not have lasted long; within two days, Freihofer's and several other large bakeries asserted that all of their employees were at work.[66] Nonetheless, German bakers had reached out, at least temporarily, to Polish fellow workers.

The 1910 general strike shows how German workers could imagine themselves as belonging to a larger collectivity of "class-conscious workers" regardless of "nationality," in the UGT's words. The strength of that drive for labor solidarity, in fact, was sufficient to threaten the ethnic unity of the United German Trades itself. For some UGT unions did not go on strike, citing contracts they had reached with employers. These included Typographia No. 1, which represented typesetters at German-language newspapers, and, most important, the brewery unions—the federation's strongest. Employees at the city's breweries, including brewers, drivers, bottlers, and firemen, were represented by five unions, which operated under a joint local executive of the United Brewery Workers (UBW). When most of the UGT unions resolved on March 6 to join the general strike, the five brewery union locals declined. The president of Brewery Workers' Union No. 5 "stated that while that body was practically unanimous for a walkout, they refused to take the responsibility of breaking their contract with the employers," which would have entailed spoiling millions of dollars worth of beer. The joint executive's secretary traveled to Cincinnati to consult with the UBW's international executive, but that board declined to grant the Philadelphia locals permission to strike.[67]

The impasse shook the UGT. On March 13, a majority of its delegates voted, in effect, to expel the brewery unions for failing to participate in the general strike. A resolution brought by the Brotherhood of Carpenters and Joiners, No. 1051, called on "all class-conscious workers" to boycott Philadelphia beer and to refuse to recognize "any decisions of this so-called brewery workers' union." After a tense debate, the assembled UGT delegates passed the resolution by a 26–4 vote. The move threatened to splinter Philadelphia's German labor movement, as the *Tageblatt* warned. Even as the general strike wound down at the end of March, the United Workers' Singing Societies offered to mediate between the UGT and the brewery unions, in hopes of calming "dissension among the organized German workers."[68]

The brewery unions ultimately rejoined the UGT, but the split over the general strike demonstrated the willingness of German workers to place solidarity with non-German strikers over ethnic solidarity. Significantly, the German carpenter's local that drafted the expulsion resolution did so in cooperation with two other union locals that were not affiliated with the UGT and may have had non-German or ethnically mixed memberships.[69] Such cross-ethnic alliances did not, obviously, preclude an interest in maintaining German culture. Yet organized German workers, and certainly labor activists, were willing to stress class solidarity, even at the risk of weakening or breaking up their ethnically German federation. They did not share the middle-class activists' single-minded devotion to ethnic maintenance, although on occasion, and on their own terms, they could partake of the German-American identity promoted by the National Alliance. Some of the links they forged to non-German workers, moreover, persisted within the Socialist Party and the larger labor movement. As the United German Trades planned its 1914 Labor Day festivities, it arranged to invite not only German workers' organizations but Jewish unions and "the Italian tailors" as well.[70] Class interests promoted a degree of openness to "new immigrants" among German workers that ultimately would shape those workers' identities in ways not shared by middle-class Germans.

If the National Alliance's influence on German workers was episodic, it did achieve some success among the larger public in its effort to put Germans at the center of American history. Germantown residents, whatever their ethnic background, knew with certainty after the 1908 commemoration that their neighborhood was German at its historical roots and that Germans played an important role in the nation's as well as the town's founding. In his comments on Pastorius, Mayor Reyburn, after all, had told them exactly that. The alliance's campaign of words and monuments—to Steuben, to Muhlenberg, to Herkimer—likely had a similar effect. If nothing else, non-German Philadelphians by 1914 knew that German Americans could claim a pedigree stretching back to the start of European colonization—that they were, indeed, "old immigrants." The historical offensive waged by Hexamer and other alliance leaders, however, did not achieve its primary goal of reinvigorating German America. The city's *Vereinswesen* was in far worse shape on the eve of World War I than it had been at the turn of the century. The war would render its situation completely untenable. Displays of public Germanness, like those in Vernon Park in the fall of 1908, would prove impossible once the United States went to war with Germany and problematic after 1919. The Pastorius monument had the misfortune of reaching completion in the spring of 1917; the War Department promptly encased it in a huge box. By the time the container came down in 1920 and the monument finally was dedicated, in a modest ceremony, many German Philadelphians had begun to cast around for alternatives to a German-American identity that had proven far too costly.

PART THREE

Storm, 1914–1919

CHAPTER SEVEN

European War and Ethnic Mobilization

ON the day in 1914 that German troops marched into Belgium and drew Britain into a general European war, the Philadelphia *Public Ledger* made a plea on behalf of the city's foreign-born residents. "Territorially, we are far removed from the scene of struggle, but as a nation, the 'melting pot' of all nations, we have ties of blood, of customs, of tradition, with all Europe," the *Ledger* declared. Native-born Philadelphians, therefore, should follow the federal government's neutral lead and cultivate "a spirit of restraint and toleration. We should show only sympathy and silent understanding in the presence of these men and women of foreign birth whose hearts are torn with emotion."[1]

Whatever spirit of restraint Philadelphians mustered in early August 1914 proved fragile and fleeting. The European war unleashed passions among the city's ethnic groups that spurred their political mobilization. As immigrant reservists flocked to their consulates and crowds cheered calls for Slavic liberation and Irish independence, many German residents, too, rallied to the homeland cause. Men and women of the city's *Vereinswesen* launched war relief campaigns, and German newspapers defended Germany's actions. Indeed, the fighting in Europe brought to German Philadelphia a measure of the ethnic unity long sought by middle-class spokesmen. While the National German-American Alliance won prominence as the preeminent voice of German America, its Philadelphia-based leadership cooperated with working-class socialists and Catholics who had kept their distance from secular, middle-class *Vereine* before the war. Thus fortified, those middle-class leaders moved aggressively to defend Germany's honor, to lobby for an approach to neutrality they felt would not favor Britain, and to forestall American military intervention on behalf of the Allies.

Yet the war also rallied partisans of the Allied cause, especially among Philadelphians of English or colonial background. Some declared their sympathies immediately. Others initially sought a neutral stance, in the spirit of President Woodrow Wilson's call for impartiality "in thought as well as in action,"[2] only to be alienated by Germany's conduct of the war and, to some extent, the aggressive tone taken by German newspaper editors and alliance leaders. For Charles Hexamer and his circle pursued a remarkably unsubtle campaign to shape American neutrality, one that, whatever its merits, struck many non-German-American observers as a dangerous injection of ethnic passions into foreign policy at a moment of particular peril for the United States. Hexamer took an ethnic movement that began with goals of cultural maintenance and attempted to make it a force in high politics. This step instead helped prompt a mounting series of attacks on German-American activists and eventually on German Americans in general as disloyal "hyphenates" who put their ties to Germany above America's best interests.

The reaction, reflected during the neutrality period in campaigns for "Americanization" and military "preparedness," did not stop at denouncing ethnic-group activity in the political sphere. Its demands for national unity would culminate in an attack on the very legitimacy of cultural ethnic separatism and a call instead for a "100 percent Americanism." The National Alliance would prove both a victim of and, to some extent, an inadvertent catalyst for a new kind of American nationalism, one with far less room for culturally pluralist conceptions of the nation and "hyphenated" ethnic-American identities. That nationalism would reach full force in the anti-German panic that followed American intervention. But its elements took shape during the neutrality period, enough so that by early 1916, the *Public Ledger* itself would endorse "[t]he patriotic business of driving the hyphen out of life in America."[3]

CLOSING RANKS, CONTESTING NEUTRALITY

As Europe lurched into war in late July and early August 1914, Philadelphians could see all about them echoes of the nationalistic fervor that was sweeping capitals across the Atlantic. "War Spirit Rife Among Foreign Residents Here: Austro-Hungarians, Servians, Germans and Britons Ready to Fight," a *Public Ledger* headline announced on August 1. Throngs of military reservists reported for duty to the Philadelphia consulates of Austria-Hungary, Germany, France, and Belgium, as each nation in turn declared war. "[T]he fatherland needs all of us," declared one weeping registrant at the German consulate.[4] Hundreds of Serbs, along with representatives from the city's Bohemian and Croatian communities, rallied on August 2 to hail calls for a Slavic war of liberation against the Austro-Hungarian Empire. The same day, a downtown meeting called by Irish nationalists heard hints that the war could be used to advance Irish independence and raised more than $5,000 for the nationalist Irish Volunteers.[5] Many foreign-born Philadelphians and their children, unable to join the homeland armies, turned to raising funds for the wounded, widows, and orphans the war was bound to produce. Serbians, Austrians, and Germans all organized campaigns for war relief during August, and by October city residents had formed committees to provide such aid for English and Belgian war sufferers.[6]

Some Philadelphians who traced their European immigrant ancestors to the colonial period found it difficult to stay neutral "in thought" at the war's outbreak. "I began as a violent partisan of the Allies," George Wharton Pepper later recalled. When Germany violated Belgian neutrality on August 4, this lawyer of colonial German descent felt immediately that the United States had to aid in punishing the malefactor.[7] Few Philadelphians likely shared Pepper's interventionist views, but many came to sympathize with the Allies, especially after the invasion of Belgium. The *Public Ledger*'s editors noted of American sentiment on August 9 that "our average attitude, while not unfriendly [to Germany], distinctly favors Germany's chief rivals, England and France. For this reason, at the outbreak of the war American opinion, with few exceptions . . . placed the blame of the catastrophe upon the Kaiser."[8]

While some German Philadelphians had doubts about the wisdom of Germany's course, the most vocal closed ranks to defend the German government and people. For the city's secular, middle-class German associations and their leaders, this was a step taken with little if any hesitation. Their agenda was set to a large extent by Charles Hexamer, working from his position as president simultaneously of the National Alliance, the German-American Central Alliance of Pennsylvania, and the German Society of Pennsylvania. On August 3, Hexamer issued an appeal to the German-language press nationally, outlining how "the German name" could be defended "against the animosity and ignorance of a minority in our own country."[9] He was prompted in part by fears of one-sided and negative coverage of Germany's war conduct by the nation's English-language press. Editorials attacking the German cause became common by mid-August; they surfaced in the Philadelphia *North American* as well as in the New York dailies. Likewise, the cutting of the German transatlantic cables after Britain entered the war virtually ended the transmission of German accounts of the conflict to American newspapers.[10] Hexamer's appeal, however, to a degree predated these developments and amounted to something of a preemptive move. He called on alliance branches in every city to sponsor press agents who could refute, in English, "all hateful attacks" of "irresponsible reporters from English newspapers." Hexamer further declared that alliance branches should take up collections for German war relief.[11]

Through August, representatives from middle-class German associations mobilized to pursue the twin goals of war relief and the rhetorical defense of Germany. An initial meeting on August 5 to establish a German war relief fund was followed by a mass meeting at the German Society on August 9, where the hundreds attending sang "Die Wacht am Rhein" and contributed a total of $1,100 for the families of dead or wounded German soldiers. Hexamer, who presided over the gathering, announced a nationwide alliance campaign to raise $2 million in war relief, setting Philadelphia's target at $50,000.[12] Representatives from leading middle-class women's associations gathered to promote the same cause on August 17. A meeting of German pastors three days later denounced newspaper articles "which tend to incite and seek to create public sentiment against Germany"; they directed their resolutions at "the managing editor, the editor and the news editor of every paper in Philadelphia."[13]

Philadelphia's middle-class German journalists likewise took up Germany's cause.[14] By August 9, if not before, the middle-class *Morgen-Gazette* was portraying the homeland as forced into war by an England intent on destroying its main commercial competitor. The next day, the newspaper accused "the English-American press" of deliberate anti-German war reporting. It called on German Americans "and their offspring" to mount "an energetic and determined opposition against this campaign of lies" in order to avert any damage it might do to relations between Germany and the United States.[15] The *Morgen-Gazette* continued its feud with "English-American" newspapers in the days that followed, while endorsing the National Alliance's war relief campaign.[16]

Doubts about the war were voiced more openly among working-class German Philadelphians. In particular, a division of opinion surfaced among those affiliated with the city's German socialist institutions, which echoed the crisis the war precipitated within the international socialist movement. Almost all of the European socialist parties, including the Social Democratic Party of Germany (SPD), rejected the official antiwar stance of the Second International and rallied behind their governments as they entered the war. The SPD's Reichstag delegation voted on August 4 in favor of the German government's request for war credits, an action that foreshadowed the splitting of the party three years later and greatly demoralized American socialists.[17] Behind the delegation's vote lay a cluster of factors: a belief that reactionary Czarist Russia had attacked Germany; a party tradition that justified defending Germany to protect the base of future socialist successes; a class loyalty that had centered ever more on *German* Social Democratic organizations; a fear that nationalist sentiment and government repression could sweep away all of the party's laboriously won gains; and an impulse to break out of the SPD's position as a pariah by showing that its members were as patriotic as other Germans.[18]

Frederick Luebke has depicted most German-American socialist leaders as critics of the war, who viewed it as resulting from ruling-class greed and ambition and were, consequently, "devoid of sympathy for the Fatherland." In Philadelphia, however, German socialists appear to have played out a drama not unlike the SPD's. Some undoubtedly opposed the war without reservations. On August 8, days after news of the SPD's war credit vote had reached the United States, a meeting of the city Socialist Party's German branch approved a resolution declaring "its opposition to the criminal war of destruction unleashed on Europe through [the workings of] capitalism, Junkerdom, monarchy and Czarism."[19]

The *Philadelphia Tageblatt,* however, the voice of the city's German socialists, came to evince a position decidedly more friendly to the German war effort. The *Tageblatt* in 1914 retained very close ties to the Socialist Party of America (SP).[20] At the same time, the newspaper had a sentimental affinity for the SPD, holding it up as a model for American socialists. A story on an SP national committee meeting noted that, with a little more effort on the part of the delegates, one would hardly be able to find a difference between "our national gatherings and a Party Day of the German Social Democrats. That," the article went on, "is surely praise enough."[21]

This identification with the SPD facilitated the newspaper's shift to a stance more supportive of Germany and at some variance with the SP's antiwar position.[22] In the first days of August, the *Tageblatt*'s editorial page condemned the war unconditionally.[23] Word then arrived of the SPD's war credit vote. The sense of shock at the newspaper was palpable. "What are plans, what are proposals?" began the lead editorial on August 6. Social Democrats had for years pondered how to avert war, recognizing the general strike as one means to that end. "And now: when it came to 'pulling it off,' nothing came of all this." Instead, all 111 Social Democrats in the German Reichstag had voted to help pay for the war. But, the editorial continued, "they certainly must have [had] good reasons" for that step—reasons of "grim necessity." With the German Empire officially at war, any action seen as interfering with the military would have prompted the suppression of the SPD and probably of unions and other organizations seen as its allies. And this sacrifice would have been in vain, for it could not have prevented the war's outbreak, the editorial concluded.[24]

By mid-August, this defense of the SPD had evolved into a conditional one of Germany in terms that would have been familiar to German Social Democrats. "One cannot strike the reactionary Germany without also striking the progressive one," including the SPD, the *Tageblatt* editorialized on August 14. To leave Germany open to attack from autocratic Russia "would be a downright unthinkable crime. Therefore, the Social Democrats had to cooperate, and therefore a defeat of the Kaiser is not to be desired—not a defeat at the hands of the Russians." The *Tageblatt*'s backing of Germany did not mean that it approved of all German ambitions. Nevertheless, it was prepared to go rather far in supporting Germany's conduct—to the extent, in May 1915, of defending the sinking of the British liner *Lusitania.*[25]

Outside of its editorial columns, the *Tageblatt* showed a greater, and earlier, commitment to Germany's cause. In reporting the Kaiser's mobilization order, the newspaper stated on August 3 that "all real Germans" had been awaiting it for days. The next day, the *Tageblatt* ran a story accusing a Philadelphia English-language newspaper of intentionally downplaying German Philadelphia's war "enthusiasm . . . for the cause of Germandom." Whether because of its editors' ethnic sympathies or its readers', the *Tageblatt* continued to demonstrate such "enthusiasm" in its news coverage, evincing a support for Germany that went well beyond the Socialist Party's antiwar stance.[26]

The shift in opinion at the *Tageblatt* signaled a new willingness on the part of at least some German socialist and labor organizations to cooperate with middle-class associations. Before the war, the working-class *Vereinswesen* had been somewhat wary of and at times hostile toward its middle-class counterpart. The war's outbreak, however, encouraged what the *Tageblatt* described as a "unified spirit of the Germans." In essence, German Philadelphia experienced a rapprochement not unlike the *Burgfrieden* ("fortress peace") declared between the SPD and Germany's other political parties at the beginning of the war.[27] By mid-August, middle-class singing societies such as the Franklinville Gesangverein and the Schiller Männerchor had joined with a working-class singing society, the Sozialistische Liedertafel, to organize a festival for war relief. Those attending the event on August 17 were proof of "the unity of the Germans in their convictions about the European war," the *Tageblatt* declared. "There they sat next to one another, old champions of the socialist idea and comfortable bourgeois . . . and they all wholeheartedly wished victory to the German cause."[28] This cooperation broadened after August. A mass meeting on October 14 drew thousands to the Philadelphia Turngemeinde's auditorium to protest the "slanderous lies of the Anglo-American press" and to hear addresses by Hexamer and Hermann Kreimer, a "representative of labor." The audience also listened to a combined performance by the United Singers of Philadelphia and the United Workers' Singing Societies, which marked the first time the city's two German choral federations, one middle-class and one working-class, had ever sung together.[29] Philadelphia's German socialists proved willing as well to work with the National Alliance in its attempts to influence American foreign policy, at least where the alliance and the Socialist Party shared common goals. Toward the end of 1914, the alliance mounted a campaign for an embargo on arms exports from the United States—a step it saw as preserving American neutrality, since British control of the seas meant only the Allies could benefit from the arms trade. On December 11, delegates from scores of Philadelphia *Vereine* met under the auspices of the alliance's Philadelphia branch and called for legislation giving the U.S.

president the power to impose such an embargo. Among the associations represented were at least a half-dozen with ties to the city's German labor movement, including the Arbeiter Sängerbund and the United Brewery Workers. Their participation may have been eased by the fact that an embargo enjoyed some initial support within the Socialist Party nationally.[30]

German Philadelphia's *Burgfrieden* appears to have held through the neutrality period. This persistence is best illustrated by a massive charity bazaar for German and Austrian war relief held in the spring of 1916. The bazaar's president, Josef Schlenz, described it as an achievement of "a united Germandom."[31] Such claims of German unity had been made by middle-class leaders before the war, often with little basis in fact. Yet Schlenz's statement rang true. The event, which drew an estimated 250,000 visitors to the city's Convention Hall in late April and early May, certainly involved German Philadelphia's middle-class leadership. Hexamer served as honorary president, Antonie Ehrlich of the German Society's Frauen Hilfsverein was president of the women's executive committee, and John B. Mayer—the secretary of the German Society, president of the United Singers, and president by 1916 of the Central Alliance of Pennsylvania and the Philadelphia Alliance branch—took a leading role as well.[32] But the charity fair also enjoyed the large-scale participation of working-class German associations. A "Workers' Day" on April 29 featured a performance by a 300-voice choir from the United Workers' Singing Societies, and thousands of union members attended in what the *Public Ledger* called "a sort of labor day celebration." The *Tageblatt,* which had given the bazaar glowing coverage from the start, rejoiced that, in its words, "[t]he call to the workers did not go unheeded."[33] That this labor newspaper described the fair at its opening as "the greatest work that the whole Germandom of the city of brotherly love has ever undertaken,"[34] suggests that the war in Europe, during its first two years, did much to tone down German Philadelphia's class divisions.

The European war likewise muted the religious divides among German Philadelphians. The close ties some German Lutherans had long enjoyed with the city's middle-class *Vereinswesen* continued during the neutrality period. The war-relief bazaar was opened by Georg von Bosse with a "German prayer" and featured eight booths for Protestant churches— some of them assuredly Lutheran, for von Bosse's wife was involved in their administration.[35] German Catholics had kept a far greater distance from Philadelphia's secular *Vereine* before the war. This distance was reflected nationally in the "cool, almost icy" stance held toward the National Alliance by its Catholic counterpart, the German Catholic Central-Verein. The war's outbreak, however, led to a considerable thaw in relations between the two federations.[36] It also eased relations between Catholics and non-Catholics in German Philadelphia, as the 1916 bazaar demonstrated. Ordinary German Catholics showed far more enthusiasm for the bazaar than they had for the National Alliance's 1908 Pastorius celebration. The "city of booths" at Convention Hall included two stands for the Catholic Women's League (Katholischer Frauenbund) and eight for Catholic churches, among them the German national parishes of St. Peter, St. Boniface, and St. Ignatius.[37]

Indeed, the spring 1916 bazaar may have marked the moment of greatest unity in German Philadelphia's history. Middle-class activists and working-class socialists, Protestants, Catholics, and Jews—whose societies set aside a Saturday to visit the fair—all came together in a manner that impressed even outsiders. "Probably the most conspicuous feature of the big benefit is the harmony which exists among German-Americans of all creeds," the *Public Ledger* noted. "They have laid aside all religious and political prejudices in an effort to make the affair one of national pride."[38]

The bazaar signified ethnic unity across lines not just of class and religion, but of gender. The event both confirmed the long-term expansion of women's presence in the *Vereinswesen* and testified to the war's encouragement of that expansion. Almost overnight, the fighting had created war relief as a new mission for organized German America, which mobilized around that goal as much as, if not more than, foreign policy aims. And war relief made women central to ethnic mobilization. Relief was portrayed as charity to wounded soldiers, widows, and orphans in Germany,[39] and charity had long been viewed as a public activity suited to women's nurturing "nature." Women's associations such as Antonie Ehrlich's Frauen Hilfsverein, moreover, had extensive experience in organizing charity drives and fairs. Not surprisingly, then, war relief work allowed women to take an even higher profile within the *Vereinswesen*. The *Tageblatt*, for example, found the relief festival of August 17, 1914, notable because it brought together not only old socialists and upright bourgeois, but also women and men. Women participated massively in the 1916 charity bazaar, and did so to a great extent through their own organizations and the separate women's executive committee led by Ehrlich. Much of the fair's work involved raising funds by selling homemade goods at booths. Women both made these items—including "[m]ore than 100,000 pieces of embroidered work and fancy articles"—and retailed them. Ehrlich estimated that 3,000 women volunteered to serve as aides at the fair, a job that involved staffing the "city of booths."[40] Women organized many of the booths themselves as members of their female *Verein* auxiliaries or on behalf of churches or male associations; female organizers were in charge of at least fifty-four of the 144 numbered booths at the bazaar. The fair's male officials undoubtedly recognized the importance of this separate effort, as is suggested by their deference to Ehrlich, who spoke at the opening ceremony along with Hexamer, Mayer, and Schlenz.[41]

That the war drew together representatives of all of the major subcultures of German Philadelphia does not mean, of course, that all Philadelphians of German background rallied to Germany's cause. At the war's outbreak, the *Public Ledger* stated that despite the reservists' rush to report, "not a few of the German born population" were "shunning the consulates because of the fear that they can legally be compelled to return . . . for military duty against their own will." Although the National Alliance claimed growth during the war's first year, its monthly bulletin complained in May 1915 that "there are still citizens of the German race [*Stamm*] who stand outside the world of German associations and have neglected to join [the alliance] as individual members."[42] Philadelphia's most prominent German-born citizen, Mayor Rudolph Blankenburg, remained aloof throughout from Hexamer's brand of ethnic politics, becoming, in fact, an advocate of military preparedness.[43]

Buoyed by an unprecedented degree of ethnic unity, however, Hexamer and the National Alliance moved to shape America's policy of neutrality so as to keep it truly neutral, in their eyes, and avoid a war with Germany. Alliance leaders and branches played a major role in the arms embargo agitation; they likewise took the initiative in opposing the raising of an Allied war loan in the United States. As they pursued these political efforts in late 1914 and 1915, relations between the National Alliance and President Wilson steadily deteriorated. Wilson's opposition to an embargo and his overall neutrality policy increasingly drew the wrath of German-American activists. Those activists did have a case. The British had imposed a blockade on German ports, which in certain respects clearly violated American neutrality. Wilson's ultimate acquiescence in the blockade compromised his neutral stance, essentially confining access to American munitions to the Allies. The president, of course, did not see things this way. His irritation at such criticism contributed to his public questioning, beginning in the fall of 1915, of the loyalty of his critics. The feud with Wilson led some alliance activists to discuss ways to work for his defeat in the election of 1916. Hexamer and many officials of state and local branches subsequently threw themselves into the campaign for the Republican presidential nominee, Charles Evans Hughes.[44]

The alliance's increasing involvement in national politics was echoed locally in Philadelphia. The December 1914 call by city *Vereine* for an arms embargo was followed by a January 28, 1915, mass meeting on behalf of the embargo legislation, held under the auspices of the American Neutrality League. Such leagues had been founded in other cities as bridges between local alliances and Irish-American organizations, and the Philadelphia league followed this pattern. Its president was one J. Rich.

Shannon, and its January gathering involved John Mayer.[45] Mayer similarly played an important role in the alliance's plunge into presidential politics. The National Alliance, under the terms of its congressional charter, could not participate in the 1916 election, so the Central Alliance, now with Mayer as president, stepped in to assume the mantle of leadership for alliance activists nationwide. In May 1916, the Central Alliance issued invitations to a wide range of German associations, including other state alliances, for a conference in Chicago on the U.S. presidential race. That gathering made no formal endorsements, but its consensus was understood to favor Hughes. Mayer emerged as chairman of a conference committee charged with marshaling a united German-American vote and mediating between the German associations and political party leaders.[46] By the fall of 1916, then, Mayer, Hexamer, and other German Philadelphians had contributed mightily to making the "German-American vote" an issue in the presidential election.

The middle-class activists found some support for their initiatives beyond German Philadelphia. The ethnic group most open to the National Alliance's political program—aside from those with ties to the Central Powers—was the city's Irish Americans. Irish nationalist hatred of England had prompted occasional prewar cooperation between Irish and German organizations. In 1907, the National Alliance reached an agreement with the Ancient Order of Hibernians, whereby both organizations vowed to oppose immigration restriction and entanglements "with any foreign power." Not surprisingly, then, Irish nationalists in Philadelphia quickly rallied to the German cause in 1914. At an August 19 meeting at the Irish-American Club, representatives of many of the city's Irish societies passed resolutions expressing hope for a German victory over England and pledging "every effort to bring the Irish and the Germans together for their common goal: the national welfare of Germany and the national existence of Ireland."[47] Such sentiments formed the basis for eventual joint political action, like that taken in 1915 under the aegis of the American Neutrality League.

SWATTING THE HYPHEN

Far from winning major support among other groups, however, the middle-class activists helped alienate a large number of Philadelphians. Their political activities and aggressive rhetoric combined with a host of other factors to evoke a sharp reaction. For many, this reaction began with revulsion at Germany's prosecution of the war and grew by 1916 to encompass a general suspicion of self-identified German Americans as potentially disloyal "hyphenates." The National Alliance's escalating involvement in national politics served as a lightning rod for such Philadelphians. Those who had tolerated, if at times uneasily, ethnic cultural differences before the war were not prepared to countenance explicit ethnic viewpoints in foreign policy debates. Many, though not all, were Anglo-Americans or of European colonial descent, and for some the National Alliance's initiatives also challenged their view of themselves as the most "American" of Americans.

The resentments stimulated by the alliance had prewar roots. The racialized nativism that emerged beginning in the 1890s spared German Americans. Some tension still obtained, however, between exponents of Anglo-Saxon superiority and German-American activists who saw their culture as competing with Anglo-America's. American attitudes toward Imperial Germany itself, moreover, grew increasingly negative in the decades before the war. Economic competition, diplomatic clashes, and the sometimes erratic behavior of Kaiser Wilhelm II fed Americans' suspicions of German ambitions and their disdain for the German Empire's militaristic and autocratic tendencies. Such attitudes helped to shape public reaction when the conflict began. One reader wrote to the *Public Ledger* in early August 1914 to explain that Americans opposed "not the Germany of Goethe, Schiller, Koch . . . but the Germany that has armed the home circle, made a soldier of every man . . . thwarted liberty and defied independence."[48]

Others began with the intention of maintaining a neutral stance, only to be alienated by Germany's conduct of the war. The *Public Ledger* itself is a good example of this phenomenon. Conservative and soberly written, the *Ledger* at the beginning of August was painfully even-handed in its treatment of the conflict. An August 8 editorial cartoon depicted a bloody dagger labeled "War," grasped by fingers bearing the names of the belligerents. "Each Finger Has Its Share of Blame," the cartoon's caption read. At the same time, the newspaper bent over backwards to provide balanced war coverage. From August 9 until at least the end of the month, the *Ledger* frequently reprinted the day's lead editorial from the *Morgen-Gazette*.[49] The editors also took care in early August to tell readers that, with the German transatlantic cables cut, newspaper reports on military operations were coming "from sources hostile to Germany."[50]

By the end of August, however, the editors, having read the official British and German explanations for the war, moved to a position decidedly hostile to the Central Powers. Those explanations, the *Public Ledger* declared on August 25, showed that Austria had gone to war with Serbia knowing this would bring Russia into the conflict and that the German government had assured Austria of "full support . . . regardless of the consequences." Such evidence fixed "an awful responsibility" on Austria, and Berlin shared in it. Britain's publication of the diplomatic exchanges leading up to the war also appeared to sway the newspaper. The *Ledger* had striven to remain impartial when Germany violated Belgian neutrality. On learning how German officials regarded that violation, however, the editors threw up their hands. Germany's chancellor "expressed amazement that England should go to war [on Belgium's behalf] 'just for a word,' 'just for a scrap of paper.' That 'word,'" the *Ledger* declared on August 30, "was the neutrality of a sister State and that 'paper' was a treaty to which Germany had signed her name. . . . [I]s it to be wondered that other nations look askance at a power so ruthlessly exercised."[51]

A condemnation of the German government did not necessarily imply one of the German people or of German immigrants and their offspring. The *Public Ledger* could show tolerance in August 1914 for even those German Philadelphians who showed their homeland ties by vehemently protesting the "anti-German" reporting of English-language newspapers. "If they left behind them all affection for the home of their ancestors and all love for its institutions they would make poor citizens of the United States," the newspaper editorialized on August 24. Nonetheless, many Philadelphians expected such affection to be kept within certain limits. Immigrants might retain aspects of their ethnic culture, but they were not to bring homeland concerns into the political sphere, especially now that the United States was attempting to remain neutral. "Loyalty to the United States does not require disloyalty to the fatherland of any adopted citizen," the *Evening Bulletin* declared on August 19. "But it ought to be recognized and, as a warning, emphasized that these prejudices and preferences must be laid aside on the threshold of American politics. This Government is, and must be, neutral."[52] Readers of the *Public Ledger* echoed this position. The J. Bancroft, "of German descent," who on August 28 condemned "the campaign being conducted in neutral United States for Germany," stressed that "this danger of trying to involve the United States in militarism and this war is imminent."[53]

Those who harbored such expectations could not help but react with misgivings to the National Alliance's venture into high politics. As it was, the alliance's pursuit of an arms embargo in 1915 coincided with a crisis in American relations with Germany. The year opened with a Washington conference in support of an embargo attended by prominent German Americans, including Hexamer. The January 30 gathering resulted in the founding of the American Independence Union, which was to support "only such candidates for public office . . . who will place American interests above those of any other country."[54] The conference also sparked what John Higham called "the first passionate outburst of anti-German hysteria." The participants felt that Wilsonian neutrality, in favoring Britain, could only lead to war with Germany and that an embargo, while of course benefiting Germany, would help to keep the peace. To a bevy of critics, these conferees were acting, as the *Nation* put it, "in the interest of a foreign government."[55]

Days after the conference, Germany declared a "war zone" around the British Isles, within which German submarines would destroy enemy vessels without warning. Wilson then warned that he would hold Germany to "strict accountability" for the destruction of American ships and lives. The question remained as to what the United States would do to protect the alleged right of Americans to travel in safety on British passenger liners. On May 7, a U-boat precipitated a full-scale crisis by sinking the *Lusitania*, with the loss of nearly 1,200 people, including 128 American citizens. Until the end of August, when the Kaiser ordered the abandonment of unrestricted submarine operations against passenger ships, war with Germany seemed a very real possibility.[56] In the meantime, supporters of the Allies could argue with some justification that Berlin already had carried the war to American soil. Beginning in February, reports surfaced of sabotage carried out by agents operating from the German embassy in Washington. At least some of these stories were genuine; they described foiled attempts to destroy American factories and to carry bombs aboard American ships.[57]

In this climate, German-American activists increasingly came under the suspicion of acting on behalf of the German government. For a few of the most militant, such as George Sylvester Viereck, this was in fact the case. Viereck, the publisher of the *Fatherland,* a New York-based English-language weekly, cooperated with German officials in producing propaganda—an activity then quite legal. Yet the shadow of "disloyalty" began to fall on activists in general in the spring of 1915. At the May convention of the Central Alliance of Pennsylvania, Mayer recommended the drafting of a resolution "against the frequent insinuations that the Central Alliance was founded only to create a state within a state, to do the spying for and dirty work of Germany, and to pursue traitorous goals."[58]

Passions ran particularly high with the sinking of the *Lusitania*. Of this attack on "helpless non-combatants," the *Public Ledger* said: "the horror is almost inconceivable." The *Morgen-Gazette* and other German-American newspapers sought to justify the action. Such comments prompted the editors of the *Ledger* to tell German Americans, in essence, to shut up. "Certainly no one outside the ranks of German sympathizers is disposed to listen to a defense of the act with patience," the newspaper declared. "[T]he best service these can now perform for Germany is to cultivate the virtue of silence." This rebuke was mild compared to that of one reader, who wanted "all hyphenated German-Americans to report daily to the civil authorities, with imprisonment as the alternative."[59]

By the fall of 1915, worries about the allegedly divided loyalties of "hyphenated" Americans had escalated into a nationwide "anti-hyphenate" campaign. Theodore Roosevelt stood at the head of the "Swat-the-Hyphen" movement, and Wilson lent it moral authority. The president was careful not to name German Americans as such in his attacks,[60] in part perhaps because he meant them to apply as well to Irish Americans. His speeches, however, revealed a conception of American nationality that had less and less tolerance for ethnically based cultural as well as political differences. "You cannot become thorough Americans if you think of yourselves in groups," Wilson told an audience of newly naturalized citizens in Philadelphia, three days after the *Lusitania* sinking. "America does not consist of groups. A man who thinks of himself as belonging to a particular national group in America has not yet become an American." He denounced divided loyalties with even greater force in the fall, when he was joined by Roosevelt. In an October 12 speech, the former president, an aggressive proponent of intervention on behalf of the Allies, depicted as treasonous the actions of "those hyphenated Americans who terrorize American politicians by threats of the foreign vote."[61]

An onslaught of antihyphen speeches, editorials, and political cartoons followed. While these tended to decry the "disembodied category" of the immigrant with divided loyalties, they were understood to target those whom Roosevelt termed "professional German-Americans." In Philadelphia and around the country, continued revelations of alleged spying and sabotage reinforced the image of those activists as subversives and conspirators.[62] The Philadelphia *Record* suggested in October that the National Alliance's new antiloan campaign "was akin to the acts of sabotage in the munitions factories." By December, the identity of "German-American" as such was losing legitimacy in the eyes of the *Public Ledger*. Its December 21 political cartoon showed a statement from Berlin repudiating sabotage on American soil—a note labeled, "Germany to German-Americans"—being torn up by a sinister, heavy-set, mustachioed figure. Next to this ethnic caricature lay a bomb and a revolver; behind him stood a worried-looking Uncle Sam. The cartoon's caption, "Another Scrap of Paper," evoked the fate of Belgium.[63] (See figure 7.1.)

The antihyphen climate that overtook Philadelphia in 1915 both fed on and fostered two other movements that established a presence in the city: the push for immigrant Americanization, and that for military preparedness. The Americanization campaign nationally had prewar roots in the settlement house movement, the drive for patriotic education in the public schools, and the efforts of patriotic societies such as the Daughters of the American Revolution to reach adult immigrants. These societies, motivated by fear of immigrant radicalism, preached to newcomers "a loyalty that consisted essentially of willing submissiveness" to the law. As Higham argued, the emerging Americanization movement incorporated both this stress on conformity and national unity and the settlements'

ANOTHER SCRAP OF PAPER

Figure 7.1. "Another Scrap of Paper," 1915. By late 1915, even the sober *Public Ledger* was casting doubt on the loyalty of German Americans. Here, the newspaper presented the "German-American" as saboteur, complete with bomb and revolver. This sinister figure is tearing up a statement recently issued by the German government that repudiated sabotage in the United States and declared to German Americans and others that such conduct was an embarrassment to Germany. The cartoon's title plays off the German chancellor's surprise at the beginning of the war that England would come to Belgium's aid out of a treaty obligation—"just for a scrap of paper." Source: *Public Ledger*, 21 December 1915, p. 2.

"immigrant gifts" approach of valuing Old World cultures to ease immigrant adjustment.[64] But Americanization as a movement aimed at adult newcomers lacked mass support until the war, when fear of divided immigrant loyalties brought it into the public spotlight. Philadelphia played a key role in this process. The May 1915 reception for new citizens that Wilson addressed became a model for similar ceremonies held in cities around the country on July 4, under the rubric of "Americanization Day." The group created to organize that event renamed itself the National Americanization Committee and began to shift from a social welfare emphasis to one of promoting naturalization, English-language training, and "undivided loyalty to America." The extent to which the crusade for Americanization and the crusade against hyphenates had merged by early 1916 became clear at the committee conference held in January in Philadelphia. Roosevelt closed the gathering with a call for "an intense sense of national cohesion and solidarity" and cast "hyphenated Americanism" as its opposite.[65]

The preparedness campaign for a stronger national defense marched hand in hand with the rising antihyphen sentiment and increasingly helped define the terms of the Americanization movement. Indeed, Roosevelt, who backed all three movements, used his Americanization conference speech to argue for universal military training, a larger navy, and national regulation of business, all meant to provide the "proper type of preparedness to protect the nation."[66] If the Americanization movement in Philadelphia had an elite tinge—Mrs. Edward T. Stotesbury, the wife of the city's leading investment banker, was instrumental in organizing the January conference[67]—the preparedness movement was primarily an upper-class initiative. The National Security League and the American Defense Society, the principal national groups formed after the war's outbreak to agitate for preparedness, had wealthy and conservative memberships. When the league established a Philadelphia branch in July 1915, it was no surprise that the new group chose as its honorary president John Wanamaker, the department store magnate.[68] One Proper Philadelphian, A. J. Drexel Biddle, established his own military training camp on his estate in suburban Lansdowne, an easy commute for the businessmen he hoped to attract. The *Public Ledger* described the eighty "patriotic women" who met in Philadelphia in December 1915 to launch the Pennsylvania Women's Division for National Preparedness as "leaders in the life of the State." Preparedness activists did, however, attempt to reach a wider audience. The *Public Ledger,* for example, sponsored showings in December 1915 of the French government film *Fighting in France,* which the newspaper judged "a powerful stimulus to preparedness sentiment." And such agitation tended to imply that the threat facing America was German. The *Ledger* noted that viewers of *Fighting in France* could "scarcely feel assured that the United States is to be forever free from such scenes. . . . The English and Irish little thought that their young men would die to keep Teutons from [their] shores."[69]

By 1916, then, the campaigns against "hyphenated Americanism" and for Americanization and preparedness had publicly raised the question of whether the national loyalty of German Philadelphians could be trusted. The middle-class German-American activists bitterly resented such questioning of their patriotism and of their right to act politically to promote, in their view, the nation's best interests. Yet the activists brought some of this reaction on themselves. As Luebke argued, they "lacked subtlety and tact." Having spent the prewar years struggling for the recognition they felt American society owed German Americans, Hexamer and his circle remained in battle mode during the neutrality period. Their lobbying and mobilization efforts had a harsh, sledgehammer quality, and they could not resist the urge to frame their appeals in ethnic terms[70]—indeed, they relied on such appeals to help bridge the long-standing internal divisions of German Philadelphia and German America. This, however, was a politically inept approach to take in a debate over how best to keep America neutral and impartial during a world war. When Hexamer, for example, declared in May 1915 that if he were secretary of state, he would "force England to her knees in two weeks,"[71] one could have forgiven a listener for doubting his interest in a truly neutral stance. Such statements hardly seemed calculated to attract the support of Americans who were not of German or Irish background but who might have been sympathetic to an arms embargo.

The most notorious illustration of the National Alliance's tin ear for American politics was a speech Hexamer delivered in Milwaukee on November 22, 1915. Addressing a banquet given in his honor, he made an appeal for the preservation of Germandom:

> For a long time we have suffered the preachment: "You Germans must allow yourselves to be assimilated, you must be merged into the American people"; but no one will find us prepared to step down to a lesser kultur; no, we have made it our aim to draw the others up to us. . . . No people is so modest and no people is so ready to recognize the good in others and to adopt it as the Germans. . . . But we will not permit that our kultur of two thousand years be trodden down in this land. Many were born here and many are giving our German kultur to the land of their children. But that is possible only if we stand together and conquer that dark spirit of muckerdom [bigotry] and prohibition just as Siegfried once slew the dragon.[72]

Hexamer had sounded this theme, that true Americanization involved a German cultural contribution to an evolving America, for years. The address differed from his prewar speeches only in stating more explicitly than most his belief in the superiority of German culture. (*Kultur* can be translated as "culture" or, more broadly, as "civilization"). In the context of 1915, however, Hexamer's words came off as, at the least, arrogant and, at the worst, an insult to other Americans and a challenge both to the surging demand for national unity and to those Anglo-Americans who saw themselves as the guardians of an American culture. The speech, which was extensively quoted, made its way into such attacks on the National Alliance and on a separate German-American ethnic identity as Gustavus Ohlinger's influential 1916 tract, *Their True Faith and Allegiance*. In his preface to Ohlinger's book, the Philadelphia novelist Owen Wister, now affiliated with the American Defense Society, repeatedly referred to Hexamer's phrase about elevating other Americans. Only Wister turned the line into a warning about the Kaiser's plan, "[t]hrough his organized hyphens," to consume America.[73]

The controversy over Hexamer's impassioned defense of German *Kultur* points to a larger danger the National Alliance's political involvement held for German Philadelphia and German America. The National Alliance began as an organization devoted to German-American cultural maintenance. The Philadelphia-based leadership always reserved its greatest interest for the promotion of a German-American history and what Hexamer in 1907 called "our noble cultural mission." Such efforts to foster a German-American identity could be advanced because they fit well with strains of American civic nationalism prevalent within and outside German America before the First World War. American national identity, in the eyes of many nineteenth-century German-American intellectuals, was for Germans a matter of allegiance to American democratic ideals; one could be a good American and still cultivate loyalties to German culture. Likewise, mainstream American nationalism itself was comparatively flexible before the war. As Cecilia O'Leary argued, there was "a relative degree of openness about who and what should represent the nation," enough so that immigrants could "maintain dual allegiance to their homelands and the United States."[74] The European war may, in fact, have heightened that sense of dual allegiance for many German Philadelphians during the neutrality period. Certainly, the war's outbreak made a common German identity more important to Catholics and socialists who put aside earlier reservations to close ranks with middle-class and Lutheran Germans. Yet, if the 1916 bazaar is any indication, many likely understood this identity as specifically *German-American*. At that unifying event, the American flag formed "the dominant note in the scheme of decorations"; frequently, it was coupled with the German flag, expressing, as the *Public Ledger* put it, "[l]ove of Fatherland and loyalty to adopted land." Visitors to the fair cheered "Die Wacht am Rhein," but "became almost wild" in their applause for "The Star-Spangled Banner." One visitor summed up this hyphenated identity with the watchword: "True German-Americans love the Vaterland as a man loves his mother, but they love America, the land of their adoption, as a man loves his wife."[75]

Cultural hyphenation, however, was one thing; in the eyes of many Philadelphians, political hyphenation was quite another. When the National Alliance began pursuing ethnic interests not only in the cultural politics of prohibition but also in the high politics of foreign relations, it ventured onto new and uncertain ground. In a sense, the alliance departed even from earlier German-American understandings of American nationality as political, since that notion could imply a necessary separation between ethnic culture on one side and American politics on the other. Rudolph Blankenburg certainly saw things this way. The mayor, a one-time president and lifelong member of the German Society, never rejected his ethnic background in a cultural sense. Yet, as he explained in a December 1915 speech, he opposed all manner of political "hyphenation," including the "Anglo-Saxon" variant. "I am a thorough believer in Americanism of the highest type and character. To me neither German-Americans, nor Irish, Scotch, French, Italian, or Russian-Americans, *as a political entity* appeal," Blankenburg declared. The difficulty for the National Alliance was that once it took up foreign policy concerns, its "cultural mission" could be read in political terms—as a threat to the American nation. For, as Frank Trommler argued, the alliance's embrace of *Kultur* as a "vague yet exclusively German concept of higher aspirations" implied an identification primarily with a country other than the United States.[76]

Thus, the alliance's move into foreign policy opened the way for critics to attack German-American culture itself, not simply alliance politicking, as disloyal. *Kultur,* in fact, became "a most visible focus" of the wave of anti-German publications that appeared in 1915 and 1916.[77] By raising the political stakes, Hexamer and the National Alliance had helped to put at risk the cultural foundations of German America. Ohlinger, who could not pin actual acts of sabotage on the National Alliance, painted it as a sinister agent of German *Kulturpolitik,* or "cultural politics." In his view, attempts to preserve the German language amounted to threats to "the life of America."[78] Sketching a nightmare version of what Horace Kallen later would call cultural pluralism, Ohlinger predicted that foreign-language maintenance efforts "among all races" would turn America into

a polyglot of compact organizations in which Germans, Italians, Poles, Russians, and every other people will strive to preserve their peculiar customs, languages and institutions. . . . Racial feuds will disrupt the country and make of it a heterogeneous mass of warring factions. . . . Under these influences an American nation would be impossible, and without an American nation the American state would soon succumb to disintegration.[79]

Here appeared a rationale for attacking not only German-American political activity but the very elements of a self-conscious German-American
ethnicity—indeed, of any collective identity cast in ethnic-American
terms. Ohlinger's brand of American nationalism, one with little or no
room for cultural pluralism, would soon dominate nationalist thought as
"100 percent Americanism." The irony is that the National Alliance inadvertently provided him and others with an opening for this narrower
conception of the nation.

Most non-German Philadelphians were not quite ready for such offen-
sives during the neutrality period. In April 1916, the *Public Ledger* could
still maintain that it had "the highest respect for German culture—not
Kultur." Some Philadelphians, however, already had in mind ways to deal
with cultural "hyphens." As Wister put it that year, "we should effectively
discourage all papers printed in any foreign tongue which have for their
purpose the perpetuation of the string tied to the immigrant . . . and that
show any inclination whatever to elevate us to their level."[80]

CHAPTER EIGHT

Intervention, the Anti-German Panic, and the Fall of Public Germanness

THE neighbors came for Louis Schneider at midnight. The North Philadelphia baker had turned down a demand from a local Liberty Loan committee that he buy a Liberty Bond. In the spring of 1918, such refusals to support the American war effort carried a price. Schneider's "place was stormed by members of the Home Defense Reserves," as he told an agent of the federal Bureau of Investigation (BOI). The "residents" who called on Schneider in the middle of the night "[forced] him to subscribe to the Liberty Loan. He was also forced to fly the American flag at his house," according to the woman who reported him to the BOI as "pro-German." Schneider then was bundled off to a police station. After his release, he was questioned by the federal agent. Schneider, a Seventh Day Adventist and naturalized immigrant who had come to the United States thirty years before, tried to explain why he had refused the committee's demand. He had told a committee member that he could not afford to buy a bond, as his bakery business was more than $2,000 in debt. "He denied that he ever made any seditious remarks and said that he had no use for the Kaiser," the agent reported.[1]

Louis Schneider's midnight ordeal was one small incident in the larger anti-German panic that descended on Philadelphia and the nation after America entered the First World War. His harrowing encounter with vigilante neighbors and federal authorities, both bent on rooting out "pro-German" attitudes and enforcing national loyalty, captured key elements of that wartime climate. The patriotism of German Americans had already undergone two years of questioning by the time the United States declared war on Germany in April 1917. American intervention, and the federal government's campaign to mobilize support for the war, escalated that suspicion into hysteria. This anti-German panic expressed itself in vigilante attacks and governmental actions that demanded explicit demonstrations of loyalty from German Americans and the suppression of symbols of German ethnicity. German Philadelphians who failed to buy a Liberty Bond or to show sufficient respect for the war effort could expect to lose their jobs, be turned in to the police or the BOI by their neighbors, or become the victims of small-scale riots on their blocks or at their workplaces. An emerging national security apparatus required thousands of German aliens to register with the police and undertook the surveillance of the city's factories, ethnic newspapers, and *Vereinswesen* in a bid to stifle dissent along with spying and sabotage. As the panic took hold, the line between perceived disloyalty and ethnic cultural expression dissolved.

This onslaught rendered virtually impossible the public expression of a German-American ethnicity during and immediately after the war. Spoken German receded from Philadelphia's streets. Associations suspended ethnic celebrations such as the Cannstatter Volksfest-Verein's once-popular outdoor festival. The National German-American Alliance itself collapsed in 1918. Public expressions of a German-American identity would only become possible again, in a limited way, in the early 1920s. By fostering the anti-German panic and the demand for unhyphenated, "100 percent American" loyalty, the war induced many German Philadelphians to retreat from an ethnic identity, while helping to set the terms for their search for alternatives.

A "PATRIOTIC ANIMOSITY TOWARD EVERYTHING GERMAN"

German Philadelphians, and certainly their middle-class leaders, were aware well before April 1917 that if war with Germany came, they would face the most intense questioning yet of their loyalty. Ethnic strains had eased following President Wilson's reelection in November 1916. Germany's announcement on January 31, 1917, of a renewal of unrestricted submarine warfare, however, and Wilson's breaking of diplomatic relations with Berlin three days later suddenly made war seem probable. While the National Alliance promoted mass meetings and peace resolutions to stave off that prospect, Charles Hexamer in early February also backed Wilson's dismissal of the German ambassador and proposed a loyalty pledge for German Americans that promised they would fight as loyally under Wilson as they had under Lincoln.[2]

By the time Wilson asked Congress for a declaration of war on April 2, the middle-class leadership was in full-scale retreat from its earlier backing of Germany. John B. Mayer joined the executive committee of the mayor's new City Home Defense agency in late March and went on to lead the campaign to sell Liberty Bonds to Philadelphians of German background. "I can emphatically state," Mayer said in response to the president's call, "that the societies with which I am connected will do their duty to America."[3] The middle-class *Philadelphia Demokrat* echoed that pledge on April 3. The reaction the same day of the *Tageblatt*, however, showed that the cross-class unity achieved by German Philadelphia since August 1914 was coming undone. Even as Congress debated Wilson's request, the working-class newspaper clung "to the hope that [war] can and will be avoided." America could have halted German submarine operations in 1915 by insisting on its neutral right to trade with the Central Powers; hence, the subsequent conflicts over undersea warfare were the fault of the United States, the *Tageblatt* argued. "Now it must be said that the United States has no just cause for war against Germany; that Germany does not want war and has not caused it, and responsibility for it cannot be placed on Germany." As the *Public Ledger* pointedly noted, the *Tageblatt* here made "[n]o appeal to its readers to support the American Government." A stubborn adherence to this stance—consonant with the Socialist Party's official opposition to the war—would lead to the arrest of five *Tageblatt* officials in September.[4]

As the timing of the *Tageblatt* arrests indicates, the anti-German panic, in Philadelphia and elsewhere, did not emerge full-blown with America's entry into the war. Fears of spying and sabotage certainly surfaced during the spring of 1917. In late March, the National Security League relayed a report of a shoemaker "of violent pro-German sympathies" who lived in a New Jersey shore town and kept a flock of pigeons "of which he seems to take great care." More substantial grounds for concern emerged on April 10, with a massive explosion that killed 121 workers at the Eddystone Ammunition Corporation plant south of Philadelphia. The *Germantown Independent-Gazette* chided readers in late April for what it called "plot hysteria and spy hysteria," while noting that the "Eddystone horror" had intensified such alarm.[5]

As yet, however, the cultural traits and symbols that defined "Germanness" drew comparatively little hostility from non-German Philadelphians. To some extent, they followed the president's lead. In his April 2 address to Congress, Wilson had stressed that Americans opposed the German government but were "sincere friends" of the German people. They would be proud to prove that friendship to the majority of "men and women of German birth and native sympathy who live among us and . . . who are in fact loyal to their neighbors and to the Government in the hour of test." The *Independent-Gazette* explicitly endorsed the president's distinction. In late April, the newspaper ran a front-page story praising an elderly Germantown businessman who had witnessed Germany's failed democratic revolution of 1848 as a youth in Berlin. This profile featured a picture of the hardware store owner in his Union Army forage cap, above the caption, "An Anti-Kaiser German."[6]

Over the next few months, however, Philadelphians increasingly came to fear their German neighbors not simply as potential spies but as Germans per se. At the same time, demands mounted that Germans as well as other Americans provide positive demonstrations of their loyalty—that they show themselves to be, not hyphenated, but "100 percent" Americans. Behind these developments lay a frustration government officials and patriotic groups felt with the state of public support for the war.[7] They knew that American public opinion was far from unified in April 1917. The Allies might have garnered the sympathy of most Americans during the neutrality period, but actual participation in the conflict was another matter. Irish Americans as well as German Americans, pacifists as well as socialists had all loudly voiced their opposition to intervention. A substantial number of citizens were indifferent, if not hostile, to American entry when it came, while a majority, while willing to defer to their president, likely did not see the war in Wilsonian terms as a crusade for democracy. The prospect of invasion that had unified the European belligerents, moreover, was singularly lacking in a country 3,000 miles distant from the scene of battle. As David Kennedy observed, the Wilson administration therefore "was compelled to cultivate—even to manufacture—public opinion favorable to the war effort." In early April, Wilson created the Committee on Public Information (CPI) to coordinate the government's domestic propaganda and, in essence, sell its war aims to the American people. Under the leadership of the muckraking journalist George Creel, the CPI produced and distributed pamphlets, posters, short films, and press releases and recruited 75,000 citizens to serve as "Four-Minute Men" who would deliver brief, patriotic speeches in movie theaters, churches, and union halls.[8] Philadelphians felt the full force of this propaganda barrage. By April 1918, the city had 200 Four-Minute Men, who became a familiar sight at Liberty Loan rallies and movie houses. They joined indigenous efforts to promote patriotism, such as the sing-alongs organized in city parks and neighborhoods beginning in the summer of 1917. Individual blocks held their own "sings": "[t]he families on both sides of a certain street simply met together to sing over the war songs in honor of their 'boys,'" after having decorated their block with the national colors. Posters, speeches, and music appealing to national loyalty were difficult to avoid, especially during one of the five Liberty Loan campaigns. At these times, "[o]rators were on every street corner; thousands of booths were erected at places of vantage; 'four-minute men' appeared everywhere to stimulate buying."[9]

Initially, the CPI took a relatively liberal approach in its propaganda, seeking to persuade, in the best Progressive manner, by force of fact rather than fear. With time, however, the committee began to spread images of the German enemy as monstrous and bestial. A widely distributed committee poster that made its way to Philadelphia's streets in time for the Third Liberty Loan campaign of April and May 1918 depicted an American doughboy shielding a woman and child from a German soldier. Above this scene ran the appeal, "Halt the Hun!"[10] By the same token, CPI propaganda increasingly stressed a loyalty that left no room for political dissent. This reflected the views of Wilson, who tended to see wartime criticism of his administration as verging on disloyalty.[11]

For those left unenthusiastic by Creel's campaigns, there was always the remedy of coercion. Wilson had promised in April 1917 that, "if there should be disloyalty, it will be dealt with with a firm hand of stern repression," and the government's repressive means mushroomed during the war. In June 1917, Congress passed the Espionage Act, which provided for $10,000 fines and twenty-year prison terms for those who obstructed recruiting, attempted to cause "insubordination, disloyalty, mutiny, or refusal of duty" in the armed forces, or made or conveyed "false reports or false statements with intent to interfere with the operation or success of the military or naval forces of the United States or to promote the success of its enemies." Another provision allowed the postmaster general to ban from the mails any matter "advocating or urging treason, insurrection, or forcible resistance to any law of the United States." The act's wording enabled federal officials, in effect, to punish both criticism of the administration's war policies and "individual casual or impulsive disloyal utterance." These powers were then made explicit in a May 1918 amendment known as the Sedition Act, which outlawed "any disloyal, profane, scurrilous, or abusive language about the form of government of the United States, or the Constitution of the United States, or the flag of the United States," or language that might bring them "into contempt, scorn, contumely, or disrepute."[12]

The burden of enforcing these statutes fell on the Justice Department, its relatively new Bureau of Investigation, established in 1909, and the United States attorneys who represented the department around the country. While the BOI had several hundred agents, its director had gladly accepted a businessman's offer in the spring of 1917 to supplement that force with a "citizens' auxiliary" that would help to monitor enemy aliens. This American Protective League (APL) eventually boasted a nationwide membership of 250,000 volunteers. U.S. Attorney General Thomas Gregory described the APL as assisting federal authorities "in keeping an eye on disloyal individuals and making reports of disloyal utterances." In practice, APL "agents" spied on neighbors and fellow workers, opened mail, committed burglaries, and illegally arrested other Americans. They constituted "a rambunctious, unruly posse comitatus on an unprecedented national scale."[13] Philadelphia's APL chapter managed to "examine" no fewer than 18,275 people between December 1917 and November 1918. Most of these cases concerned draft status, but chapter members also made arrests for "seditious and pro-German remarks," as when an APL operative turned over to the BOI one Franz Meisel, who had allegedly stated that "the Kaiser is going to be in the White House, and President Wilson knows it—America is licked now."[14]

A variety of "patriotic" organizations also worked alongside federal authorities. These ranged from the National Security League (NSL) and the American Defense Society (ADS) to the Patriotic Order Sons of America and the Military Order of the Loyal Legion. The NSL and ADS in particular came to embody a "100 percent Americanism" that sought, in John Higham's words, "universal conformity organized through total national loyalty." This loyalty was to be expressed through visible service and the abandonment of ethnically based cultural differences—especially German or German-American ones. German *Vereine* and the German language became the special targets of these groups by the summer and fall of 1917. German-American organizations that had not publicly adopted resolutions against the German government's actions were charged by the NSL with aiding the enemy. The NSL and the ADS both were agitating by the fall against the teaching of German, which the latter group characterized as having produced, in Germany, "a people of ruthless conqestadors [sic]," making German "not a fit language to teach clean and pure American boys and girls."[15]

During the first six months of American involvement, Wilson, his administration's propaganda and investigatory arms, and the patriotic groups functioned together to intensify the "spy hysteria" and added to it a hysteria over a malevolent German culture. This emerging national climate of fear and hostility was fueled as well by arguments in mass circulation magazines and newspapers for the suppression of the German-language press. Writing in *Outlook*, Hermann Hagedorn depicted the cultural content of German newspapers as the problem: "it is the German atmosphere that makes them the menace they are." By the fall of 1917, as Frederick Luebke wrote, a "fierce hatred of everything German pervaded the country." Place names, food names, and musical offerings were altered to eliminate any trace of German content: Berlin, Iowa, became Lincoln; sauerkraut became liberty cabbage; and Beethoven was banned in Pittsburgh. German-language training was expurgated from school curricula in communities across the nation, patriotic ceremonies featured the burning of German books, and several states restricted the freedom to speak German in public. Acts of violence against German Americans mounted during the winter of 1917–1918 and peaked in April 1918 with the killing of Robert Prager, an immigrant miner who was hung by a mob in Collinsville, Illinois.[16]

As Prager's murder suggests, the anti-German panic flared most intensely in the Midwest, the region with the highest concentration of German immigrants and their descendants.[17] Philadelphia was spared the most extreme manifestations of the hysteria. No German Philadelphians were killed, although some were mobbed. Germantown, Nebraska, became Garland; but Germantown, Philadelphia, kept its name, despite demands from outsiders who assumed, as a local historian put it, "that this was a German community."[18]

Yet if the anti-German panic was somewhat less harsh in Philadelphia, it was harrowing nonetheless, traveling an arc similar to that of the hysteria nationally. During the summer of 1917, local developments combined with the efforts of the federal government and the national patriotic groups to fan fears both of espionage and of German culture. As a major industrial center producing armaments and ships, Philadelphia seemed a logical target for spying and sabotage. Suspicions aroused by the Eddystone disaster were heightened by troubles at the Frankford Arsenal: an explosion and a major fire there in April were followed by a blast in early September that killed two people. The December arrest of a "pro-German" arsenal worker for allegedly spoiling shells confirmed sabotage fears. By the summer's end, the image of the ordinary German Philadelphian as saboteur had emerged in a *Public Ledger* cartoon, "Foxy Fritz" (figure 8.1). Fritz, a portly delicatessen owner with a Kaiser-like mustache, took it as his mission to dynamite City Hall. The newspaper made him a bungling figure of fun. That the staid *Ledger,* however, could even pretend that otherwise innocuous German shopkeepers wanted "to blooie the City Hall" said much about how its readers were coming to view the German Philadelphians in their midst.[19] The city's German-language press also came under fire. In July and August the Philadelphia *North American* repeatedly attacked the *Tageblatt* as openly disloyal, while also portraying the *Morgen-Gazette* as covertly traitorous. "U.S. Sneered At by Phila. Daily German Papers; Twist News," the *North American* blared on July 23.[20]

Once German-language publications came under attack, it was but a short leap to attack the language itself and the culture it expressed. The view that German culture and German political aims were inseparable, that together they formed a subversive *Kultur,* had been promoted during the neutrality period by polemicists such as Gustavus Ohlinger. By the fall of 1917, that view echoed from the *Public Ledger*'s editorial page. On September 16, the newspaper published a long contribution from Lewis R. Harley headlined, "Kultur vs. Civilization: Shows Antagonism Every Way." Harley invoked a recent book by the Belgian scholar Franz de Hovre to portray *Kultur* as a tool of the German empire. In de Hovre's definition, *Kultur* was "the whole of the creation and achievement of the German nation: its language, science, art, literature, industry, army, education, etc., organized and controlled by the German State for the German State." Harley's article, while it drew an invidious contrast between German *Kultur* and English "civilization," did not advocate the aban-

Figure 8.1. "Foxy Fritz—He Unconsciously Helps Subway," 1917. The ordinary German Philadelphian as bumbling saboteur: Foxy Fritz, the delicatessen owner, tries to blow up City Hall but only helps workers building a subway beneath it. However comical, this cartoon hints at the fears of German spies and sabotage that characterized the initial stage of the anti-German panic, in the first months after the American declaration of war. Source: *Public Ledger,* 1 September 1917, p. 20.

donment of German learning. But it reflected the growing belief that German culture was itself a threat, a manifestation of the enemy that must be suppressed.[21]

A crude expression of this view came from the vandals who defaced statues of Goethe and Schiller in the city.[22] The most intense fury, however, was reserved for the German language itself, especially as taught in the public schools. It came to be seen as subverting those most vulnerable Philadelphians, the city's children, and so local patriotic organizations rallied to put an end to the teaching of German. By the end of the year, protests against German-language instruction were lodged with the Philadelphia school board, and a subcommittee was assigned to review German textbooks for objectionable passages. After expurgating some, the subcommittee reported in April 1918 that further action was not advisable. "Then the storm broke," as the *Philadelphia Inquirer* reported. More than a score of organizations demanded that the school board eliminate German-language study. They campaigned, in the *Inquirer*'s words, "against the poisoning of the minds of Young America through the subtle influence of German propaganda hidden in text books on German language." The matter formally came to the board through a petition submitted by twenty-four groups. Most were patriotic organizations, such as the Junior Order United American Mechanics and the Patriotic Order Sons of America. But the petition drew wider support as well; its signers included the city's Rotary Club, the Philadelphia branch of the Woman Suffrage Party of Pennsylvania, and the city Select and Common Councils, which had passed a joint resolution backing the call. Under such pressure, the board voted at its May 14 meeting—unanimously, without discussion, and "[i]n record time"—to discontinue the study of German in the city's high schools at the end of the spring term. The *Inquirer* applauded the step as long overdue: "This work should go on until not one community is left where German is taught."[23]

The school board's vote was only one sign of the "patriotic animosity toward everything German," to use the *Independent-Gazette*'s phrase, that reigned by 1918. That year saw Mayor Thomas B. Smith suspend all city advertising in German-language newspapers. German-language church services likewise came under a cloud. St. Thomas' Evangelical Lutheran Church in Germantown was urged to drop the language from its liturgy, and by December 1918, the Pennsylvania Ministerium was reviewing whether it should remain a German-speaking congregation. The general execration of *Kultur* was effectively if crudely demonstrated in a political cartoon the *Inquirer* ran on its front page on May 12. The sketch caricatured the Kaiser as a chicken atop a dung heap titled, "Kultur[']s Record of Shame"[24] (figure 8.2).

ENFORCING LOYALTY: THE STATE, EMPLOYERS, WORKMATES, AND NEIGHBORS

For thousands of German Philadelphians, the anti-German hysteria of late 1917 and 1918 had consequences far more severe than canceled language classes. Many experienced the war years as a personal ordeal. Residents of German background were subjected to an unprecedented degree of surveillance by federal authorities, factory managers, fellow workers, and neighbors. German Philadelphians regularly encountered petty harass-

MONARCH OF ALL HE SURVEYS   —Copyright, 1918, by The Philadelphia Inquirer Co.

Figure 8.2. "Monarch of All He Surveys," 1918. By 1918, the anti-German panic had broadened into an attack on German culture, depicted as malevolent, subversive, and, here, shameful. This cartoon turned the Kaiser into a chicken and equated *Kultur* with his excrement. Source: *Philadelphia Inquirer,* 12 May 1918, p. 1.

ment, job discrimination, and demands that they buy Liberty Bonds to prove their loyalty; behind such indignities lay a threat of violence. Those who voiced resentment—of the intimidation they suffered, of a war they considered unjust, of the demonization of Germany—might find themselves out of a job, denounced to the authorities, or surrounded by a mob.

Americans of German background were among the first to encounter the "surveillance state,"[25] that collection of federal agencies and quasi-legal affiliates that emerged during World War I to keep track of domestic disloyalty and, as frequently happened, dissent. In Philadelphia, the task of surveillance was taken up by the BOI, working in cooperation with the APL and with U.S. Attorney Francis Fisher Kane; by agents of the U.S.

Army's Military Intelligence Division; and by the Navy Department's Office of Naval Intelligence and the Aide for Information of the Fourth Naval District. Military intelligence officers were particularly concerned with averting sabotage and disruptive accidents in the many Philadelphia factories working on government contracts. The army and navy both established Plant Protection Sections that used inspections and "inside agents" to guard against these eventualities. In the army's case, Plant Protection agents would work with a manufacturer's preexisting system of labor spies. The J. G. Brill Company in West Philadelphia, for example, accepted Military Intelligence's "plan of Interior Organization . . . for incorporation with [its] own service."[26] These federal authorities cooperated with Philadelphia police, although there is evidence of considerable friction between what was then a notoriously corrupt police force and the BOI.[27] Finally, the Philadelphia-based Pennsylvania Council of National Defense, a state-sanctioned volunteer body chaired by George Wharton Pepper, collected reports of disloyalty and disaffection.[28]

Perhaps the single largest class of German Philadelphians to encounter federal oversight were German immigrants who had not naturalized. With the declaration of war, these people technically became "alien enemies." Wilson invoked the sole surviving provision of the Alien and Sedition Acts of 1798, which gave him the power to regulate, arrest, and deport unnaturalized subjects of a hostile power during wartime. By his proclamation, alien enemies were technically barred from coming within one-half mile of forts, arsenals, and munitions plants. Given the prevalence of war-related production in Philadelphia's factories and the many German aliens they employed, U.S. Attorney Kane hesitated to enforce this rule.[29] Eventually, a system of permits was set up under which unnaturalized Germans deemed reliable could work in "restricted areas."[30] In the fall of 1917, Wilson tightened restrictions, requiring all German aliens fourteen years of age or older to register and forbidding them to move without permission. By early 1918, Philadelphia police had registered 6,481 German aliens in the city. Those found to be "to the danger of the public peace and safety" were sent to an internment camp at Gloucester City, New Jersey. Nationwide, by the end of 1918, federal internment camps held more than 6,000 enemy aliens.[31]

The hand of the federal government descended as well on the *Vereinswesen*. The National Alliance, through which Philadelphia's middle-class activists had tried to rationalize German America's associational life, became an inevitable target. Although its officers strove to present the alliance as loyal and law-abiding, and the Central Alliance of Pennsylvania made an impressive showing in Liberty Bond sales, the national organization could not escape the enmity it had earned during the neutrality period. Across the country, alliance branches began to fold or change their names. In January 1918, Senator William H. King of Utah introduced a bill to repeal the National Alliance's congressional charter of 1907. From late February to mid-April, a subcommittee of the Senate Judiciary Committee held hearings on the measure. The first and principal witness called was Gustavus Ohlinger, who repeated his charges that the alliance represented a pan-German threat to American unity. The organization, indeed, "was operating in favor of the German general staff," in that its activities worked against the creation of "a red hot, flaming national spirit" in the United States. That the alliance had sinned against the wartime demand for national unity—by causing, in Ohlinger's words, "opposition to processes of assimilation" and encouraging "a scramble of disjointed nationalities"—was clear from Senator King's questioning of Adolph Timm. King pressed the Philadelphian and long-time alliance secretary to admit that Hexamer's speeches had "urged the German people to maintain their racial distinctions and not become assimilated with and absorbed into the population of our country." The senator evidently saw such advocacy of "Germanism" as a call for German Americans "to constitute themselves a bulwark for Deutschland."[32] Timm put in a faltering performance, but the contemporary climate allowed him little room for an effective defense. To explain the alliance in its own, prewar terms, as an organization that sought to maintain German America so that it could contribute its culture to an evolving America, would have been futile. By 1918, such cultural pluralist arguments were no longer accepted as legitimate. Hence, when King asked Timm, the onetime editor of the alliance's official bulletin, whether that publication's policy was "to urge vigorous unity of the Germans for the purpose of maintaining Germanism," Timm could only answer with a denial: "I do not think so."[33]

The outcome of the hearings was a foregone conclusion; on July 2, 1918, Congress repealed the act that had given the National Alliance its charter. By then, however, the alliance had ceased to exist. Bowing to the inevitable, the executive committee met in Philadelphia on April 11 and agreed to dissolve the national organization, turning its assets over to the American Red Cross.[34] Charles Hexamer did not take part in this final act. In failing health, he had resigned from the presidency of the National Alliance in November 1917, his place taken by Georg von Bosse's son, the Lutheran pastor Siegmund von Bosse. Hexamer had already withdrawn, to some extent, from the city's middle-class *Vereinswesen*, declining in late 1916 to accept another term as president of the German Society of Pennsylvania. After American intervention, his world, like his health, collapsed. He was put under surveillance, expelled from the Art Club and the Manufacturers Club of Philadelphia, to which he had belonged for years, and even refused service in stores. He retreated into seclusion, finally succumbing to his illness in 1921.[35]

Individual *Vereine* in Philadelphia likewise became targets of federal surveillance and investigations. In June 1918, the BOI searched the basement of the German Society building for records of the defunct National Alliance, trying to track down correspondence between Hexamer and a Cincinnati alliance official that allegedly related "to the preparation of a certain list of German sympathizers who could be relied upon to work for the German cause." It seems likely that this rumored list of 16,000 names of draft-age men was in fact drawn up by the alliance to demonstrate its loyalty to the United States. At the Senate hearing in March, Timm had described how the organization was preparing "a statistical compilation of Americans of German birth or extraction, serving in the U.S. Army or Navy during the present war."[36] A BOI agent, aided by an assistant U.S. attorney, interviewed Mayer (now the German Society's president), the society's treasurer, its second vice president, and Timm. The agent came up with some alliance bills and memoranda that appeared to date from the neutrality period, but nothing more incriminating. Federal authorities likewise kept tabs on the Philadelphia Turngemeinde and the German Hospital.[37] Smaller associations with lower profiles, such as the Fischler Sangerbund and the Karpathen Saengerbund, also came under federal scrutiny, although no evidence of wrongdoing on their part emerged.[38] In addition, agents of the BOI and the Office of Naval Intelligence undertook to visit German, Austrian and Hungarian societies, whether in search of draft violators or to gauge the extent of pro-German sentiment.[39]

Ordinary German Philadelphians, too, could fall under the investigatory gaze of BOI and Plant Protection agents. The records of the U.S. attorney's office for 1917 and 1918 document more than fifty cases of Philadelphians accused of or investigated for talk or behavior that was either allegedly pro-German or of a suspicious "German" nature. These cases, most of which date from 1918, include letters written to U.S. Attorney Kane denouncing neighbors, workmates, and tenants, reports filed by BOI agents, and referrals from other agencies and private companies.[40] This documentation reflects matters that made their way to Kane's office; the actual number of such cases handled by the BOI was almost certainly higher, for the bureau evidently conducted pro-German investigations that are not noted in Kane's files.[41] Similar investigations were undertaken by the Plant Protection Section of Military Intelligence, mostly in relation to allegedly pro-German factory workers.[42] Taken together, the material preserved by Kane's office and the Plant Protection Section provides a unique window onto how ordinary German Philadelphians experienced the anti-German panic.

It is difficult to glean from the material preserved by federal authorities how common resentment about the war was among German Philadelphians and what form it took. Many of the denunciatory letters in Kane's files simply accused a particular individual of "pro-German" sentiments, as with a note from "An American" who reported a widow as "a great

German sympathizer." Accusatory letters that related a suspect's statements or actions may, of course, have done so falsely. Investigators' reports appear somewhat more trustworthy, yet they, too, frequently passed along second-hand accusations. Relatively rarely did an investigator hear questionable language at first hand, as when one was told by the wife of an enemy alien that "she had not bought any Liberty Bonds or Thrift Stamps . . . because she was a German subject and that her sympathies were with them, because she had relatives fighting in the German Army, and she would not help the United States to buy ammunition to kill the Germans."[43]

These letters and reports, however, do suggest the kinds of offenses that might draw down the wrath of neighbors, fellow workers, and employers. Sometimes, the mere fact of being a German immigrant could trigger suspicion. The superintendent of the Brill Car Works in West Philadelphia, for example, put a German-born cabinet maker with sixteen years at the plant "under constant observation, both at his home and at the works, for about two months, not on account of anything he . . . had done or said, but, because he is a German and picks as his friends and associates other Germans employed at the works." The superintendent found nothing suspicious, and concluded that the man "was a loyal citizen."[44] More frequently, informants cited provocative language or an unwillingness to display such signs of loyalty as the flag. An anonymous "patriotic citizen" complained to Kane about a second-generation German immigrant of draft age "saying he would rather go to jail than fight against the Germans. He refuses to hang out an American flag and his wife says he will not hang out any flag if it cannot be a German one." The U.S. attorney handed this letter over to the BOI for investigation.[45] Kane likewise forwarded to the bureau an unsigned note denouncing one man who "will not let an American flag fly from his house." The letter went on to attack several neighbors, apparently on the same block. "The one 3446 will not allow her children to speak only german [sic] and Otto at 3447 Schwell and Robb 3445 and 3440 they all stick together. . . . [T]he whole bunch of Huns got together and made little of the country."[46]

Perhaps the standard most frequently invoked to gauge the loyalty of ordinary German Philadelphians was whether they had purchased Liberty Bonds. A manager at the American Asbestos Company in suburban Norristown wrote that "we consider the Liberty Bond test the best test as to whether [our workers] are backing up the Government."[47] Manufacturers in Philadelphia similarly cited the success of Liberty Loan campaigns on their shop floors as proof of the national allegiance of their workforces.[48] Many other Philadelphians employed this "test" as well. When seven householders in the Thirty-ninth Police District would not pledge to buy bonds after being canvassed in the spring of 1918, the district's Liberty Loan Committee chairman forwarded their pledge slips to the U.S. attorney. "The men say that these particular individuals appear to be pro-german [sic] in sentiment, and would bear investigation," the chairman wrote. Kane promised to have the BOI "investigate all the people that you have mentioned."[49] Kane wrote elsewhere that "it is a man's right to refuse to subscribe to either Liberty bonds or the War Chest. Of course, a refusal to subscribe to the Loan, coupled with disloyal remarks, might be evidence to be considered with other matters in determining a man's loyalty." Given the significance attached to the bonds, German Philadelphians felt under considerable pressure, if not coerced, to purchase them. The German-born wife of a worker at Midvale Steel complained to one informant that "this was a fine free country when they make you buy liberty bonds whether you want them or not."[50]

The consequences of expressing pro-German sympathies, failing to put out a flag, or refusing to subscribe during a loan drive could be severe. As these cases show, such actions could trigger denunciations and investigations by federal authorities. It is not clear how many of the fifty-five cases in Kane's files led to formal prosecutions, but the experience of talking with a federal agent could be intimidating enough. Agents often gave suspects who were not charged a verbal warning. When the BOI investigated a Midvale Steel worker who had been dismissed from his previous job at a munitions plant for allegedly being "Pro-German" and a "dangerous" character, the man told an agent that if the latter "could prove anything on him to 'go to it.'" This naturalized citizen was promptly taken down to headquarters, where he "apologized . . . for his defiant manner. He was given a good strong talk and after the usual warning was released." As this case also indicates, "pro-German" statements could get one fired. One firm reported to the Plant Protection Section that "if we find anyone showing any indications of being disloyal, we get rid of him."[51]

The ultimate sanction against pro-German talk or behavior was violence. In the charged atmosphere of wartime Philadelphia, residents could and did take the law into their own hands. German workers at the Edward G. Budd Manufacturing Company discovered this the hard way. The Budd plant produced steel helmets and aerial bombs for the Army, employing 3,100 men and 100 women.[52] Two former workers complained in July 1918 of "a large number" of unnaturalized Germans and Hungarians at the plant who were "pro-German in feeling." These informants related the tale of "a German named Al. Wertz," who inadvertently revealed his opinion of the wartime demand for loyalty one day when the plant was burning an effigy of the Kaiser:

During the proceedings Wertz turned to a lot of the Germans near him and thinking no other people were within hearing, and said that he wondered what they were going to do now with the Kaiser, how they were going to burn him, face up or face down? Wertz said . . . that they ought to burn the Kaiser face down so they (the Americans) could kiss his _____.[53]

This remark "was overheard by someone not intended," and an enraged crowd of workers apparently took off after Wertz, for he "escaped from the plant by jumping out the window in his overalls, leaving his street clothing and watch and chain behind him." Other employees ran into similar trouble. When a troop train steamed past the factory on March 28, 1918, eight German and Austrian workers were heard to make "slurring remarks about the troops." One, a German named William Burk, allegedly said "that he would rather put his hand under a trip-hammer than fight for the United States." The following day, "the Americans" at the plant refused to go to work unless the company fired the eight men; Burk "was made to get down on his hands and knees and apoligize [sic] and kiss the Flag." All eight lost their jobs.[54]

Neighborhood pressures on German Philadelphians to demonstrate national loyalty could be just as intense. These ranged from informal harassment or ostracism to mob actions. One German-born woman told a BOI agent in December 1918 that she was "sorry she can't speak better English, as some of her neighbors have made it very unpleasant for her on this account in the last two years." The woman, accused of being pro-German, stated that she loved the United States and had bought Liberty Bonds and War Savings Stamps. More-or-less subtle coercion was exerted through neighborhood gatherings in support of the war, whether "block sings" or such crowd events as the "roast" that followed a flag-raising ceremony in Kensington. Residents discovered an oil painting of the Kaiser and a German flag; these objects were "rushed by a crowd of 1,000 persons to a big bonfire. . . . Amid fire and smoke, yells and the strains of The Star Spangled Banner, they vanished into oblivion and ashes."[55] Crowd intimidation could escalate to mob attacks, as Louis Schneider discovered and as a West Philadelphia woman suggested in informing on her neighbors, a family named Rampe. "These people . . . are constantly creating disturbances by their pro-German talk and behavior," she complained. "There have been several near riots here recently and, if something is not done, there is liable to be a repetition of deplorable (though in some ways commendable) law-lessness."[56]

Curbing the *Tageblatt*

Government intimidation and social pressures could operate independently, but they also could work together to coerce German Philadelphians into positive displays of national loyalty. The prime example of this phenomenon in wartime Philadelphia was the arrest and prosecution of editors and officers of the Philadelphia *Tageblatt*. Two of the newspaper's editors and three other *Tageblatt* officials ultimately were convicted of violating the Espionage Act of 1917 by publishing articles slanted so as to support the German war effort. The *Tageblatt* affair entered the larger history of American civil liberties when it joined a string of other Espionage and Sedition Act cases reviewed by the United States Supreme Court after the war. Dissents in these cases by Justices Oliver Wendell Holmes Jr. and Louis D. Brandeis laid the foundations for the case law governing freedom of speech and, in particular, for the "clear and present danger" standard in First Amendment law.[57] The affair's significance for German Philadelphia, however, lies in its dynamics. The *Tageblatt* case illustrates how the emerging anti-German panic, a sensationalistic press, and a nation-state given vastly greater domestic powers by the war could combine to force a major German-American institution into line—and to some degree curb its usefulness as a vehicle for ethnic identity.

The *Tageblatt*'s collision with the federal government grew out of its recalcitrance over American participation in the war. The newspaper clearly resented that participation, both on general antiwar grounds and because it meant war with Germany. The bills of indictment against the *Tageblatt* included facsimile reproductions of more than three dozen stories and editorials it published between April and September of 1917. These reveal a lively distaste for conscription, the Wilson administration, and the Allies, and a bent for reporting the war in ways that celebrated German successes. On May 10, for example, the *Tageblatt* decried the prospect of draftees serving "the fatherland of the dollar as mere cannon fodder."[58] A June 6 editorial referred to the Wilson administration as "autocratic and imperialistic." The newspaper, moreover, had not shaken the habit of describing German advances in favorable terms. A May 9 headline announced "A Brilliant Success of German Troops," while a July 7 story on the sinking of an American steamer by a German submarine carried the headline, "Got Her Already."[59]

Such coverage left the *Tageblatt* open to charges of disloyalty, and in the summer of 1917 the *North American* began its campaign against the working-class daily. While the *North American* aimed some shots at the *Morgen-Gazette*, it concentrated most of its fire on the *Tageblatt*, publishing a series of stories in July and August under the byline of reporter Einar Barfod. Barfod had an easy story: all he had to do was to pick up the day's *Tageblatt*, scan it for provocative statements, translate them, and write his own article. The result was a barrage of reports under sensational headlines such as: "Defeat of U.S. Men by Kaiser's Troops, Plea of *Tageblatt*," "*Tageblatt* Squirts More German Poison against U.S. Cause," and, "Ach, Yes! *Tageblatt* 'Dopes' Its War News to Suit Holy Kaiser."[60]

These stories evoked an explosive reaction. *North American* readers made their anger known to U.S. Attorney Kane. By the end of August, one correspondent was warning him of "trouble, perhaps bloodshed," if "immediate action" were not taken to suppress the *Tageblatt* and jail its editors for treason. "Undoubtedly the indignation of the people is growing, judging from the comments one hears on every side." The U.S. attorney, in fact, was "very largely of the opinion" this correspondent expressed.[61] Since at least mid-July, Kane had been looking into the *Tageblatt*'s coverage, and through August he pondered how to bring the newspaper's "very objectionable propaganda . . . within the terms of the law."[62] As he explained to Attorney General Gregory on August 27, a successful prosecution of the *Tageblatt* under the new Espionage Act would involve the difficult task of proving the falsity of statements it had made to promote the success of the nation's enemies. Kane also heard calls to bring charges of treason, despite the probability, as one correspondent put it, that "a conviction cannot be got."[63]

Ultimately, the U.S. attorney decided to proceed on both legal fronts. On September 10, 1917, acting on a warrant that invoked the Espionage Act, federal agents raided the *Tageblatt* offices and arrested the newspaper's managing editor, Martin Darkow, and its business manager, Herman Lemke. In the next few days, authorities detained the editor in chief, Louis Werner; an editorial writer, Waldemar Alfredo, who was subsequently released; and two officers of the Philadelphia Tageblatt Publishing Association—its president, Peter Schaefer, and its treasurer, Paul Vogel.[64] On September 15, Darkow, Lemke, Werner, Schaefer, and Vogel were indicted for violating the Espionage Act by making "false reports with intent to promote the success of the enemies of the United States." This indictment, which was later expanded, essentially charged the defendants with intentionally falsifying dispatches in ways that would weaken the American cause and strengthen that of Germany. They had, for example, published a story regarding a handful of suicides among American troops under the headline, "Many Suicides in Pershing's Army Reported."[65] Kane, however, also won an indictment from the federal grand jury that charged Werner and Darkow with treason.[66]

Kane knew he was venturing into unknown legal territory by seeking treason convictions against the editors of a newspaper. At the trial in March 1918, the U.S. attorney tried to make the case, as he noted afterward, that the publication of certain articles by Werner and Darkow amounted not simply to disloyal expression, but to treasonous acts. The "inevitable effect" of those articles, Kane maintained, "would be an obstruction of the government's war programme." Even in 1918, however, this argument was too much for the trial judge. He directed the jury to return a verdict of not guilty, and Werner and Darkow were acquitted.[67]

The Espionage Act indictment remained, however, and here the defendants' luck ran out. In September 1918, after a five-day trial, a jury took less than two hours to find all five men guilty of conspiracy to violate the Espionage Act. As editors, Werner and Darkow also were convicted of writing and editing articles and headlines that showed they had altered dispatches taken from other newspapers to bear a false, and seditious, meaning. Both were sentenced to five years in prison, while Lemke received a two-year prison sentence, and Schaefer and Vogel were given jail terms of a year each.[68] On appeal, the Supreme Court reversed the convictions of Schaefer and Vogel but affirmed those of Werner, Darkow, and Lemke. Writing for the majority, in a decision handed down in March 1920, Justice Joseph McKenna dismissed the contention that the *Tageblatt* convictions violated the freedoms of speech and of the press guaranteed by the Constitution. Brandeis, in a dissent concurred in by Holmes, invoked the "clear and present danger" test Holmes had first formulated in early 1919. Here, Brandeis pointed to the hysteria of the war years: "[N]o jury acting in calmness could reasonably say that any of the publications set forth in the indictment was of such a character or was made under such circumstances as to create a clear and present danger either that they would obstruct recruiting or that they would promote the success of the enemies of the United States." To hold that they could be suppressed as false "subjects to new perils the constitutional liberty of the press," and those perils would persist long after the war. "In peace, too, men may differ widely as to what loyalty to our country demands; and an intolerant majority, swayed by passion or by fear, may be prone in the future, as it has often been in the past, to stamp as disloyal opinions with which it disagrees."[69]

In peace, many Philadelphians evidently thought better of the convictions that threatened three old men, two of them seriously ill, with imprisonment. More than 10,000 people signed petitions asking President Wilson to pardon Werner, Darkow, and Lemke. Even Kane, now in private practice, agreed that the defendants' pardon applications should be granted. Noting that "we are now to all intents and purposes, at peace with Germany," he told his successor in April 1920 that "[a]ll that justice required has been already secured and it would serve no good purpose now to send any one of the three defendants to jail." Within two months, Wilson pardoned the three.[70]

While the *Tageblatt* defendants ultimately survived their ordeal, their case illustrates how the anti-German panic and the unprecedented wartime powers of the federal government could combine to mute one of the major voices of German Philadelphia. Federal authorities never actually shut the newspaper down, even in the immediate wake of the September 1917 raid. But postal officials invoked the Espionage Act to revoke the *Tageblatt*'s second-class mailing privileges on September 21, effectively ending its circulation outside Philadelphia.[71] Under federal legislation passed in October 1917, the newspaper was forced to file English translations of articles on "political subjects" with the Post Office Department, and Kane's office continued to monitor its contents. The U.S. attorney also appears to have made a deal with the publishers in March 1918 that guaranteed a curbing of the *Tageblatt*'s tone. That month, Darkow and Werner resigned from the newspaper, and its publishers "then promised me that its policy would be all that the government desired," Kane told Gregory in May. Monitoring of the newspaper showed that "the publishers . . . have carried out their promises." That Kane employed an element of coercion in extracting those promises from the newspaper's officials is evident from his description elsewhere of what he told them at the time: "Of course, I could only say to them that they would be entitled to have their subsequent conduct taken into consideration."[72] As a threat to the Wilson administration, the *Tageblatt* had been tamed. As a vehicle for voicing the concerns of working-class German Philadelphians and expressing the German component of their identities, it had been crippled.

The Fall of Public Germanness

In early 1919, Louis Werner scolded the chairman of a public meeting on the *Tageblatt*'s future for having induced him to address the gathering. In a letter submitted to the newspaper, Werner reminded readers that he and his fellow defendants were still appealing their case and were only free on $35,000 bail. How anyone could expect them to discuss the newspaper in a public meeting under these conditions "is beyond my understanding," Werner wrote, the more so in that four detectives and a police officer were rumored to have been in attendance. The former editor was unwilling to risk further damage to his case and that of the other defendants by speaking in public meetings, "as long as the state of war exists. On the other hand, we are completely prepared to provide all desired information in private meetings."[73]

Werner's legal plight was not, of course, shared by most German Philadelphians in 1919. In a larger sense, however, his withdrawal from the public stage reflected a more general retreat—that of German ethnicity from public view. The hysteria of the war years forced German Philadelphians, for their own safety, essentially to abandon most public expressions of German and German-American identity. Non-German Philadelphians caught up in the anti-German panic took their own steps to efface public symbols of Germanness and German culture, as we have seen. The social pressure reflected in those acts, however, also induced German Philadelphians themselves to hide such symbols.

This cultural self-policing could reach ludicrous extremes. In the spring of 1918, for example, John P. Nicholson, the commander in chief of Philadelphia's Military Order of the Loyal Legion, wrote to U.S. Attorney Kane complaining about the insignia used by a brewery's delivery wagons. "[I]t is about time that the 'Imperial Eagle,' which is so prominently displayed on the Blinders of the harness of the Bergner & Engel Co. should be removed," Nicholson harrumphed, "especially when they are made an instrument of disloyalty, and women, as I witnessed, would pull the horse's head down for the purpose of kissing the Eagle, when the teams are delivering beer." Kane, who had already spoken with the company's president, called "Mr. Bergner" in again and learned that he had painted out the eagles on his wagons "and is going to obliterate them from his blankets and elsewhere in his business, substituting the American eagle wherever possible." Self-policing, however, could extend to symbols with greater local resonance than the eagles on Bergner & Engel beer wagons. The German Hospital, one of the pillars of the city's middle-class *Verein-swesen*, changed its name to Lankenau Hospital during the war, taking the name of the man who figured centrally in its early growth.[74]

The fear of violence that lay behind such alterations surfaced in a remarkable way in June 1918, as German associations prepared to take part in a July 4 "Parade of Nations" organized in response to a nationwide call from Wilson. The parade would see thousands of immigrants and their children marching, ethnic group by ethnic group, down Broad Street and toward Independence Hall, where they would pledge their loyalty to the United States. Some of these marchers, in fact, would enliven the procession by wearing their "native costume"—but not the Germans. They were specifically instructed to wear only dark suits and straw hats, and to leave behind the banners of their *Vereine*.[75] "Neither Verein flags nor Verein badges, nor any other flag, banner, or badge, may be displayed, except for pure American ones," the now-tamed *Tageblatt* told its readers. As the newspaper reported, "it is obvious that no items will be shown that could give offense."[76] At the same time, the *Tageblatt* assured potential marchers that the authorities would guarantee their safety. In a twice-repeated phrase, the newspaper told German participants that they would find "protection under the star-spangled banner."[77]

Vereine that traditionally had put versions of a German ethnic identity on display likewise felt forced to withdraw from public view. The German Society of Pennsylvania, which had regularly celebrated German Day every October in the years leading up to the declaration of war, chose not to mark it in 1917 and 1918, "due to the war situation."[78] The Cannstatter Volks-fest-Verein found it impossible to hold its yearly outdoor festival in 1917 "because of the outbreak of war with Germany," and was not able to put one on again until 1920. Even then, the festivals of 1920 and 1922 were one-day affairs, unlike the three-day celebrations that preceded American intervention. By 1922, the association found its membership figures suffering appreciably due to Prohibition; potential members presumably found it difficult to imagine a Cannstatter event without beer. Membership that year was down to 751, compared with 1,015 in 1916. The Volksfest-Verein's troubles in this regard were an indirect outgrowth of the national anti-German hysteria. Prohibition activists used the image of the subversive German-American brewer in their successful wartime campaign for the Eighteenth Amendment. Even before the Volstead Act took effect, drys persuaded the federal government to enact a wartime ban on the manufacture of beer and wine, which went into force on May 1, 1919.[79]

Perhaps the most striking sign of the sinking public profile of German ethnicity was the shrinking public use of the German language. German Philadelphians, it appears, began to avoid speaking it in the open. Across the city during the war, Louis Werner's daughter, Minna, recalled, "the use of German on the streets dropped off very considerably." English even began to make significant inroads into the city's dwindling German-language press. In 1918, the *Morgen-Gazette* merged with the Philadelphia *Demokrat* to form the *Philadelphia Gazette-Democrat*. This left the *Tageblatt* as the only exclusively German-language daily in the city, for the new newspaper boasted that it published its columns "in both English and German," making it "the leading English-and-German newspaper in the country."[80]

A retreat from public German identity carried out on so wide a scale could not help but have some impact on private expressions of Germanness. Wartime pressures could hit close to home, in the form of door-to-door canvassing for Liberty Bonds, or even reach inside, as Schneider found. Those pressures in turn could dampen ethnic identity in fundamental ways. Esther Schuchard Browne, for example, who grew up in Kensington, recalled how the war heightened her family's distance from things German. Her father was born in Illinois to an immigrant family that had to return to Germany after the death of his father, a Lutheran pastor. Browne's father came back to the United States as a young man. After America entered the war, he told her German-born mother that "she should stop immediately talking German, and especially in the streets, and she'd better stop talking it at home, too . . . to get out of the habit," Browne said. "Because she would just . . . call down insults and unpleasant experiences on herself." As a result, English became the common language at home for Browne and her siblings. Similarly, some individuals sought to obscure their German origins by changing a basic element of their identity: their names. August Schwimmer, a painter at a ship repair company who was the American-born son of a German immigrant, confessed to a BOI agent in May 1918 that he had been using the name August Henry Stone. "He said his reason for assuming the name of Stone was it sounded more English, he was unable to get employment under the name of Schwimmer," the agent reported. Another Philadelphian, George Washington Ochs, entered a court petition for a change of last name to Oakes. "Your petitioner," this man wrote, "has no purpose or reason in changing the spelling of his father's name, except the desire to relieve his sons of a Teutonic appellation which he believes will arouse hostility and prove an unnecessary burden in their future social, personal, commercial, and professional relations."[81]

The shock of the war had a lasting legacy. The pressures from ordinary Philadelphians and a more powerful wartime state embodied in the anti-German panic rendered public expressions of German ethnic identity virtually impossible during the war, and problematic thereafter. Only gradually would those expressions reappear in the 1920s, and then they would be markedly subdued. The war likewise narrowed American nationalism in a way that made it very difficult to claim a specifically German-American identity. The definition of true Americanism as unhyphenated had emerged with force during the neutrality period, but American intervention brought it to dominance. This happened in no small part because the state itself became, for the first time, "a major participant in articulating the nationalist discourse and in enforcing a specifically antiliberal, chauvinistic conception of the nation," as Cecilia O'Leary wrote. "One hundred percent Americanism" singled out German Americans as well as Irish Americans during the war years, but it would soon enough confront all immigrant groups. That potential was apparent even at the 1918 Parade of Nations, which the *Inquirer* interpreted as showing "that the 'melting pot' has welded the Nation into one people, under one flag and under one Constitution."[82] Such views could not accommodate the paired German and American flags of the 1916 war relief bazaar or the brand of cultural pluralism preached by the National Alliance. Indeed, the wartime state greatly encouraged 100 percent Americanism by destroying the alliance, for that act silenced a powerful voice for a pluralist idea of the nation. At the same time, the *Tageblatt*'s curbing showed the rightward tilt of state repression. The government went after the newspaper primarily because it seemed pro-German. Yet the *Tageblatt*'s opposition to American intervention was driven both by ethnic resentment and socialist commitments. When the Justice Department brought the newspaper to heel, it managed to tame a radical voice, in line with the government's larger repression of leftist antiwar dissent.[83] The new American nationalism was narrower in political as well as ethnocultural terms; if it had little room for hyphenated Americans, it had less for hyphenated Americans with left-wing views.

Georg von Bosse, that tireless champion of Philadelphia's *Deutschtum,* felt the shift in climate. "After thirty years of activity [in America], I am powerfully drawn back to the old homeland," he wrote in 1920. "I feel alien among this people, more alien than ever."[84] Von Bosse would nurse his resentments and try to maintain his piece of Philadelphia's Germandom. Others, especially the children of immigrants, would take stock of the subdued ethnicity that was their lot in the 1920s and reach for new identities.

PART FOUR

Reshaping Identities in the 1920s

CHAPTER NINE

An Ethnicity Subdued

IN the fall of 1920, the wooden box that for three years had encased Germantown's monument to its immigrant founders finally came down. The memorial, conceived by the National German-American Alliance to commemorate the German role in American history, had been finished in the spring of 1917, just in time for the War Department to board it up. The government took "this precaution because of misconceptions that prevailed as to the purposes of the memorial," in the delicately chosen words of the *Germantown Independent-Gazette*. Those "misconceptions" persisted after the First World War. Controversy raged during 1919 over whether a female figure adorning the monument was, in fact, "Germania triumphant," as one local critic put it.[1] Even after an investigation by the Site and Relic Society of Germantown found "nothing unpatriotic" about the boxed-up statue, a local branch of the Junior Order United American Mechanics denounced it as "typifying a form of so-called civilization and kultur that Americans will want to forget."[2]

It was thus with some caution that a committee of local notables arranged what were later called "modest dedicatory ceremonies" for the "Founders' Monument." On November 10, 1920, at Vernon Park, Mayor J. Hampton Moore formally accepted the memorial on behalf of the city of Philadelphia from a representative of the War Department. The dedication featured singing by Germantown High School students, speeches from the mayor and descendants of the "Pioneers of 1683," and a crowd of onlookers numbering in the thousands. "Nothing spectacular was attempted, but a simple program was carried out with good effect," the *Independent-Gazette* reported.[3]

Without question, the statue's dedication was a simpler affair than the unveiling of its "cornerstone" on the same site a dozen years before. But the 1920 event also marked a virtual erasure of the German-American ethnic presence that had loomed so large in 1908. Then, some 10,000 National Alliance members and delegates from the city's *Vereine* had marched with Germantowners to Vernon Park, and alliance president Charles Hexamer himself had spoken. By 1920, Hexamer was dying, the National Alliance was dead, and only one representative of Philadelphia's *Vereinswesen* was to be found on the roll of the arrangements committee: John B. Mayer, president of the German Society of Pennsylvania. The monument itself bore echoes of the National Alliance's devotion to German-American history; the closing speaker took care to point out one panel depicting "the service of the Germans in American wars." Yet the focus of the 1920 dedication was on the town founders themselves, as the afternoon's speeches attested. By reading German-American history out of the monument's meaning, the ceremony averted what the *Independent-Gazette* referred to as "antagonism."[4]

The careful unveiling of the Germantown Founders' Monument, calculated to avoid "undue splutter and demonstration,"[5] reflected in microcosm German Philadelphia's situation during the 1920s. That the monument could see the light of day at all suggested an ebbing of the hysteria of the war years. Yet, as the caution of the arrangements committee indicates, enough anti-German feeling remained to keep the public profile of German ethnicity in the city low. As the decade progressed, ethnic associations such as the German Society would take tentative steps back into public view, but never again would they act with the aggressiveness of the years before 1917. The subdued public face of German Philadelphia, however, also owed something to deeper structural factors. Prohibition and an ongoing dearth of German immigrants battered the *Vereinswesen*, which continued its long-term decline. Secular associations, German Catholic parishes and German Lutheran congregations faced falling memberships, mergers, or extinction.

For those who left the *Vereinswesen*, and even for some who stayed, the 1920s marked a turning point, a time when many German Philadelphians reshaped their identities so as to distance themselves from their German origins. The story of those redefinitions is told in the book's final chapters. To some extent, however, such reworkings reflected both division and change within the *Vereinswesen* itself. For that world did not simply shrink. It also altered internally during the interwar years, as some associations, particularly working-class *Vereine* and German Catholic parishes, increasingly acquired multiethnic memberships.

THE SECULAR *VEREINSWESEN*: OLD TROUBLES AND NEW MEMBERS

Looking back in 1929 over a decade of dwindling enrollments, an observer of the city's German Lutheran Sunday schools pinned hopes for their survival on a renewed "strong immigration of fellow believers from Europe."[6] Such wishes were fated to disappointment. In 1920, Philadelphia's German-born population numbered 39,766, a figure about half that at the turn of the century. By 1930, the number of German-born had fallen by another 1,800; ten years later, it was down to 27,286. The decline was slowed but not halted by a slight upsurge in German immigration to the United States in the 1920s that peaked at mid-decade. Ethnic Germans, of course, came to the city from Austria, Hungary, and other nations aside from Germany. Yet the overall number of native speakers of German, too, was in decline. German was the mother tongue of 55,702 white, foreign-born Philadelphians in 1920; by 1930, that figure had fallen to 52,489.[7]

Declining immigration, combined with wartime persecution, translated into a significantly smaller secular *Vereinswesen*. This much seems clear from a comparison of figures provided by a 1911 national directory of German-American organizations and a 1933 accounting published by the *Philadelphia Gazette-Democrat*. Between those two years, the number of German singing societies in Philadelphia fell from sixty-one to thirty-eight, while the total of German veterans' organizations dropped from thirty-three to nineteen. The city likewise lost two of the eight *Turnvereine* that had existed in 1911.[8]

The city's middle-class associational world was a shadow of its former self in the 1920s. The German-American Central Alliance of Pennsylvania had managed to survive the war, but it was a hollowed-out structure. In 1910, the Central Alliance's Philadelphia branch counted 179 member *Vereine*; it claimed sixty-six in 1932.[9] The German Society of Pennsylvania did maintain a fairly stable male membership, but only until the end of the 1920s. The society listed 609 male members in 1925 and 640 in 1929.[10] As a 1944 history of the society noted, however, "[i]n the last twenty years . . . our losses by death have exceeded the gain in new members."[11] The Women's Auxiliary of the society, on the other hand, not only retained its prewar membership edge over the society but to some extent flourished. Although the war years dented its rolls, the auxiliary by 1925 claimed 971 members, more than had belonged during the mid-1910s. Membership nevertheless fell toward the end of the decade, reaching 744 in 1929.[12] The 1920s brought harder times to the Cannstatter Volksfest-Verein. As a 1923 history of the group noted, its "yearly festivities" were "instrumental in keeping our members together," and their wartime interruption presumably contributed to the jolting drop in membership it suffered between 1916 and 1922. However, the history explicitly blamed what it called "the disastrous Prohibition [law]" for the Volksfest-Verein's membership woes, and the Volstead Act also seems to have hurt the group financially. Repeal, unfortunately, coincided with the Great Depression. As one chronicler wrote, the quarter-century after 1923 "was not especially successful for the association, for the alcohol law and later the Depression greatly damaged the Verein."[13]

Verein officials had complained before the war about a lack of interest in German associational life among the rising generation. That the war and Prohibition likely accentuated that indifference is suggested not only by the troubles of once-popular organizations such as the Volksfest-Verein, but also by the stagnant readership of the *Gazette-Democrat,* the city's largest German-language daily. The *Gazette-Democrat,* formed in 1918 by the merger of the Philadelphia *Demokrat* with the *Philadelphia Morgen-Gazette,* had a respectable circulation of 51,612 in 1925. This figure, however, barely exceeded the combined 1915 readership of its two predecessors.[14] The *Gazette-Democrat* essentially maintained this level into the 1930s, showing a 1935 circulation of 50,160. Yet the newspaper undoubtedly was losing readers within Philadelphia at a greater rate than these numbers suggest, for it appears to have sustained its circulation figures by buying up a series of failing German-language journals outside of the city. By 1940, in any event, readership had fallen to 41,750.[15]

Ultimately, the *Gazette-Democrat* faced the same dilemma as the rest of institutional German Philadelphia: German immigrants formed its base, and without substantial replenishments from Germany, that base was dying off. The nature of the newspaper's readership is suggested by a collection of complaint letters triggered by the John Wanamaker Department Store's 1932 decision to eliminate its daily advertising in the *Gazette-Democrat.* This cost-cutting measure induced at least 132 subscribers to write to the newspaper in protest. Thirty-four of these letters survive. Their authors complained, in essence, that they had relied on Wanamaker's advertisements as a guide to shopping and wanted them back. Not surprisingly, almost all of the letters were from female writers, suggesting that the *Gazette-Democrat,* like other German-language newspapers at the turn of the century and after, had successfully implemented a strategy of recruiting women readers.[16]

That female readership, however, was as vulnerable to erosion as the *Vereinswesen* in general. Almost half of the thirty-four letters addressed to this German-language newspaper were in English. In nearly a quarter of the letters, moreover, the authors identified themselves as long-time *Gazette-Democrat* readers, with six writers stating that they had taken the newspaper and its predecessors for at least twenty years.[17] This suggested that a significant segment of the daily's subscribers were of middle age or older, an audience the newspaper would lose to death in the not-too-distant future. That younger readers, particularly the children of immigrants, were less than attached to the *Gazette-Democrat* is indicated by two letters, written in English, by women on behalf of their mothers.[18] As Mrs. A. Castor wrote:

> This paper of yours has been in our family for years[.] my Mother is german and enjoys reading your paper and I of course am interested in the ad. of Wanamakers it being the only paper we buy now and Wanamaker ad is not in any more[.] I feel I must drop your paper and buy a paper with the Wanamaker ad

in it as I do all my shopping there and yet my Mother does not want to give it up[.][19]

For these correspondents, the *Gazette-Democrat*'s loss of Wanamaker's advertising was more a matter of concern for their parents' generation; given their language skills, they could always subscribe to an English-language paper "with the Wanamaker ad in it."

Such complaints suggest as well that consumer culture continued to attract German Philadelphians, in ways that enabled some to de-emphasize their ethnic identity while partaking of new collective identities of consumption, including those open especially to women. Certainly, the women who wrote to the *Gazette-Democrat* in German had no trouble thinking of themselves as both ethnic Germans and department store shoppers. Castor, however, had reached the point where her identity as a consumer clearly outweighed any ethnic sense of self. She was quite ready to drop a German-language newspaper out of devotion to Wanamaker's.

Indeed, postwar changes in the nature of mass culture made it an even more powerful competitor for the attention of German Philadelphians. Commercial culture, of course, was still subject to ethnic interpretations. In Chicago, as Lizabeth Cohen argued, ethnic audiences in the early 1920s could talk back to the screen at silent movies or tune into "ethnic nationality hours" on their radios. The *Philadelphia Tageblatt* in 1924 still carried advertisements for recorded German music.[20] As Cohen also noted, however, mass culture grew more uniform and less open to ethnic interpretations toward the end of the 1920s, with the advent of talking pictures and national commercial radio networks. Significantly, the *Gazette-Democrat* of 1928 reflected such uniformity. The newspaper's section of vaudeville and film reviews, which ran to three columns of English copy, was already reviewing "talkies" that year. The *Gazette-Democrat*, like the *Tageblatt* in 1924, could also provide an entire column of radio listings with no mention of any "nationality" hour, let alone a German-language one.[21]

The degree to which such nationally produced, commercialized entertainment could enter into the homes of German Philadelphians is suggested by the *Gazette-Democrat*'s coverage of the July 1928 prize fight in New York between Gene Tunney, the world champion, and challenger Tom Heeney. The newspaper's readers evidently took a great interest in the match, for the *Gazette-Democrat* provided ample coverage, running the report of Tunney's victory at the top of its front page. One retailer considered that interest great enough, in fact, to direct advertising, in German, at those readers, promising the day before the bout that they could have a radio installed in time to listen to the fight broadcast. "Der Tunney-Heeney Kampf in Ihrem Heim" ("The Tunney-Heeney Fight in

Your Home"), this advertisement blared.[22] What the German-language headline promised to bring into the home as well was an English-language broadcast that promoted collective identities grounded in mass culture. Even in this private realm, German Philadelphians could become fight fans and join a community of listeners eavesdropping on a national sporting event.

Like its middle-class counterpart, Philadelphia's working-class *Vereinswesen* suffered from the effects of the war, Prohibition, and declining immigration. The basic structure of that associational world survived World War I. In the 1920s, as at the turn of the century, the United German Trades served as the umbrella group for German union locals and as the focus of a complex of German socialist institutions, including the *Tageblatt*, three labor lyceums, the United Workers' Singing Societies, and the German branch of the Socialist Party of America.[23] Nevertheless, indications exist that this world, too, was shrinking. Most obviously, the *Tageblatt* experienced a massive loss of circulation. The newspaper had actually seen its readership rise from 12,500 in 1915 to 17,500 in 1920, despite the prosecution of its editors and reflecting, perhaps, the militancy of the postwar strike wave. By 1930, however, circulation had plummeted to 3,362. Within three years, control of the *Tageblatt* passed to the publisher of the *Gazette-Democrat*, which would absorb the *Tageblatt* completely in the 1940s.[24]

Membership figures for other organizations affiliated with the United German Trades are difficult to come by. The UGT itself, however, appears to have suffered a net loss in its constituency of German union locals between the turn of the century and the mid-1920s. While the *Tageblatt* asserted in 1924 that "many thousands of organized German-speaking workers stand behind" the federation, the UGT had only fifteen locals under its jurisdiction that year—five fewer than in 1899 and ten fewer than in 1910. Among the departed unions were locals representing cigar makers and packers, textile workers, leather workers, woodworkers, and tailors.[25] Six of the remaining locals had members who worked in brewing or brewing-related trades, compared with three such locals in 1899.[26] Thus, by 1924, nearly half of the UGT's locals depended on the brewing industry.

Unfortunately for the UGT, the ascendance of its brewery unions coincided with the triumph of Prohibition. The Volstead Act, in defining intoxicating liquors as those with an alcohol level of 0.5 percent by volume, forbade the manufacture of beer. The act, which took effect in January 1920,[27] had a devastating impact on the brewing industry and its workers. Some of the dozen breweries that defined the Brewerytown neighborhood attempted instead to produce "near beer"; others turned to manufacturing soda, yeast, or ice; still others closed. An *Evening Ledger* reporter in 1926 described the neighborhood's shuttered breweries standing "like great empty shells beside railroad tracks." Many Brewerytown workers were forced out of the trade. George J. Beichl, who grew up in the neighborhood in the 1920s and 1930s, recalled that a number of former brewery workers took jobs at meat-packing plants located elsewhere in the city.[28] Repeal came too late for Brewerytown; only one of its original breweries managed to reopen there temporarily in the mid-1930s. Such conditions nationally severely weakened the United Brewery Workers, the parent organization of Philadelphia's brewery unions. The threat Prohibition posed locally to those unions and, in turn, the UGT, can be gauged from the ferocity with which the labor federation attacked the "insane and immoral Volstead Act."[29]

The membership losses that plagued middle-class associations during the 1920s were visited as well on working-class clubs, as the experience of the Germania Turn Verein von Roxborough und Manayunk demonstrates. The Turn Verein, while not directly under the UGT's jurisdiction, seems to have had a primarily working-class orientation. It numbered machinists, a textile worker, and a bartender among its officers and directors in 1921,[30] advertised in the *Tageblatt,* and rented space to the Lace Makers' Union.[31] The Turn Verein's adult male membership, which had fallen from 145 in 1900 to seventy-nine in 1910, appears to have risen slightly by 1920. Within ten years, however, it had dropped again, to fifty-three in 1929 and to twenty-four the following year, perhaps reflecting the impact of the Great Depression.[32]

The case of the Germania Turn Verein, however, points to changes in the secular *Vereinswesen* that went beyond its dwindling size. For the secular associations that survived into the 1920s and beyond increasingly became sites for ethnic mixing, as non-Germans began to join them. This trend reached into some middle-class associations, but it was particularly evident among working-class clubs such as the Germania Turn Verein and Brewerytown's Fairmount Liedertafel, which more and more took on the character of neighborhood social centers—in part, it seems, due to Prohibition.

The Germania Turn Verein, in fact, had had a substantial non-German contingent since the turn of the twentieth century. Twenty-eight percent of the club's male members in 1900 bore clearly non-German surnames.[33] That proportion dropped slightly by 1920, but it rose sharply over the following decade, reaching 45 percent in 1929.[34] In all three years, the great majority of these non-Germans carried surnames that were either English or Irish, but a handful had surnames of apparent southeast European derivation. Of the club's twenty-four non-German members in 1929, for example, one had a possibly Italian surname, while another had an apparently Slavic one.[35]

What could have attracted these non-German members to an ethnic German gymnastics club? Part of the answer may lie in Prohibition. Despite the Volstead Act, which forbade the manufacture and sale of intoxicating beverages—although not their purchase or, under some exemptions, their possession—the Germania Turn Verein continued to maintain a bar and to buy and serve beer, at least during the early 1920s. The association's directors, for example, voted in February 1921 to "pay the bartenders $5.00 per Sunday." Club members in July discussed the need to obtain better beer, as "the beer from Hohenadel's Brewery of late [has been] very bad." The Turn Verein, of course, could have been serving near beer, but the beverages consumed on the premises likely were stronger stuff, given the complaint lodged against one Irish-surnamed member for "un-Turner-like behavior." Accused of speaking "very indecently" in the Turn Verein's hall, he admitted the charge, but stated by way of explanation that he was drunk at the time.[36] If the Germania Turn Verein in fact evaded Prohibition, it would not have been alone in doing so. Philadelphia through the 1920s was "ostentatiously wet," and "high-powered beer" reportedly made its way to market from illicit local breweries. The Fairmount Liedertafel, a Brewerytown club affiliated with the United Workers' Singing Societies, relied on bootleggers for its beer supply, George Beichl recalled. The Germantown Maennerchor apparently made its own, for police in 1928 confiscated about 60 cases of "home brew" from the Maennerchor building.[37] Such *Vereine* could and, in some cases, did prove attractive to nearby residents of varying ethnic backgrounds seeking more than near beer.

As its membership grew increasingly diverse, the Germania Turn Verein also changed in character. Once defined by a commitment to gymnastics as a specifically German form of sport, the association broadened its focus during the 1920s and became noticeably lukewarm about its ties to the larger turner movement. Gymnastics remained a central feature of the club; John A. Eichman III, who grew up in Roxborough, recalled taking gymnastics lessons there for a season during the 1920s. But the association began to add activities that lacked German ethnic overtones. Early in the decade, for example, the Turn Verein founded a baseball team, which played under the management of an Anglo-American member, Thomas Craighead.[38] At the same time, the club began to withdraw from its involvement with the national American Turnerbund. Citing "insufficient preparation," the Turn Verein declined to participate in the 1921 national turner festival in Chicago. By 1928, the club's members had decided that "financial difficulties" prevented them from paying dues to the American Turnerbund or the Turnerbund's local district. They likewise resolved to cancel the Turn Verein's subscription to the national turner newspaper, noting that "no one reads it anyway."[39] Over the 1920s, too, English apparently became the club's predominant language. Eichman's gymnastics class was conducted entirely in English. A linguistic watershed was reached in January 1929, when the Turn Verein's longtime secretary ceased writing the association's minutes in German, switching—without comment and for good—to English.[40]

With its rising non-German membership and increasing use of English, its decreasing emphasis on gymnastics and declining interest in the turner movement, and its availability as a place to get a drink, the Germania Turn Verein more and more came to resemble a social center for residents of varying ethnic backgrounds in Manayunk and Roxborough. This much is suggested by a stinging letter the district president of the Turnerbund—now the American Turners—addressed to the club in 1942. He noted that in the past four years, the "Roxborough Germania Turners" had "failed to participate in Turner activities or to have representation at the District Executive meetings and annual Conventions"; the Middle Atlantic District therefore would have to consider suspending the club. The president's reproof summed up the Turn Verein's apparent transition from German sports club to neighborhood center: "Roxborough for almost a century was a leader in the Turner movement, but in the past decade has, from all reports, become merely a social honky-tonk."[41]

The Germania Turn Verein was not an aberration. Other working-class associations appear to have taken similar paths in the 1920s and 1930s. George Beichl, who attended gym classes at the Columbia Turn-Verein in Brewerytown during the late 1920s, remembered that "there was nothing German about it, uniquely German." The language commonly used in classes and by adult members was English. Perhaps the sole reminder that the club had had a German ethnic character, Beichl jokingly suggested, was that it had a bar. "It became just a social club, and then everybody . . . belonged to it, you didn't have to be German or anything." The Fairmount Liedertafel, located in the same neighborhood, apparently retained a stronger sense of German ethnic identity, but it too began to attract non-German members. Beichl started attending German-language plays and concerts at the singing society as a grammar-school student in the 1920s, and he later became a singing member. The primary language used by those who sang and socialized at the Liedertafel's headquarters in the 1920s was German, he recalled, as was, for the most part, the clientele. But the society's bar began to draw Irish members, a change that was clear by the 1930s and that, even after repeal, was encouraged by the city's blue laws. "Clubs were great because you could drink beer on Sundays," Beichl remembered. "[T]hat's why a lot of Irish belonged to the Fairmount Liedertafel. They would serve beer on Sunday [when] the saloons were closed." Most of the Liedertafel's Irish members lived nearby and were social rather than singing members in the 1930s. An appreciable number, however, did mix with members of German background at Liedertafel dances and events. Irish men would dance with German women, and Irish members participated in the society's German wine festival. The Liedertafel, like the Germania and Columbia *Turnvereine*, had evolved into a neighborhood club, as Beichl characterized it.[42]

The trend toward ethnic mixing was less evident, but still apparent, in some middle-class associations. Organizations such as the German Society limited membership to those with at least some German ancestry.[43] The Cannstatter Volksfest-Verein, however, attracted a small but growing number of non-Germans. The Volksfest-Verein counted nine members with English, Scottish, or Irish surnames in 1912, out of a total membership of 1,120. By 1923, the association's shrunken membership roll listed thirteen such individuals.[44] By the late 1910s, some of the choral societies affiliated with the United Singers of Philadelphia likewise had taken in Irish members. Moreover, the cooperation between German and Irish associations fostered by the First World War appears to have continued in the postwar years. The Philadelphia Turngemeinde, for example, routinely granted the use of its hall in the late 1920s to such groups as the Catholic Sons of Derry and the County Cork Men's Society.[45]

"Dying Congregations" and Mixed Parishes

"Church Germans" after the First World War faced challenges similar to those that confronted the secular *Vereinswesen*. Both Catholics and Lutherans grappled with a decline in German-language congregations. German Lutheran churches would, by and large, remain German preserves. German Catholic parishes, however, began to take in more parishioners of more diverse ethnic backgrounds.

"What is the true calling of German-American Catholics?" the Reverend John E. Rothensteiner asked on the front page of *Nord Amerika* in May 1924. German Catholics, he answered, had a mission to contribute their best traits to the nation and to American Catholicism. By rendering the latter spiritually warmer, deeper, and more earnest, they could help bring German Americans of other faiths back to the Catholic Church.[46] These lines echoed the arguments of prewar secular activists that German Americans had a role to play in shaping a nation in the process of becoming. But Rothensteiner departed from such views in insisting that German-American Catholics, rather than pursuing ethnic separatism, truly would have to fuse with other elements of the population:

We will, however, succeed in this [mission] the more easily and more completely, the more uniformly our race [*Volkstum*] melts with the other peoples
of America and, as it apportions from its own estate, also receives from [that
of the others.] The view that everything German is absolutely splendid, but that
everything American, Irish, Italian often is good for nothing, is an un-German
conceit. . . . We German Americans do not want and are not able to found a
new Germany; rather, history and our own instincts prescribe that we fuse our
race with all of the other elements into the great American people of the
future.[47]

In this process, the German language itself inevitably would yield. Yet the
coming generation, while gaining a better facility with English, would remain "German in character . . . though it might clothe everything in
American forms. Only take care that [they] remain good Catholics."[48]

In asserting that German ethnic distinctiveness would survive the transition to English, Rothensteiner seconded the views of other German
Catholic spokesmen across the nation during the 1920s, which was not
surprising, since his article came to *Nord Amerika* by way of the national
press service of the German Catholic Central-Verein.[49] Yet his frank endorsement of a brand of assimilation that came close to ethnic submer-
sion, and his acceptance of the loss of the German language, also reflected
the condition of Philadelphia's German Catholic subculture. Like the secular *Vereinswesen*, German Catholic Philadelphia continued to dwindle
in the 1920s. Moreover, its remaining national parishes became, as one
local priest put it, "more and more Americanized" in terms of English-
language use.[50] They likewise increasingly became sites for ethnic mixing.

The city's German national parish system had virtually ceased its expansion in the 1890s, acquiring only one more parish thereafter—St.
Henry's, in 1916. The first decades of the twentieth century, moreover,
saw a gradual but steady decline in overall German parish membership.
In 1900, a total of 23,395 men, women, and children belonged to the
city's eleven German parishes. The corresponding figure for 1921, including the parishioners of St. Henry's, was 21,221; by 1930, it was down
to 19,561.[51] Over thirty years, total German parish membership had
dropped by one-sixth. Part of this decline stemmed from the loss in 1928
of West Philadelphia's German national parish, St. Ignatius. The Catholic
Nord Amerika's circulation traveled a similar downward course, from
6,000 in 1905 to 3,500 in 1941.[52]

German parishes altered in nature as well as in number, most obviously
through an accelerated transition to English. Even before World War I,
churches such as St. Peter's had become essentially bilingual. After the
war, the balance in these parishes seems to have shifted toward English.

One priest dated this change to the war and the subsequent tailing-off of immigration. "While in former years most services were held in the mother tongue, it has become an exception today when on Sunday more than one sermon is preached in German and a rarity, indeed, if German is still taught in school," he wrote in 1934.[53] George Beichl, a member of the German national parish of St. Ludwig in Brewerytown from his birth in 1918 until he left the neighborhood in the early 1950s, recalled that the church offered German services until the 1940s. Yet he remembered English sermons as predominating in masses before that point. English likewise was the language of the schoolyard and the classroom at St. Ludwig's parochial school, which Beichl attended from 1923 to 1931. Before the First World War, he remembered hearing, morning classes were conducted in German and afternoon ones in English. By the 1920s, however, instruction was entirely in English, with the exception of a German-language course that ended after Beichl finished the third or fourth grade. On the playground, among the second-generation immigrants who predominated in the student body, English ruled. If Beichl's fellow students used German at all, they did so at home, and then, apparently, with reluctance. "They'd say, 'Aw, the old man always talks to me in German.'"[54] German proved somewhat more durable in the services held at St. Mary of the Assumption in Manayunk. John Eichman's family belonged to St. Mary's until they moved to the suburb of Bala Cynwyd in the late 1930s. Eichman, who was born in 1917, recalled that of the four masses held on Sunday morning, two featured German sermons, and two sermons in both German and English. Yet the parish school, which Eichman attended beginning in the early 1920s, discontinued the teaching of German after his first year.[55]

By the 1920s, moreover, these "German" national parishes had become more and more ethnically mixed. A small degree of ethnic mixing had obtained at the turn of the century, even in such flagship parishes as St. Peter's. As the next chapter describes, the admixture there had become much more evident by the 1920s, and this was true of other parishes, especially their parochial schools. "In my classroom, there were two Italians and one Pole, and I don't know how many Irish," George Beichl recalled of St. Ludwig's school. One of the Irish pupils became Beichl's closest friend during his grammar school years. Such students "would have to come in under special dispensation, because they didn't belong, really, to the ethnic parish. But they lived there."[56] In addition, more and more children of ethnically mixed marriages were entering German parishes. John Eichman recalled that there were few, if any, immigrant members of St. Mary's parish, although parishioners, "for the most part . . . had some connection" with Germany, having parents or grandparents born there. Among these second- and third-generation parishioners, ethnic intermarriage was not uncommon. Eichman himself, the son of a prosperous businessman, was "three-quarters Irish." He was a great-grandson of German and Irish immigrants on his father's side and a third-generation Irish immigrant on his mother's side. Eichman recalled there being many such German-Irish families in the parish, as well as some other mixed families. Their children were especially evident at St. Mary's parochial school. Eichman estimated that between one-third and one-half of the students in his classes were of mixed parentage. The most common such mixes were German-Irish, but some students were of German-Polish background. The school also took at least a few pupils of other national-ities, including a close friend of Eichman's who was of Czech background, although children of solely German descent were the most common.[57]

For German Lutheran congregations, the 1920s presented a crisis of even greater proportions, perhaps, than that faced by German Catholics. In the first two decades of the century, the German Conference of the Evangelical Lutheran Ministerium of Pennsylvania added two Philadel-phia congregations. The conference's twenty-one city churches in 1920 had 7,045 communing members, a small increase over the corresponding figure for 1900.[58] Over the 1920s, however, total communing member-ship in the city's German Conference churches fell by one-fifth, reaching 5,631 in 1930.[59] Given such losses, German Lutheran spokesmen saw lit-tle hope for the future. "The German congregations are dying congrega-tions," O. Kline, writing in the Philadelphia-based *Lutherischer Herold*, declared in 1929. Kline traced the roots of their decline to the war, im-migration restriction, and a lack of interest on the part of postwar Ger-man immigrants. "The war was carried into the souls of the children, it became almost a crime to belong to a German congregation," this author wrote. Of those Germans who arrived after the war, "only a few find their way to the German church."[60]

Facing decline, German Lutheran churches began to resort to what Kline doubtfully called the "cure" of introducing English-language ser-vices, "in order at least to retain the younger members of the congrega-tion."[61] By the mid-1920s, St. Michael's German Lutheran Church in Kensington offered an evening English service on Sundays, along with its morning German service. Esther Schuchard Browne, who was born in 1915 and attended St. Michael's in the 1920s and 1930s, recalled that the English service drew "the young generation." Nonetheless, "a lot of peo-ple broke away, the younger people," to English Lutheran churches after the First World War.[62] St. Marcus' German Lutheran Church likewise of-fered Sunday services in both German and English by the time Alberta Schilling Brosz began attending it in the late 1920s. Brosz, born in 1912, had started out in Sunday school at St. Marcus' in the early 1920s, but those classes, held in English, apparently did little to reinforce a sense of the congregation as German. At the beginning, at least, "I wasn't really aware that that was a German Lutheran church," she recalled.[63]

The city's German Lutheran churches also seem not to have served as sites for ethnic mixing, at least not to the extent that some German Catholic parishes did. While Browne had German, Irish, and English neighbors on her block in Kensington, for example, St. Michael's was made up "largely of German Americans," she said.[64] Indeed, it seems unlikely that the city's German Lutheran congregations would attract many members who were not ethnically German, given the nature of Lutheranism in Philadelphia. The Pennsylvania Ministerium had nothing like the plethora of nationalities that crowded the city's Catholic churches. German immigrants had founded the ministerium in the eighteenth century; their descendants, along with later arrivals from Germany, made up the vast majority of Philadelphia Lutherans. In the mid-1920s, the city had a handful of Scandinavian Lutheran congregations affiliated with other synods, along with a Slovak Lutheran church and four Missouri Synod churches that catered, in turn, to Lettish, Lithuanian, Polish, and African-American congregants. Aside from its German and English churches, however, the Ministerium itself sponsored only a Lettish and an Italian congregation, both of which belonged to the Philadelphia English Conference.[65] Consequently, Philadelphia Lutheranism in general, and the Ministerium in particular, had far less potential for ethnic mixing than Catholic Philadelphia.

A Cautious Activism

In the spring of 1924, officials of the Philadelphia branch of the German-American Central Alliance of Pennsylvania busied themselves with preparations for a Whitsuntide festival. The event, which was being put on for the first time in years, had once drawn a range of German associations. The Philadelphia branch wanted to revive it in part to foster greater unity among German clubs and congregations. The time for that "reunification" had arrived, "for we must realize that we have to profess our solidarity more publicly," the branch declared.[66]

This plea for a higher public profile reflected the degree to which German societies remained wary of such exposure. In fact, some associations that had survived the war did take careful steps onto the public stage in the 1920s. By 1922, "the combined German societies" were again commemorating the landing of Pastorius, with a gathering at Schützen Park. The following year's celebration apparently regained the title of "German Day."[67] Anti-German feeling had eased enough by 1928 that the Philadelphia Chamber of Commerce could cooperate with German-American,

Irish-American, and Anglo-American notables in honoring three visiting aviators, the "Bremen Fliers." Similarly, a 1932 commemoration of the centenary of Goethe's death, attended by German Americans and Anglo-Americans alike, represented "the most impressive homage to a great German in these parts" since before the United States entered World War I, a historian of the German Society noted.[68]

By the early 1920s, then, Philadelphia had room again for public Germanness—but only of a certain sort. What these events had in common was their unexceptionable nature. They offered no evidence that German Americans were reaching for political power as an ethnic group and thus differed strikingly in tone from the activities and rhetoric of the National Alliance. That such a nonthreatening, low-key public stance was German Philadelphia's preferred postwar approach is suggested by the fact that the *Vereinswesen*'s most prominent endeavor of the 1920s was the provision of charitable relief to war-torn Germany, in particular its undernourished children. This effort, in which the German Society and its Women's Auxiliary played a central role, saw German Americans in Philadelphia and across the country raise huge sums to fund feeding centers in Germany administered by the American Friends' Service Committee. Operating with the endorsement of Herbert Hoover's Relief Administration, the program lasted into the mid-1920s. Such relief work had an obvious emotional appeal to German Philadelphians, but it also allowed them cautiously to reenter public life with an image—as feeders of starving children—that few could find threatening. The shift toward such charitable activity, like the wartime relief efforts, likely allowed women to continue expanding the place they had staked out in the *Vereinswesen*. The Women's Auxiliary took a "greater and greater" share in all of the society's charitable work during and after World War I, to the point that its contribution began "to outweigh that of the men's side," according to a society history.[69]

Those who sought a more aggressively political role for German Philadelphia quickly discovered that postwar tolerance had its limits. When, for example, activists in 1921 sought to hold a mass meeting at the city's Metropolitan Opera House to protest the Allied occupation of the Rhineland, they found their lease of the hall revoked at the last minute, "at the instigation of the American Legion and other patriotic organizations on the plea that it would hurt the feeling of our former ally, France." Moreover, anti-German animus occasionally resurfaced later in the 1920s. Even the effort to feed German children drew fire, delivered by that unreconstructed nativist, Owen Wister. Wister attacked the program in a 1924 letter to its director, the former commander of American occupation troops on the Rhine. "[T]hat you who wore your country's uniform when Americans were dying to save our civilization from Germany's assault, should be Germany's spokesman, will surprise many more Americans than, Yours truly," the novelist closed.[70] Public representations of German America likewise were subject to ridicule that carried echoes of the war. The Founders' Monument in Germantown, for example, continued to draw derisive comments with an ethnic edge into the 1930s. Margaret Zinser, who grew up in Germantown in the interwar years, recalled classmates in grammar school making fun of the monument at least in part because of its German connotations. As the 250th anniversary of Germantown's founding approached in 1933, a local monthly, *The Beehive,* went on a campaign against the memorial; as it asked, "does Germantown want a monument to German or any other brand of culture in her historic park in place of a monumental tribute to the Founders?" Over the following months, the *Beehive* repeatedly ridiculed "Brunehilde," as it dubbed the female figure atop the monument.[71]

The remnants of Philadelphia's *Vereinswesen,* then, found themselves contending with the legacy of the anti-German panic through and beyond the 1920s, as did all Philadelphians of immigrant German background. Their struggle with that legacy would constitute one factor in the reshaping of identities that marked German Philadelphia in the 1920s. So, too, however, would population shifts in the neighborhoods they inhabited, shifts examined in the next chapter.

CHAPTER TEN

Changing Neighborhoods

THE identities Philadelphians of German ancestry crafted in the postwar period were profoundly shaped by the city's changing ethnic and racial makeup. The years leading up to World War I brought waves of newcomers from southern and eastern Europe. The war itself triggered the first Great Migration of black Southerners to the North and, consequently, a sudden expansion of Philadelphia's African-American community. These developments, coupled with local population shifts, altered the ethnic nature of the neighborhoods within which German Philadelphians made their homes. Residents of German background were presented with greater opportunities to mix with—or define themselves against—a greater diversity of peoples. How some made use of such changes to reshape their identities is the topic of the final two chapters. This chapter provides context for those redefinitions by focusing on the process of ethnic and racial succession as it affected the Girard Avenue district and Germantown. By examining how these two neighborhoods had changed by the 1920s and how their German residents chose to mix with, or avoid, their new neighbors, we can better understand how space, class, and religion fostered different varieties of assimilation for German Philadelphians.

IMMIGRANTS, MIGRANTS, AND NEIGHBORHOOD CHANGE

Philadelphia's population in 1920 remained markedly less immigrant and more African-American than that of other large Northern cities. In New York and Chicago, first- and second-generation immigrants made up more than 70 percent of the population; only 54 percent of Philadelphians fell into that category. In contrast, Philadelphia that year had a greater percentage of black residents than did New York, Chicago, Pittsburgh, or Detroit.[1] Nevertheless, the city had experienced substantial change in the nature of its immigrant population and the size of its African-American community. Philadelphia maintained a comparatively strong concentration of "old immigrants" in 1920. Yet the first two decades of the century had brought a large influx of Russian Jewish and Italian newcomers, along with smaller numbers of Poles, Hungarians, Slovaks, and other "new immigrants." By 1920, such south and east European immigrants formed a slight majority among Philadelphians born abroad.[2] The First World War had halted this immigrant stream while increasing the demand for armaments and other goods from Northern factories. In the resulting labor short-age, companies that had never hired African Americans began accepting and even recruiting black laborers, triggering a massive northbound mi-gration. Roughly 40,000 black Southerners arrived in Philadelphia during the war years, fleeing the threat of violence posed by lynching and gaining access to previously closed, semiskilled jobs in stevedoring, construction, and shipyard work. The return of white workers from the war temporar-ily dampened this influx, but it recommenced during the early 1920s; about 10,000 black migrants moved to Philadelphia annually between 1922 and 1924.[3] The wartime migration helped to push the proportion of African Americans in the city's population up to 7.4 percent in 1920 (see table 10.1).

With these demographic changes came changes in residential patterns. Many new immigrants tended to settle at first in the poorer sections of the central and southern wards, a pattern that brought Russian and east Eu-ropean Jewish settlements, as well as a "Little Italy," to South Philadel-phia and Russian Jews to Northern Liberties in the late nineteenth cen-tury. After 1900, members of these groups increased their presence in other parts of the city, with east European Jews moving west and north

TABLE 10.1
Ethnic Composition of Philadelphia, Girard Avenue District, and Germantown, 1920 (Percent of Total Populations)

	Philadelphia	Wards 16 and 17	Germantown
German stock	8.2	15.5 (±4.3)	6.3 (±0.9)
Native white of native parentage	38.3	18.9 (±4.9)	51.4 (±3.2)
Irish stock	12.2	5.0 (±1.9)	16.8 (±2.4)
British stock*	5.4	0.8 (±0.4)	10.5 (±1.3)
Russian stock**	11.3	17.6 (±11.7)	1.3 (±0.8)
Hungarian stock	1.3	22.9 (±8.5)	0.3 (±0.3)
East European stock***	4.0	15.4 (±4.8)	1.0 (±0.4)
South European stock†	7.7	1.2 (±1.0)	3.5 (±2.3)
Other Northwest European stock	1.3	1.0 (±0.5)	1.7 (±0.5)
Other††	8.2	1.8 (±2.2)	7.3 (±2.8)
Of mixed foreign parentage	2.2	—	—
Total (N)	1,823,779	3,215	9,110

Source: Percentages for Philadelphia are population figures, derived from U.S. Depart-ment of Commerce, Bureau of the Census, *Fourteenth Census of the United States, Taken*

continued

TABLE 10.1
Continued

in the Year 1920, vol. 2, *Population, 1920: General Report and Analytical Tables,* 944; and vol. 3, *Population, 1920: Composition and Characteristics of the Population by States,* 896 (Washington, D.C., 1922). Percentages for the Girard Avenue district and Germantown are derived from the author's census samples.

Note: Figures in parentheses are 95 percent confidence intervals for each proportion, corresponding to the 0.05 level of significance (see appendix).

"Stock" includes immigrants and their second-generation children. The population figures for Philadelphia are generally but not completely comparable to those for the two sample areas. The published 1920 census defined second-generation white immigrants from a given country as native whites with both parents born in that country, or with one parent so born and one native parent. Native whites with one parent born in one foreign country and the other in a different foreign country, however, were defined as being "of mixed foreign parentage," and were not included in individual countries' stock totals. These individuals are accounted for in the Philadelphia column under the category, "of mixed foreign parentage." For the sample areas, I followed the published census' definition of the second generation, with the exception that, for technical reasons, my totals for individual countries do include persons of mixed foreign parentage, with such individuals assigned to a given country according to their father's place of birth. In addition, my aggregation of the categories "German stock," "Russian stock," "East European stock," and "Other" differ somewhat for Philadelphia as a whole and for the sample areas, due in part to the Census Bureau's decision to calculate 1920 country totals on the basis of 1910 boundaries.

*Includes immigrants from England, Scotland, and Wales.

**Includes immigrants from Russia, Lithuania, Estonia, and Latvia.

***Includes immigrants from Bohemia, Romania, Austria, and, for the sample areas, Poland (except prewar West Prussia). For Philadelphia, Polish immigrants are divided among the overall totals for Germany, Russia, and Austria (assigned to East European stock). This approach is necessitated by the published census, which assigned to those states immigrants from, respectively, prewar German Poland, Russian Poland, and Austrian Poland.

Immigrants and their children from Austria were assigned to the Northwest European category in 1900 but to the East European category in 1920; the latter approach seemed more accurate for Philadelphia, given the nature of the published census's aggregation in 1920 and the many ethnic Slavs in the Austrian group. If the 1920 categories are reaggregated to make them comparable with those for 1900 (by shifting Austrians from the East European to the Other Northwest European category), the proportions for 1920 appear as follows: of Philadelphia's population, 0.5 percent is East European stock and 4.7 percent is Other Northwest European stock; of individuals in the Girard Avenue district sample, 9 percent (±4.0 percent) are East European and 7.4 percent (±2.7 percent) are Other Northwest European; of individuals in the Germantown sample, 0.5 percent (±0.4 percent) are East European and 2.1 percent (±0.5 percent) are Other Northwest European.

†Includes immigrants from Italy, Spain, Portugal, and Greece.

††Includes African Americans and immigrants from countries outside Europe, including Canada, South America, and China. For Philadelphia, but not for the sample areas, "Other" also includes the published census category of "Europe, not specified," which totaled 126 Philadelphia residents.

Blacks—categorized as "Negro" in the published census—made up 7.4 percent of the city's population, 6.1 percent (±2.8 percent) of the Germantown sample, and 1.6 percent of the Girard Avenue sample in 1920. African Americans composed 1.5 percent of the actual population of the Sixteenth and Seventeenth wards that year; Bureau of the Census, *Fourteenth Census,* vol. 3, *Population, 1920: Composition and Characteristics,* 897.

to neighborhoods such as Strawberry Mansion, along the Schuylkill River, and small Italian enclaves growing in parts of North Philadelphia and Germantown.[4] African Americans began the century relatively dispersed. In the late nineteenth century, a majority of black residents lived in South Philadelphia, but they were not highly segregated residentially. Blacks were beginning to move to new parts of the city, however, and during and after the 1910s, they experienced greater segregation. Areas of African-American concentration appeared not only in South Philadelphia but also north and west of the city center.[5]

As African Americans and new immigrants moved into new neighborhoods, many white residents of older immigrant background—Anglo-Americans, Irish, and Germans—moved out. West Philadelphia became a commuter suburb favored by the Irish; Irish, Scots-Irish, and German residents grown more affluent moved to Germantown and Chestnut Hill;[6] and other Germans pushed north from Kensington and Brewerytown to Olney and beyond. This process of ethnic and racial succession was nicely captured in 1926 by one observer describing population shifts since 1900:

> The older "downtown" homes of many immigrating Irish families were largely taken by multitudes of Italians, Poles and refugee Russian Jews. Marked material prosperity had by this time come to people of Irish stock, who moved to West Philadelphia and similar sections. In like manner, the great German population which, 50 years ago, occupied the Girard avenue and Columbia avenue quarter, gravitated towards Olney, where the second and third generations occupy handsome houses, owned by themselves. More recent immigrants are driving them still further northward, so to say; just as in the period since the World War tens of thousands of Negroes have driven the scions of European immigrants to West Philadelphia and various localities in North, Northeast, Northwest and Southwest Philadelphia.[7]

The northward drift of German immigrants and their children, already apparent before the First World War, continued during and after the 1910s. In 1920 as in 1910, the Twenty-ninth Ward, encompassing Brewerytown, had the highest concentration of German immigrants in the city, while the old strongholds of the Sixteenth and Seventeenth wards and Kensington's Nineteenth Ward ranked among the top six such wards in Philadelphia. The wards ranked second and third, however, were the Forty-third, which sat squarely on the northbound corridor of settlement, and the Thirty-fifth, in the far northeast. These figures also indicated a good degree of dispersion, for none of the concentrations was high at the ward level; of the Twenty-ninth Ward's population, only 7.3 percent was immigrant German.[8]

Some of this movement, however, clearly resulted in the creation of new German neighborhoods, as the case of Olney shows. Located in the Forty-second Ward, near the city's northern border with suburban Montgomery County, Olney had emerged by the 1910s as a recognized German suburb.[9] The section sustained relatively high concentrations of first- and second-generation German immigrants during the interwar period. Census tract data for 1930 show that two tracts in the neighborhood had German-stock populations exceeding 20 percent, at a time when the Twenty-ninth Ward's most German tract was 28 percent German-stock.[10] That Olney drew migrants from the city's older German neighborhoods is suggested by the history of St. Paul's Independent Lutheran Church. St. Paul's Independent, a fixture of the Sixteenth Ward since 1871, essentially picked up and moved to Olney in the 1920s; its congregation completed construction of a new church there in 1926. St. Paul's Independent, in fact, was catching up with its congregants. "Since so many members left the neighborhood of the [old] church . . . and moved to the northern part of the city," a church history recounted, "Pastor Meyer and most of the members of the church saw that the time was coming when the church had to follow its members."[11]

The church's new home was German enough to sustain a business district offering a variety of ethnic services and products. Olney was "famous for the Teutonic eateries, markets, butcher shops and bakeries that filled the neighborhood." These amenities drew temporary as well as permanent migrants. George Beichl, who developed an interest in the zither after hearing it played at the Fairmount Liedertafel, recalled taking the trolley from Brewerytown to Olney for zither lessons given by a Mr. Zapf. Zapf, an immigrant, subsequently opened a music store that became an Olney landmark. Olney thus may have helped to sustain certain aspects of a German identity for outsiders as well as residents between the world wars, serving, in Kathleen Conzen's formulation, as "a cultural reference point and source of services supporting the ethnic side of life."[12]

ETHNIC SUCCESSION ALONG GIRARD AVENUE

Racial and ethnic succession, however, could also tell against German ethnic identity. The experience of the Girard Avenue district shows how succession could change the neighborhoods of those who stayed in ways that encouraged their mixing with others. As the district grew smaller, less German, and less Protestant, its remaining German residents found themselves increasingly associating, on their streets and in local Catholic parishes, with the Irish and a variety of newcomers from eastern and southern Europe.

The Girard Avenue district remained heavily industrial and industrially diverse in the 1920s. Leather works, paper box factories, dye houses, iron foundries, and a host of other manufactories peppered the neighborhood

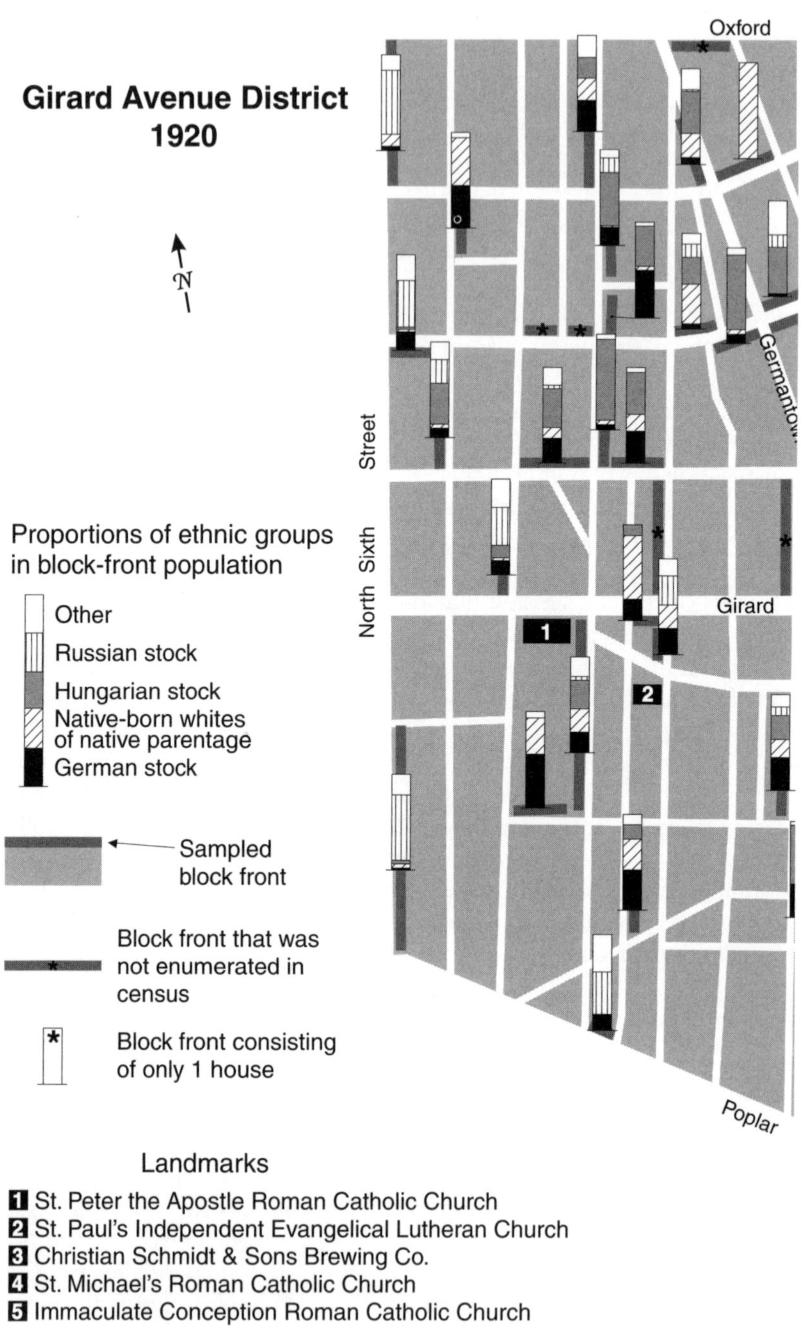

Map 10.1. Girard Avenue District, 1920. The area north of Girard Avenue corresponds to the Seventeenth Ward; the area south of Girard Avenue is the Sixteenth Ward. Sources: Author's census sample; George W. Bromley and Walter S. Bromley, *Atlas of the City of Philadelphia* (Philadelphia, 1895); George W. Bromley and Walter S. Bromley, *Atlas of the City of Philadelphia (Central):*

South Street to Lehigh Ave., Wards 5 to 20, 28, 29, 31, 32, 37 & 47 (Philadelphia, 1922); Sanborn Map Company, *Insurance Maps of Philadelphia, Pennsylvania* (New York, 1917), vol. 8; Ernest Hexamer and Son, *Insurance Maps of the City of Philadelphia* (Philadelphia, 1901–1920), vols. 4, 8 (for more specific publication information, see appendix, note 3).

and dominated its southeastern reaches. The area, in fact, grew increasingly industrial in terms of land use after 1900.[13] That the neighborhood retained a predominantly working-class orientation is suggested both by its industrial character and by an analysis of a random sample of block fronts drawn from the 1920 manuscript census (see map 10.1). Only 1 percent of the working individuals in this Girard Avenue district sample were employers, for example. In contrast, of the working population in a corresponding Germantown sample, 5 percent employed others. While the latter figure is not large in absolute terms, it does hint that Germantown in 1920 retained a stratum of major proprietors that was by and large lacking in the Sixteenth and Seventeenth wards.[14]

As the district became more industrial, it suffered a considerable loss of residents, particularly Germans and Protestants. Between 1900 and 1920, the population of the Sixteenth and Seventeenth wards fell by more than one-sixth, to 27,740.[15] The proportion of first- and second-generation German immigrants in the wards declined at an even faster rate, from 44.6 percent in 1900 to 15.5 percent in 1920 (see tables 2.2 and 10.1). This exodus involved German Catholics as well as Protestants. The German Catholic parish of St. Peter's, which counted between 7,000 and 7,500 parishioners in 1900, could claim only 4,404 by 1921. About half of these parishioners in the latter year were listed as Hungarian, but whether their ethnicity was German or Magyar was unspecified, suggesting the possibility of an even steeper decline in the number of ethnically German Catholics.[16] Lutheran churches, however, suffered losses that threatened the very existence of German Lutheranism in the neighborhood. The departure of congregants impelled St. Paul's Independent to leave the Sixteenth Ward altogether. St. Jacobus' German Lutheran Church saw its communing membership fall from 962 in 1900 to 658 in 1920; by 1930, the congregation was down to 354 members. St. Paul's German Lutheran Church held its own in the first two decades of the century, but over the 1920s its communing membership also fell, from 507 to 369.[17] Such losses appear to have been part of a larger Protestant exodus from the neighborhood. "For a generation, Protestant churches have been leaving this territory," the director of the Pennsylvania Ministerium's Lutheran Settlement, located on the eastern edge of the Girard Avenue district, declared in 1920. The president of the settlement's parent organization, the Inner Mission Society, similarly described the neighborhood in the mid-1920s as "strongly Roman Catholic." Here, the district reflected the general experience of older neighborhoods in the urban North described by John McGreevy: Catholics were "significantly more likely to remain in particular neighborhoods than non-Catholics" because they were anchored by immovable parishes, the property of which was registered in the name of the local diocese. Parish priests, in fact, implored parishioners not to move away. In contrast, Protestant churches like St. Paul's Independent *could* sell their old buildings and leave, and their mobility encouraged Protestant flight.[18]

German-born residents and their children nonetheless maintained a sizable presence in the Girard Avenue district; indeed, they were overrepresented in the neighborhood, compared with the city as a whole. Yet they were no longer the area's largest group, and the ethnic background of their neighbors had changed dramatically. In the twenty years after 1900, newcomers from Russia—almost all of them Russian Jews—and from eastern Europe, especially Hungary, poured into the Sixteenth and Seventeenth wards. By 1920, first- and second-generation Hungarian immigrants made up the largest single ethnic group in the district, composing 23 percent of all individuals in the sample. Native whites of native parentage, although a smaller group in 1920 than in 1900, retained their second-rank position (19 percent), but Russian-stock individuals ranked third (18 percent). German-stock residents had fallen to fourth place; they were trailed by immigrants and their children from other east European countries (15.4 percent) (see table 10.1).

The shift in population may have appeared less dramatic than these figures would indicate. Given the time that had passed since the peak years of German and Irish immigration, many of the neighborhood's "native whites of native parentage" likely were third- or fourth-generation immigrants whose forebears had arrived from Germany or Ireland in the nineteenth century. Moreover, a large proportion of the new arrivals from what had been the Austro-Hungarian Empire were ethnic Germans. German was the mother tongue of 79 percent of the 470 Hungarian immigrants in the sample. In fact, of the sample's 1,313 immigrants, nearly half (47 percent) had German as their native language. The persistence of German as an immigrant tongue probably reinforced the perception that the vicinity "of Fifth Street and Girard Avenue" remained one of Philadelphia's "German neighborhoods," in the words of the city's 1937 *WPA Guide*. Joseph Gruninger, who was born in 1935 and grew up in St. Peter's parish, recalled that the neighborhood around the church was "predominantly of Germanic descent—if not from Germany itself, then German-speaking from someplace else."[19]

Yet the arrival of immigrants from eastern Europe and Russia did change the look, feel, and sound of the Girard Avenue district. In the years after 1900, Jewish newcomers brought synagogues to Girard Avenue; turned Marshall Street, one block west of the Sixteenth Ward, into a major open-air marketplace; and hawked fruits and vegetables from stands that lined Second Street from Vine to Girard. Second Street likewise became home to Polish taverns and dance halls, while a Magyar-language newspaper opened its office in the Seventeenth Ward.[20] German Hungarians

TABLE 10.2
Ethnic Composition, by Percent, of the "Average" German-Stock Resident's
Block Front: Girard Avenue District and Germantown, 1920 (P* Indices)

	Wards 16 and 17	Germantown
German stock	26.2	11.5
Native whites of native parentage	21.8	50.9
Irish stock	5.4	15.3
British stock*	0.7	11.0
Russian stock	9.4	1.5
Hungarian stock	20.3	0.3
East European stock**	12.1	1.5
South European stock***	1.2	1.9
Other Northwest European stock	1.2	2.0
Other†	1.7	4.2
Total	100.0	100.1

Source: Author's census samples.

Note: A population parameter can be reliably inferred from each of the above results, as each result falls within the 95 percent confidence interval of the corresponding resampled mean P* (see appendix). The Germantown column totals 100.1 percent, due to rounding of individual results.

"Stock" includes immigrants and their second-generation children, with the second generation defined as native born with both parents or father born in specified country or, if father is native, with mother born in specified country. If parents are born in different foreign countries, birthplace of father determines parentage of native born.

*Includes immigrants from England, Scotland, and Wales and their children.

**Includes, among others, immigrants from Poland, Bohemia, Romania, and Austria and their children. If Austrians are shifted from the East European to the Other Northwest European category to make them comparable with those categories for 1900 (see table 10.1), P* results for 1920 are as follows: in the Girard Avenue district sample, the average German-stock resident's block front is 6.6 percent East European stock and 6.7 percent Other Northwest European stock; in the Germantown sample, the average German-stock resident's block front is 0.9 percent East European stock and 2.6 percent Other Northwest European stock.

***Includes immigrants from Italy and Spain and their children.

†Includes African Americans and immigrants from non-European countries (including Canada, South America, and Asia) and their children. The P* value for German-stock Germantowners in regard to black residents specifically was 3.3 percent, although this did not fall within the 95 percent confidence interval of the corresponding resampled mean P*. No corresponding P* value for the Girard Avenue district was calculated, given the very small number of African Americans living there in 1920.

brought their own brand of ethnic distinctiveness to this mosaic, and at times they could be at odds with German-born residents and their descendants. Gruninger, himself the son of an immigrant German-Hungarian father and a mother of German and Swiss-German descent, remembered hearing of class distinctions between the two groups in the 1910s and 1920s. "People born in Germany tended to be . . . more skilled laborers or craftsmen. People born in Hungary seemed to be more of the farmer class," he recalled. These distinctions may have carried over into stereotypes that applied specifically to Hungarians, whether they were Magyar or German. "If you were associated in any way . . . with Hungary, all right, you had a hard head and big hands," Gruninger remembered from his youth. "My father . . . would say, 'After all, what would you expect, I'm a hard-headed hunky.'" The tag "hunky" itself set German Hungarians off from neighbors with forebears from Germany proper. "A Hungarian was a Hungarian regardless of what language they spoke, so you called them a 'hunky,'" Gruninger said.[21]

For its German-stock residents, then, the Girard Avenue district in the 1920s was no longer as strongly German a neighborhood as it had been in 1900. This difference extended to the streets where they lived, as can be seen from the ethnic composition of sampled block fronts in 1920 (see map 10.1) and an analysis using the P^* statistic. In 1900, the average German-stock resident lived on a block front that was 53 percent German-stock, 25 percent native white of native parentage, and 10 percent Irish-stock (see table 2.4). Twenty years later, the Girard Avenue district's average German-stock resident lived on a block front that was only 26 percent German-stock and 22 percent native white of native parentage, 20 percent Hungarian-stock, 12 percent east European-stock, 9 percent Russian-stock, and 5 percent Irish-stock. (If Austrians, many of whom were German speakers, are factored out of the east European category, its sample P^* drops to 6.6 percent. See table 10.2).

Ethnic succession did more than make German-stock residents a minority. For them, it also appears to have promoted an increased degree of mixing across ethnic lines. Local factories may have been the site for at least some of this interaction, as is suggested by reports they filed during World War I with the U.S. Army's Plant Protection Section. In 1918, for example, the Ajax Metal Company's foundry in the Sixteenth Ward employed 292 workers. Eight were American citizens of German descent; they shared the shop floor with larger numbers of Russians, Poles, Austrians, Italians, and workers of British background. The 158 workers who produced blankets and duck cloth the same year at the Seventeenth Ward textile firm of Dornan Brothers were predominantly of British background, but they included as well thirty-two employees of German descent, three Austrians, five Poles, and two Italians.[22] It is impossible to

know whether workers at these factories were divided into ethnically segregated work gangs, or whether new immigrant employees were shunted
off into unskilled labor. However, given the relatively small size of the
workshops, chances for ethnic mixing would appear higher than they
might at a large plant.

The clearest examples of ethnic mixing involving Germans, however,
emerge from the district's Catholic parishes. Although the territorial
parish of St. Michael was known around the neighborhood as "the Irish
church,"[23] it was less Irish by the early 1930s than it had been at the turn
of the century. In 1901, 89 percent of donors to the parish's fall collection
had clearly or possibly Irish surnames. That proportion fell to 79 percent
in a list of 1,102 donors to the "Christmas, Monthly and Offertory Collections" published in the parish's monthly bulletin in February 1933. In
the intervening years, the proportion of clearly German surnames had
more than doubled, from 4.1 percent in the 1901 collection list to 10.1
percent in the 1933 list. Moreover, the parish had begun to attract a small
number of Italians and east Europeans. Twenty-six of the surnames on the
1933 list were clearly Italian, while another five were clearly of Slavic derivation.[24]

St. Peter's similarly was drawing an increasingly diverse mix of people
to its doors. "Dutch Pete's," as local residents called the church,[25] was
still a recognized German national parish, and its members remained predominantly ethnic German. Yet the church attracted a sizable non-
German contingent that appears to have grown during the 1920s. St.
Peter's had a small, non-German admixture at the turn of the century, and
such an admixture was clearly part of the active congregation at the close
of World War I, as a surname analysis of donors to the parish's Christmas
collection for 1920 indicates. Of the 916 individuals who made donations, 789 (86.1 percent) had clearly or possibly German surnames; the
remaining 127 donors (13.9 percent) had clearly non-German surnames.
Of those 127 non-German contributors, slightly more than half had surnames of clearly Irish, clearly British, or either Irish or British derivation,
but nearly a third (forty individuals) had surnames that were clearly
Slavic. One individual had an Italian last name.[26] This non-German contingent increased perceptibly over the 1920s. By 1930, the number of
donors to the church's Christmas collection had fallen to 771, but 150 of
them, or 19.5 percent, carried clearly non-German surnames. This group
had roughly the same proportion of clearly Slavic to Irish or British names
in 1930 as it had ten years before, but it was becoming a larger part of a
shrinking parish.[27]

Relations between ethnic Germans and non-Germans in the parish were
not always easy. The transition to English may have made St. Peter's more
welcoming to its ethnic outsiders. Where the parish's 1912 bulletin was

essentially bilingual, its 1921 counterpart appeared entirely in English, save for the occasional German-language advertisement.[28] The church apparently still accorded German sermons a greater importance than English ones in the early 1920s; during Lent, the Sunday high mass had the German sermon, while the English sermon was relegated to the evening service. By the 1940s, however, as Gruninger recalled, German was used only for confessions on Saturdays and in one morning mass of the several masses held on Sundays. [29] The parish bulletin also appears to have at least given a nod to non-German readers. The publication, for example, declared in 1921 that St. Malachy's prophecy that "the Church of God in Ireland shall never fail" should "be familiar to all interested in Ireland's present-day determination to have freedom," and in April 1927 it printed a priest's letter describing "A Sick-Call in Poland." Yet more private correspondence and recollections reveal some ethnic tensions. A notation on the St. Peter's 1930 annual report to the archdiocese, for example, suggested a degree of exasperation on the part of its priests with some Hungarian parishioners—whether German or Magyar is not clear. This note stated that the parish had 3,500 members, "of these about 800 Hungarians, ignorant socialists, who in spite of all our efforts cannot be brought to church. . . . They claim to be Catholics, but this Catholicity ends there."[30] Helen U., a Slovak woman who grew up in the Girard Avenue district and attended St. Peter's parochial school in the 1920s, recalled feeling "discriminated against a little bit" when it came to church functions. "[M]y parents always had a hard time getting a seat" at St. Peter's Church "for first communion or any of those things," she remembered. "You know, like my parents were not quite accepted at these functions." When her sister received a mathematics medal at graduation, "some of these Germans didn't think it was right, 'cause they gave it to this foreigner over there."[31]

St. Peter's school, in fact, can be seen as something of a barometer of relations between Germans, Irish, and eastern European immigrants in the neighborhood. The school drew at least some non-German students as early as 1912, when a few English, Irish, and Slavic names appeared on its honor roll. Some new immigrant groups, however, apparently only made use of the school until they could find an alternative. Helen U. recalled that in the fourth grade, "all these Slovak people were taking their kids . . . out of St. Peter's and sending them down" to the newly opened parochial school of St. Agnes', the Slovak national parish church in Northern Liberties. St. Agnes' had built the school, she said, partly because of the difficulties Slovak children faced at St. Peter's school.[32] Similarly, in 1926, "the Ukra[i]nian children left St. Peter's [school] to go to St. Basil's Home," according to a parish history. Polish and Irish students, however, appear to have remained at St. Peter's. Joseph Gruninger recalled that his classmates in the 1940s were mainly of German, German Hungarian, and Austrian German background, but that there were "[n]ot many . . . but some" of Irish and Polish origin. As with St. Mary's in Manayunk, some of these students came to St. Peter's as the children of ethnic intermarriages. Asked why St. Peter's would have Irish students, Gruninger noted that "[t]here was a lot of intermarriage between Germans and Irish and between Germans and Italians," as well as between Irish and Italians, in the neighborhood.[33]

Ultimately, then, St. Peter's can be seen as a German ethnic institution that, in a changing neighborhood, reflected and, to an extent, fostered social mixing between Germans and their Irish and eastern European neighbors. Gruninger, who grew up playing mostly with children of German and German Hungarian background, also numbered among his friends some who were the offspring of ethnically mixed marriages. Helen U., who stayed at St. Peter's school until she graduated, noted that the distance she sensed "didn't stop me from making fun, [and] making friends" with her ethnically German classmates, "[f]riends that I've had all my life." It is telling that George N., a Slovak resident of South Philadelphia born twelve years after Helen U., would in his youth travel up to St. Peter's for "Sunday dances," presumably at the parish hall.[34] Not without friction, but gradually, the Girard Avenue district's German Catholics were learning during the interwar period to live with—and even to socialize with—new immigrants.

OLD RESIDENTS AND OUTSIDERS IN GERMANTOWN

Philadelphia's population shifts had a very different impact on Germantown. In that suburb, they brought growth and highlighted divisions between more established, middle-class residents of northwest European background and a small but rising number of Italian and African-American newcomers. Within this context, Germantown's residents of immigrant German origin remained entrenched in the neighborhood's northwest European social worlds.

As neighborhoods like the Girard Avenue district lost residents in the early twentieth century, more suburban areas like Germantown gained. Between 1910 and 1920 alone, the population of the Twenty-second Ward, encompassing Germantown, Mount Airy, and Chestnut Hill, grew by 22 percent.[35] The housing boom that accompanied this rise did not change Germantown's fundamental division between a middle-class west side of comfortable homes and a more working-class east side. Maps from the 1920s show the east side as dotted with small knitting, yarn, and hosiery mills, as well as paper box factories, machine shops, and such larger establishments as the Scatchard woolen mill. The west side remained a well-off commuter suburb, although it was losing some of its cachet. Most of the upper-class, "Proper Philadelphian" families that kept estates there in the 1890s had moved away by the First World War.[36]

Germantown's growth in some ways made it more than ever a bastion of long-settled northwest Europeans. The neighborhood's proportion of native whites of native parentage actually rose between 1900 and 1920, to 51 percent. This increase likely marked the appearance of third-generation descendants of nineteenth-century immigrants from Britain, Ireland, and Germany, for the proportions of first- and second-generation immigrants from those countries all had fallen by 1920. Irish, British, and German newcomers and their children remained the neighborhood's largest immigrant groups. Nevertheless, Germantown by 1920 had begun to feel the impact of both the new immigration and the Great Migration, as table 10.1 indicates. Italian-born residents and their children—who made up almost all of the individuals in the "south European" category, itself 3.5 percent of the population—had emerged as the fourth-largest immigrant group, trailed by a scattering of east Europeans and Russian Jews. African Americans also had increased their numbers: their proportion in the population (6.1 percent) was now roughly as large as that of German immigrants and their children (6.3 percent).

Black Germantown was growing even before the Great Migration. One observer noted of Germantown in 1912 that "a large number of the better class of Negroes have settled [there] within the past ten years." By 1915, a survey estimated that between 3,500 and 4,000 African Americans lived in the neighborhood, some scattered and others gathered into five distinct concentrations. The survey found some doctors, schoolteachers, carpenters, and printers in this population, along with a majority of laborers and domestic servants. Together, they supported nine churches, including St. Catherine's, a "colored" Catholic church. Whatever success black residents achieved, however, they still faced pervasive discrimination, in the form of, among other things, segregated elementary schools.[37]

In their own way, Germantown's Italians also represented an outsider presence to longer-established white residents. As early as 1900, the *Germantown Independent-Gazette* had referred to a "Little Italy" on Germantown's east side. By 1914, east-side Italians had their own national Catholic chapel, Holy Rosary. The chapel's school was enlarged that year, one journalist noted, as a consequence of the fact that "[t]he Italian Catholic population of East Germantown has increased so rapidly during the past few years." In 1920, the east-side "Italian colony" was large enough to support Italian clubs and a building and loan association. However, to the *Independent-Gazette,* it still seemed unknown terri-

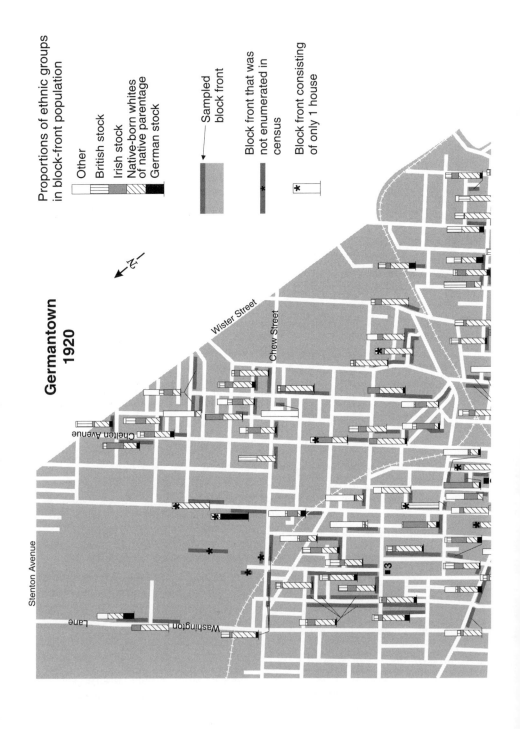

Germantown 1920

Proportions of ethnic groups in block-front population

- Other
- British stock
- Irish stock
- Native-born whites of native parentage
- German stock

Sampled block front

Block front that was not enumerated in census

Block front consisting of only 1 house

Stenton Avenue

Washington Lane

Chelten Avenue

Wister Street

Chew Street

Landmarks

1 Vernon Park
2 St. Vincent de Paul Roman Catholic Church
3 St. Thomas' Evangelical Lutheran Church
4 Trinity Lutheran Church
5 Germantown Cricket Club
6 YMCA
7 Market Square Presbyterian Church

Map 10.2. Germantown, 1920. Sources: Author's census sample; George W. Bromley and Walter S. Bromley, *Atlas of the City of Philadelphia, 22nd Ward* (Philadelphia, 1923, corrected to 1928); Sanborn Map Company, *Insurance Maps of Philadelphia, Pennsylvania* (New York, 1924–1926), vols. 22, 23; Ernest Hexamer and Son, *Insurance Maps of the City of Philadelphia* (Philadelphia, 1893–1922), vols. 16, 21, 28, 29, 33 (for more specific publication information, see appendix, note 3).

tory, a somewhat exotic locale that made its presence felt through the "[t]er-rific detonations of fireworks" Italian Germantowners set off on saints' days.[38]

Many Germantown residents who descended from nineteenth-century German immigrants seem to have remained at some remove from neighborhood German ethnic institutions, for only two of these survived into the 1920s: the Germantown Maennerchor and St. Thomas' Lutheran Church. St. Thomas' retained a congregation of just over ninety members, but it announced in 1925 that it would add an English-language service, apparently in an effort to hold onto the rising generation.[39] At the same time, first- and second-generation German immigrants continued to mix with the neighborhood's other northwest Europeans. In residential terms, such mixing was even more apparent in 1920 than in 1900. This can be seen by mapping the ethnic composition of a random sample of German-town block fronts (see map 10.2) and through a P^* analysis of that sample. The average German-stock resident of Germantown in 1920 lived on a block front that was only 11.5 percent German-stock; the corresponding figure for 1900 was 18.6 percent (see tables 10.2 and 2.4). That average German of 1920 had fewer neighbors of immigrant Irish (15.3 percent) or British (11 percent) background but more who were native whites of native parentage (50.9 percent). Of his or her neighbors in the sample, only 1.9 percent were of south European stock, while just 3.3 percent were black. German-stock residents thus seem to have avoided living next to Italians and African Americans.

Many Germantowners of immigrant German background likewise stayed within northwest European worlds socially, although ones often divided by religion. The Business Men's Association of Germantown, for example, listed 202 members in its 1928 directory, most of whom had English, Scottish, or Irish surnames. Thirty-one members had clearly German surnames, including three of the group's charter members—Frederick W. Kaplan, Henry W. Pletcher, and Charles J. Schaefer, all second-generation German immigrants. Only a handful of members, however, carried what could have been Russian Jewish surnames, and no Italian names at all appeared in the membership list.[40] Many German-stock residents also availed themselves of religious denominations cast in northwest European molds. Catholics of German background continued to attend the neighborhood's Irish-dominated territorial parishes, which were kept clear, by and large, of Italian and African-American members by the existence of Germantown's "colored" and Italian national parishes. The Church of St. Vincent de Paul, for example, remained overwhelmingly Irish, to judge by a list of donors to the parish's 1930 Easter collection. Of the 1,071 individuals on the list, seventy (6.5 percent) had clearly German surnames, but only seven had clearly Italian and two had clearly

Slavic surnames.[41] Other residents of German background turned to St. Michael's Lutheran Church, the Pennsylvania Ministerium's English Lutheran congregation in Germantown. Margaret Zinser, a lifelong member, recalled the congregation in the interwar period as including some children of German immigrants, along with "Anglo-Americans" and members of colonial German descent.[42]

The lines that separated these northwest European worlds from African-American and new immigrant Germantowners could be quite stark. At the extreme, among some white Protestant residents, they shaded into forms of racism and nativism that had a particular hold in Germantown during the 1920s. The neighborhood had a set of nativist lodges that dated to the nineteenth century, including units of the Junior Order United American Mechanics, the Order Independent Americans, and the Patriotic Order Sons of America.[43] Joining these older groups was the Ku Klux Klan, with an ideology even more anti-Catholic than it was antiblack. During the interwar period, the Klan showed particular strength among white Protestants in suburban neighborhoods, such as Germantown, who were "concerned about the northward spread of nearby 'alien' communities, whether Catholic, black, or Jewish." In the mid-1920s, Germantown's klavern was the largest in Philadelphia, with more than 1,200 members.[44]

Most Germantowners, of course, did not burn crosses in the 1920s. But the views expressed in their most extreme form by the Klan—a fear of new immigrants and African Americans as racial threats to America—had their counterparts in more diffuse suspicions among Philadelphians of northwest European background as to the fitness of south and east European newcomers for American life. How some children of German immigrants drew on such sentiments to cast their identities in a more "American" light is the topic of the next chapter.

CHAPTER ELEVEN

Middle-Class Germans: American Identity and the "Stock" of "Our Forefathers"

As Congress waged its last debates over the nation's new system of restrictive immigration quotas in the spring of 1929, a correspondent to the *Lutherischer Herold* called on readers to fight the lowering of the quota for German immigrants. "[I]t is absolutely necessary," this contributor declared, "that Americandom of German birth and descent . . . push for a further postponement" of the national origins quotas.[1] That phrase—an "Amerikanertum deutscher Geburt und Abstammung"—would have been virtually unknown before World War I. It said much about how German Philadelphians had reconceived their relation to the nation. Many came to stress their adherence to "Americandom" over their ethnic origins, rather than balancing the two between a hyphen. This move toward a primarily "American" sensibility was one of several developments that contributed to a fundamental reworking of identities in the 1920s, as many German Philadelphians de-emphasized or abandoned the ethnic labels of "German" or "German-American."

This chapter and the next explore several of the major paths that second- and third-generation German immigrants traveled away from German origins. Their routes were shaped by ethnic and racial succession, by the conformist climate of "100 percent American" nationalism ushered in by the First World War, and by the rising, and related, tide of racialized nativism that culminated in the immigration restriction acts of 1921 and 1924—and ultimately in the national origins quota system. Yet the fault lines that had long divided Philadelphians of German background also played a role: the ways in which those Philadelphians redefined their identities tended to vary by class and religious affiliation. This chapter examines how some middle-class and Lutheran residents descended from nineteenth-century German immigrants evinced an American identity keyed to their self-perceived status as insiders in a nation where southern and eastern Europeans were outsiders. These identities could be expressed in relatively neutral ways, as when a mission teacher took the role of an "American" working among "Italians." But such an "American" sense of self could also draw on the categories of racialized nativism to depict new immigrants as coming from less desirable "stock" than northwest Europeans. American identities of that stripe were much less available to working-class Catholics and blue-collar workers in general; they retreated from their ethnic origins largely on different paths, which the last chapter will describe.

"Americans" First

Attacks on "hyphenated Americanism," while they abated somewhat after 1919, remained a staple of political discourse in the 1920s. "There is no such thing as Irish-American and there is no such thing as Italian-American," roared a delegate to the 1926 state convention of the Patriotic Order Sons of America, held in Philadelphia. "If we are Americans we are Americans only." The *Philadelphia Tageblatt* was impelled to defend the "healthy and justified hyphen" against a 1924 declaration by Pennsylvania's U.S. Senator David A. Reed that immigration restriction would end "the frightful 'hyphen' and the 'hyphen vote' in our country."[2]

Such attacks reflected what Gary Gerstle has described as "the powerful nationalism that settled over America in the 1910s and 1920s, suffocating the hyphenated identities that had thrived in the beginning of the century." This "new equation between national loyalty and a large measure of political and social conformity," in John Higham's words,[3] spelled a climate within which many children and grandchildren of German immigrants embraced or took for granted identities as "Americans," with little or no stress on their ethnic background. This stance—a sharp contrast to some Germans' prewar ambivalence about "America"—comes through very strongly in the recollections of second-, third-, and fourth-generation German immigrants who grew up in Philadelphia during the interwar years. "We considered ourselves as full-blooded Americans," John Eichman said of his family in the 1920s and 1930s. "We didn't think of ourselves in terms of . . . the nationality of our ancestors who came to this country." Eichman, of fourth-generation German and third-generation Irish descent, recalled asserting that identity while hanging out with friends in the Roxborough and Manayunk of the 1920s. "[I]f somebody said to me, 'You, you no-good Irish punk,' okay, or 'You're a G——d—— German,' . . . my retort would be, 'I'm a full-blooded American.'" Esther Schuchard Browne had similar memories of her youth in Kensington. She had "a tie with German background" through her German-born mother's correspondence with relatives in Germany; nevertheless, "I thought of myself as an American, first of all." Browne, like Eichman, claimed this identity among her contemporaries during her grade school years: "I used to think I was American, and then they said to me, 'You're not American—you're, you're German!' 'I am *not*!'" she would reply. Even George Beichl, whose interest in German culture eventually led him, in the 1970s, to the presidency of the German Society, recalled that he "never" thought of himself as a "German American." Rather, he would call himself an "American," while also referring to himself as being "of German descent."[4]

"American," however, was a fought-over category that, for many Americans, carried its own ethnic and racial meanings. American nationalism, as Gerstle argued, had a racial tradition that had long cast whiteness as intrinsic to Americanness.[5] By the 1920s, that tradition took a particular form. As chapter 5 described, many European Americans had come to see Americans of northwest European descent, whether of colonial or nineteenth-century immigrant background, as a group with a greater claim to white and American identity than "new" south and east European immigrants. This understanding was both racial and temporal: Americans of English, German, Scandinavian, and even Irish origin were considered superior to Italians, Poles, and Russian Jews because they possessed a superior racial stock in common with the country's early settlers and the founders of the nation. A crucial factor in cementing this view was the rise of a racialized nativism that "scientifically" divided Europeans into "races" of Nordics, Mediterraneans, Alpines, and Jews. "Nordic" joined and at times fused with categories such as "old stock" and "American race stock" as a way of talking about those of northwest European background supposed to be the truest of Americans. Ultimately, these views helped to reshape the American body politic. The Johnson-Reed Act of 1924, which limited immigration quotas for a given country to 2 percent of the number of foreign-born residents of that nationality present in the 1890 census, drew directly on racial nativists' arguments in favoring northwest European immigrants.[6]

For some by the early 1920s, then, "American" meant northwest-European American.[7] Yet, as this meaning did not go uncontested, terms such as "old stock" and "Nordic" were used to specify who, exactly, qualified as the best sort of American. Crucially, these terms invited Americans of German background to join the northwest European club, and such language proliferated at virtually the same moment as those Americans were ordered to drop their hyphens. The debate over immigration restriction in particular popularized "Nordic" as a category that included Germans. Naaman H. Keyser, Germantown's premier local historian, could offhandedly refer to the Founders' Monument in 1922 as "a memorial to the pioneers of one of the greatest branches of the Nordic race." The term even found its way into the *Tageblatt,* which, while denouncing the Johnson-Reed bill, spoke of "the German, yes, the entire Nordic immigration."[8]

Embracing Racial Nativism

By the early 1920s, some second-generation German immigrants had begun to accept the invitation terms like "old stock" and "Nordic" represented. They adopted an American identity framed as the common, and venerable, racial possession of northwest Europeans. The clearest evidence of this shift is the fact that children of German immigrants belonged to organizations that increasingly espoused such views, organizations dedicated to excluding or "Americanizing" new immigrants.

The city's nativist groups drew the strongest lines between "Americans" and "new immigrants." Among these organizations were the Junior Order United American Mechanics and the Patriotic Order Sons of America. As we have seen, the Junior Order's founding council, Germantown's Washington Council, No. 1, seemed relatively unaffected before World War I by the racial nativism of national JOUAM leaders. By 1914, a series of schisms had left the Washington Council unaffiliated with the order's state or national bodies. The council did, however, belong by 1915 to the local Federation of Councils, comprising four such bodies in Philadelphia. In 1923, the federation claimed 2,500 members, 525 of them in the Washington Council.[9]

The four federation councils retained the Junior Order's traditional anti-Catholic bent at least into the 1910s, to judge from their monthly newsletter, *The Federation News*. A 1915 issue, for example, reported on an alleged effort "to increase the influence of the Pope." The same issue, however, demonstrated that the councils were taking enthusiastically to the burgeoning antihyphen movement. The newsletter took "pleasure" in reprinting a *Philadelphia Inquirer* editorial declaring that naturalized immigrants should learn English: "[T]hey are no longer—or should not be—German-Americans, Italian-Americans, Irish-Americans . . . or anything else but plain Americans." The federated councils likewise rallied wholeheartedly behind the campaign that culminated in the Johnson-Reed Act. "Let's all work for absolute restriction of Immigration," the *Federation News* declared in March 1924. "There are too many foreigners here already. Remember our motto—America for Americans." Just who "Americans" were was made clear in resolutions adopted by the federation that month endorsing a precursor of the act. These complained that "[i]mmigrants coming from non-English speaking races are colonizing largely in industrial centers, continuing to speak their own language and failing to become Americanized." Accordingly, "[t]hose races by their failure to assimilate become a menace to American institutions and American ideals." The federation then signaled that the races in question were new immigrant ones by introducing a time element: "After reviewing the class of Immigrants for the last twenty-five years or more coming from those races, we feel that it is for the best interests of our Country and our American institutions, that Immigration should be drastically checked."[10]

It seems clear that among those who resolved "unanimously" to pass these resolutions at the federation's March 12 meeting were a number of officers and delegates of German descent. The page of the *Federation News* that carried the resolutions also listed, two columns away, the federation's five officers and four council deputies; of these nine individuals, three had clearly German surnames: Louis R. Kleiber, Jacob Bumm Sr., and George Calvin Klein, a Washington Council member who served as federation secretary. Such surnames also appeared among the officers of Washington Council's Veteran Association, which had F. P. Beitenman as its secretary and John H. Shultz as its second vice president in 1924.[11] These five individuals, of course, may have been of colonial German ancestry; the three who could be traced in the 1920 manuscript census were native whites of native parentage.[12] But the federation numbered at least some second-generation German immigrants among its rank-and-file members, including three in Germantown: John C. Vogelsang, a stationary engineer; John L. Zimmerman, a self-employed paperhanger; and Frederick W. Kaplan, the Germantown hat store proprietor and charter member of the Business Men's Association.[13]

Kaplan's case is particularly interesting. He appears to have been a long-time member of Washington Council; his advertisement in the June 1915 *Federation News* noted that he was a "Member of Washington Council," and a short 1922 biography likewise numbered the "American Mechanics" among his affiliations.[14] He also seems to have embraced an American identity over an ethnic German one. As chapter 6 described, Kaplan was one of a number of sons of German immigrants who helped organize the 1908 celebration of Germantown's founding but who chose to do so as a member of the Founders' Day Committee, rather than of the "German Citizens of Germantown" committee. Kaplan likewise had unimpeachable patriotic credentials: since at least 1908, he had served as the frequent, if not only, chairman of the Business Men's Association's Fourth of July committee, which organized the annual Independence Day festivities at Vernon Park.[15] Kaplan may not have ignored his ethnic background completely; his committee did plan to include an "exhibition of Gym. team of the Turngemeind [*sic*]" in the 1919 celebration. But his affiliations suggest he would have agreed that "[t]he hyphen has no business to be placed before the word American," to quote the *Inquirer* editorial reprinted by the *Federation News*, one page away from the advertisement for Kaplan's store.[16] One can presume as well from his continued membership in the Washington Council that this son of German immigrants saw himself as "American" in a way south and east European "races" would not or could not be.

Like the older JOUAM, the Patriotic Order Sons of America (POSA) was founded in Pennsylvania and expanded in the late nineteenth century through much of the country. The POSA seems to have added racial nativism to its antiradical and anti-Catholic repertoire somewhat later than the Junior Order. Where the latter group forwarded extensive statements to the Dillingham Commission in 1910 decrying southeast European immigrants, the POSA submitted a one-page resolution that called for the restriction only of "undesirable and the less assimilative aliens."[17] By the early 1920s, however, the Patriotic Order had done some catching up. It agitated vigorously for what became the Johnson-Reed Act, and its monthly journal, the Philadelphia-based *Camp News,* indulged in racial nativist language. "It was the Nordic races solely who planted our civilization and launched our Government, and not until about 1890 did the hordes of southern and eastern Europe begin to over-run our shores," the newspaper's front page proclaimed in April 1924. "When the Nordic races cut home ties and come to America they do so determined to become a part of the country to which they immigrated. . . . Now those who come, from other sources, come only for the easy money there is in America."[18]

In the early 1920s, too, Philadelphians of German descent were well-represented among those who led the POSA's local councils, or "camps." The city had ninety-four POSA camps in 1920, and lists of their recording secretaries in 1920 and 1924 are peppered with German surnames— Auman, Fritz, Hefterich, Doderer, Rohlfing, and Barth, among others.[19] Of those who could be located in the 1920 manuscript census, some were native whites of native parentage and might have been of either nineteenth-century or colonial immigrant background.[20] At least four, however, were second-generation German immigrants: William A. Hammer, a house painter; John Schmidt Sr., an operator in a horse blanket mill; Maurice H. Rasener, a self-employed publisher; and Frederick Baumert, a dry goods salesman.[21] That such immigrant sons may not have been uncommon among the POSA rank and file is suggested by an anecdote in the April 1924 *Camp News* about a dispute between two members over "the immigration subject." Both had some immigrant parentage. "God bless their daddies if they were immigrants—they are the kind of immigrants we want, for they brought into the world some real Americans, and in just one generation, all assimilated," the newspaper declared. POSA membership could provide the sons of German newcomers with just that sense of being "real Americans," as defined against new immigrants. As the *Camp News* stated in its next breath, "[b]ut God save us from what we are getting now—close the gates."[22]

Where groups such as the Junior Order and the Patriotic Order sought primarily to exclude new immigrants, organizations such as the Americanization Committee of Germantown hoped to reform them. The committee was one of a number of agencies engaged in "Americanization" work in Philadelphia during the 1920s. The Philadelphia Chamber of Commerce's Americanization Committee sought early in the decade to coordinate the efforts of the public schools, social welfare agencies, manufacturers, patriotic groups, and women's organizations. Americanization of this ilk stressed naturalization; teaching immigrants to speak, read, and write English; and the inculcation of "city-wide patriotism and loyalty." Its sponsors also had an interest in combating political radicalism. The chamber of commerce urged patriotic organizations to "[m]eet the arguments of the 'soap-box' orator with the truth." The city's Americanizers seem to have focused on a very specific kind of foreigner, however: the new immigrant. Of the 528 students registered for city Americanization classes in the 1921–1922 school year, 97 percent came from southern or eastern Europe; only four were born in Germany.[23]

The Americanization Committee of Germantown shared these predilections, for the middle- and upper-class women who made up the organization trained their sights on the Italians of the east side. The committee grew out of the Woman's Club of Germantown, itself founded in 1917. The Woman's Club, a member of the national General Federation of Women's Clubs, resembled its sister associations in that body in mixing impulses toward sociability and political activism.[24] Club members attended citizenship classes as well as poetry readings and teas. The Americanization Committee had its origins in meetings held in the winter of 1918–1919, under the leadership of Ida Kane, the chair of the club's Patriotic Committee. In 1919, a social worker "at a little settlement among the large Italian population over on our East Side, asked our interest and assistance," and Kane and her associates began their work in East Germantown. When the settlement closed early in 1920, they decided to continue their east-side efforts under the name of the Americanization Committee of Germantown.[25]

The committee operated under the auspices of the Woman's Club, in conjunction with a number of other Germantown organizations. Working out of an east-side "Americanization room," the committee's paid staff and volunteers conveyed "practical instruction," while seeking to encourage "American ideals of cleanliness and right living, as well as loyalty to the flag and country." By 1921, the group was offering English classes for men, sewing and cooking classes for women, and gymnastics, dancing, and scouting troops for children.[26] Like the would-be Americanizers of Mexican newcomers in Los Angeles studied by George Sánchez, the committee soon focused its attention on mothers and their children and then primarily on "the children of the foreign-born." Committee members hoped that through American-born daughters, they might influence the immigrant home, or at least the homes of the second generation. By the end of the decade, they sponsored a "Little Mothers Club," where "the children, guided by volunteer teachers, follow a program of home routine."[27]

Whatever their impact on Italian Germantowners, the efforts of the Americanization Committee spoke volumes about how its members saw themselves. By the committee's very name, those who belonged to it considered themselves "Americans" who had something to teach immigrants about what being American meant. But the opposition between "American" and "foreign-born" carried still more meaning. Committee members—unlike many nativists—obviously considered east-side Italians capable of becoming Americans, but they feared them as well. "These people are our neighbors, with families frequently of from 5 to 15 children," Kane wrote in 1921. "It has been estimated that in 30 years they will outvote us 6 to 1. If this country is to be safe for us and for our children, must we not educate them, teach them our language, our laws, the fundamentals of our Government which stands for liberty, but not for license?"[28] At the bottom of this fear, moreover, lay a perception of racial difference, one keyed to a sense that Americanizers—and, hence, true Americans—shared a common northwest European racial stock with roots in America that trailed back to colonial times. This view emerged with full force in the committee's 1925 annual report, which began with a nod of approval to the Johnson-Reed Act:

> The recent check upon immigration is a most hopeful sign for the future of our country—but we nevertheless have with us an enormous percentage of alien-born of less desirable stock than that from which our forefathers came. When we consider the average American family with its one or two children as against the immigrant family of Central or Southern Europe with perhaps a dozen children, the necessity for work among these coming Americans is quite apparent—and assumes great importance.[29]

Presumably, the committee's members, who were listed on the page opposite this declaration, shared the more "desirable stock" of "our forefathers." That these members shared a sense of being Americanizers racially distant from their Italian clients is likewise suggested by a poem, titled "The Big Problem," that appeared in the 1925 and 1921 annual reports. As the work's first stanza put it: "He's a hunkie or a wop, he's a dago or a Greek. / And the language of our country is a tongue he cannot speak. . . . / He's a power for good or evil[,] he will hate us or revere / And become a friend or traitor from the way we treat him here."[30]

Who, then, were these members? Certainly, they were middle- or upper-class. Among the husbands of the women listed on the Americanization Committee's 1925 roster were the president of a paper box company, a company executive secretary, a lawyer, a doctor, and a schools superintendent, along with a clerk and a commercial salesman. Kane herself, now the group's second vice chairman, was married to a securities broker.[31] The committee thus had a more elite tinge than the nativist orders, which took in some skilled as well as low-white-collar workers. Crucially, however, the committee roster also represented a northwest European ethnic mix, a collection of English, Scotch-Irish, Irish, and German surnames. Of the body's twenty-five members, seven had surnames that were clearly of German derivation: Mrs. William E. Buehler, Mrs. W. H. Betz, Mrs. W. H. Bossert, Mrs. R. E. Steckle, Mrs. George Wertsner, Mrs. David Wallerstein, and Mrs. Lewis D. Ziegler. Five of these individuals could be traced in the 1920 manuscript census. Three were native whites of native parentage.[32] Such members may, again, have had either colonial or nineteenth-century immigrant forebears. At least one of the committee members, however, was a second-generation German immigrant. Nellie C. Wallerstein was born in Pennsylvania in 1867; her father and mother both were German-born. Wallerstein's lawyer husband, David, was also a Pennsylvania native, with a mother born in that state and a father born in Germany. In 1920, Nellie and David Wallerstein lived on Germantown's west side with their two children.[33] Nellie Wallerstein appears to have become involved with the Americanization Committee through the Woman's Club, for she served on the club's Program Committee in 1919 and 1920. She joined the new Americanization Committee in the first year of its existence and, from available records, appears to have belonged to it at least through 1925.[34] The remaining committee member carrying a German surname, Anna E. Wertsner, was, in fact, an English immigrant married to a native white of native parentage; she had arrived in the United States as a young child in 1874. Wertsner's presence illustrates the committee's racial understanding of "desirable stock," for while she was "alien-born," her English origins put her squarely within the "stock . . . from which our forefathers came."[35]

LUTHERANS AS AMERICANIZERS

By the early 1920s, then, at least some second-generation German immigrants were coming to see themselves as Americans by virtue of their membership in a common northwest European group defined by race and time. One's parents might have arrived in the nineteenth century, but if they came from Germany, they belonged to the same "stock" as "our forefathers" who had settled in the colonial period, or to "Nordic races" that immigrated before 1890. Such views, however, represented only one end of a range of stances taken by the Philadelphia descendants of nineteenth-century German immigrants in the 1920s. Another, more moderate response was to see oneself as American in opposition to new immigrants, without necessarily invoking racialist rhetoric, although the implication remained that real Americans were of northwest European background. This was the tack taken by some Lutherans of German immigrant origin who sought to win new immigrants, especially Italians, for the Lutheran faith.

That children and grandchildren of nineteenth-century German Lutheran immigrants might adopt an "old stock" American identity as they entered "English" Lutheran churches would not be surprising, given the strength of such views among "English Lutherans" of colonial German descent. The English Lutherans who dominated the Pennsylvania Ministerium and its newly created parent synod, the United Lutheran Church in America (ULCA), had an almost testy sense that their forefathers, too, were founders of the nation. "From the early days of its colonization North America has felt the influence of the Lutheran Church, which existed here three years before the Pilgrim Fathers set foot upon New England soil," the Ministerium's short-lived Committee on Americanization declared in 1920. *The Lutheran,* the Philadelphia-based weekly that served as the ULCA's official organ, shared this perspective—not surprisingly, since its editor in chief, the Ministerium pastor George Washington Sandt, served in 1921 and 1922 as president of the Pennsylvania German Society.[36] The newspaper, however, seemed ready to consider the children of nineteenth-century Lutheran immigrants from northwest Europe as sufficiently American. "In recent years, much of the immigration from Southern Europe and Russia has been anything but desirable," the *Lutheran* observed in May 1924. "[T]here is a marked difference between the present-day immigrants and those who have come from the States bordering on the Baltic, several generations ago. The middle and the northwest has been greatly enriched by these now thoroughly Americanized citizens from Northern Europe." The *Lutheran*'s "Young People" feature similarly depicted American civilization in July 1924 as "a fusing of many nationalities," all of them northwest European. The article then provided another term for readers to describe their fused nationality when it contrasted the "Spanish population" in the southwest with "the older American stock." "Old stock," in fact, seems to have been a key term in the Pennsylvania Ministerium's sense of itself. In 1927, the synod published a survey of its congregations that had asked about "favorable" influences toward Lutheranism in the community. Under the heading, "Of Character of People," congregations reported such favorable community traits as, "[f]airly stable," "middle class," and "old stock."[37]

Available evidence, however, suggests that Philadelphia Lutherans of nineteenth-century immigrant background may have conceived of their

American identities in more subtle terms. Margaret Zinser, a fourth-generation immigrant on her father's side, recalled that members of that branch of the family called themselves American, without bringing up their German ancestry. But while she remembered hearing the term "old-stock American" in the 1920s, she did not think her family referred to themselves that way.[38] At least some Lutherans of German immigrant background appear to have cast themselves as Americans in opposition to new immigrants, while leaving racialist language aside, as can be seen in the case of the Ministerium's Inner Mission Society.

The Inner Mission Society of the Evangelical Lutheran Church was founded in 1902 by Philadelphia Lutherans with an interest in social service work. By 1914, the Society had established its Lutheran Settlement at the eastern edge of the Girard Avenue district. The institution offered its neighbors the usual range of clubs and classes but brought a specifically religious outlook to its work, acquiring its own congregation and Sunday school.[39] By 1916, the Inner Mission Society had also taken control of the Martin Luther Neighborhood House, a South Philadelphia settlement established in 1910 by St. Peter's English Evangelical Lutheran Church as part of its mission work among the area's Italian immigrants. The society transferred responsibility for the Neighborhood House to the ULCA's Immigrants Mission Board in 1923, but within less than ten years it was again running the South Philadelphia settlement and would do so until 1949.[40]

The society and its two settlement houses appear to have drawn a mix of English Lutheran and German Lutheran officers and staff. In 1915, the president of the society's Board of Managers was the Reverend J. F. Ohl, who had ancestors in America before the Revolution; George Washington Sandt, of Pennsylvania German background, was also a member of the panel. Yet the board likewise included at least two German-born pastors, the Reverend E. F. Bachmann and the Reverend R. G. Bielinski.[41] The society's longtime treasurer, the manufacturer George Hofstetter, was born in Germany as well.[42] Similarly, the Reverend Gustavus Henry Bechtold, the director of the Lutheran Settlement from 1914 to 1922, and the Reverend Joseph S. Schantz, the settlement's pastor before and after Bechtold's administration, were both native whites of native parentage. Anna P. Hess, on the other hand, a veteran teacher at the Martin Luther Neighborhood House, was the American-born daughter of a German-born father and a mother who was herself a second-generation German immigrant.[43] Hess had opened a kindergarten for Italian children at St. Peter's Church in 1908; the Neighborhood House, which in part grew out of that experiment, employed her as its director of religious instruction into the early 1920s, if not longer. Hess also worked, at least occasionally, at the Lutheran Settlement. By the end of 1932, she was one of four editors of the society's newsletter, *The Inner Missionary*, and she became the director of the Neighborhood House by 1934.[44] Hess's sister, Emma, had joined her there as a kindergarten teacher by 1916.[45]

Settlement work brought the society's staff and volunteers in contact with a range of immigrant peoples, not only the Italians of South Philadelphia but also the polyglot residents of the Sixteenth, Seventeenth, and Eighteenth wards. In the early 1910s, the population around the Lutheran Settlement "consisted of people of German descent, Hungarians and Slavs, with a group of Jewish people on the west side," according to a history of the institution published in the *Inner Missionary* in 1936. Music classes at the settlement drew "[f]ive nationalities" in 1919. The *Inner Missionary* provides a window onto how society members and workers viewed these immigrants and their children. The newsletter appears to have been edited from the Lutheran Settlement, presumably by Bechtold, while he was director; after Bechtold left, Schantz served as editor until his death in 1931.[46] The main motive behind the settlement and the Neighborhood House was religious. As the newsletter stated in 1916, "[t]he primary function of The Settlement is always the preaching of the Gospel."[47] Bechtold in particular, however, saw Americanization as an important aspect of settlement work. The *Inner Missionary* in 1919 described both settlements as "laboratories": "America has been called a 'melting pot' and the settlements are the workshops where the contents are analyzed, their possibilities and defects noted."[48]

Significantly, in "analyzing" such contents, the newsletter tended to place "people of German descent" in the "American" category, as against new immigrants. Discussing "the Americanization of the incoming millions" in 1916, the *Inner Missionary* noted that "we are working among the Slovaks, the Letts, and the Italians," and added that the Lutheran Settlement was constantly "coming in contact with a great many" of what it called "real Magyars." The article, however, never mentioned the neighborhood's German-stock residents, although the settlement obviously dealt with some of them. Bechtold made the distinction clear when describing the population around the Neighborhood House. "While the immediate neighborhood is predominantly Italian there are quite a number of other nationalities within easy reach," he wrote in 1920. These included Jews, "a large Syrian colony," and "many unchurched Americans, quite a few of whom are of German extraction."[49]

Whether most of the first-, second-, and third-generation German immigrants who belonged to or worked for the Inner Mission Society saw themselves as Americans aiding foreigners is difficult to determine. Bechtold himself may have been a third-generation immigrant, a circumstance that seems the more likely because—unlike Schantz—he was born in Philadelphia, with its large nineteenth-century population of German immigrants, rather than the city's Pennsylvania German hinterland.[50] But Anna Hess, for one, did cast herself in such an "American" light. Reflecting in 1923 on her fifteen years at the Neighborhood House, Hess described that settlement's origins in terms that put her on the American side of an effort to reach Italians. As Italians moved into the South Philadelphia neighborhood, "the Americans left for other parts of the city," she recalled. The resulting loss in congregants forced sixteen area churches to shut their doors, and St. Peter's, "being in the section affected, found itself threatened with a similar fate." However, the pastor's wife, Lillian Cassaday, resolved to win the newcomers for Lutheranism. Cassaday enlisted Hess in this effort, and the latter opened St. Peter's kindergarten for Italian children at Cassaday's request. In remembering Cassaday's dedication to this cause, Hess signaled that she saw herself as acting with the congregation of St. Peter's, a congregation that, she had just implied, was American, like the sixteen that had closed. Cassaday "saw in those little dark-eyed children the souls which Christ died to save, and it seemed to her that we, as Christians, have a duty toward these people—that in our zeal for foreign missions we dare not overlook those at our own doors."[51]

Anna Hess, and perhaps her sister Emma as well, thus seems to have situated herself as an American in opposition to the first- and second-generation Italian immigrants she sought to reach. Other Philadelphians of immigrant German background also crafted such situational American identities during the 1920s, as the recollections of some attest. These identities could carry a temporal element. Esther Browne recalled perceiving that "there was an awareness . . . [and] a measurement or a degree of worth . . . having . . . been an American citizen or born in this country for several generations." Young, second-generation German immigrants likewise could measure the difference between themselves and "new immigrants" in terms of different customs and accents. Some schoolchildren gauged this distance in terms of how the latter's parents dressed. "I know that the babushka or the scarf tied around the head [of a parent], when I was going to school, that . . . to us kids meant, they just came over on the boat, . . . that's what we used to say," Browne remembered. "We used to feel sorry for those kids," the children of Polish and Russian immigrants, she added. "Because their parents were dressed differently . . . from the norm."[52]

American identities of this kind were not confined to Lutherans, for middle-class Catholics could hold them as well. Perhaps the most vivid example is John Eichman's sense of being a "full-blooded American." Eichman, of course, socialized with classmates of east European background at St. Mary's parochial school. Yet his encounters with other new immigrants, in particular the children of Polish immigrants, could leave a sense of difference that was quite strong. His daily walk from his Roxborough home to St. Mary's school, for example, took him through a section of Manayunk that "was practically all Polish." About twice a year, on his way through "the Polish turf," some young sons of that neighborhood's immigrants would corner him and start a fight that the outnumbered Eichman inevitably would lose. By his early teens, Eichman became a familiar enough sight on his route that "the Polish kids" stopped beating him up. But accents continued to mark some "Polish kids" as different. "Some of them, you could tell they were Polish" from their speech, he said. Such perceptions, in turn, helped to shape Eichman's sense of American nationality. Crucially, for Eichman and his friends, a Polish accent excluded even a second-generation Polish immigrant from the category of "full-blooded American." "A kid would judge another kid by the way he talked, you know?" he recalled. Eichman did say that he and his friends would consider most of the children of Manayunk's Polish immigrants to be "full-blooded Americans," but with reservations. As he put it: "Yeah, they were full-blooded Americans. But . . . they were different."[53]

Some middle-class and Lutheran Philadelphians of German background, then, forged American identities in the 1920s by drawing lines between themselves and south and east European immigrants. Such identities were not uniformly the same. Some had a more racialist tinge than others. Gender also seems to have played a role in shaping how exclusive one's American self-image might be. While the male nativist orders stressed the exclusion of new immigrants, women such as Anna Hess and the members of the Americanization Committee were more interested in changing them. Those women dealt with immigrants in what amounted to a social-work context, and such work was particularly open to women because it stressed service to others—a gender expectation that also reinforced a more inclusionary, if at times patronizing, approach.

These American identities also were not exclusively middle-class. The heavily white-collar ranks of the nativist orders could include skilled workers like John Vogelsang and William Hammer, much as the Protestant and predominantly middle-class Germantown YMCA attracted some skilled workers in 1900. Many workers and Catholics, however, were hesitant to define "America" in terms quite so narrow. Increasingly, some would fall back on a larger distinction—that between black and white—when it came to shaping their sense of self.

CHAPTER TWELVE

Workers and Catholics: Toward the "White Ethnic"

ON an August day in 1921, the German Catholic church of St. Ignatius said a painful farewell to a well-liked parishioner. "Mr. Sangmeister took leave with tears in his eyes," the church's rector, the Reverend Theodore Hammeke, reported in the parish bulletin. "The unpleasant housing conditions in West Philadelphia have driven him and his exemplary family away from us to Germantown." The German-born Hammeke[1] did not have to spell out for his readers what made conditions in their neighborhood "unpleasant." He was more frank, however, when writing to his archbishop, Dennis Cardinal Dougherty. Three years earlier, Hammeke had asked Dougherty what he should do with requests from African-American Catholics to hold their services and Sunday school at St. Ignatius'. "The catholic negroes of West Phila. . . . have urgently requested me to let them do so in our church and school because they expect better results here, a more convenient centre of our negrodom," Hammeke told the archbishop in October 1918. "Though I expect trouble and objections from my own parishioners, who are crowded out of this neighborhood by them[,] I could not well refuse permission, and we had some thirty people here the last two Sundays."[2]

The "crowding out" of Mr. Sangmeister was a small episode in a larger drama that played itself out across Philadelphia during the first Great Migration. That drama greatly influenced how some German Philadelphians reshaped their identities in the 1920s and after. Like their middle-class and Lutheran counterparts, many working-class and Catholic residents of immigrant German background felt the pull of an American identity that overshadowed German ethnic ties. For them, however, the distinction between northwest-European Americans and "new immigrants" had relatively little purchase. What increasingly mattered instead was the color line between European Americans in general and the African Americans then flooding into Philadelphia.

By the 1920s, Catholics and workers of German origin—often the same people—had begun to mix in parishes and neighborhood clubs with new immigrants as well as Irish residents. These encounters carried their own conflicts, but they occurred against a backdrop of rising racial tension between European Americans and African Americans, especially those moving into new parts of the city traditionally considered "white." The Great Migration did not cause the city's Catholic and working-class Germans to "become white" in any simple sense; German Philadelphians by and large already thought of themselves as white at the turn of the century. Rather, the influx of black migrants significantly raised the *salience* of whiteness for German residents in working-class neighborhoods and Catholic parishes—crucially, at the same time as those residents were mixing with non-Germans of different European backgrounds. Hence, color lines, which became more important as "national" lines faded, increasingly set the terms under which many German workers and Catholics integrated with their Irish, Polish, and Italian neighbors. We can only observe the beginnings of this process here; its results would not become fully apparent until after the Second World War. Yet, by the early 1930s, some of the elements were in place for what a later generation would call a "white ethnic" identity—an identity whose bearers retained some sense of ethnic identification but also shared with other European "ethnics" an overarching self-perception as white, working-class, and, usually, Catholic.

WORKERS AND THE "BLACK PERIL"

The impulse to give one's "American" identity precedence over an ethnic German sense of self also emerged among working-class and Catholic Philadelphians of German ancestry in the 1920s. Catholics from working-class backgrounds such as George Beichl, along with middle-class Catholics such as John Eichman, felt this pull. It was a fixture of working-class life in the streets around St. Peter's during the 1940s, Joseph Gruninger recalled. "People categorized themselves as being first American, and then they would mention their descent," he said. "At least within my family or . . . within my neighborhood, there was such a great emphasis placed on being an American, being a good American, being a patriotic American, speaking English—all of those things took precedence over maintaining the fact that you were of a certain heritage." No doubt the Second World War had something to do with the strength of this feeling, yet Gruninger remembered his mill-worker father holding such views, which, according to family lore, dated to the 1910s. Working-class socialists, even German-speaking ones, sensed this imperative. By 1924, the *Philadelphia Tageblatt,* in a manner similar to the *Lutherischer Herold,* could refer to German Americans as "Americans of German heritage."[3]

Working-class Germans, however, seemed much less likely than middle-class Germans to exclude south and east Europeans from their conception of "American." Although some skilled workers joined nativist orders, the *Tageblatt* consistently rejected arguments that defined "new immigrants" as inadequately American, as the newspaper's coverage of the immigration restriction debate shows. Despite its few, isolated references to "Nordics," the *Tageblatt* had nothing but scorn for what became the Johnson-Reed Act. The legislation, in proposing to end America's role as an asylum for the oppressed, represented a "radical break with one of the proudest traditions of Americanism," the newspaper declared in April 1924. The *Tageblatt*'s editors likewise had little use for the racialized nativism behind the legislation, to judge from a syndicated article they ran in early April. "Of all the arguments offered for restricting immigration, the race-theoretical one is probably the stupidest," this piece declared. "The Nordic man is no less a historical myth than the Aryan man." The same article, however, underlined the limits on the *Tageblatt*'s understanding of who could qualify as American. Unlike European countries, the author concluded, "America can assimilate all white elements," and by "white" he understood Poles and Italians as well as Germans. This view of the United States as a country "of the white man"[4] was not new. But its use in this context pointed to the greater salience that whiteness had acquired among working-class German Philadelphians over the previous decade—the decade that launched the Great Migration.

German Philadelphians were no strangers to whiteness at the turn of the century. Yet, as chapter 5 described, many did not seem deeply invested emotionally in the white component of their multiple identities. The *Tageblatt* itself evinced a degree of indifference toward black Philadelphians. Its distanced tone may have reflected residential isolation, for the vast majority of Germans lived in North Philadelphia, away from the traditional black settlement areas in South Philadelphia. North Philadelphia, however, was already drawing increasing numbers of black residents after 1890, and the Great Migration greatly accelerated that movement. By 1920, 40 percent of Philadelphia's black population lived there, with many concentrated in four central wards that lay between Northern Liberties and Brewerytown.[5]

Such population shifts within the city and the larger migration from the South made African Americans much more of a presence in the minds of German Philadelphians. The *Tageblatt* had betrayed its considerable misgivings as early as 1903 at the mere possibility of a large-scale labor migration of black Southerners to the North. As that migration became a reality, the newspaper's stance toward blacks in Philadelphia hardened, shifting from indifference to concern and, at times, pronounced fear and hostility. By the early summer of 1918, the *Tageblatt* was running editorials on "The Negro Problem of the North" and "Why the Negroes Leave the South." Such statements were not unsympathetic, but they did contain a note of apprehension. "It is clear . . . that the in-migrated Negro labor in the North is to be reckoned with permanently, and that the labor movement has to come to terms with it, economically and politically," the latter editorial concluded.[6] The racial violence that followed attempts by blacks to ease a severe housing shortage by moving into white neighborhoods, however, brought a different response. In July 1918, an African American who had just moved into a house on a white block in South Philadelphia was attacked by a white mob. The assault set off four days of rioting in South Philadelphia that killed four people and injured several hundred. A year before, the *Tageblatt* had denounced the East St. Louis, Illinois, race riot as a "pogrom" of whites against blacks, noting cuttingly that "[w]hen an American has nothing else to be proud of, then he's proud that he's a white." A riot in Philadelphia was another matter; it apparently induced the editors to show on which side of the color line they stood. Reporting on one incident in which a black man accused of theft was beaten by a crowd of whites, the newspaper had this to say: "It turned out here that the nigger-skull doesn't resist everything, for [the man] had a deep head-wound."[7]

By the early 1920s, the tone of the *Tageblatt* regarding the city's burgeoning black population had turned from apprehension to fear. "Are We Threatened by a Black Peril?" asked one 1923 headline, which ran above a story on a fourfold increase in African-American arrivals during the first half of the year. The article displayed some sympathy for black Southerners fleeing mistreatment at the hands of "the whites." Yet, in reference to a forthcoming report by social welfare agencies on the migrant upsurge, the story concluded, "[o]ne may anxiously await what [they] will report and recommend—how one will meet the presumed evil." At the same time, the newspaper's references to blacks grew increasingly nasty. In June 1924, a racist cartoon even found its way into the Sunday page of jokes and caricatures, a feature traditionally devoted to German ethnic themes. This vicious drawing depicted an "African Family Idyll" of a mother, father, and three children, all linked by chains running from the nose ring of one parent to that of the other (see figure 12.1). By this point, the editors had learned American English's leading racial slur well enough to refashion it into an insult applicable to Old World politics: "Verniggerung," or, roughly translated, "niggerfication." Denouncing the Treaty of Versailles in a 1924 editorial, the *Tageblatt* accused the Entente powers of "sinking back to the level of Negro civilization" in dealing with Germany "like a wild colonial people," an apparent reference to the use of African troops in Europe. "Finally, one defends one's country, one's women, and children—not without impunity—with niggers and Congo slaves; the moral niggerfication of the victorious powers precedes the physical."[8]

The African-American presence loomed larger for working-class German Philadelphians on the edges of their neighborhoods as well as in the pages of the *Tageblatt*. *The Inner Missionary,* discussing black "colonies"

Afrikanisches Familien-Idyll.

Figure 12.1. "African Family Idyll," 1924. The *Philadelphia Tageblatt*'s hardening tone toward blacks provides one index of the rising salience of white identity for working-class German Philadelphians during the first Great Migration. This racist cartoon depicts a black family linked by a chain running from the father's nose ring to the mother's. While not the *Tageblatt*'s first racist illustration, the cartoon appeared in an unusual place: on the Sunday jokes and caricatures page, which traditionally was given over to German ethnic themes. The placement suggests that readers most committed to ethnic German concerns were increasingly familiar with such stereotypical views. Source: *Philadelphia Tageblatt*, 29 June 1924, p. 15.

in North and South Philadelphia, including some just west of the Girard Avenue district, noted in 1919 that "[t]hese sections are adjacent to the Settlement and Neighborhood House and we are aware of the spreading out and infiltration of these people." A May 1924 *Tageblatt* report told of how a "Negro mob" had assaulted a policeman at Third Street and Fairmount Avenue, in the heart of what had been heavily German Northern Liberties and just south of the Sixteenth Ward. A month earlier, black-white racial tensions erupted either in the Seventeenth Ward itself or just over its boundary with the Eighteenth Ward. A crowd of factory workers led by a police officer chased an African-American man for several blocks after he allegedly attempted to rape a seven-year-old girl. The officer caught up with the suspect but had to pull his revolver to keep the mob from lynching the man. The suspect was taken to the East Girard Avenue police station; the crowd followed and threatened to storm the building. It took a squad of twelve officers to get the man out of the station.[9]

Such racial conflict was not omnipresent. White responses to new African-American neighbors in the 1910s and 1920s could vary drastically "not only from one neighborhood to another but also from block to block," one historian observes. Large areas of the city remained off-limits to blacks, and white flight occurred in parts of North and West Philadelphia; in other parts of those sections, stable racially mixed blocks emerged.[10] Nonetheless, color lines of varying degrees grew up around some of North Philadelphia's working-class neighborhoods. Those that encircled Brewerytown helped to define the limits within which Germans and other European Americans in the neighborhood mixed with one another. Brewerytown in the 1920s bordered on an area that had grown increasingly African-American with the Great Migration. The Twenty-ninth Ward had attracted Southern black migrants, who were concentrated at the ward's eastern end, in an area that had been virtually all-white before 1916. Brewerytown took up the ward's western half. In 1930, the census tract that covered the heart of Brewerytown had a population that was 28 percent German-stock, 40.1 percent native white of native parentage, and 5.4 percent Irish-stock, with smaller proportions of Polish-stock, Russian-stock, and Italian-stock residents. Only 1.1 percent of this tract's residents were "Negro." The adjoining census tract on the east was 50.5 percent black, 21 percent native white of native parentage, and only 8.2 percent German-stock.[11] This stark racial geography is reflected in George Beichl's recollection of "the black neighborhood" near Brewerytown as being "east of Twenty-fourth Street," with Brewerytown itself running from about Twenty-sixth Street west to Fairmount Park. As Beichl remembered it, the boundary between "the black neighborhood" and Brewerytown was not entirely sealed. He recalled trips with an Irish classmate to "play ball with some of the African Americans up there, around Twenty-fifth and Master," in the late 1920s, and Beichl would walk through this African-American section during the early 1930s to get to high school. Blacks, however, "were not welcome in the swimming pool" run by the city at Twenty-sixth and Master. "I guess blacks were admitted, but they wouldn't go in, because . . . they figured they might be beaten up, or something," he said. The Fairmount Liedertafel had Irish and German members, but no African-American ones: "Oh, that line was rigid," Beichl recalled.[12]

The degree to which such exclusion reflected a self-consciously white identification is unclear; Beichl did not recall Liedertafel members referring to themselves as "white." Yet white Brewerytowners clearly drew a line between themselves and their new black neighbors to the east—a color line, certainly in the sense that it kept out blacks specifically. Occasioned by the Great Migration, this "rigid" line meant the Liedertafel would bring German and Irish neighbors together on the basis, at some level, of a common European background. Hence, the Great Migration helped to lend a "white" aspect to the mixing of working-class Germans with non-Germans, just when that mixing was getting underway. A similar dynamic would shape the interwar experience of German Catholics.

German Catholics into "White Catholics"

Philadelphia Catholics of German background, like working-class German Philadelphians, tended not to see themselves as part of a northwest European group ranged against a set of new immigrant "races." The evocations of a larger "Germanic" group voiced by some secular middle-class and Lutheran figures at the turn of the twentieth century found little resonance in the pages of *Nord Amerika*. Similarly, John Rothensteiner's 1924 vision of the German "race" merging with "other elements" of the American population listed Italians as well as the Irish among those elements. To be sure, some middle-class Catholics did distinguish themselves from certain new immigrant groups, as Eichman's experience shows and as the case of Germantown's Henry Pletcher suggests. When Pletcher, an active member of an Irish-dominated parish, died in 1931, a friend wrote that his immigrant parents "were of the old stock."[13] Yet the experience of getting to know fellow classmates and parishioners of south or east European background in the increasingly mixed "German" parishes of the 1920s told against such conceptions. Despite his run-ins with the "Polish kids," Eichman did count a Czech classmate at St. Mary's as one of his close friends.

Catholicism thus could provide a kind of pan-European common ground for German Catholics, one that was encouraged by the official pronouncements of the Archdiocese of Philadelphia and the workings of diocese-wide lay associations. Dennis Dougherty, the city's archbishop from 1918 to 1951, was a fierce opponent of nativism and interpreted restriction as an attack on Catholics. Attempts to "crush or to restrict Italian immigration into the United States" spring "chiefly from religious bigotry," he told an audience in April 1924. The official archdiocesan newspaper, the *Catholic Standard and Times,* made its disdain for racialized nativism clear in a 1928 editorial lauding the honesty of a man who found a bag of money and returned it to its owner. "Mr. Labowski, while not of Nordic descent is, all must agree, a type of man that this country needs," the editors acidly noted.[14]

Such inclusive language was to some extent merely rhetorical. Many Italians and other new immigrants held to their own national parishes, and the interwar period was punctuated by ethnic conflict within the archdiocese, especially between Irish and Italian Catholics. Dougherty sanctioned the creation of Italian national parishes in neighborhoods where incoming Italians met with hostility from Irish members of territorial churches.[15] Yet by the late 1920s, some Irish, German, and new immigrant individuals had begun to find common ground within pan-diocesan voluntary associations and their parish branches. In 1928, the *Standard and Times* described a striking number of such branches with officers bearing German and Irish surnames, and in some cases Italian surnames as well. The officers installed by Chapter No. 1 of the Daughters of Columbus in January 1928, for example, were mostly Irish, but some were named Schott, Scherr, and Travascio. Similarly, the Holy Name Society of West Philadelphia's Transfiguration parish had mainly Irish officers that year, but the group's advisory board included names such as Hofbauer and Weigman, and a Constantine Picirrillo served as an alternate delegate to the society's Diocesan Union. Organizations such as the Daughters of Columbus and the Catholic Daughters of America offered these diverse memberships an identification that was at once Catholic and "American."[16] Such branches formed the building blocks of pan-diocesan associations within which German Catholics were taking leadership roles. For example, the Alliance of Catholic Women of the Archdiocese of Philadelphia, created in 1916, brought together members from "all the auxiliaries, of orders, hospitals and homes," from the Catholic Daughters of America to the German-American League of Catholic Women and "the Irish and Italian societies," as the *Standard and Times* described it. The alliance president, just finishing her term in the spring of 1928, was Mrs. Henry A. Beisser.[17]

Where German Philadelphians were concerned, however, pan-Catholic views tended to stop at the color line. Rothensteiner saw German Catholics fusing with "all of the other elements" of the American nation, but when enumerating such groups he confined himself to European Americans. To some extent, this stance may have reflected the fact that relatively few African Americans were Catholic. A list of "foreign churches" compiled by the archdiocese early in the 1920s showed only two of the city's forty-one national parishes as "colored"; they had a combined membership of about 2,300, which amounted to just 1.8 percent of all national parish members in Philadelphia. The list neglected to mention St. Catherine's Chapel in Germantown,[18] but its congregation would not have raised the overall total of black Catholics significantly. Correspondingly, African-American Catholics had a low profile in the archdiocese. As a *Standard and Times* columnist noted in 1928, after the count of "colored" parishes had risen by one, "It will surprise even some residents of Philadelphia to know that we now have four parishes devoted exclusively to Negroes."[19]

The case of that fourth parish illustrates how the Great Migration made whiteness both much more salient for Catholics of German background and instrumental in creating a sense of Catholic community that reached beyond German-stock believers. For the new "colored" parish in West Philadelphia was Mr. Sangmeister's old church—St. Ignatius', which had been founded as a German national parish thirty-five years before. The arrival of black Southerners during the First World War jeopardized the German parish's very existence, as its members fled before what they saw as a deluge of African-American residents entering the neighborhood. For parishioners who stayed during the 1920s, racial succession helped set the terms by which they mixed with fellow parishioners of non-German, but European, background. By the time the archdiocese handed the church over to a fledgling black congregation in 1928, the "German" parish's remaining members appear to have found the distinction between blacks and whites of more importance than internal divisions among Germans, Irish, and eastern Europeans. They had become "white Catholics."

The transformation of St. Ignatius' grew out of the larger process of neighborhood racial succession. Like North Philadelphia, West Philadelphia had seen its black population grow after the turn of the century and increase sharply with the Great Migration. The concentration of African Americans in St. Ignatius' ward, the Twenty-fourth, rose from 7.3 percent in 1910 to 13.5 percent in 1920 and 23.7 percent in 1930. In 1920, the church's immediate neighborhood was nearly 30 percent black.[20] The influx into West Philadelphia met with varying white responses. These included intermittent violence, especially in wards that lay further west and south of the Twenty-fourth. From the turn of the century on, blacks who tried to buy or rent in the "West End," for example, had their houses stoned. When an African-American chauffeur moved there in 1914, a crowd of "[s]everal hundred white residents . . . gathered before [his] house . . . and, after demands for the immediate removal of the family, smashed the windows and terrified the inmates," the *Public Ledger* reported.[21]

The wartime Great Migration brought the issue of racial succession to a head. For the parishioners of St. Ignatius', the change seemed nothing short of disastrous. Theodore Hammeke described his church in 1920 as holding a core of more than 100 "old German families" who were "scattered over all West Phila[delphia]." "Their and my ambition and heart's desire was to build a [new] church as a Souvenir of our Silver Jubilee," the rector told Dougherty that year. After these members had collected $50,000 and received permission to build, Hammeke continued, "the unfortunate war brought along the extraordinary influx of negroes into this neighborhood." In response, parishioners began to leave; the building fund sat unused. "If the influx of the colored element keeps on . . . at the present rate it may be necessary to change the parish into a colored peoples [*sic*] congregation within 5 years," the rector warned.[22]

Hammeke's words were prescient. The membership of St. Ignatius' dropped precipitously through the 1920s, from about 900 in 1921 to an estimated 325 in 1927. Meanwhile, West Philadelphia's black population grew to the point that Dougherty decided, in 1924, to found an African-American parish there. He entrusted this task to the Reverend Vincent A. Dever, a racial liberal who had served him as something of aide on matters concerning black Catholics.[23] Over the next several years, Dever worked to organize the new parish of the Holy Saviour. Holy Saviour's black congregants worshipped for a while in a house across the street from the German church; they subsequently held services in St. Ignatius' basement. In the summer of 1928, they finally moved upstairs. Dougherty apparently decided that, given the rising membership of Holy Saviour and the dwindling size of St. Ignatius', it was time to transfer the latter's physical plant to the former. By the end of July 1928, Dever had taken over St. Ignatius' church, rectory, school, and convent. Dougherty instructed Dever to acquire the parish name as well, so that "St. Ignatius' Parish be hereafter known as the parish for the colored."[24]

The crisis of the German parish of St. Ignatius forced its members to face some fundamental questions about who they were. Even before the African-American influx, they may have wondered how "German" St. Ignatius' was. Like other German national parishes, it had acquired an ethnically mixed congregation by the early 1920s. Hammeke described St. Ignatius' in 1920 as made up of four types of parishioners. First, the church had between 130 and 150 "very good families . . . whose heads come from the other side [of the Atlantic] and are used [to] and prefer German singing, praying and preaching." Second, there were "about 120 families partly of German birth or extraction who want to belong to this parish but for convenience sake often attend the nearest English church." Third, St. Ignatius' attracted "about 100 English families living in the neighborhood"; most of these belonged to a local territorial parish, but they "very often attend here and have their children in our school." Lastly, Hammeke knew of "over 100 families . . . who are shifters or catholics by name only who find the German priest when they are in trouble."[25] A surname analysis of a list of donors to the parish's 1921 block collection suggests that the "English" families of St. Ignatius' in fact were largely a mix of Irish, English, and eastern European residents. Of the 308 individuals who gave to the collection, 237, or 77 percent, had clearly or possibly German surnames. Nearly one-quarter (23 percent) of all donors, however, had clearly non-German last names. These seventy-one non-Germans included eighteen individuals with clearly Irish surnames, nineteen with clearly British surnames, eighteen with surnames of either British or Irish derivation, and eight with clearly Slavic surnames; one individual had an Italian last name.[26]

The Great Migration presented this ethnically mixed congregation with a dilemma. Hammeke wrote in 1920 that the rector of a nearby territorial parish had suggested a number of years before that St. Ignatius' might have to take in formally "those of his parishioners who live near and mostly attend our church." This would amount to declaring St. Ignatius' to be "an English-speaking" parish, as Dougherty put it.[27] "Nothing was done then," Hammeke recalled, "but later when the influx of negroes seemed to endanger the parish and to discourage the parishioners I tried to cheer them by telling them that I would hold out with them and ask for those families when necessity would compel me to do so." If some parishioners appeared ready for such a step, others—particularly among the founding German families—seemed reluctant. Hammeke noted that if he left St. Ignatius', "I have reasons to fear that a change of the same into an English or mixed congregation soon after my departure would be a blow to and considered as a betrayal of a trust by the about hundred good families," these being "old German families." Parishioners thus contemplated either remaining, at least officially, a German church, with its attendant risk of going under, or abandoning that status to become an "English" parish. In essence, the latter step would amount to becoming a "white" church, since no one was suggesting that St. Ignatius' recruit *black* members to stay afloat. Hammeke saw such a transition as a move toward becoming American. "In case I should be changed[,]" he told Dougherty, "a zealous native German-American priest . . . might be best able to lead the old Germans over into American ways and find out the proper time for a change in the character of the parish."[28]

Although St. Ignatius' eventually would become a "colored" parish rather than an "English" one, its mixed congregation appears in the meantime to have matched a dwindling interest in German ethnic concerns with a continuing, and perhaps increasing, identification as "white." This much is suggested by a review of the parish bulletin, the *St. Ignatius' Monthly Calendar,* in the years leading up to 1928. While the *Calendar* was published almost entirely in English, it reflected a range of German, Irish, and even Slovak ethnic interests, at least until Hammeke left the parish in 1924. The bulletin usually contained a "pastor's diary" recounting events of the previous month, and these indicate parishioners' continuing involvement in such causes as charitable relief for Germany.[29] Yet the diary also recorded a "St. Patrick's Novelty Euchre" and the founding, in the parish hall, of a branch of the American Society of Irish Independence, as well as a talk by the nephew of a Slovak parishioner on "conditions in his home land." After Hammeke's replacement by an American-born priest, the Reverend Francis P. Regnery, however, the diary feature ceased, and the bulletin ran primarily generic material that said little about the parish or its ethnic concerns.[30]

The *Calendar* nonetheless continued to reflect a distanced view of African Americans, as signaled by the occasional appearance under both Hammeke and Regnery of stories allegedly written in black "dialect."[31] The bulletin also described at least one activity, a minstrel show, that suggested the children of German and Irish immigrants in the parish were cultivating a common white identity. The 1922 production by the St. Ignatius Catholic Club featured the stock characters of blackface minstrelsy: an "Interlocutor," "End Men" with the surnames of Callan and Trainer, and "Minstrel Men" with surnames including McNamee, Flannigan, Maenner, and Yaeger. Such shows were popular parish entertainments, and they could serve to unite Catholics across a range of European ethnicities in the common endeavor of "blacking up." A 1928 production scheduled for the hall of St. Agatha's parish in West Philadelphia, for example, had a cast with a mix of Irish, Italian, Slavic, and German names.[32] What stands out about St. Ignatius' show, however, is that it was specifically an initiative of the parish's young men, the Catholic Club being the "Young Men's" society.[33] The production suggests that members of the parish's rising generation were learning to cross ethnic lines by playing at being black, a step that in turn emphasized their common whiteness.

That the relative salience of whiteness rose during the 1920s for the parishioners of St. Ignatius' is suggested as well by one of the last issues of the *Calendar* to appear before the church changed hands. The bulletin's May 1928 issue contained no indications that the parish was or ever had been German. It was filled with generic, admonitory stories, one of which told of a woman who had converted to Catholicism in part because she felt "the communion rail" had a leveling effect. "Young and old, black and white, poor and rich, native and alien, there they knelt, and all were equal when all were pure enough worthily to receive the bread of angels."[34] Regnery's approval of this article for one of his bulletin's final issues was telling. "German" had ceased to be a category that mattered in the pages of the *Calendar,* but its readers were expected to recognize that color played an important role in organizing their Catholic world: there were "white" Catholics and "black" Catholics, and the bulletin's readers, presumably, numbered among the former.

The "white Catholic," in fact, would be a figure increasingly invoked across the urban North in the wake of the Great Migration, as distinctions between European Catholic groups receded and changing neighborhood demographics highlighted the dichotomy between "black" and "white." This development was well expressed in a Brooklyn pastor's 1938 observation that his parish, "once an Irish German congregation[,] is composed at present of six thousand white people and four hundred

Catholic negroes. . . . The presence of Negroes contributes to the rapid exodus of the Catholic Whites." As the historian John McGreevy argued in citing this comment, "Irish and Germans, in other words, became 'Catholic whites' only in the context of African-Americans moving in large numbers to a particular area. Ethnicity was flattened into race."[35] In Philadelphia, this flattening, too, was under way. Middle-class areas like West Philadelphia and working-class neighborhoods such as Brewery-town and the increasingly Catholic Girard Avenue district experienced the "infiltration" of African Americans, whether along their borders or in their streets. As we have seen, European-American residents of these sections often did not hesitate to take racial matters into their own hands; they did so at the same time as they increasingly crossed the internal lines between Germans, Irish, and new immigrants. This mixing did not go unnoticed by local priests. A pastor of one of the city's black parishes noted in 1936 that "finally the various National Catholic Immigrant groups— Polish, German, Irish, Italian etc. are slowly merging and are gradually losing their spirit of European parochialism." Such observers, in turn, looked at these Catholics and saw "whites." As early as 1923, Dever, in arguing for an eventual end to separate African-American parishes, declared it necessary "that white Catholics realize that Christ having instituted the Church for all, its opportunities and energies should be given to all." Seven years later, he would put the last stragglers from the old St. Ignatius' in the same category. As he told Dougherty in 1930, "I have followed Your Eminence's instruction to discourage the attendance of white people. Those who still come are mostly the kind who do not contribute."[36]

In the rising salience of whiteness for working-class Germans and German Catholics, one can see hints of future developments. On a rainy day in 1968, Peter Binzen, a reporter for the *Philadelphia Bulletin,* walked into a Kensington bar to hear "the barkeep and his lone customer . . . exchanging views on a favorite subject: niggers." The customer, "a white-trash nigger hater," was making little headway with the bartender, a man "who looked to be of German extraction." "There's good whites and good niggers," Binzen recalled the bartender as saying. "Bad whites and bad niggers." The reporter saw the barkeep as someone who "wasn't going to put up with a lot of nonsense," including the customer's rantings. But the German-looking man behind the bar had accepted color categories, however expressed, as fundamental to life in working-class Kensington. He was part of a world that Binzen described as "Whitetown," inhabited by "'ethnics'" who resisted the territorial encroachments of black North Philadelphians. The "white workingman" of neighborhoods like Kensington was, more than likely, "the son or grandson of immigrants. . . . Whether of Irish, Italian, German, Polish, Russian, or Ukrainian extraction, he was a hundred per cent American and proud of it," Binzen wrote. He was also "usually Roman Catholic."[37]

Binzen's portrayal verged on caricature, but it did describe a type widely recognized, in and outside of Kensington, as the "white ethnic." The term was popularized in the late 1960s and early 1970s through the "white ethnic revival," which saw many second- and third-generation European immigrants rediscover their ethnic roots. The revival had different facets, from intellectual declarations of the persistence of European ethnicities and popular assertions of "ethnic pride" to a cultural and political mobilization among residents of working-class Northern neighborhoods who felt threatened by black militancy and civil rights gains.[38] Scholars have divided sharply over the sources, strength, and, indeed, reality of the revival.[39] Some have depicted the period's neighborhood mobilizations as "far less 'ethnic' than 'white,'" with ethnic identity serving as "the legitimating ideology of white resistance to black mobilization." Nevertheless, "white ethnics" themselves, along Binzen's lines—working-class, patriotic, often Catholic—were widely recognized as a social reality and a political force in the urban North, especially as they fought busing and neighborhood integration.[40]

"White ethnics" in a sociological and political sense, however, did not emerge out of nowhere in the 1960s. Recent scholarship has found their antecedents in the working-class resistance to neighborhood integration, mobilized across European ethnic lines, that flared in the 1940s and 1950s in cities such as Chicago and Detroit.[41] In Philadelphia, one historian argues, Italian Americans increasingly "yielded to a growing white ethnic consciousness" in the 1960s and 1970s, as they joined with other European ethnics to oppose the Whitman Park housing project in South Philadelphia and, eventually, to elect Frank Rizzo as a "law-and-order" candidate for mayor. Yet the Whitman Park controversy dated to the mid-1950s; it was one of a set of battles during that decade waged against city public housing plans by residents of white, working-class neighborhoods. The 1950s likewise saw continuing, sometimes violent white resistance to African Americans seeking homes in Kensington, Manayunk, Roxborough, Olney, and other neighborhoods.[42]

The degree to which the neighborhood battles of the postwar period drew working-class and Catholic Germans into coalitions with other European "ethnics" bears further research, although the presence of such conflict in traditionally German Olney is suggestive. But one can plausibly suggest a line running from Binzen's 1968 "Whitetown" through the 1950s and back to the interwar period. For the *Bulletin* reporter described one legacy, three decades later, of the ethnic mixing and rising white consciousness experienced by some working-class and Catholic Philadelphians of immigrant German background in the 1920s and 1930s. The "white ethnic" as such did not yet exist in interwar Philadelphia. But elements fundamental to that figure's makeup—a fervent patriotism, a heightened racial consciousness, and a sense of commonality with other Catholic or working-class immigrants—did emerge in the twenty years after the First World War. As some German Philadelphians became "white Catholics" and patriotic, color-conscious workers, they pointed the way toward the white ethnic.

Pluralism, Nationalism, Race, and the Fate of German America

THE decades that followed the 1920s did little to revive a sense of German ethnic identity among German Philadelphians and much to keep that identity repressed. The 1930s did see the abrupt rise of a second German American Bund, a Nazi movement that found some support in Philadelphia. But the bund was overwhelmingly an organization of postwar German immigrants, and it collapsed even before the United States entered a second war against Germany. World War II did not bring a second anti-German panic. Some individuals, however, did experience harassment due to their ethnic background, and the war's revelations of Nazi atrocities contributed to the reluctance of many to advertise their German heritage, a reluctance that continues to this day.

These developments are beyond the scope of this book; they are sketched briefly below to illustrate how Philadelphians of nineteenth-century immigrant German background continued to maintain a low ethnic profile. Their ethnic reticence, however, has a larger significance. That the children and grandchildren of German immigrants reshaped their identities after the First World War in particular ways throws light on the workings of assimilation, the intertwined fates of pluralism and American nationalism, and the changing nature of white identity in the twentieth century. German Philadelphia's story has its own peculiarities, but aspects of it echo the German experience in other large American cities. The German-American experience as a whole can likewise appear idiosyncratic. Yet what happened to German America represents, to some degree, an extreme version of the changes wrought in other immigrant ethnic groups by the larger assimilative pressures and processes of the past century. The retreat from German-American identity during and after World War I played a key role in the demise of an earlier, more pluralist America and the rise of a more exclusive and conformist American nationalism. The resort by some German Americans to new forms of identity encouraged a divide within whiteness between "old stock" Americans and those who would come to be called "white ethnics"—a fault line that has persisted, under various headings, down to our own day. Members of other European ethnic groups had to respond to these changes, even as they helped to shape them. If they did not share German America's fate—at least, not to the same extent—they negotiated a landscape irrevocably altered by that fate.

THE 1930S AND AFTER

Eight decades after the Great War's end, those willing to look can find traces of the German Philadelphia that was. The German Society of Pennsylvania retains its quarters on Spring Garden Street; the Cannstatter Volksfest-Verein still draws a crowd to its festival, now a fixture of the Labor Day weekend. Later in September, a downtown parade commemorates the birthday of the Revolutionary War general Friederich von Steuben. Enough singing societies remain to sustain the United Singers of Philadelphia, which, however, "now includes members of many ethnic backgrounds," as the federation's secretary notes.[1]

Philadelphia's *Vereinswesen*, then, never vanished completely. Yet, as one historian writes, "[w]hat remained by the late twentieth century . . . was but a small fragment of the old institutional German America." Most of the landmarks of that German Philadelphia are gone; some are transformed beyond recognition. The *Philadelphia Tageblatt* folded in the 1940s and *Nord Amerika* in the 1950s.[2] The *Philadelphia Gazette-Democrat*, too, has departed, although the New York newspaper that inherited it still runs a page of news for Philadelphia readers. St. Thomas' German Lutheran church and St. Henry's national parish are memories, as are so many other German-language congregations. St. Peter's claims some parishioners of German descent. But this bilingual church now makes Spanish rather than German its alternate tongue, reflecting the latest wave of newcomers—many from Puerto Rico—to settle in the Girard Avenue district.[3]

More enduring than German associational life has been the reticence about German origins that emerged from the First World War. In conducting survey research in the Albany, New York, area during the mid-1980s, the sociologist Richard Alba found that roughly a third of native-born whites reported having German ancestry, but only about 20 percent claimed a German identity.[4] Philadelphians of immigrant German background who grew up during the interwar period bear witness to a similar tendency to downplay or pull away from a German heritage that has only grown with time. "I probably thought more about being German than I realized," Alberta Brosz recalled of her earlier years. "You know, I kind of grew out of it." "Oh, it has waned," George Beichl said of that ethnic sense—if not for himself, then for others.[5]

The retreat from a German identity, rooted in the experience of World War I, ultimately was encouraged by the events of the 1930s and 1940s.

The single largest exception to this generalization might seem to be the emergence in the 1930s of the short-lived German American Bund. A Philadelphia branch of the bund's predecessor, the Friends of the New Germany (FNG), formed early in 1933. The FNG renamed itself the Amerikadeutscher Volksbund, or German American Bund, in 1936. Both organizations had a high degree of visibility in Philadelphia. Rallies such as a June 1938 gathering to celebrate Germany's annexation of Austria featured "Hitler" salutes and bund "organization policemen" in paramilitary uniform.[6]

The "enormous publicity" generated by such actions, combined with the specter of Nazi aggression in Europe, proved the bund's undoing, however, as Philip Jenkins argued. By 1938, bund activities in Philadelphia were sparking riots. The local bund also began to attract greater attention from state and federal investigators. Germany's steps toward war in 1939, culminating in the September invasion of Poland, spelled the rapid disintegration of the local and national organization, as membership plummeted, finances ran low, and prosecutors closed in. "After December 1939, no one, including the Bundists, considered the Amerikadeutscher Volksbund effective," Sander Diamond wrote.[7]

The bund undoubtedly represented, among other things, an assertion of a particular kind of ethnic German consciousness. But it would be misleading to portray that assertion as evidence of a resurgence of ethnic identity among most German Philadelphians, and certainly those descended from nineteenth-century immigrants. First, the bund itself was quite small. One recent estimate put the number of bundists nationwide at about 6,500, while Jenkins suggested that Pennsylvania as a whole might have held up to 3,000. The anti-Nazi activist A. Raymond Raff counted 400 known current and former bund members in and around Philadelphia in 1939. The following year, the FBI set out to estimate the number of bund supporters and members and came up with a figure of "perhaps 8,000" people "influenced" by the organization in the greater Philadelphia area.[8]

Second, the bund was, by and large, a creation of immigrants who came to the United States after the First World War. Diamond estimated that between 1933 and 1935, no more than 10 percent of the FNG's national membership was made up of native-born Americans of German extraction or naturalized Americans who had arrived before 1900. By the decade's end, bund membership nationally included several thousand Americans of German background, but the group's core "remained constant—German nationals and recently naturalized citizens of the United States." The Philadelphia bund did draw some American-born supporters. Its first leader, Gerhard Kunze, was born in nearby Camden, New Jersey, and Siegmund von Bosse, Georg von Bosse's son, became an open sympathizer. Nonetheless, Philadelphia bundists tended to be recent ar-rivals: of the 200 members of the city's original bund society, 138 were aliens, most of them German citizens.[9]

Relatively few nineteenth-century immigrants or their descendants, then, took the step of joining the bund. Whether many sympathized with the bundists is a more difficult question. Jenkins argued that the bund "created a Nazi-influenced coalition within the German American com-munity" and, until 1938, had little problem in making its presence felt within the city's older *Vereinswesen*. As he pointed out, a popular meet-ing place for bundists was the hall of one of the leading middle-class *Ve-reine*, the Philadelphia Turngemeinde. The bund certainly appears to have co-opted some officials of the German-American Central Alliance of Pennsylvania. Fred Gartner, the alliance's president in 1932, served as an attorney for a local bund newspaper and spoke at bund meetings, where he allegedly gave the stiff-armed Nazi salute.[10] Siegmund von Bosse like-wise became the Central Alliance's president in 1939. At the same time, however, an energetic opposition to the bund emerged within the *Verein-swesen*, spearheaded, above all, by the German American League for Cul-ture. Organized in 1938 to fight Nazi influence, the league and its Phil-adelphia branch claimed the loyalty of twenty local German associations by the following year. As Jenkins wrote, the group's activism "ensured that the great majority of German societies were increasingly distanced from Bund sympathies." Hitler's attack on Poland appears to have solid-ified this stance, for it evoked what Jenkins called "broad opposition to Nazi policies in the established German community of Philadelphia."[11]

Indeed, the bund's ultimate legacy for ethnic identity may have been to create yet another stereotype for Philadelphians of German ancestry to avoid—that of the German as Nazi goon, half menacing and half comi-cal. The first years of the Second World War brought a proliferation of political cartoons featuring "swastika-clad Bund members speaking in stage-German accents" and opposing national defense measures. A Sep-tember 1940 cartoon in the *Philadelphia Inquirer* pictured a "ludicrous" bundist taking issue with the new Selective Service Act: "Dot's Un-American, dictatorial—und besides, I don't like it!" he complained, to be answered by the cartoon's caption, "Sez Who?"[12]

The actions of the Third Reich in Europe, from the territorial bullying of the 1930s to the unleashing of war in 1939 and of the Holocaust in the 1940s, gave Americans of German descent still more incentive to down-play their ethnic background. "Hitler was in fact doing the kind of things Allied propagandists had accused the Kaiser of two decades earlier," as Frederick Luebke aptly wrote. "It was no time to take pride in German heritage." American intervention in this second war did not bring a rep-etition of the anti-German backlash of the first. Authorities did arrest Philadelphia bund leaders in the days after Pearl Harbor.[13] But government propaganda, rather than fostering doubts about German-American loyalty, stressed a brand of "cultural pluralism" centered on "a belief in the right of every individual . . . to life, liberty, and the pursuit of happiness, irrespective of creed, color, or nationality." This message sought to mute rather than exacerbate ethnic divisions, at least those among European Americans. Some Philadelphians of German descent did encounter anti-German feeling. Esther Schuchard Browne recalled a colleague confronting her as France fell in the spring of 1940. "He was very nasty to me, and said, 'Oh, I suppose you're very happy . . .' that the Germans marched on Paris," despite Browne's protestations that "'this whole thing is the saddest thing.'" Brosz remembered that someone in her neighborhood would "paint swastikas on our pavement. . . . [T]hat's the kind of things they did during the war if you were German." Beichl, however, who saw combat in Europe as a U.S. infantryman, said he "never noticed" any anti-German feeling at home in Philadelphia during the war years. Gruninger had similar recollections: "I didn't experience anything, nor did I hear anybody in the family talk about anything, that would indicate any hostility towards me or my family or my neighbors due to our German descent."[14]

These perceptions, while conflicting, suggest that anti-German sentiment in Philadelphia was relatively mild during the second war, certainly compared to the first. The cumulative effect of both conflicts, however, was to keep German ethnic identity subdued. In Browne's view, the waning of that identity over her lifetime in Philadelphia stemmed, at least in part, from the fact that "we had two wars with Germany. And bam, that . . . closed any . . . even talking about or even owning up to your background as German or as German-American." The years since the 1940s have witnessed little impetus to reverse this ethnic seclusion. Philadelphians of German background may have taken a few cues from the "ethnic revival" of the late 1960s and early 1970s, as might be suggested by the fact that the city's first Steuben Day parade took place in 1970. By and large, however, they remain remarkably quiet about their ancestry. Kathleen Conzen's 1980 assessment of German-American ethnicity still holds true for Philadelphia today: "an occasional *Maifest* revival or lecture series on German-American culture signifies that the offspring of immigrants have joined to some extent in the national search for an ethnic heritage, but there is little to suggest the renewal of a viable German-American culture."[15]

THE PHILADELPHIA CASE AND GERMAN AMERICA

With its long history of German immigration, its substantial German population, and its status as the headquarters of the National German-

American Alliance, early twentieth-century Philadelphia occupied a position of strategic importance within German America. Whether German America was German Philadelphia writ large is another matter. Any case study raises the issue of representativeness; here, one must ask whether a story like German Philadelphia's could be told for Germans in other American cities. A full answer to that question requires further research. With few exceptions, existing studies of urban German communities tend not to venture past 1920.[16] Current scholarship suggests, however, that German Americans in some other large cities experienced at least some of the changes undergone by German Philadelphians, despite marked differences in their urban environments.

At first glance, and in several respects, German Philadelphia diverged from other, better-known urban German communities. Although Philadelphia's German-born population was the third largest among American cities in 1900, the proportion of German immigrants in Philadelphia's overall population that year (5.5 percent) was relatively low. German-born concentrations were noticeably higher in New York City (9.4 percent) and, above all, in cities along the Great Lakes and in the Midwest, including Milwaukee (18.9 percent), Cincinnati (11.7 percent), Detroit (11.2 percent), Cleveland (10.7 percent), Buffalo (10.4 percent), St. Louis (10.2 percent), and Chicago (10.1 percent).[17] In contrast to Philadelphia and other eastern cities, cities such as Buffalo, Detroit, St. Louis, and Milwaukee also evinced markedly greater German residential concentrations in the nineteenth century.[18]

Higher concentrations of Germans likely helped fuel a stronger sense of public Germanness in large Midwestern cities after World War I than in the urban Northeast. Even in the 1920s, Chicagoans could celebrate German Day on a scale that dwarfed anything Philadelphians might manage; the 1923 festivities at Chicago's Municipal Pier drew a crowd of 100,000. More recently, some Midwestern cities have promoted large-scale, public celebrations of German ethnicity as tourist attractions, including Cincinnati's Downtown Oktoberfest, begun in 1976, and Milwaukee's annual German Fest, which dates to 1980.[19] This level of public recognition stands in stark contrast to the low German ethnic profile that obtains today in the urban mid-Atlantic, despite the fact that the region ran a strong second to the Midwest as a destination for nineteenth-century German newcomers. Public Germanness remained quiescent in the late twentieth century in Philadelphia, Albany, and even New York City. When Nathan Glazer and Daniel Patrick Moynihan surveyed New York's ethnic groups in the early 1960s, they found that "the Germans *as a group* are vanished. . . . [G]enerally speaking, [there is] no German component in the structure of the ethnic interests of the city." Glazer and Moynihan did see signs of a possible "mild" resurgence of German ethnic identity. Yet the force of their comments about the "disappearance of the Germans" was striking, the more so because their study, *Beyond the Melting Pot,* was one of the earliest and most influential scholarly declarations of the persistence of ethnicity.[20]

In some respects, then, Philadelphia fits into a larger pattern of regional differentiation, representing the German-American experience more in mid-Atlantic than Midwestern cities. Yet to stop here would be to miss important similarities in the assimilatory processes encountered by German Americans in Philadelphia and the urban Midwest. The German populations of Midwestern cities, too, confronted a long-term decline of associational life beginning in the 1890s. Even before World War I, falling readerships prompted mergers of German-language newspapers in Milwaukee, Cleveland, and St. Louis. Some individual *Vereine* likewise suffered membership losses before 1914 in St. Louis, Buffalo, and Cincinnati. James Bergquist interpreted the increasingly frequent demands for ethnic solidarity "in all the German urban communities in the 1890s" as a reaction to their decline and to worries over the ethnic loyalty of second- and third-generation immigrants.[21]

Once America intervened in World War I, moreover, anti-German hysteria proved even more intense in the Midwest than in the mid-Atlantic. Violence against German Americans occurred most commonly in Midwestern states. Midwestern cities likewise witnessed vandalism against symbols of German culture, the removal of German from public school curricula, the replacement of German street names, the arrest of German residents deemed disloyal, and the folding of additional German newspapers and *Vereine.*[22] The anti-German panic, coupled with Prohibition, also forced an extended retreat from public Germanness in parts of the urban Midwest. Don Tolzmann argued that Cincinnati's remaining German institutions survived after the war by adopting a strategy of making themselves "as low-key, subdued, and publicly invisible as possible." The result was a "public submergence of German-American ethnicity" that lasted at least into the early 1930s. In Buffalo, another historian has argued, most German Americans "abandoned ethnic group activity altogether" after 1918.[23]

In Midwestern cities, too, therefore, some proportion of first- and second-generation German immigrants were departing German America in the early twentieth century. Comparatively little is known about their destinations, but some parallels with the Philadelphia case emerge here as well. The most striking parallels concern the ultimate fates of workers and Catholics. Recent scholarship suggests that, just as in Philadelphia, some working-class and Catholic Germans in the urban Midwest drew closer to fellow workers or believers of Irish and new immigrant background in ways that presaged the emergence of the "white ethnic."

Chicago provides perhaps the best example of these developments. At the turn of the twentieth century, Germans were the largest immigrant ethnic group in Chicago's industrial workforce. Unionized German workers belonged to the "predominantly Anglo-American" Chicago Federation of Labor, while radical ones joined the German section of the multiethnic Socialist Party (SP). In venues such as the unions, the SP, and the shop floor, German immigrants and their children experienced both conflict and, at times, a measure of common ground with the city's growing number of new immigrants. Working-class Germans also felt the lure of the new mass culture. In a manner not unlike the *Tageblatt,* the radical *Chicagoer Arbeiter-Zeitung* ran advertisements for Riverview Park, the city's premier amusement park, and described working-class festivities that increasingly incorporated movies. Radicals, in fact, used mass culture to facilitate cross-ethnic alliances. Riverview Park was a popular site for SP picnics that brought together German, Bohemian, and Italian comrades.[24]

The road to such transethnic cooperation was long and bumpy, to say the least. Strikes after World War I in steel and meatpacking failed in part because of divisions between skilled German, Irish, and American-born workers on the one hand and unskilled eastern European workers on the other. Chicago unionists would succeed in closing such rifts only in the 1930s, through the organizing campaigns of the Congress of Industrial Organizations (CIO). That success, as Lizabeth Cohen argued, owed much to the continuing spread of mass culture, as well as to the Depression and the common experience of voting for the Democratic Party and its New Deal. The rise of chain stores, chain movie theaters, and network radio provided workers with a new kind of common ground, one the CIO drew on to build a "culture of unity" across European ethnic and even, to an extent, black-white racial lines. While Cohen rarely identified German-American workers as such in her account of the CIO, its ranks in Chicago presumably included children and grandchildren of German immigrants who joined the "integrated working-class culture" she described.[25]

Many of Chicago's German Catholics followed a similarly rocky path to common ground with the Irish and new immigrants. Germans lost ground within Chicago Catholicism in the early twentieth century. Thirty-one of the city's 253 Catholic parishes in 1929 were German national parishes, but that figure represented a loss of five national parishes since 1915. The average membership of German parishes also fell between 1900 and 1930, from over 7,000 to just under 4,000. As in Philadelphia, some of this decline involved a shift of German Catholics into heavily Irish territorial parishes. At the same time, a number of nominally German parishes became increasingly mixed ethnically. St. Boniface acquired many Polish and Slovak parishioners, especially after World War I; St.

Philomena's "German character faded" following the war, as Polish and Irish newcomers entered the area; and St. Gregory's parish experienced a "great influx of . . . Celtic parishioners" during the interwar period that changed it "into a truly cosmopolitan American parish."[26]

As in Philadelphia, these changes did not occur without a good deal of interethnic friction. German parishioners at St. Boniface resented the arrival of new Polish members. Many Poles, in turn, fiercely resisted the campaign waged by George Mundelein, Chicago's archbishop from 1915 to 1939, to centralize and "Americanize" the archdiocese. As Cohen argued, this battle intensified Polish Catholics' commitment to Polish identity, at least in the short term, while the archbishop's attempts to turn Italians into American Catholics inadvertently helped to solidify an Italian identity. Nonetheless, over time, the archbishop's efforts would encourage a greater degree of pan-Catholic awareness and mixing among Chicago's European ethnics, even as they retained specific ethnic identities. Seminary students met those of other backgrounds under training instituted by Mundelein; Italians moving to new neighborhoods increasingly worshipped in territorial churches. The working-class majority among Chicago Catholics, meanwhile, reached across internal ethnic lines more and more during the 1930s in the ways described by Cohen.[27]

By the 1940s, however, the city's European ethnic workers and Catholics would create for themselves yet another kind of common ground—one defined by a white racial identity.[28] European-American workers often willing to tolerate African Americans on the job fought to keep blacks from moving into their neighborhoods and parishes. Crucially, these mob actions involved a mix of rioters. Most appeared to be working-class Catholics of both "old" and "new" immigrant background. Such mixing was not characteristic of the massive race riot of 1919, which had been spread in part by Irish-American gangs and from which Slavic immigrants, to some extent, had abstained. As early as 1928, however, a diverse group of European ethnics in and around the heavily working-class suburb of Pullman cooperated to exclude African-American residents through the use of restrictive covenants.[29] While the 1930s saw relatively few black-white clashes, renewed migration from the South subsequently led black residents facing a severe housing shortage to challenge existing racial boundaries in older neighborhoods. They encountered white mobs at newly purchased homes and housing projects that admitted blacks in the 1940s and battles over the use of neighborhood facilities in the 1950s. These incidents included a series of large-scale riots between 1946 and 1953.[30] As Arnold Hirsch described, the mobs involved were dominated by working-class Catholics, with most yielding a majority of arrestees drawn from Irish and new immigrant backgrounds. Yet some proportion of Germans consistently appeared on arrest lists; nearly one-quarter of the twenty-nine people arrested at a 1949 riot in the Englewood section, for example, were German, while just over half were Irish, and smaller proportions were of Anglo-American and Slavic background. The crowds that touched off the riot were mobilized by a group of block organizations launched at a gathering at Visitation parish hall—a group quietly encouraged by the parish's Irish-born pastor. At Englewood and elsewhere, rioters from a variety of European backgrounds acted together against a perceived African-American "invasion"—as "whites" defending a "white" neighborhood and, as John McGreevy argued, as white Catholics defending an immovable parish from a non-Catholic influx seen as both a racial threat and a threat to parish institutions.[31]

The Germans in those crowds, it would seem, had assembled multiple identities along lines anticipated in interwar Philadelphia. Whether workers, Catholics, or both, they asserted collective identities keyed to whiteness and, to some extent, to Catholicism and working-class status. They shared those identities with others primarily of Irish and new immigrant background. All concerned likely "knew" that they were German, or Irish, or Polish, but that awareness was subordinated to the "overriding concern" to keep African Americans out. This particular configuration of identities and common grounds was not limited to Chicago. It took shape across the urban North. Violence aimed at keeping African Americans out of white neighborhoods erupted during and after the 1940s in Cleveland, Detroit, Newark, and Cincinnati, as well as Philadelphia. Those resisting black "invasion" in Detroit were also primarily working-class Catholics of different ethnic backgrounds—Italian, Irish, Slavic, and German, among others, to judge from the surnames of activists in the homeowners' associations studied by Thomas Sugrue.[32] By the early 1970s, some of these Catholics and workers would come to celebrate their ethnic identities as part of that period's "white ethnic revival," a development that emerged at least partly in reaction to and emulation of the militancy of the Black Power movement.[33] Yet their collective sense of being "white ethnics"—indeed, their ability to be both white and ethnic without contradiction—would hinge as much on their identification with whiteness as on their investment in a particular ethnic identity. In that sense, the foundations of "white ethnicity" were laid in the housing clashes of the 1940s and 1950s and, further back, in the processes that brought Catholics and workers of German background closer to their Irish and new immigrant counterparts between the world wars.

One can draw some fairly strong parallels, then, between Philadelphia and parts of the urban Midwest in terms of the assimilation of German workers and Catholics. Whether similar parallels exist in regard to Lutheran and middle-class Germans is more difficult to say. There has been comparatively little research addressing their fate in Midwestern cities.[34] The existing work points in different directions. While Chicago saw hostility between Germans and Slavs, especially during World War I, some Germans during the interwar period cooperated with new immigrant and Irish residents in property owners' associations dedicated to keeping middle-class neighborhoods "white." Yet other evidence suggests a continuing divide between new immigrants and Protestant or middle-class Germans. A 1967 survey of two small Midwestern cities found that while relatively high proportions of Germans married each other, German Protestants who married out preferred spouses of Scandinavian or British background, while German Catholics more frequently selected Irish and Polish spouses.[35] The most intriguing evidence along these lines is offered by the career of John J. Weitzel, the second-generation German immigrant who lobbied for immigration restriction as a national officer of the Junior Order United American Mechanics. Weitzel appeared to define himself in 1910 as a "real American" in opposition to south and east European immigrants who differed "racially from the original settlers of the country." Crucially, his American identity was shaped in Cincinnati. There, he pushed for restriction and cultivated good relations between the order and local Germans. Weitzel was an organizer of the Hamilton County Immigration Bureau, which seems to have had a nativist tinge; as a bureau officer, he "visited the foreign colonies of Cincinnati in 1905 and his report thereof created quite a stir." At the same time, "when the Germans of Cincinnati took exceptions to the objects of the Junior Order," Weitzel stepped in and helped to establish "peace and harmony." Significantly, this rapprochement appears to have been with Protestants, for it resulted in "a large parade given by the German Protestant Orphan Association," in which members of the Junior Order participated.[36]

Whether John Weitzel was an aberration or symptomatic of larger trends requires further research. His case, however, suggests the possibility that the transformations undergone by Lutheran and middle-class Germans in Philadelphia echoed through other parts of German America. Perhaps in this respect, and certainly in the way some of its workers and Catholics anticipated the "white ethnic," German Philadelphia's story is representative of German America's. Yet the "white ethnic revival" also revealed the limits of that representativeness. For in Midwestern cities, unlike Philadelphia, the 1970s' renewal of interest in European ethnicities could result in large-scale celebrations of public Germanness.

Here, German Philadelphia matters for a different reason: it underscores the importance of space in shaping assimilation. The city today shares a low German profile with other urban centers in the mid-Atlantic, where Irish immigrants tended to outnumber Germans in the nineteenth century.[37] In contrast, the urban Midwest's greater concentration of German settlers likely shaped the incorporation of its German population in ways that ultimately allowed for a greater expression of public German-ness. Similarly, the mid-Atlantic's distinctive colonial history may have made it particularly fertile ground for the fashioning of "old stock" identities. Such identities linked Americanness to membership in a northwest European group thought to share a racially superior stock with colonial-era settlers. This definition of "American" had a particular resonance for the descendants of nineteenth-century German immigrants in the mid-Atlantic. The region had had an extremely diverse European population from the seventeenth century on, and German settlers had played an important role in its colonial history. Prewar definitions of "old stock" in Philadelphia naturally included residents descended from German as well as English colonial settlers. After World War I, second-generation German immigrants there could plausibly claim to share the racial "stock" of colonial "forefathers," to use the language that Nellie Wallerstein encountered at the Americanization Committee of Germantown. Such identifications, however, may have had less purchase for Germans in other regions. In New England, the "stock" of "our forefathers" was necessarily English, presuming—as Americanizers and nativists did—that only European-American forefathers counted as such. To the extent the Midwest had such settlers of colonial vintage, they were likely to be French fur traders—as was the case with the sites of Milwaukee and Chicago in the eighteenth century.[38] This did not prevent John Weitzel from defining himself as a "real American" in old stock terms. Yet the Midwest offered alternative ways to stress oldness, such as the figure of the nineteenth-century pioneer, and Germans there may have fashioned American identities that relied on memories of local settlement as well as those keyed to the colonial period. To chart such varying paths toward ethnic integration demands attention to what Kathleen Conzen has called "pluralisms of place"[39]—to the ways in which different local "mainstreams," with varying ethnic compositions, have arisen and flourished in different parts of the United States. The Philadelphia case therefore suggests a larger lesson. Rather than seeking to craft a uniform model of assimilation that applies equally everywhere, scholars should consider how local conditions may inflect assimilatory processes, even as they tease out aspects of those processes that transcend specific localities and regions.

THE GERMAN CASE AND ETHNIC AMERICA

If German Philadelphia was, in some respects, representative of German America, then how typical was German America of the general immigrant ethnic experience in the twentieth century? Not very, one is tempted to reply at first. Certainly, in a number of ways, the German-American experience was idiosyncratic. No other large immigrant group was subjected to such strong, sustained pressure to abandon its ethnic identity for an American one. None was so divided internally, a characteristic that made German Americans especially vulnerable to such pressure. Among the larger groups that immigrated in the century after 1830, none—despite regional variations—appears to have muted its ethnic identity to so great an extent.

The pressure imposed on German Americans to forsake their ethnic identity was extreme in both nature and duration. No other ethnic group saw its "adoptive fatherland" twice enter a world war against its country of origin. To this stigma, the Third Reich added the lasting one of the Holocaust. In her study of ethnic identity in the 1980s, sociologist Mary Waters noted that the "effect of the Nazi movement and World War II was still quite strong" in shaping "popular perceptions of the German-American character," enough so that some individuals of mixed background often would acknowledge only the non-German part of their ancestry.[40]

Japanese Americans, of course, suffered far more during the Second World War. More than 100,000 of them, native-born citizens as well as aliens, were forcibly evacuated from the West Coast to inland internment camps. The criterion for internment was Japanese ancestry alone: Japanese Americans belonged to "an enemy race," according to the Army commander who recommended removal. This racial justification, however, hints at the fundamentally different nature of the climate experienced by Japanese Americans. Until at least the 1950s, the pressures on them ran toward exclusion from, rather than inclusion in, the nation. Americanization efforts, with the exception of those in Hawaii, tended to pass over Asian residents as racially "unassimilable." Such judgments reflected a long history of legal and popular efforts, going back to the mid-nineteenth century, to exclude Asians from American life on racial grounds.[41] The state and many ordinary European Americans refused to recognize Asians as potentially American. In contrast, they pressured Germans to accept precisely that American identity in place of a German one.

The burden of "enemy" status made those pressures far greater for Germans than for other European ethnic groups. To some extent, American intervention in World War I actually helped fuel ethnic nationalism in the United States among Poles, Czechs, Lithuanians, Italians, and east European Jews, who felt their desires for existing or prospective homelands stood to gain from an Allied victory. Indeed, some historians have depicted the following decade as one when immigrants transcended local or regional homeland affiliations to craft or further consolidate national identities as Poles, Czechs, and Italians. Such groups escaped the fury of

"100 percent Americanism" during the war, in part because of their obvious stake in the defeat of the Central Powers.[42]

Many Irish Americans, in contrast, had little enthusiasm for aiding England, and they proved more vulnerable to the wartime "antihyphen" climate. A number of newspapers with Irish nationalist leanings were actually banned from the mails in 1918. One historian has argued that such pressures accelerated a shift among Irish Americans toward an identity as "militant Catholic Americans," a stance that "made a casualty out of their uniquely Irish identification and outlook," as "purely Irish ethnic organization membership declined." This interpretation, however, must be qualified by the fact that Irish nationalist activity intensified during and immediately after the war, as many Irish Americans became swept up in the events leading to the creation of the Irish Free State.[43] It made a difference for the long-term viability of Irish-American identity that the Irish homeland not only did not go to war with the United States but, in fact, emerged during the interwar years as a sovereign nation.

German-American identity fell victim not only to a peculiar set of events, but also to an extraordinarily high level of internal diversity. All ethnic groups have internal divides, whether of class, religion, gender, politics, or homeland region. What distinguished German America was that it incorporated not just some but *all* of these divisions. Irish Americans, for example, had lost their status as primarily a proletarian group by 1900, yet they were united by religion and politics. "Irish American" had come to mean Irish Catholic; the vast majority of Irish Americans subscribed to some form of Irish nationalism conflated with American patriotism; and Irish-American voters were overwhelmingly Democrats. The power of this synthesis, Kerby Miller argued, explains the survival of Irish-American identity despite the ebbing of organized Irish-American nationalism after the Free State's founding. For German Americans, however, religion and party politics were sources of division rather than of unity.[44] Across such divides, activists like those in the National Alliance promoted a common identity only with great effort and with limited, episodic success. They could draw on aspects of a shared culture, such as German-language use and mixed-sex leisure. But these were wasting assets: even before the First World War, the use of German was fading, while mass culture had co-opted German forms of sociability. The subcultures of German America, meanwhile, had ample opportunity for contact, however testy, with non-German counterparts. The latter beckoned as destinations when the cost of being German-American rose too high.[45]

The trajectories followed by Americans of German background in the twentieth century, then, are to some extent singular. They vary in important respects from those taken by Americans of Irish, Polish, Italian, Japanese, and other immigrant ancestries. This, however, is far from the end of the story. First, German America's singularity depends in part on the angle from which one views it. The fate of the group's subcultures, that is, was far less idiosyncratic than that of the group itself. Members of those subcultures, to some degree, coaligned with and shared the fates of constituents of other ethnic groups. This was the case most obviously with German workers and Catholics who swelled the ranks of the urban North's white ethnics along with working-class Italians, Irish, and Slavs.

Second, and relatedly, the forces that upended German America had an impact, albeit less extreme, on other ethnic groups—an impact that itself was shaped by what happened to German America. This was especially true of the rise of mass culture and the new collective identities it opened to women in particular. Elsie Spalde's pursuit of mixed-sex leisure and female *Gazette-Democrat* readers' devotion to department-store shopping were hardly German monopolies. German festive culture, including its heterosocial nature, helped to shape mass culture, but women of many ethnic backgrounds embraced that culture and the consumption-oriented identities it offered.[46]

In more subtle ways, German America's collision with an increasingly exclusive and conformist American nationalism presaged a larger struggle for all ethnic groups; indeed, it helped alter the very context within which those groups crafted their identities. The campaign for "100 percent Americanism" was at its heart an attack on ethnic pluralism. During the war years, that attack focused on German and Irish Americans. But it would broaden by the 1920s, helping to fuel a renewed nativism—by turns antiradical, anti-Catholic, and racial—the drive to pass and enforce Prohibition, and coercive Americanization campaigns. These efforts targeted immigrants in general and newcomers from Asia and southern and eastern Europe in particular, especially through a draconian brand of immigration restriction. They amounted to "a disciplinary project breathtaking in its scope," in Gary Gerstle's words, one supported by a federal government made more powerful by the war.[47]

That project, and the conformist nationalism behind it, were not all-powerful. The Supreme Court struck down some of the harshest Americanization measures, Prohibition ended, and Poles, Italians, and other groups continued to construct ethnic-American identities during these years. Clearly, however, conformist nationalism "weakened the pluralist character of pre-1917 America and accelerated national integration," as Gerstle argued. Immigrant groups found their freedom to fashion their own ethnic identities considerably narrowed. They now had to "couch their programs in the language of Americanism."[48] Even northwest European groups felt these pressures. In 1925, Norwegian Americans marked a century of Norwegian immigration by staging a massive celebration in Minneapolis and St. Paul. The event, as described by April

Schultz, celebrated both American and Norwegian nationalism, offering a "safe" ethnicity that nevertheless "hinged on Norwegian Americans as a unique, 'peculiar' people." Schultz saw that public stance as a "profound challenge" to the "forces of Americanization." Nonetheless, the fact that the organizers of the Norse-American Immigration Centennial felt so compelled to stress the compatibility of Norwegian and American ways—symbolized, for example, by a "living" Norwegian flag that metamorphosed into an American one—suggests that they, too, had to bend to the imperatives of a conformist American nationalism.[49]

That brand of nationalism reigned for roughly half a century. It only collapsed in the 1960s, when a failed war in Vietnam, racial crises at home, and mounting affirmations of particularistic identities—above all, black nationalism—led many Americans to question the primacy of the American nation.[50] As long as "Americanism" enjoyed that primacy, however, ethnic groups had to operate on its terms, which recognized the legitimacy of cultural pluralism only grudgingly if at all. The emergence of this narrower nationalism in the 1910s, ironically enough, owed much to German Americans. Their ordeal during World War I was a turning point, a key moment when conservative Americanizers, patriotic groups, and the federal state succeeded in delegitimizing concepts of the nation that today would be called multicultural. For German America represented the strongest bearer of a pluralist alternative. German-American activists had long held that German Americans should maintain their ethnic distinctiveness to preserve their best cultural traits, so that these could be contributed to the nation as a whole—a nation still in the process of becoming. The National Alliance, for all of its at times overblown rhetoric, was a bulwark of this kind of thinking. Despite their losses and divisions, moreover, German Americans were still the largest immigrant group in the 1910s and one of the most prosperous and respected. They were a very visible reminder that American society could not be viewed simply as Anglo-American. Conformist nationalism could not succeed unless its advocates discredited this rival center of ethnic power and disabled its rival, culturally pluralist, vision of the nation. The war let them do both: *Kultur* became anathema, and its champion, the National Alliance, crumbled amid an investigation by a Senate committee.

Paradoxically, however, conformist nationalism also succeeded because it managed to recruit some of its own victims. This phenomenon remains little-studied by historians, who tend to stress efforts by elites to impose their style of nationalism on ordinary Americans.[51] Yet German Philadelphians who abandoned their hyphens clearly were welcomed as allies in efforts to exclude or "Americanize" new immigrants. The tendency to fall in with Americanization drives, moreover, was not limited to German Americans. At least some Norwegian Americans in the upper Midwest sympathized with English-only efforts in the public schools, while the Irish-dominated Knights of Columbus organized elaborate patriotic programs for "Americanization Day" in 1915.[52] Winning the allegiance of Americans who were not of English background likely was crucial to the success of conformist nationalism, given the size of that population and the legitimacy conferred by such conversions.

Such recruitment, moreover, also strengthened the racialist side of this new nationalism. German Philadelphians who worked in the Junior Order United American Mechanics or the Patriotic Order Sons of America during the 1920s helped reinforce the message that "Nordics" made the best Americans. To an extent not generally recognized, members of all ethnic groups had to grapple with that message. Germans were not alone among northwest European ethnics in trying to turn it to their advantage. The organizers of the Norse-American Centennial likely were aided in their attempts to present a "safe" ethnicity by the fact that Norwegians were, after all, "Nordic." Schultz did not dwell on this aspect of the celebration,[53] but her narrative provides indications that the planners tapped the discourse of racialized nativism, including the idea that only northwest Europeans were racially fit for self-rule. As one Norwegian American suggested to the planning committee, "the keynote of the pageant should be that men of Norse blood have those qualities that make for desirable American citizenship."[54] Similarly, a Chicago Swedish newspaper in 1923 called for both restricting immigration from southeastern Europe and encouraging it from the rest of the continent, since the latter was needed "to reinforce the western European human stock which is already here."[55] South and east European immigrants were on the receiving end of such racial nationalism. Yet even they were not immune to what Gerstle termed "the allure of Nordic Americanization." In the 1930s, American Communists like Stjepan Mesaros and Joseph Cohen changed their names to give them more of a northwest European ring—becoming, respectively, Steve Nelson and Joe Clark—while ethnic workers revealed a yearning for "Nordic" ancestors in their adulation of the Founding Fathers.[56]

By its nature, Nordic Americanization had a limited constituency. It was always more available to Americans of English, German, or Scandinavian background, Protestant belief, and middle-class status. One could argue, moreover, that it had a limited lifespan. In one reading, the tumult of the 1960s that brought down conformist nationalism likewise crippled that variant of racial nationalism that presumed the superiority of a WASP elite; proponents of the "white ethnic revival" now felt empowered to break out of what Michael Novak called the "Nordic jungle."[57] Another reading, offered by Matthew Jacobson, sees the "hierarchy of white races" expressed in the Johnson-Reed Act as flattening between the 1920s and the 1960s into a "monolithic whiteness." Immigration restriction, the Great Migration, and even civil rights agitation worked to turn "race" into primarily a black-white issue, with former Nordics, Celts, and Slavs now marshalled on the white side of this color line and differentiated under the culture-based concept of "ethnicity."[58]

Both readings have much to recommend them. They may, however, overlook the persistence within European America of a division that, in an earlier incarnation, separated new immigrants from "old stock" Americans. Richard Alba has discerned a growing "social integration among persons with European ancestry," evidenced especially by a rise in intermarriage among non-Hispanic whites across both ethnic and religious lines that dates at least to the late 1940s. One might see this development as the structural underpinning of an emerging "monolithic whiteness." Alba himself notes that such evidence undermines the idea that the descendants of European immigrants were merging into more limited, religious solidarities as Protestants, Catholics, and Jews, a view advanced by mid-twentieth-century scholars as the "triple-melting-pot thesis."[59] When he turns to the identities of Americans of European ancestry, however, Alba finds a situation more fractured than monolithic. His 1980s survey research in the metropolitan Albany area confirms that many whites retained ethnic identities, although these were "not typically anchored in strongly ethnic social structures," amounting more to attachments to a few ethnic symbols—"symbolic ethnicity," in Herbert Gans's phrase.[60] At the same time, such identities were expressed most commonly and most intensely by new immigrant groups and less so by "the old-stock groups originating in northern and western Europe, such as the English, Germans, and Scots." For the latter groups, ethnic identity was "relatively faint"; 40 to 50 percent of such respondents said their ancestral background held no importance for them at all. Many, in fact, "claim no identity other than the American one."[61]

To Alba, these findings suggest the emergence, especially in the metropolitan Northeast and Midwest, of a broader, "European-American" group among whites. The European Americans are composed of those who retain different ethnic identities, yet understand those identities in terms of a shared historical memory of immigration, discrimination in the new land, and hard work that led to economic security or upward mobility as well as to a stronger American nation. This European-American account emerged partly in response to the civil rights movement, which challenged the fairness of the system under which European ethnics eventually "made it." In this and other respects, Alba's European-American group seems to overlap to a great degree with the collectivity commonly known as "white ethnics." Alongside the European Americans, however, lies an "older, unhyphenated American identity" that seems to take in many of those in the old-stock groups. As Alba notes, his concept of a new, European-American group "may have more validity for the descendants of historically recent immigrations from southern and eastern Europe than for old-stock Americans, who can rely on the continued prestige of an older, more exclusive American identity."[62]

Alba's work suggests not only that whiteness remains somewhat fractured, but that its major fault line descends from the division that emerged in the early twentieth century between "old-stock" or "Nordic" Americans, including "old immigrants," on the one hand and new immigrants on the other. A great deal, of course, has changed since then. The distinction between "European" and "unhyphenated" Americans today is far less salient than that between the "older American stock" and south and east European "races" in the 1910s and 1920s. If whiteness today is not monolithic, it certainly functions as an overarching collective identity for Americans of every European background, one that carries far more social, cultural, political, and economic weight than internal divisions between "European Americans" and "unhyphenated" ones. The ethnoracial distinctions that matter most in American society at the turn of the twenty-first century are those dividing whites from blacks and, to a lesser extent, Latinos, as well as those dividing blacks from Latinos and Asians, as the low rates of intermarriage across those lines suggest.[63]

Nonetheless, the divide between whites who claim an ethnic identity and those who identify only as "American" still has political consequences. It speaks to differing notions of American nationality. "Unhyphenated" identity seems linked in part to a family's longtime presence in America. "European-American" identity, on the other hand, is grounded in an immigration saga seen as perhaps "the defining American experience"; here, ethnic identities become "ways of claiming to be American." But that immigration saga is painted in terms of self-sacrifice, individual mobility, ethnic mutual aid, and, by implication, no government aid. However faulty this historical memory may be, many whites invoke it to measure the success, or shortcomings, of the newest wave of immigrants and of African Americans. Often enough, it allows them to ignore deeply entrenched structures of racial discrimination and to argue against government remedies for such discrimination.[64]

The fault line within today's whiteness, then, matters, for white and nonwhite Americans alike. This, in turn, suggests a final reason why we should care about the fate of German America. For German Americans not only straddle that fault line; they have a great deal to do with its construction. The choices they made during and after the 1920s both anticipated the split found by Alba and contributed to it. Nativists largely of colonial background popularized the idea of a deep divide between northwest-European "Americans" and southeast European immigrants before the First World War. But that divide only became a social reality when northwest Europeans who derived from the nineteenth-century mass migrations and who were not "Anglo-Saxon" joined in this racialized American identity. The middle-class and Lutheran Germans who took that step in Philadelphia did so in the wake of the war, under the pressures of "100 percent Americanism" and the influence of the immigration restriction campaign. Their working-class and Catholic counterparts, on the other hand, found a broader solidarity in a pan-European whiteness. It was not that German workers and Catholics "became white" in the late 1910s and 1920s but that they became more so. For them, whiteness gained importance as an alternative to a specifically German ethnic identity, because the latter was under attack just as the former was growing more salient with the Great Migration. Over time, both workers and Catholics would mix increasingly with the Irish and new immigrants in a manner that anticipated and, finally, resulted in the emergence of "white ethnics." By the 1960s, the pattern found by Alba was already in place: whites who stressed their ethnic identities on one side, and those, especially of old stock background, who held to an unhyphenated American identity on the other.

German Americans remained, even here, divided. Alba found that respondents of German as well as English background had a relatively low sense of ethnic identity, often identifying simply as "American" in his survey. At the same time, some subjects did strongly assert a German ethnic identity.[65] Americans of German background could still be found among both the "white ethnics" and the "unhyphenated Americans."

This tendency to divide may be one factor behind the curious absence of German Americans from much scholarly and popular writing on ethnicity in the twentieth century. Germans tend to fall out of overviews of immigration and ethnic history as they wend their way past 1900 and, especially, World War I.[66] In part, of course, this likely reflects the waning of German-American identity itself. It is difficult to study a group whose members are making themselves scarce; and, for precisely that reason, German Americans do not fit the "models of pluralistic ethnic maintenance" that have prevailed in recent immigration historiography, as Conzen noted.[67] Moreover, immigration historians and sociologists have studied the new immigrants and their descendants to a far greater extent than they have Americans descended from old immigrants.[68] But the historical fissures in German-American life likely play a role as well. Because German Americans straddled so many class and religious divides, they were hard to categorize; observers may have found it easier, therefore, to pass over them. Popular writing, for example, could readily lump Protestant and middle-class Germans into the category of "White Anglo-Saxon Protestant," while ignoring German Catholics and workers. Michael

Novak, who drew a rather tight southern and eastern European circle around his "unmeltable ethnics" and cast WASPs as their main antagonists, dismissed the Germans as having been "speedily absorbed into Anglo-American life"[69]—a view that would have surprised Kensington.

And yet it is that continuing diversity among Americans of German background that may most merit study. Some aspects of German America's fate were singular; others spoke more to the experience of ethnic America than we have realized. As singular as German America's internal diversity was, however, it suggests a larger conclusion about the nature of racial identity in America: even today, class, religious, and other fissures make it less than completely monolithic. The German case points to the wide range of ways that the members of one European ethnic group could conceive of their whiteness, given that group's internal divisions, and to the power of those class and religious divides to shape such racial self-conceptions. For some middle-class second-generation German immigrants could cast themselves as the racial superiors of new immigrants in the interwar years, even as German workers and Catholics were joining with those south and east Europeans on the common ground of whiteness. And in the late twentieth century, whiteness, while it conferred significant uniform privileges, carried some distinctly different meanings for "white ethnics" and "unhyphenated Americans." The ultimate success of such self-definitions among Americans of German background spelled a final irony. The new identities conveyed real privileges; they likewise carried little hint of the ordeal their bearers had endured to acquire them.

The Neighborhood Census Samples

THIS book's description of the Girard Avenue district and Germantown rests in part on an analysis of samples drawn from federal manuscript census returns for those neighborhoods. The samples were designed to provide a picture of the class and ethnic makeup of the neighborhoods in 1900 and 1920 and to determine the extent to which German-stock residents mixed with their neighbors residentially. This appendix describes the design of the four samples taken—one for each neighborhood in each census year—the measures used to analyze them, and the methods employed to gauge the reliability of results.[1]

THE SAMPLE DESIGN

The sampling methodology grew out of a set of questions relating to the assimilation of German Philadelphians. I wanted to gain a sense of the range of that assimilation at the beginning of the century by comparing the German experience in two neighborhoods: one with a heavily German population and one where Germans formed a small minority. In particular, I wished to determine the extent to which Germans mixed with residents of other ethnic backgrounds, and whether they tended to mix with some groups rather than others. Ultimately, the type of mixing I chose to measure was residential. This came down to the question of whom first- and second-generation German immigrants tended to have as neighbors; literally, with whom did they share their streets?

Olivier Zunz offered a model for answering this question in his fine study of ethnicity and class in Detroit, *The Changing Face of Inequality*. Zunz employed a sample design that had as its smallest component the block frontage—one side of a city block. His actual sampling unit was a cluster of six such block fronts, made up of a city block and two of the four fronts "across the street" from that block. Zunz located and coded the households along sampled fronts in the federal manuscript census for 1880, 1900, and 1920. This approach allowed him to measure the ethnic composition of individual fronts, blocks, and complete clusters.[2]

In many respects, my sample design was modeled on Zunz's. However, I chose as my sampling unit the single block frontage. I felt a random sample of such block fronts in a given neighborhood would prove less complicated to execute while still providing a fine-grained picture of whom Germans lived next door to. One could learn thereby the ethnic composition of individual fronts, in essence determining the ethnic mix among the neighbors who lived along one side of a length of street. One could ascertain as well whether that mix varied in different areas of the neighborhood, and, in the aggregate, whether German residents tended to share their block fronts mainly with other Germans or, instead, with non-German neighbors of particular ethnic backgrounds. Taken together, the fronts could yield estimates for the neighborhood's population characteristics, in particular its class and ethnic makeup.

The sample design involved the drawing of random samples of block fronts in the Girard Avenue district, composed of the Sixteenth and Seventeenth wards, and Germantown in 1900. All of the fronts in each neighborhood were inventoried using turn-of-the-century fire insurance maps. These beautifully drawn maps show the location and street address of every house on each street. One of the small ironies of this study of assimilation is that the primary maps used were created by the Philadelphia firm of Ernest Hexamer & Son. The son in the business was the same Charles Hexamer who led the battle against assimilation as president of the National German-American Alliance. The Hexamer maps allowed me to create sampling frames consisting of every residential block front in the Girard Avenue district and Germantown.[3] From the Girard Avenue district's inventory of residential fronts, my statistical consultant, Michael Guilfoyle, drew a 15 percent simple random sample of fronts with more than one house on them and a separate 15 percent simple random sample of fronts carrying only one house. The first sample allowed an analysis of neighboring that would not be skewed by "100 percent German" fronts consisting of a single German-stock family. The two samples combined permitted the computation of population estimates for the entire neighborhood. One should note that while these were simple random samples at the block-front level, they amounted to cluster samples at the level of households and individuals.

In an attempt to reduce the number of fronts to be coded, the Girard Avenue sample of fronts with two or more houses was further broken down into subsamples. Only three of these four subsamples were coded. The resulting cases were weighted to account for the absence of the fourth subsample; all Girard Avenue figures given in this study are the weighted figures. The overall sample, then, was stratified, in terms of its subsamples and the separate sample of single-house fronts. The final Girard Avenue sample for 1900 included a total of sixty-nine block fronts. With the aid of the Hexamer maps, I was able to find the households along these fronts in the 1900 manuscript census and code them;[4] the resulting weighted sample held 3,936 individuals.

Germantown presented a particular problem: its German-stock residents were a small enough group that a simple random sample might have garnered too few for statistical analysis. The 1900 Germantown sample was stratified, therefore, to ensure that a sufficiently large number of German-stock individuals were drawn. I went through the neighborhood's manuscript census returns and, for every residential front, cataloged the number of residents with at least one parent born in Germany. Residential fronts with more than one house were divided into three strata—those with no German-stock residents, those with one or two, and those with three or more—and a 15 percent simple random sample was drawn from each stratum. These three strata, taken together with a 15 percent sample of single-house fronts, yielded a total of 131 block fronts holding 6,181 individuals.

Rather than draw entirely new samples for 1920, I replicated the 1900 samples, locating the households that appeared on their fronts in the 1920 manuscript census. Since the Sixteenth and Seventeenth wards had lost population in the intervening two decades, with very few new residential fronts emerging during that time, it was not deemed necessary to draw an additional Girard Avenue sample for 1920. The neighborhood's population decline was reflected in the reduced size of its 1920 sample, which contained sixty block fronts with 3,215 individuals. Germantown, on the other hand, grew enormously during this period. Correspondingly, an additional 15 percent sample of residential fronts with two or more houses was drawn from an inventory of the neighborhood's new residential fronts, as was an additional 15 percent sample of single-house fronts. The overall 1920 Germantown sample thus had six strata and totaled 163 block fronts containing 9,110 individuals.

ANALYZING THE SAMPLES

Measures used to analyze the samples included frequency distributions showing the neighborhoods' ethnic and class makeup and cross-tabulations illustrating the class composition of particular ethnic groups. Two aspects of the analysis deserve particular explanation: the P^* statistic and the scheme of occupational classification applied to the 1900 samples.

The P^* index, as used in this study, summarizes the degree to which the "average" German-stock resident in a neighborhood lived on a block front with other Germans or with members of other ethnic groups. The index allows one to describe residential ethnic mixing in the Girard Avenue district and Germantown, how it changed over time, and how it differed between the two neighborhoods. Technically, the P^* statistic is an exposure index, measuring the degree to which members of different groups "physically confront one another by virtue of sharing a common residential area," in the words of Douglas Massey and Nancy Denton. In this it differs from the more familiar index of dissimilarity, which measures the extent to which the spatial distribution of a group's members departs from a theoretical even distribution. P^* indices thus aim to determine "the *experience* of segregation as felt by the average minority or majority member." They also allow one to compare the isolation a given group experiences and its interaction with a number of other groups.

For a given group X—here, a neighborhood's German-stock residents—one may compute a P^* isolation index, measuring the extent to which group members are exposed only to one another, and a series of P^* interaction indices, measuring the extent to which members of group X are exposed to members of group Y, group Z, and so forth. The isolation index is computed as the group X weighted average of each spatial unit's group X proportion:

$$_xP^*_x = \sum_{i=1}^{n} [x_i / X][x_i / t_i]$$

where x_i and t_i are the numbers of X members and the total population of unit i, respectively, and X represents the number of X members in the entire neighborhood. The interaction index is computed as the group X weighted average of each spatial unit's group Y proportion:

$$_xP^*_y = \sum_{i=1}^{n} [x_i / X][y_i / t_i]$$

where y_i is the number of Y members of unit i. Both of these indices can vary between 0 and 1. If more than two groups are present, then the sum of the isolation index plus each interaction index (showing group X's interaction with group Y, group Z, and so forth) will equal 1.[5] The indices can also be expressed in percentage form. Thus, for example, the average German-stock Germantowner in 1900 lived on a block front that was 19 percent German-stock, 16 percent British-stock, 20 percent Irish-stock, and 39 percent native white of native parentage. (Table 2.4.)

Historians seeking to delineate the class structure of the nineteenth- and early-twentieth-century United States have long made use of the occupational titles provided in the manuscript census. To examine the class composition of the Girard Avenue district and Germantown in 1900, I first had to order these titles into class categories. To do so, I followed the classification scheme employed by Zunz, which divided occupations into four larger categories: high white-collar, low white-collar, skilled, and semiskilled and unskilled. Zunz sorted occupations into these four categories "on the basis of a broad agreement among historians who had already developed occupational coding schemes," including Stephan Thernstrom in his study of Boston and Theodore Hershberg in his work on nineteenth-century Philadelphia.[6] The high white-collar category, for example, took in professionals, major proprietors, and major managers and officials, while low white-collar workers included petty nonmanual proprietors, clerks, salesmen, and low-level managers and officials.

The lines between these categories were not always easy to define, given the limited amount of information available in the census. To the extent possible, I replicated Zunz's approach, making use of his list of titles in the 1900 census ordered by class category. In addition, I referred to lists of occupational titles organized by class that Walter Licht developed for an analysis of adolescent workers in late-nineteenth- and early-twentieth-century Philadelphia.[7] In a number of cases, I referred to city directories for more information on particular individuals or consulted works by labor historians when the status of certain titles seemed particularly unclear.[8]

For a number of reasons, I did not attempt to order occupational titles from the 1920 census into a scheme of class categories. The 1920 census offers three occupation variables: trade, profession, or line of work; industry, business, or establishment in which at work; and whether employer, salary or wage worker, or working on own account. These open the possibility of developing more refined occupational coding approaches, such as the twelve-category scheme devised by Zunz.[9] However, the greater number of class levels employed in such approaches would have made it more difficult to achieve statistically significant results from the 1920 samples, especially given the smaller size of the Girard Avenue sample. I instead made use of the last variable to classify working individuals in the two 1920 samples as employers, self-employed, or wage or salary workers. While this classification is rough at best, it does allow one to compare the class structures of the Girard Avenue district and Germantown in 1920. (See note 14 to chapter 10.)

ASSESSING THE RELIABILITY OF RESULTS

How is one to know whether the results derived from the neighborhood census samples are reliable estimates of actual population parameters? One can gain a sense of the overall validity of the samples themselves by seeing how well they predict known population parameters. For individual

results, the reliability of simple proportions, such as the percentage of individuals in a sample who are German, can be gauged by calculating confidence intervals around those estimates. The P^* results are more difficult
to assess; this study employs resampling techniques to verify whether its
P^* indices accurately reflect their parameters in the population.

For simple proportions, I calculated standard errors and confidence
intervals; the latter are presented in parentheses next to their corresponding proportions in the individual tables. I made use of a set of equa-
tions that Zunz employed to derive the variances and, hence, standard
errors for proportions estimated from his stratified samples. These formulas are as follows: we wish to estimate from a sample the population
proportion

$$R = X/Y$$

where Y is the number of all persons in the population, and X is the number of those persons having a particular attribute—say, German birth. R
then is estimated by

$$r = x/y$$

where x and y are sample estimates of X and Y. The estimated variance
of r is given by

$$Var(r) = \frac{1}{y^2}[Var(x) + r^2 Var(y) - 2rCov(x, y)]$$

where

$$Var(y) = \sum_{h=1}^{H} \sum_{a=1}^{a_h} (y_{ha} - \bar{y}_h)^2$$

$$Var(x) = \sum_{h=1}^{H} \sum_{a=1}^{a_h} (x_{ha} - \bar{x}_h)^2$$

and

$$Cov(x, y) = \sum_{h=1}^{H} \sum_{a=1}^{a_h} (x_{ha} - \bar{x}_h)(y_{ha} - \bar{y}_h)$$

Here, H is the number of strata, a_h is the number of clusters—in this case,
block fronts—in stratum h, x_{ha} and y_{ha} are the sample totals for the ath
block front within the hth stratum, and $\bar{x}_h$ and $\bar{y}_h$ are the sample stratum
means for x and y in stratum h.

The standard error of r then is given by

$$SE(r) = \sqrt{Var(r)}$$

while the 95 percent confidence interval around r corresponding to the .05 level of significance is derived by multiplying the standard error by 1.96.[10] These calculations are extremely time-consuming. For this reason, I did not provide confidence intervals for certain sample proportions that were based on very small numbers of cases; these results seemed, in any case, unlikely to prove statistically significant. (See tables 2.1 and 2.3.)

The representativeness of a sample also can be gauged by seeing whether known population parameters fall within the confidence intervals around their corresponding sample estimates.[11] Such known parameters are available for three of the four samples. The Girard Avenue district was defined by the Sixteenth and Seventeenth wards, and some population proportions are given for those wards in the published census. These strengthen the case for the validity of the district samples. In 1900, for example, 70.07 percent of the combined wards' population was native-born. The proportion of native-born individuals in the 1900 sample was 71.23 percent, with a 95 percent confidence interval of ±3.1 percent. The population parameter thus fell well within the estimate's confidence interval. Similarly, in 1920, 5.03 percent of the wards' population was German-born, a proportion comfortably contained within the confidence interval of ±1.57 percent that spanned the sample proportion of 4.83 percent for individuals born in Germany.[12] No such published figures exist for Germantown, but I determined in my review of the neighborhood's manuscript returns for 1900 that 7.4 percent of its residents were either born in Germany or had at least one German-born parent. The corresponding proportion in the 1900 Germantown sample was 8.45 percent, with a 95 percent confidence interval of ±1.45 percent, again encompassing the known population parameter.

Determining the reliability of the samples' P^* estimates required a somewhat different approach. The P^* statistic has been used most commonly to analyze aggregated census data, such as that for census tracts; hence, formulas to generate confidence intervals for this statistic are not readily available. I instead worked with Guilfoyle to apply resampling techniques to the samples. Resampling, also known as bootstrapping, involves taking many subsamples of the sample itself, with the aim of generating an estimate of the sampling distribution of a given statistic.[13] In this case, Guilfoyle wrote a computer program to draw 200 random samples, each with a sampling fraction of 25 percent, from each of the four neighborhood samples. These results were combined to calculate a set of mean resampled P^* indices and their standard deviations. Multiplying the standard deviations by 1.96 in turn generated 95 percent confidence intervals around the resampled indices. The test of reliability for the original sample P^* indices was whether they fell within the confidence intervals around the resampled indices to which they corresponded. Results for individual P^* indices are indicated in tables 2.4 and 10.2. For 1920, these verified the reliability of the original sample P^* indices as estimates of population parameters. For the 1900 samples, resampling showed indices for larger groups to be quite reliable estimates. In the case of a number of groups, however, P^* indices of 4 percent and under could not be so verified.

Notes

RTC	Roxborough Turners Collection, Balch
SRS	Site and Relic Society of Germantown, GHS
YMCA	Young Men's Christian Association of Germantown Collection, UA

INTRODUCTION

1. This finding represents my analysis of published data from the 2000 census. In samples taken in 1990 and 2000, the U.S. Bureau of the Census asked respondents to write in their "ancestry or ethnic origin" and allowed for up to two responses; U.S. Census Bureau, 1990 Census of Population, *Detailed Ancestry Groups for States,* 1990 CP-S-1-2 (Washington, D.C., 1992), E-14; U.S. Census Bureau, 2000 Census of Population and Housing, *Summary File 3: Technical Documentation* (Washington, D.C., 2002), D-4. The 1990 data showed that German was the most frequently reported ancestry group, with 58 million people "reported as being solely or partly of German ancestry." The ten next-largest ancestry groups, in decreasing order of size, were Irish, English, Afro-American, Italian, Mexican, French, Polish, American Indian, Dutch, and Scotch-Irish; Census Bureau, *Detailed Ancestry Groups,* III-1.

As of this writing, the Census Bureau was preparing but had not yet issued an equivalent ancestry ranking for 2000. The bureau had, however, generated tables with results for more than 100 specific ancestry groups from the Census 2000 Summary File 3 data set. This data set is based on a sample of approximately 19 million housing units (about one in six households) that received the 2000 census long-form questionnaire; "Summary File 3 (SF 3)," press release available at www.census.gov/Press-Release (accessed 19 March 2003). The data are weighted to represent the total population. Table PCT18 provides totals of first and second ancestry responses for each ancestry. German is the table's largest specified ancestry group, with 42.9 million responses. The table does list one larger category: "Other groups," with 81.5 million responses. This catchall category covers European and other ancestry groups too small to be listed separately, along with Hispanic, Asian, African American, American Indian, and other groups that the Census Bureau counted in its 100 percent enumeration (through questions on race and Hispanic origin on the short form questionnaire). See U.S. Census Bureau, Census 2000 Summary File 3, Table PCT18, at http://factfinder.census.gov (accessed 19 March 2003); Census Bureau, *Summary File 3: Technical Documentation,* 6-95–6-97; U.S. Census Bureau, American Community Survey, "2000–2001 Ancestry Code List," at www.census.gov/acs (accessed 19 March 2003); U.S. Census Bureau, "Frequently Asked Questions about Ancestry," at www.census.gov/population (accessed 19 March 2003).

Is any single ancestry group within PCT18's "Other groups" category larger than the German group? One can approximate the size of the largest of those "Other groups" by examining responses to the race and Hispanic origin questions in the 100 percent enumeration. The race question allowed respondents to mark one or more races. The broad categories then reported by the Census Bureau were White, Black or African American, American Indian and Alaska Native, Asian,

Native Hawaiian and Other Pacific Islander, and Some other race. The broadest definition for each of these categories, given the multiple responses possible on the question, was the given race alone or in combination with one or more other races. The largest such category after White was African American; 36.4 million people reported themselves as Black or African American alone or in combination with other races, while 11.9 million reported Asian alone or in combination, and 4.1 million reported American Indian and Alaska Native alone or in combination. See U.S. Census Bureau, *Overview of Race and Hispanic Origin: 2000,* by Elizabeth M. Grieco and Rachel C. Cassidy, Census 2000 Brief, C2KBR/01-1 (Washington, D.C., March 2001), 1–3, 5–8. These three categories together total 52.4 million responses; that figure would account for nearly two-thirds of the 81.5 million responses in PCT18's "Other groups" category, leaving it with a remainder of 29.1 million. It seems unlikely that any group within that remainder would equal or exceed the German group's 42.9 million responses. This is particularly the case if one breaks ancestry down as the Census Bureau did in 1990, by subgroup within the Hispanic category and some race categories. While 35.3 million U.S. residents described themselves as Hispanic or Latino in 2000, for example, the largest subgroup within that population (Mexican) numbered 20.6 million people; U.S. Census Bureau, *The Hispanic Population: 2000,* by Betsy Guzmán, Census 2000 Brief, C2KBR/01-3 (Washington, D.C., May 2001), 2, 3 (table 1).

2. Kathleen Neils Conzen, "Patterns of German-American History," in *Germans in America: Retrospect and Prospect. Tricentennial Lectures Delivered at the German Society of Pennsylvania in 1983,* ed. Randall M. Miller (Philadelphia, 1984), 15.

3. Richard D. Alba, *Ethnic Identity: The Transformation of White America* (New Haven, Conn., 1990), 321, 59. Alba distinguishes between "self-image (identity) and knowledge of an objective family past (ancestry)"; ibid., 49.

4. Kathleen Neils Conzen, "Germans," in *Harvard Encyclopedia of American Ethnic Groups,* ed. Stephan Thernstrom (Cambridge, Mass., 1980), 409, 422; John Higham, *Strangers in the Land: Patterns of American Nativism, 1860–1925,* 2d rev. ed. (New York, 1981), 196.

5. Russell A. Kazal, "Revisiting Assimilation: The Rise, Fall, and Reappraisal of a Concept in American Ethnic History," *American Historical Review* 100 (April 1995): 437–471. I largely draw from this article for the account presented in this paragraph and the two that follow.

6. Rudolph J. Vecoli, "Return to the Melting Pot: Ethnicity in the United States in the Eighties," *Journal of American Ethnic History* 5 (Fall 1985): 11; Donna R. Gabaccia, "Liberty, Coercion, and the Making of Immigration Historians," *Journal of American History* 84 (September 1997): 573.

7. On this point, see John Higham, "Ethnic Pluralism in Modern American Thought," in *Send These to Me: Immigrants in Urban America,* rev. ed. (Baltimore, 1984); and Philip Gleason, "The Odd Couple: Pluralism and Assimilation," in *Speaking of Diversity: Language and Ethnicity in Twentieth-Century America* (Baltimore, 1992).

8. Will Herberg, *Protestant-Catholic-Jew: An Essay in American Religious Sociology* (Garden City, N.Y., 1956); Milton M. Gordon, *Assimilation in American Life: The Role of Race, Religion, and National Origins* (New York, 1964).

9. Kathleen Neils Conzen, David A. Gerber, Ewa Morawska, George E. Pozzetta, and Rudolph J. Vecoli, "The Invention of Ethnicity: A Perspective from the U.S.A.," *Journal of American Ethnic History* 12 (September 1992): 3–41.

10. The phrase "imagined community" is borrowed from Benedict Anderson's now-classic analysis of nationalism, *Imagined Communities: Reflections on the Origin and Spread of Nationalism,* rev. ed. (London, 1991). Examples of studies along the lines suggested here include: Lizabeth Cohen, *Making a New Deal: Industrial Workers in Chicago, 1919–1939* (Cambridge, 1990); James R. Barrett, "Americanization from the Bottom Up: Immigration and the Remaking of the Working Class in the United States, 1880–1930," *Journal of American History* 79 (December 1992): 996–1020; Gary Gerstle, *Working-Class Americanism: The Politics of Labor in a Textile City, 1914–1960* (Cambridge, 1989); Gary Gerstle, "The Working Class Goes to War," *Mid-America* 75 (October 1993): 303–322; Gary Gerstle, *American Crucible: Race and Nation in the Twentieth Century* (Princeton, N.J., 2001); David R. Roediger, *The Wages of Whiteness: Race and the Making of the American Working Class* (London, 1991); David R. Roediger, "Whiteness and Ethnicity in the History of 'White Ethnics' in the United States," in *Towards the Abolition of Whiteness: Essays on Race, Politics, and Working Class History* (London, 1994); James R. Barrett and David Roediger, "Inbetween Peoples: Race, Nationality, and the 'New Immigrant' Working Class," *Journal of American Ethnic History* 16 (Spring 1997): 3–44; Matthew Frye Jacobson, *Whiteness of a Different Color: European Immigrants and the Alchemy of Race* (Cambridge, Mass., 1998); John T. McGreevy, *Parish Boundaries: The Catholic Encounter with Race in the Twentieth-Century Urban North* (Chicago, 1996); Arnold R. Hirsch, *Making the Second Ghetto: Race and Housing in Chicago, 1940–1960* (Cambridge, 1983); Thomas J. Sugrue, "Crabgrass-Roots Politics: Race, Rights, and the Reaction against Liberalism in the Urban North, 1940–1964," *Journal of American History* 82 (September 1995): 551–578; Thomas J. Sugrue, *The Origins of the Urban Crisis: Race and Inequality in Postwar Detroit* (Princeton, N.J., 1996); David Nasaw, *Going Out: The Rise and Fall of Public Amusements* (New York, 1993); and Michael Rogin, *Blackface, White Noise: Jewish Immigrants in the Hollywood Melting Pot* (Berkeley, Calif., 1996).

11. Kazal, "Revisiting Assimilation," 438–439. The definition of assimilation as a process of homogenization is taken from Harold J. Abramson, "Assimilation and Pluralism," in *Harvard Encyclopedia of American Ethnic Groups,* ed. Thernstrom, 150.

12. Gordon, *Assimilation,* 24, 29. Gordon's definition of an ethnic group seems to me the most useful; I prefer it to concepts of ethnicity as "primordial," which grow out of the work of Clifford Geertz and Harold Isaacs, although I recognize that ethnic groups may also operate as interest groups in the sense proposed by Nathan Glazer and Daniel Patrick Moynihan, *Beyond the Melting Pot: The Negroes, Puerto Ricans, Jews, Italians, and Irish of New York City* (Cambridge, Mass., 1963). For a brief review of these concepts of ethnicity, see Conzen et al., "Invention of Ethnicity," 4.

13. This use of identity draws on the theory of the self-concept employed in contemporary social psychology. I have shied away from theories of ethnic identity, like those of Erik Erikson, that locate it in deep structures of the psyche. Such psy-

choanalytic approaches are difficult to implement in the absence of actual subjects and hence pose particular problems for historians. This description of theories of identity is taken from the very useful overview provided in Alba, *Ethnic Identity,* 21–26. In conceptualizing identity, I have drawn as well on Liam O'Boyle Riordan, "Identities in the New Nation: The Creation of an American Mainstream in the Delaware Valley, 1770–1830" (Ph.D. diss., University of Pennsylvania, 1996), 49–62.

14. Riordan, "Identities in the New Nation," 54, 49 (quotation), 53; Alba, *Ethnic Identity,* 22–23. Lesley Ann Kawaguchi explored the concept of multiple ethnic identities in her account of nineteenth-century German Philadelphia, drawing on the work of Charles Keyes and Milton Gordon; Lesley Ann Kawaguchi, "The Making of Philadelphia's German-America: Ethnic Group and Community Development, 1830–1883" (Ph.D. diss., University of California, Los Angeles, 1983), 64–66. See also Gordon, *Assimilation,* 25–27.

15. Riordan, "Identities in the New Nation," 53.

16. John Higham, "Integrating America: The Problem of Assimilation in the Nineteenth Century," *Journal of American Ethnic History* 1 (Fall 1981): 9.

17. John A. Hawgood, *The Tragedy of German America: The Germans in the United States of America during the Nineteenth Century—and After* (New York, 1940). One of the few recent works to support Hawgood's position is Melvin G. Holli, "Teuton vs. Slav: The Great War Sinks Chicago's German *Kultur,*" *Ethnicity* 8 (December 1981): 406–451.

18. Guido Andre Dobbert, *The Disintegration of an Immigrant Community: The Cincinnati Germans, 1870–1920* (New York, 1980); James M. Bergquist, "German Communities in American Cities: An Interpretation of the Nineteenth-Century Experience," *Journal of American Ethnic History* 4 (Fall 1984): 9–30. See also Frederick C. Luebke, *Bonds of Loyalty: German-Americans and World War I* (DeKalb, Ill., 1974), and Philip Gleason, *The Conservative Reformers: German-American Catholics and the Social Order* (Notre Dame, Ind., 1968).

19. Jacobson, *Whiteness of a Different Color,* 93; Gerstle, *American Crucible.*

20. U.S. Census Office, *Census Reports: Twelfth Census of the United States, Taken in the Year 1900,* vol. 1, *Population* (Washington, D.C., 1901–1902), lxix, 796–801.

21. The general interpretation of American pluralism in this paragraph is derived from Alba, *Ethnic Identity,* especially chap. 8; the interpretation of the German-American role is mine. For a more detailed discussion of the significance of that role, including citations of other secondary works pertaining to it, see the conclusion.

CHAPTER ONE
GERMAN PHILADELPHIA: A SOCIAL PORTRAIT

1. Oswald Seidensticker and Max Heinrici, *Geschichte der Deutschen Gesellschaft von Pennsylvanien. 1764–1917,* 1. Teil, *Von der Gruendung im Jahre 1764 bis zur Jubelfeier der Republik 1876,* by Oswald Seidensticker; 2. Teil, *Von 1876 bis 1917,* by Max Heinrici (Philadelphia, 1917), 275–277 (hereafter Seiden-

sticker, *Deutsche Gesellschaft,* I; and Heinrici, *Deutsche Gesellschaft,* II); *Phila-delphia Sonntags-Journal,* 24 November 1901, p. 5. Cited issues of the *Sonntags-Journal* are on microfilm at the GSP.

I generally have not provided the original German versions of quotations trans-lated into English in the text. The great majority of these German originals appear in the dissertation on which the book is based; see Russell A. Kazal, "Becoming 'Old Stock': The Waning of German-American Identity in Philadelphia, 1900–1930" (Ph.D. diss., University of Pennsylvania, 1998).

2. Heinrici, *Deutsche Gesellschaft,* II: 277, 381; *Sonntags-Journal,* 24 Novem-ber 1901, p. 5.

3. *Sonntags-Journal,* 24 November 1901, p. 5; *Philadelphia Tageblatt,* 16 No-vember 1901, p. 4. For member choirs of the UWSS as of 1898, see *Kalender, Philadelphia Tageblatt, 1899* (Philadelphia, n.d.), 36 (in VPL); for its UGT affili-ation, see *Tageblatt,* 5 October 1901, p. 2. Unless otherwise noted, *Tageblatt* ci-tations are to microfilmed holdings in GSP and Balch.

4. Heinrici, *Deutsche Gesellschaft,* II: 277. The quotations are a subjunctive-tense paraphrase of Hexamer's words, indicating that his language is recounted verbatim except for verb tense.

5. *Sonntags-Journal,* 24 November 1901, p. 5; Heinrici, *Deutsche Gesellschaft,* II: 279. On these regional societies, see Lesley Ann Kawaguchi, "The Making of Philadelphia's German-America: Ethnic Group and Community Development, 1830–1883" (Ph.D. diss., University of California, Los Angeles, 1983), 307–308.

6. German America's diversity has long been a theme of German-American his-toriography. See, for example, Kathleen Neils Conzen, "Patterns of German-American History," in *Germans in America: Retrospect and Prospect. Tricenten-nial Lectures Delivered at the German Society of Pennsylvania in 1983,* ed. Randall M. Miller (Philadelphia, 1984); Philip Gleason, *The Conservative Re-formers: German-American Catholics and the Social Order* (Notre Dame, Ind., 1968); and Frederick C. Luebke, *Bonds of Loyalty: German-Americans and World War I* (DeKalb, Ill., 1974).

7. Lincoln Steffens, "Philadelphia: Corrupt and Contented," *McClures* (July 1903), cited in Caroline Golab, *Immigrant Destinations* (Philadelphia, 1977), 11, 11n; ibid., 11, 171 (app. B).

8. Calculated from figures in U.S. Census Office, *Census Reports: Twelfth Cen-sus of the United States, Taken in the Year 1900,* vol. 1, *Population* (Washington, D.C., 1901–1902), 876–877, 884–885, 892–893. "Foreign stock" denotes those with at least one parent born abroad.

9. Proportions here and in the next paragraph are taken from Theodore Hersh-berg, Alan N. Burstein, Eugene P. Ericksen, Stephanie W. Greenberg and William L. Yancey, "A Tale of Three Cities: Blacks, Immigrants, and Opportunity in Phil-adelphia, 1850–1880, 1930, 1970," in *Philadelphia: Work, Space, Family, and Group Experience in the Nineteenth Century,* ed. Theodore Hershberg (New York, 1981), 465 (table 1).

10. Golab, *Destinations,* 168–169 (app. A); Census Office, *Census Reports: 1900,* 1: 639.

11. Golab, *Destinations,* 19 (table 4); Gary B. Nash, *Forging Freedom: The For-mation of Philadelphia's Black Community, 1720–1840* (Cambridge, Mass.,

1988), 2, 5–7 and passim; W.E.B. Du Bois, *The Philadelphia Negro: A Social Study* (Philadelphia, 1899; reprint, 1996), 74.

12. Census Office, *Census Reports: 1900,* 1: 796–801, 876.

13. Kathleen Neils Conzen, "Germans," in *Harvard Encyclopedia of American Ethnic Groups,* ed. Stephan Thernstrom (Cambridge, Mass., 1980), 406–407; Harry M. Tinkcom, Margaret B. Tinkcom, and Grant Miles Simon, *Historic Germantown: From the Founding to the Early Part of the Nineteenth Century; A Survey of the German Township* (Philadelphia, 1955), 3–6; Aaron Spencer Fogleman, *Hopeful Journeys: German Immigration, Settlement, and Political Culture in Colonial America, 1717–1775* (Philadelphia, 1996), 4–8, 86, 102–103.

14. Fogleman, *Hopeful Journeys,* 81–84, 99; Owen S. Ireland, "Germans Against Abolition: A Minority's View of Slavery in Revolutionary Pennsylvania," *Journal of Interdisciplinary History* 3 (Spring 1973): 693.

15. Conzen, "Germans," 409, 410 (table 2), 406, 406 (table 1), 413 (table 4).

16. Ibid., 411, 413; Fogleman, *Hopeful Journeys,* 80, 37–38, 56, 60–65; Mack Walker, *Germany and the Emigration, 1816–1885* (Cambridge, Mass., 1964), 47, 157, 161–167.

17. James F. Connelly, ed., *The History of the Archdiocese of Philadelphia* (Philadelphia, 1976), 35; Conzen, "Germans," 417, 410.

18. Fogleman, *Hopeful Journeys,* 152, 149, 149n; Don Yoder, "The Pennsylvania Germans: Three Centuries of Identity Crisis," in *America and the Germans: An Assessment of a Three-Hundred-Year History,* ed. Frank Trommler and Joseph McVeigh, vol. 1, *Immigration, Language, Ethnicity* (Philadelphia, 1985), 42–43; Jürgen Eichhoff, "The German Language in America," in *America and the Germans,* ed. Trommler and McVeigh, 1: 231; Fredric Klees, *The Pennsylvania Dutch* (New York, 1961), 3; Yoder, "Pennsylvania Germans," 43–44.

19. Robert C. Williamson, "The Survival of Pennsylvania German: A Survey of Berks and Lehigh Counties," *Pennsylvania Folklife* 32 (Winter 1982–83): 64, 66; Eichoff, "German Language," 230; Don Yoder, "The 'Dutchman' and the 'Deitschlenner': The New World Confronts the Old," *Yearbook of German-American Studies* 23 (1988): 7. Thirty-two German-language newspapers were published in German crescent counties in 1888; their number fell to twenty-one by 1900 and to six by 1917; Homer Tope Rosenberger, *The Pennsylvania Germans, 1891–1965* (Lancaster, Pa., 1966), 70, 71 (table).

20. Yoder, "'Dutchman' and 'Deitschlenner,'" 15, 2, 5–6; Yoder, "Pennsylvania Germans," 53; *The Pennsylvania-German Society: Sketch of Its Origin, with the Proceedings and Addresses at Its Organization* (Lancaster, Pa., 1891; reprint, 1907), 69–71, 85.

21. Mark Allen Hornberger, "The Spatial Distribution of Ethnic Groups in Selected Counties in Pennsylvania 1800–1880: A Geographic Interpretation" (Ph.D. diss., Pennsylvania State University, 1974), 38; U.S. Census Office, *Statistics of the Population of the United States at the Tenth Census (June 1, 1880)* (Washington, D.C., 1883), 525.

22. E. Digby Baltzell, *Philadelphia Gentlemen: The Making of a National Upper Class* (Glencoe, Ill., 1958; reprint, Chicago, 1971), 93, 168–170; Rosenberger, *Pennsylvania Germans,* 73, 503; Samuel Whitaker Pennypacker, *The Autobiography of a Pennsylvanian* (Philadelphia, 1918), 229–230, 31, 55, 112.

23. Conzen, "Germans," 413; Walter Licht, *Getting Work: Philadelphia, 1840–1950* (Cambridge, Mass., 1992), 4–10; Golab, *Destinations,* 31–32.

24. Golab, *Destinations,* 30–32; Philip Scranton, *Figured Tapestry: Production, Markets, and Power in Philadelphia Textiles, 1885–1941* (Cambridge, 1989), 7, 21, 236–237, 196 (table 4.10).

25. Licht, *Getting Work,* 8; Kawaguchi, "Philadelphia's German-America," 124–125; Hershberg et al., "Tale of Three Cities," 471 (table 4). On the German "middle-rung" pattern in the nineteenth century, see Kawaguchi, "Philadelphia's German-America," 154, 157; Bruce Laurie, George Alter, and Theodore Hershberg, "Immigrants and Industry: The Philadelphia Experience, 1850–1880," in *Philadelphia,* ed. Hershberg, 109.

The 1900 figures and the corresponding data in table 1.1 are derived from a systematic random sample of 1 percent of all manuscript census households in Philadelphia, drawn by researchers in association with the Philadelphia Social History Project. I sorted the sample's occupational titles into classes, following the approach taken with the 1900 neighborhood census samples (see the appendix). The 1900 Philadelphia sample can be found at the Demography Library of the Population Studies Center, University of Pennsylvania, Philadelphia, and on the center's website, www.pop.upenn.edu/world/usa/pshp (accessed 29 July 2002). For a fuller description of the sample, see David Hogan, "Working Paper No. 12: Data Base: School and Census Data Sets," in "The Organization of Work, Schooling and Family Life in Philadelphia, 1838–1920: Final Report," principal investigator Michael B. Katz (Graduate School of Education, University of Pennsylvania, 1983). My thanks to Michael Guilfoyle for his help in working with these data.

26. Conzen, "Germans," 413–414.

27. For larger cities in 1900, the Census Bureau published a detailed breakdown of the workforce by occupational title, cross-tabulated by first- and second-generation immigrant background. The analysis below draws on these aggregate data for Philadelphia, from which are derived all figures for 1900 in the remainder of this section. See U.S. Department of Commerce and Labor, Bureau of the Census, *Special Reports: Occupations at the Twelfth Census* (Washington, D.C., 1904), xix, xxii, xxvii, 672–679 (table 43).

28. This definition is that of Suzanne Model, "The Ethnic Niche and the Structure of Opportunity: Immigrants and Minorities in New York City," in *The "Underclass" Debate: Views from History,* ed. Michael B. Katz (Princeton, N.J., 1993), 164, 164n.

29. Laurie et al., "Immigrants and Industry," 109–116, 102–104.

30. Figures for 1880 are taken from ibid., 110–111 (table 13), 108 (table 12). These percentages are only roughly comparable, since the 1880 figures are for males eighteen years of age and older, while those for 1900 are for males age ten and older.

31. Ken Fones-Wolf, *Trade Union Gospel: Christianity and Labor in Industrial Philadelphia, 1865–1915* (Philadelphia, 1989), 108; *Official Labor Directory of Philadelphia and Vicinity: Published under the Auspices of the United German Trades Unions of Philadelphia* (Philadelphia, n.d.), 7–9, 13–15 (in VPL; from internal evidence, this pamphlet appeared no earlier than 1894 and possibly as late

as 1897); *Tageblatt Kalender 1899,* 35; Karl Minster, "Die Arbeiterbewegung in Philadelphia im Jahre 1901," in *Kalender des Philadelphia Tageblatt für das Jahr 1902* (Philadelphia, n.d.), 44–45 (in VPL).

32. Kathleen Neils Conzen, "Immigrants, Immigrant Neighborhoods, and Ethnic Identity: Historical Issues," *Journal of American History* 66 (December 1979): 608–610; Alan Nathan Burstein, "Residential Distribution and Mobility of Irish and German Immigrants in Philadelphia, 1850–1880" (Ph.D. diss., University of Pennsylvania, 1975), 34, 134, 138.

33. Burstein, "Residential Distribution," 132–134, 84, 138; Alan N. Burstein, "Immigrants and Residential Mobility: The Irish and Germans in Philadelphia, 1850–1880," in *Philadelphia,* ed. Hershberg, 182 (map); Kawaguchi, "Philadelphia's German-America," 460–464.

34. Burstein, "Residential Distribution," 149–150, 147 (table IV-2).

35. James M. Bergquist, "German Communities in American Cities: An Interpretation of the Nineteenth-Century Experience," *Journal of American Ethnic History* 4 (Fall 1984): 9; *German Day 1892* (Philadelphia, n.d.), 42–43.

36. All figures cited in this and the following paragraph for 1910 represent my calculations from data provided in U.S. Census Bureau, *Thirteenth Census of the United States, Taken in the Year 1910,* vol. 3, *Population: Reports by States . . . Nebraska-Wyoming* (Washington, D.C., 1913), 605–608.

37. George W. Bromley and Walter S. Bromley, *Atlas of the City of Philadelphia, 22nd Ward* (Philadelphia, 1899), "Outline and Index Map"; *Der Deutsche Lutheraner,* 6 June 1918, p. 273; *Minutes of the 153d Annual Convention of the Evangelical Lutheran Ministerium of Pennsylvania and Adjacent States . . . 1900* (Philadelphia, n.d.), 98; *Philadelphia Morgen-Gazette,* 30 October 1915, p. 6. *Deutscher Lutheraner* holdings and the published Ministerium minutes are in LTSP; *Morgen-Gazette* citations are to holdings in Balch.

38. *Sonntags-Journal,* 7 October 1900, p. 1. The quotations are from a reporter's description of Learned's speech.

39. Conzen, "Patterns," 25–30.

40. *Tageblatt,* 5 October 1901, p. 2; *Sonntags-Journal,* 12 October 1902, p. 5; *German Day 1892,* 39–43.

41. *German Day 1892,* 42; Kawaguchi, "Philadelphia's German-America," 308.

42. Seidensticker, *Deutsche Gesellschaft,* I: 58; Kawaguchi, "Philadelphia's German-America," 262, 257, 271, 298, 320 (table 5.1); *1846–1906: 60. Stiftungsfest des Philadelphia Schützen-Verein, abgehalten in den Tagen vom 19. bis 21. November 1906* (Philadelphia, [1906]), 133 (in GSP).

43. Kawaguchi, "Philadelphia's German-America," 257, 262, 290, 313–314.

44. Karl J. R. Arndt and May E. Olson, *The German Language Press of the Americas,* vol. 1, *History and Bibliography 1732–1968: United States of America,* 3d ed. (Munich, 1976), 575; *Official Labor Directory,* 11–13; *Tageblatt Kalender 1899,* 40–42, 36; *Tageblatt Kalender 1902,* 50; *Tageblatt,* 5 October 1901, p. 2. The *Tageblatt*'s banner identified it as the "official organ" of the UGT; *Tageblatt,* 3 October 1901, p. 1. On nineteenth-century German labor activism, see Ken Fones-Wolf and Elliott Shore, "The German Press and Working-Class Politics in Gilded-Age Philadelphia," in *The German-American Radical Press: The*

Shaping of a Left Political Culture, 1850–1940, ed. Elliott Shore, Ken Fones-Wolf and James P. Danky (Urbana, Ill., 1992).

45. *Tageblatt Kalender 1899,* 35–36; *Tageblatt,* 30 September 1901, p. 2. The Socialist Labor Party, Philadelphia Section, was a UGT member in the 1890s; *Tageblatt Kalender 1899,* 35.

46. *Tageblatt,* 20 April 1899, p. 4.

47. Conzen, "Germans," 416; Richard J. Evans, "Religion and Society in Modern Germany," in *Rethinking German History: Nineteenth-Century Germany and the Origins of the Third Reich* (London, 1987), 131, 147; *German Day 1892,* 34–39.

48. Josef Bernt, "Deutsche Katholiken in Amerika," in *Das Buch der Deutschen in Amerika,* ed. Max Heinrici (Philadelphia, 1909), 250. The membership figure is my calculation drawn from the *Archdiocese of Philadelphia, Annual Report . . . January 1, 1900, to January 1, 1901* (in PAHRC) for each of the eleven parishes, which I identify as: Holy Trinity, St. Peter, Assumption B.V.M. (St. Mary), St. Alphonsus, St. Bonifacius, Our Lady Help of Christians, St. Bonaventura, St. Ludwig, St. Ignatius, St. Aloysius, and St. Vincent. Sources for this list include Joseph L. J. Kirlin, *Catholicity in Philadelphia: From the Earliest Missionaries Down to the Present Time* (Philadelphia, 1909); a list of German parishes in *Nord Amerika,* 15 September 1900, p. 5; and Francis Xavier Roth, O.S.A., *History of St. Vincent's Orphan Asylum of Tacony, Philadelphia: A Memoir of Its Diamond Jubilee, 1855–1933* (Philadelphia, 1934) (in PAHRC).

Two other parishes—All Saints and St. Elizabeth—appear to have been partly German at the turn of the century. A 1907 almanac describes All Saints as "[e]mbracing all Catholics living in Bridesburg, except Polish Catholics; also German Catholics living in Frankford"; *The Catholic Standard and Times Almanac for 1907* (Philadelphia, n.d.), 13. On St. Elizabeth's, see Roth, *St. Vincent's,* 45; *Nord Amerika,* 15 September 1900, p. 5; *St. Elizabeth's Parish: 100th Anniversary, 1872–1972* (Philadelphia, n.d.), 8 (in PAHRC); *Archdiocese of Philadelphia, Annual Report of the Church of St. Elizabeth's, Philadelphia: Religious and Financial Statistics, January 1, 1900, to January 1, 1901.* My thanks to the Archdiocese of Philadelphia for granting me permission to examine its parish annual reports and other parish records. Quotations in this book from the parish annual reports are reproduced courtesy of PAHRC (The Philadelphia Archdiocesan Historical Research Center).

49. Membership calculated from figures provided in *Minutes of the 153d Annual Convention of the Ministerium, 1900,* 84–119.

50. *Public Ledger Almanac, 1901* (Philadelphia, n.d.), 22; *Lutherisches Kirchenblatt,* 14 April 1900, p. 117. The Evangelical Lutheran Synodical Conference of America was the Missouri Synod's parent body, and its communicants in Philadelphia in 1906 numbered only 772; U.S. Department of Commerce and Labor, Bureau of the Census, *Special Reports: Religious Bodies: 1906,* pt. 1, *Summary and General Tables* (Washington, D.C., 1910), 392; E. Clifford Nelson, ed., *The Lutherans in North America* (Philadelphia, 1975), 322, 377. *Kirchenblatt,* 14 April 1900, p. 117, lists two more Lutheran congregations outside the Ministerium in Philadelphia and implies that they are German; one, however, is "Lettish" by name, and judging by their confirmation numbers, both were extremely small.

As the Census Bureau noted in 1906, communicant membership in Protestant churches was "practically adult membership;" the bureau attempted to control for the broader membership definition of the Catholic Church by adjusting its figures downward by 15 percent; U.S. Census Bureau, *Religious Bodies: 1906*, pt. 1: 24. Even by this measure, German Catholics still outnumbered German Lutherans in Philadelphia.

51. *Public Ledger Almanac, 1901,* 33. In 1906, the German Philadelphia classis of the Reformed Church in the United States—the one Reformed polity of four in the country with roots in German immigration—counted 7,494 members. These were, however, divided among twenty congregations, suggesting that the classis took in many congregations beyond the city limits. U.S. Department of Commerce and Labor, Bureau of the Census, *Special Reports: Religious Bodies: 1906,* pt. 2, *Separate Denominations: History, Description, and Statistics* (Washington, D.C., 1910), 579; U.S. Census Bureau, *Religious Bodies: 1906,* pt. 1: 590.

52. Hugh McLeod, "Weibliche Frömmigkeit—männlicher Unglaube? Religion und Kirchen im bürgerlichen 19. Jahrhundert," in *Bürgerinnen und Bürger. Geschlechterverhältnisse im 19. Jahrhundert,* ed. Ute Frevert (Göttingen, 1988), 135–136; *Nord Amerika,* 12 May 1900, p. 5; Harriet R. Spaeth, ed., *Life of Adolph Spaeth, D.D., LL.D: Told in His Own Reminiscences, His Letters and the Recollections of His Family and Friends* (Philadelphia, 1916), 329.

53. Jay P. Dolan, "Philadelphia and the German Catholic Community," in *Immigrants and Religion in Urban America,* ed. Randall M. Miller and Thomas D. Marzik (Philadelphia, 1977), 71; Dennis Clark, "A Pattern of Urban Growth: Residential Development and Church Location in Philadelphia," *Records of the American Catholic Historical Society of Philadelphia* 82 (September 1971): 167–169; Dennis Clark, *The Irish in Philadelphia: Ten Generations of Urban Experience* (Philadelphia, 1973), 143; Connelly, ed., *History of the Archdiocese,* 64, 86, 113, 273.

54. See, e.g., *Catholic Standard and Times,* 30 December 1899, p. 8; and ibid., 13 January 1900, p. 8. The *Standard and Times* is held on microfilm at Ryan Memorial Library, St. Charles Borromeo Seminary, Wynnewood, Pennsylvania.

55. Dolan, "Philadelphia," 74–77.

56. Gail Farr Casterline, "St. Joseph's and St. Mary's: The Origins of Catholic Hospitals in Philadelphia," *Pennsylvania Magazine of History and Biography* 108 (July 1984): 309–314, 289; Dolan, "Philadelphia," 75; Roth, *St. Vincent's,* 30, 46, 53–54, 47–50; Arndt and Olson, *German Language Press,* 566. On the Central-Verein, see Gleason, *Conservative Reformers.*

57. For a few among many examples in 1900 in *Nord Amerika,* see 27 January, p. 4; 10 March, p. 1; 24 March, pp. 1, 4; 21 April, p. 4; 28 April, p. 5; 5 May, p. 6; 26 May, p. 1; 2 June, p. 4; 18 August, p. 8; 8 September, p. 4; 15 September, p. 5; 22 September, p. 4; 29 September, p. 4. All citations below to *Nord Amerika* are likewise for 1900; these issues are in PAHRC.

58. Examples of "German-American Catholic" or "German-American Catholics" can be found in *Nord Amerika,* 24 March, p. 4; 9 June, p. 4; 25 August, p. 3; 6 October, p. 4.

59. For examples, see *Nord Amerika,* 14 July, p. 4; 15 September, p. 6.

60. *Nord Amerika,* 21 July, p. 8; 11 August, p. 1; 6 October, p. 4; 17 February, p. 4.

61. *Nord Amerika,* 3 March, p. 8; 10 March, p. 8; 14 April, p. 8; 28 April, p. 5; 23 June, p. 1. For other invocations of the *Kulturkampf's* memory, see ibid., 14 July, p. 1; 21 July, p. 4; 7 April, p. 1, p. 4.

62. Dolan, "Philadelphia," 77; Joseph J. Casino, "From Sanctuary to Involvement: A History of the Catholic Parish in the Northeast," in *The American Catholic Parish: A History from 1850 to the Present,* ed. Jay P. Dolan, vol. 1, *Northeast, Southeast, South Central* (New York, 1987), 60.

63. Colman J. Barry, O.S.B., *The Catholic Church and German Americans* (Washington, D.C., 1953), 134–136, 313–315; Gleason, *Conservative Reformers,* 29–39; Philip Gleason, "'Americanism' in American Catholic Discourse," in *Speaking of Diversity: Language and Ethnicity in Twentieth-Century America* (Baltimore, 1992), 277–281; Roth, *St. Vincent's,* 51.

64. See, e.g., *Nord Amerika,* 5 May, p. 4; 17 February, p. 4.

65. Ibid., 31 March, p. 4.

66. Ibid. For pejorative uses of "Amerikanismus," see *Nord Amerika,* 17 March, p. 4; 8 September, p. 1.

67. Nelson, ed., *Lutherans in North America,* 49; David A. Gustafson, *Lutherans in Crisis: The Question of Identity in the American Republic* (Minneapolis, 1993), 39; U.S. Census Bureau, *Religious Bodies: 1906,* pt. 1: 392, 395; *Public Ledger Almanac, 1901,* 20–21.

68. *Public Ledger Almanac, 1901,* 20–21, Nelson, ed., *Lutherans in North America,* 234–235, 222–224; Gustafson, *Lutherans in Crisis,* 62, 89, 103, 84.

69. Gustafson, *Lutherans in Crisis,* 56, 104–107, 121, 160, 162–163; Nelson, ed., *Lutherans in North America,* 234–235.

70. Gustafson, *Lutherans in Crisis,* 47, 90–91, 117, 119, 107–109, 163; Nelson, ed., *Lutherans in North America,* 140, 259.

71. *History of the Evangelical Lutheran Synod of East Pennsylvania, with Brief Sketches of Its Congregations* (Philadelphia, [1892]), 8, 15–19, 38 (in LTSP); Nelson, ed., *Lutherans in North America,* 374, 334, 311, 356.

72. *Kirchenblatt,* 13 October, p. 321; 3 February, p. 36; *Der Kirchenbote,* 27 October, p. 3. All citations to *Kirchenblatt* and *Kirchenbote,* here and below, are for 1900; these newspapers are in LTSP. For attacks on Methodists, Baptists, and Christian Science, see *Kirchenblatt,* 24 February, p. 60; 17 March, pp. 84–85; 25 August, p. 268.

73. *Kirchenbote,* 8 December, p. 3; *Kirchenblatt,* 10 February, p. 46. On antiecumenicism, see also *Kirchenblatt,* 3 March, p. 70; 19 May, p. 155. On the Christian Endeavor Society, see Nelson, ed., *Lutherans in North America,* 302.

74. Nelson, ed., *Lutherans in North America,* 205; David L. Scheidt, "The Ministerium of Pennsylvania and Its Linguistic Constituencies, 1865–1916," unpublished paper, cited in ibid., 259. The newspaper ran a six-part series in 1900 dealing with the professors' departure and other conflicts, titled, "Ein Artikel des *Lutheran*"; *Kirchenblatt,* 10 February, p. 46; 17 February, p. 54; 24 February, pp. 61–62; 3 March, p. 70; 10 March, p. 77; 17 March, p. 85.

75. *Kirchenblatt,* 20 October, p. 332.

76. *Kirchenbote,* 13 October, p. 3; *Kirchenblatt,* 10 March, p. 75; 20 October, p. 332.

77. *Kirchenbote,* 31 March, p. 1; *Kirchenblatt,* 27 January, p. 30; 17 November, p. 364; 27 October, p. 341; *Kirchenbote,* 31 March, p. 2.

78. Figures calculated from *Archdiocese of Philadelphia, Annual Report[s]* of parishes for 1900 and *Minutes of the 153d Annual Convention of the Ministerium, 1900,* 84–119.

79. Kawaguchi, "Philadelphia's German-America," 66–70, 23–25, 309–318.

80. Conzen, "Patterns," 27; *Cannstatter Volksfest-Verein, Philadelphia: Geschichte des Vereins von der Gründung in 1873 bis zum Goldenen Jubiläum im September 1923* (Philadelphia, [1923]), 41 (in Balch).

81. Kawaguchi, "Philadelphia's German-America," 401–402; Eugene P. Willging and Herta Hatzfeld, *Catholic Serials of the Nineteenth Century in the United States: A Descriptive Bibliography and Union List,* 2d ser., pt. 5, *Pennsylvania* (Washington, D.C., 1964), 66–69; Arndt and Olson, *German Language Press,* 566. Bernt served as the German Society's agent after 1896; Heinrici, *Deutsche Gesellschaft,* II: 463.

82. *Tageblatt,* 7 October 1901, p. 1.

83. In part, this was because the leading middle-class, secular societies had more of a Protestant orientation than they might wish to admit. A central figure in the growth of the German Hospital, for example, was J. D. Lankenau, a financier and Lutheran layman who worked with the German Conference pastor Adolph Spaeth to bring seven Lutheran deaconesses to the hospital from Germany in the 1880s. By 1900, thirty-five Lutheran deaconesses worked at the institution, and its sixteen-member board of trustees included three Pennsylvania Ministerium pastors. See Nelson, ed. *Lutherans in North America,* 299; *Kirchenblatt,* 24 March, p. 93; 16 June, p. 187; 10 February, p. 43.

CHAPTER TWO
TWO NEIGHBORHOODS

1. Ratio calculated from population figures for Germantown and Wards 16 and 17, together with the Girard Avenue district German-stock proportion in table 2.2. For the population figures, see notes 8 and 38, below.

2. Calculated from data in U.S. Census Bureau, *Thirteenth Census of the United States, Taken in the Year 1910,* vol. 3, *Population: Reports by States . . . Nebraska-Wyoming* (Washington, D.C., 1913), 605–608.

3. Ernest W. Burgess, "The Growth of the City," in *The City,* ed. Robert E. Park, Ernest W. Burgess, and Roderick D. McKenzie (Chicago, 1925), 50–51, 56–58; Paul Frederick Cressey, "Population Succession in Chicago: 1898–1930," *American Journal of Sociology* 44 (July 1938): 61. This discussion draws on Olivier Zunz's account in *The Changing Face of Inequality: Urbanization, Industrial Development, and Immigrants in Detroit, 1880–1920* (Chicago, 1982), 42–45.

4. Kathleen Neils Conzen, "Immigrants, Immigrant Neighborhoods, and Ethnic Identity: Historical Issues," *Journal of American History* 66 (December 1979): 604–606; Theodore Hershberg, Alan N. Burstein, Eugene P. Ericksen, Stephanie W. Greenberg, and William L. Yancey, "A Tale of Three Cities: Blacks, Immigrants, and Opportunity in Philadelphia, 1850–1880, 1930, 1970," in *Philadelphia: Work, Space, Family, and Group Experience in the Nineteenth Century,* ed. Theodore Hershberg (New York, 1981), 474, 467–469.

5. Kenneth A. Scherzer, *The Unbounded Community: Neighborhood Life and*

304 • Notes to Chapter Two

Social Structure in New York City, 1830–1875 (Durham, N.C., 1992), 209, 137–160, 204. For an account of aspatial networks among one immigrant group in Philadelphia, see Robert Zecker, "'All Our Own Kind Here': The Creation of a Slovak-American Community in Philadelphia, 1890–1945" (Ph.D. diss., University of Pennsylvania, 1998).

6. Alexander von Hoffman, *Local Attachments: The Making of an American Urban Neighborhood, 1850 to 1920* (Baltimore, 1994), xxii, xviii, xxiii; Conzen, "Immigrant Neighborhoods," 606; Zunz, *Changing Face of Inequality,* 46–47, 50–57, 139.

7. Von Hoffman, *Local Attachments,* xix; Scherzer, *Unbounded Community,* 11; Caroline Golab, *Immigrant Destinations* (Philadelphia, 1977), 112.

8. The wards together had 33,696 residents in 1900; U.S. Census Office, *Census Reports: Twelfth Census of the United States, Taken in the Year 1900,* vol. 1, *Population* (Washington, D.C., 1901–1902), 345.

9. For depictions of Girard Avenue as the northern border of Northern Liberties, see *Philadelphia Tageblatt,* 21 June 1900, p. 1; and William B. Richter, *North of Society Hill, and Other Stories* (North Quincy, Mass., 1970), 119. For contemporary maps showing structures with the Kensington name south of Girard, see George W. Bromley and Walter S. Bromley, *Atlas of the City of Philadelphia* (Philadelphia, 1895), plate 13; and Ernest Hexamer and Son, *Insurance Maps of the City of Philadelphia* (Philadelphia), vol. 4 (1889, corrected to 1903), vol. 8 (1879, corrected to 1895).

10. Maps generated by the Philadelphia Social History Project (PSHP) show this German cluster in 1880 as centered on the Sixteenth and Seventeenth wards. These "DENPRINT" maps are kept at the PSHP repository, VPL. In 1910, Ward 16 ranked third and Ward 17 fifth among the city's forty-seven wards in terms of proportion of German-stock residents; U.S. Census Bureau, *Thirteenth Census of the United States,* 3: 605–608.

11. *Philadelphia Press,* 17 May 1905, p. 7. *Press* citations are to microfilmed holdings in FLP.

12. *Press,* 29 April 1905, p. 7; Hexamer and Son, *Insurance Maps,* vols. 4, 8; Bromley and Bromley, *Atlas of the City of Philadelphia,* plates 13, 15.

13. Bromley and Bromley, *Atlas of the City of Philadelphia,* plate 13; Walter Licht, "Work: Case Studies of Philadelphia Firms," in "The Organization of Work, Schooling and Family Life in Philadelphia, 1838–1920: Final Report," principal investigator Michael B. Katz (Graduate School of Education, University of Pennsylvania, 1983), 115; Richter, *North of Society Hill,* 21; *Public Ledger Almanac, 1901* (Philadelphia, n.d.), 33.

14. Harry W. Pfund, *A History of the German Society of Pennsylvania* (Philadelphia, 1944), 16; Federal Writers' Project, Works Progress Administration, *WPA Guide to Philadelphia* (reprint, Philadelphia, 1988; originally published as *Philadelphia: A Guide to the Nation's Birthplace* [Philadelphia, 1937]), 102; *Press,* 22 September 1907, p. 7.

15. *1900: Boyd's Co-Partnership and Residence Business Directory of Philadelphia City* (Philadelphia, 1900), 77–79, 85; *Official Labor Directory of Philadelphia and Vicinity: Published under the Auspices of the United German Trades Unions of Philadelphia* (Philadelphia, n.d.), 7; Bromley and Bromley, *Atlas of the*

City of Philadelphia, plate 13. The Mozart Harmonie was a member of the middle-class United Singers of Philadelphia; *Official Souvenir Program, Twenty Third National Sängerfest of the Nord Oestliche Sängerbund of America, Philadelphia, June 29–July 4, 1912* ([Philadelphia], 1912), 101 (in GSP).

16. *Minutes of the 153d Annual Convention of the Evangelical Lutheran Ministerium of Pennsylvania and Adjacent States . . . 1900* (Philadelphia, n.d.), 84–117; *Lutherisches Kirchenblatt,* 14 April 1900, p. 117.

17. Georg von Bosse, *Ein Kampf um Glauben und Volkstum: Das Streben während meines 25jährigen Amtslebens als deutsch-lutherischer Geistlicher in Amerika* (Stuttgart, 1920), 11, 14, 45–46, 157–159.

18. Proportions calculated from the membership list in *Fünfundzwanzig Jahre in der Deutsch-Lutherischen St. Paulus-Gemeinde, St. John und Brown Straße, in Philadelphia* (Philadelphia, 1895), 76–87 (in LTSP).

19. Ibid., 76–87, 32–33, 47–48, 52–53, 33–40.

20. Von Bosse, *Glauben und Volkstum,* 28–29, 159.

21. Oswald Seidensticker and Max Heinrici, *Geschichte der Deutschen Gesellschaft von Pennsylvanien, 1764–1917,* 1. Teil, *Von der Gruendung im Jahre 1764 bis zur Jubelfeier der Republik 1876,* by Oswald Seidensticker; 2. Teil, *Von 1876 bis 1917,* by Max Heinrici (Philadelphia, 1917), 589, 466; von Bosse, *Glauben und Volkstum,* 23, 25, 27.

22. Von Bosse, *Glauben und Volkstum,* 41, 25, 31.

23. Ibid., 32.

24. *Archdiocese of Philadelphia, Annual Report of the Church of St. Peter's, Philadelphia: Religious and Financial Statistics, January 1, 1900, to January 1, 1901,* PAHRC. The parish boundaries are described in *Souvenir of the Re-Opening of St. Peter's Church: 1842–1901* (Philadelphia, 1901), 115 (in PAHRC).

25. *Souvenir of St. Peter's,* 118, 61, 75, 84.

26. *Nord Amerika,* 12 May 1900, p. 5. St. Peter's one clearly female-oriented beneficial society, St. Ann's Beneficial Society for Women, counted 180 members in 1900, while the St. Peter's Young Men's Society alone claimed 275; *Souvenir of St. Peter's,* 118; *Annual Report of the Church of St. Peter's [1900].*

27. Baptismal Register [1900], vol. 7 (1897–1909), St. Peter the Apostle Roman Catholic Church, Philadelphia; the register is among the PAHRC's microfilmed parish records.

The book's surname analyses are based on the author's judgment of a given surname's derivation. Surname analysis is not an exact science. Names may be of unclear ethnic origin, have more than one possible ethnic derivation, or have been assimilated from another cultural area or language. Given such difficulties, I have throughout used consciously conservative standards. Surnames are classified as clearly of a certain derivation, possibly of that derivation, or, conversely, as clearly *not* of another derivation. The aim was to produce conservative estimates of surname origin, which these standards appear to do. For example, my initial analysis of the 1900 membership roll of the Germania Turn Verein, based on my own judgment of surname origin, produced a tally of twenty-nine members with clearly non-German surnames. When I analyzed the roll again, this time checking every name in each of six surname dictionaries, I determined that forty-one members had non-German surnames (see chap. 9). The dictionaries are: Elsdon C. Smith,

Dictionary of American Family Names (New York, 1956); George F. Jones, *German-American Names* (Baltimore, 1990); Horst Naumann, ed., *Das große Buch der Familien Namen. Alter-Herkunft-Bedeutung* (Niedernhausen, Ts., 1994); Hans Bahlow, *Deutsches Namenlexikon* (Munich, 1967); Edward MacLysaght, *The Surnames of Ireland,* 3d ed. (Dublin, 1978); P. H. Reaney and R. M. Wilson, *A Dictionary of English Surnames,* 3d ed. (London, 1991).

In addition to employing my own judgment, I carried out some surname analyses with these reference works as an aid, checking some or all names on certain lists against one or more of the dictionaries. These analyses are so denoted in the notes.

In analyzing St. Peter's baptismal register, I checked the surname of every Hungarian-born father and of every father born in Austria or Austria-Hungary in Smith, *American Family Names;* Jones, *German-American Names;* Bahlow, *Deutsches Namenlexikon;* and Naumann, ed., *Buch der Familien Namen.*

28. Baptismal Register [1900]. The surname of every American-born father was checked in two or more of the following: Smith, *American Family Names;* Jones, *German-American Names;* Bahlow, *Deutsches Namenlexikon;* Naumann, ed., *Buch der Familien Namen;* MacLysaght, *Surnames of Ireland;* Reaney and Wilson, *English Surnames.* I checked the surname of each mother paired with an American-born father of clearly or possibly Irish background in all six of these surname dictionaries.

29. Marriage Register (1898–1908), St. Peter the Apostle Roman Catholic Church, Philadelphia, pp. 6–9.

30. *Souvenir of St. Peter's,* 15, 103, passim; *St. Paulus-Gemeinde,* passim.

31. St. Michael's had a Catholic population of about 6,000 in 1900; the corresponding figure for Immaculate Conception was 4,500; see, for each parish, *Archdiocese of Philadelphia, Annual Report . . . January 1, 1900, to January 1, 1901.*

32. *St. Michael's Kalendar* 3 (November 1900): 5. This and the other Catholic parish bulletins cited in the book are held in the Parish Calendars Collection, PAHRC.

33. *St. Michael's Kalendar* 4 (December 1901): 25–38, 15, 17. Of the 178 individuals on the list with clearly non-Irish surnames, sixty-nine had clearly German surnames, fifty-six had surnames clearly of British (English, Welsh, or Scottish) derivation, and twenty had last names that were clearly either British or German. Twenty-five individuals had surnames that were clearly non-Irish but could not otherwise be classified. In analyzing the list, I checked each name that appeared either questionably Irish or non-Irish in at least one of the six surname dictionaries cited in note 28. Surnames denoted as clearly or possibly Irish include some names of English derivation that came into common use in Ireland over time; see MacLysaght, *Surnames of Ireland.*

34. *St. Michael's Kalendar* 2 (November 1899): 6.

35. Marriage Register [1900], vol. 3 (1897–1908), St. Michael's Roman Catholic Church, pp. 20–28, PAHRC.

36. *Press,* 14 November 1905, p. 7.

37. *Press,* 11 May 1905, p. 7.

38. Germantown's population in 1900 was 37,766, a figure I calculated by to-

taling the populations of the enumeration districts covering the neighborhood in the federal manuscript census; U.S. Census Office, *Twelfth Census of the United States* (1900), Population Schedules for Philadelphia County, Microfilm, NAP (hereafter Philadelphia Census Schedules [1900]). I counted 2,802 German-stock residents in the same enumeration district returns, with "German-stock" defined in the most inclusive sense, as meaning any resident either born in Germany or with at least one parent born in Germany. Hence, 7.4 percent of Germantown's actual population was German-stock, under the broadest definition. The sample proportion of 8.2 percent in table 2.2 is based on a slightly more restrictive definition of "stock."

39. Aaron Spencer Fogleman, *Hopeful Journeys: German Immigration, Settlement, and Political Culture in Colonial America, 1717–1775* (Philadelphia, 1996), 103; Harry M. Tinkcom, Margaret B. Tinkcom, and Grant Miles Simon, *Historic Germantown: From the Founding to the Early Part of the Nineteenth Century; A Survey of the German Township* (Philadelphia, 1955), 3–6; Stephanie Grauman Wolf, *Urban Village: Population, Community, and Family Structure in Germantown, Pennsylvania, 1683–1800* (Princeton, N.J., 1976), 128.

40. Wolf, *Urban Village,* 153, 206–216, 131–132, 140–142, 103, 51–52.

41. Philip Scranton, *Figured Tapestry: Production, Markets, and Power in Philadelphia Textiles, 1885–1941* (Cambridge, 1989), 187 (table 4.6), 189 (table 4.7). In the mid-nineteenth century, workers and manufacturers in Germantown textiles were overwhelmingly English-born; Philip Scranton, *Proprietary Capitalism: The Textile Manufacture at Philadelphia, 1800–1885* (Cambridge, 1983), 227, 236, 237 (table 7.2).

42. Edward W. Hocker, *Germantown, 1683–1933: The Record That a Pennsylvania Community Has Achieved in the Course of 250 Years; Being a History of the People of Germantown, Mount Airy, and Chestnut Hill* (Philadelphia, 1933), 168–170, 271; E. Digby Baltzell, *Philadelphia Gentlemen: The Making of a National Upper Class* (Glencoe, Ill., 1958; reprint, Chicago, 1971), 197–201, 122.

43. I use "mainstream" here in a sense similar to that proposed by Kathleen Neils Conzen, who has described particular communities where the descendants of non-Anglo settlers became the mainstream *locally;* Conzen, "Mainstreams and Side Channels: The Localization of Immigrant Cultures," *Journal of American Ethnic History* 11 (Fall 1991): 5–20.

44. Wolf, *Urban Village,* 210; S. A. Ziegenfuss, *A Brief and Succinct History of Saint Michael's Evangelical Lutheran Church of Germantown, Pennsylvania, 1730–1905* (Philadelphia, 1905), 10–11, 31–34 (in LTSP); Hocker, *Germantown,* 66–67; *History of the Evangelical Lutheran Synod of East Pennsylvania, with Brief Sketches of Its Congregations* (Philadelphia, [1892]), 156; *1855–1930: St. Thomas-Bote: Fest-Ausgabe anlässlich der Feier des Fünfundsiebzigjährigen Jubiläums der Ev.-Luth. St. Thomas-Gemeinde* (Philadelphia, 1930), 3–4 (in LACP).

45. *Germantown Independent-Gazette,* 17 November 1905, p. 1; Wolf, *Urban Village,* 215; Hocker, *Germantown,* 134, 142–146, 188–189; *Germantown Telegraph,* 9 May 1902, p. 1; Guy S. Klett, "Some Phases of Presbyterian Beginnings

in Germantown," *Germantowne Crier* 3 (December 1951): 21. Unless otherwise noted, *Independent-Gazette* citations are to holdings at GHS or microfilmed holdings at FLP. *Telegraph* citations are to GHS holdings.

46. Wolf, *Urban Village,* 128. The Bringhursts were of "old Philadelphia," according to the *Independent-Gazette,* 12 January 1900, p. 8.

47. See, e.g., the *Telegraph*'s description of the Shoemakers' venerable "American ancestry," and the *Independent-Gazette*'s classing of the Rittenhouses, Keysers, and Kulps under the heading, "Some Old Mennonite Families"; *Telegraph,* 21 March 1902, p. 1; *Independent-Gazette,* 19 January 1900, p. 5. On these families' colonial German ancestry, see also *Dirck Keyser Newsletter* 1 (September 1988): 2; and news clipping dated 1914, both in Keyser Family File, Biographical Files, GHS; *Telegraph,* 13 June 1902, p. 1 (Wistar); Charles F. Jenkins, *The Guide Book to Historic Germantown,* 3d ed. (Germantown, Pa., 1915), 20 (Keyser, Rittenhouse, Saur).

48. Wolf, *Urban Village,* 110, 149–150.

49. Germantown Borough was the southern third of the colonial-era German Township. The borough's, and thus the sample area's, boundaries ran roughly from Stenton Avenue on the east, to Wister Street on the southeast, to Roberts Avenue on the south, to Wissahickon Avenue on the west, to Washington Lane on the north; John Daly and Allen Weinberg, *Genealogy of Philadelphia County Subdivisions,* 2d ed. (Philadelphia, 1966), 51.

50. George W. Bromley and Walter S. Bromley, *Atlas of the City of Philadelphia, 22nd Ward* (Philadelphia, 1899), plates 6, 1.

51. *Germantowne Crier* 3 (September 1951): 26; Earle W. Huckel, "Germantown at the Beginning of the Century," in ibid., 11.

52. *Verhandlungen der Ver. Staaten Gross-Loge D.O.H. In General-Sitzung versammelt am 5., 6., und 7. September 1900, zu Chicago, Ill.* (Reading, Pa., 1900), 52; *Verhandlungen der Ver. Staaten Gross-Loge des Deutschen Ordens der Harugari. In General-Sitzung versammelt am 2. und 3. September 1908, zu Davenport, Iowa.* (Reading, Pa., 1908), 78–79; *Press,* 5 December 1905, p. 7; *Independent-Gazette,* 1 December 1905, p. 1. The Harugari *Verhandlungen* are available on microfilm at the New York Public Library, New York.

53. News clippings dated 1912 and 1916, "Beneficial Societies," Subject Files, GHS; news clipping dated 1915, "Germans and German-Americans," Subject Files, GHS; *Deutsch-Amerikanisches Vereins-Adressbuch für das Jahr 1911. German-American Directory 1911* (Milwaukee, Wis., 1911), 60 (in GSP).

54. *Minutes of the 153d Annual Convention of the Ministerium, 1900,* 90; *Independent-Gazette,* 9 March 1900, p. 5; Parish Register, p. 61, St. Thomas' Evangelical Lutheran Church, LACP; 6 March 1900, Church Council Minutes, St. Thomas' Evangelical Lutheran Church, LACP; "Communicanten am heil. Osterfest 1901," Verzeichnis über die Gemeinde Glieder der Deutschen evangelisch lutherischen St. Thomas-Kirche zu Germantown, Pa., LACP.

55. St. Thomas' Parish Register, pp. 10–11.

56. Ibid. The American-born grooms' surnames were checked in MacLysaght, *Surnames of Ireland,* and Reaney and Wilson, *English Surnames.*

57. *Constitution and By-Laws of the Germantown Business Men's Association*

(Germantown, Philadelphia, 1897), 2, in "Germantown Businessmen's Association," Business Box 1, PBC; *Telegraph,* 10 January 1902, p. 1.

58. Undated news clipping in 3 December 1906 and 9 September 1907, "Meeting Minute book, 1906–1913," folder 103, box 8, URB47, BMAG-UA.

59. The following analysis was conducted by linking the names of signers of the Association's 1898 charter to the 1900 federal manuscript census for Germantown and to obituaries in the GHS Obituary Files and Bulletin Collection. This linkage was accomplished with the aid of the 1900 *Boyd's* city directory. Some names were also linked to the 1900 membership roll of the Germantown YMCA (see below). The charter is found in folder 1, box 1, URB47, BMAG-UA.

60. On the candy "manufacturer" and retailer Robert H. Hurst, see *Souvenir of the Germantown Business Men's Parade and Demonstration, October 1896* (Germantown, Philadelphia, 1896), unpaginated [33], "Germantown Business Men's Association," Business Box 1, PBC.

61. "C. J. Wister Dies at Chestnut Hill," *Philadelphia Inquirer,* 4 July 1954, and "Men and Things," *Evening Bulletin,* 29 August 1928, "Wister, Charles J.– & Mrs. (Elizabeth)–Dead," Bulletin Collection; "Lewis Wynne Wister," news clipping dated 11 June 1919, "Wister, Lewis Wynne–Dead, & Mrs. (Elizabeth W.)–Dead," Bulletin Collection; Baltzell, *Philadelphia Gentlemen,* 76; *Boyd's [1900],* 770; Philadelphia Census Schedules (1900), Enumeration District 482, p. 11b. Woods' factory is depicted in Bromley and Bromley, *Atlas of the City of Philadelphia, 22nd Ward,* plate 6.

62. Two of the seven had American-born mothers and foreign-born (in these cases, English-born) fathers.

63. Wolf, *Urban Village,* 228 (Bockius); *Independent-Gazette,* 16 October 1908, p. 8 (Tull).

64. Philadelphia Census Schedules (1900), E.D. 491, p. 6b (Schaefer); E.D. 493, p. 16a (Kaplan); E.D. 494, p. 4b (Pletcher).

65. *Telegraph,* 10 January 1902, p. 1. On Kyle, see Philadelphia Census Schedules (1900), E.D. 493, p. 10a; "Kyle, John, 1842–1914," Obituary Files, GHS. On Hoffman, see *Souvenir of the Germantown Business Men's Parade,* unpaginated [28]; *Germantown Guide,* 30 December 1899, p. 2.

66. 4 January 1901, "Board of Directors Minutes, 1897–1900," folder 6, box 1, URB47, BMAG-UA; "A Cemetery Needed," *Germantown Guide,* 3 February 1906, in 5 February 1906, "Meeting Minute book, 1906–1913," and minutes of this meeting.

67. "Past presidents of the BMA of Gtn.," folder 3, box 1, URB47, BMAG-UA; "Monthly Meeting and St. Patrick's Day Smoker," 8 March 1910, folder 19, box 21, URB47, BMAG-UA; "Business Men Have Jolly Evening Out," *Independent-Gazette,* 24 January 1908, in 4 February 1908, "Meeting Minute book, 1906–1913." One indication, aside from newspaper coverage of banquets, that most association social affairs were all male is a program for an association-sponsored function in May 1907, titled "Our Ladies' Night," "Germantown Businessmen's Association," Business Box 1, PBC.

68. *Independent-Gazette,* 12 January 1900, p. 4; "German Society Is 30 Years Old," newspaper clipping dated 1912, "Beneficial Societies," Subject Files, GHS;

Independent-Gazette, 1 December 1905, p. 1; *Beehive* 20 (January 1932): 9; *Germanopolis: 225th Anniversary of the Settlement of Germantown by Francis Daniel Pastorius: The First Permanent German Settlement in America; Official Historical Souvenir Book of Germantown* (Philadelphia, 1908), unpaginated [45, 49] (in Library, GHS). *Beehive* holdings are at GHS.

69. Hocker, *Germantown,* 245; *23rd Annual Report of the Young Men's Christian Association of Germantown, Philadelphia, Pa.* (Philadelphia, 1894), 8, in box 1, acc. 260, YMCA; *Record,* January 1900, 2; April 1900, 6; September 1900, 1; February 1900, 1; and June 1900, 1 (all in box 5, acc. 260, YMCA).

70. *25th Annual Report of the Young Men's Christian Association of Germantown, Philadelphia, Pa.* (Philadelphia, 1896), 10, in box 1, acc. 260, YMCA; *23rd Annual Report,* 37. Proportions calculated from the YMCA's 1900 membership roll; "Y.M.C.A. of Germantown Membership Record, 1894–1903," 133–155, in box 7, acc. 260, YMCA.

71. These figures represent my analysis. I checked every potentially German surname on the membership list in Jones, *German-American Names,* and some further in Bahlow, *Deutsches Namenlexikon,* and Naumann, ed., *Buch der Familien Namen.* A number of surnames were checked in Smith, *American Family Names,* MacLysaght, *Surnames of Ireland,* and Reaney and Wilson, *English Surnames.* The possibly southeastern European surnames on the list were Cohn (two members), Kissileff and Lewisson (both identified on the roll as Jewish), Petri, Seka, Stankowitch, and Vila; "Y.M.C.A. of Germantown Membership Record [1900]," 147, 154, 153, 146, 150, 133, 151. The British-or-German designation applies to surnames that clearly belonged to one or the other category, such as Miller or Brown.

72. "Y.M.C.A. of Germantown Membership Record [1900]," 142, 143. Men of colonial descent among the 132 members with German surnames included Lewis W. Wister and E. M. Wistar; ibid., 155, 146.

73. The 1900 roll listed eighty-nine members with occupational titles classifiable as blue-collar skilled. Of these members, fifty-two (58 percent) worked as machinists, in textiles, or in the building trades. Of the twenty skilled workers with clearly German surnames, eleven (55 percent) worked in metals, textiles, the building trades, or printing. I was able to trace eight of these twenty in the 1900 federal manuscript census; three were native whites of native parentage, one was a native white with an American-born mother and a father with birthplace unknown, one was German-born, and three were second-generation German immigrants on one or both sides.

74. "Y.M.C.A. of Germantown Membership Record [1900]," 142, 143; Philadelphia Census Schedules (1900), E.D. 496, p. 11b (Gonaver and Gruhler). The membership roll identifies Gonaver as a Catholic, age sixteen; the manuscript census puts his age at eighteen.

75. Philadelphia Census Schedules (1900), E.D. 489, p. 21a; "Y.M.C.A. of Germantown Membership Record [1900]," 150; *Record,* August 1900, 6; and June 1900, 9, in box 5, acc. 260, YMCA; *Independent-Gazette,* 13 April 1900, p. 1. On the Turnerbund, see Henry Metzner, *History of the American Turners,* 3d rev. ed. (Rochester, N.Y., 1974). On organized sports, see John Higham, "The Reori-

entation of American Culture in the 1890's," in *The Origins of Modern Consciousness,* ed. John Weiss (Detroit, 1965).

76. *Telegraph,* 11 April 1902, p. 1; Lloyd M. Abernethy, "Progressivism, 1905–1919," in *Philadelphia: A 300-Year History,* ed. Russell F. Weigley (New York, 1982), 532.

77. Joseph L. J. Kirlin, *Catholicity in Philadelphia* (Philadelphia, 1909), 501, 458; *Archdiocese of Philadelphia, Annual Report of the Church of St. Vincents [sic] de Paul's . . . January 1, 1900, to January 1, 1901; Monthly Magazine, Parish of St. Vincent de Paul, Germantown, Phila.* 4 (September 1900): 4–6.

78. Marriage Register [1900], vol. 2 (1898–1923), Church of St. Vincent de Paul, Germantown, Philadelphia, pp. 50–55, PAHRC. The remaining two German matches paired a German groom with a possibly English bride and a German bride with a groom who was Irish or English by surname. One groom of eastern European background took an Irish bride, as did one groom of Italian background. German surnames in the register were checked in Jones, *German-American Names;* Bahlow, *Deutsches Namenlexikon;* Naumann, ed., *Buch der Familien Namen.*

79. *Monthly Magazine* 4 (July 1900): 26–29; *Monthly Magazine* 4 (August 1900): 7. German surnames on the contributors' list were checked in Jones, *German-American Names;* Bahlow, *Deutsches Namenlexikon;* Naumann, ed., *Buch der Familien Namen.*

80. *Archdiocese of Philadelphia, Annual Report of the Church of St. Ignatius, Philadelphia, Religious and Financial Statistics, January 1, 1906, to January 1, 1907.*

81. *Beehive* 20 (October 1931): 15; "Henry W. Pletcher Dies Suddenly," undated news clipping, and "Henry W. Pletcher As I Knew Him," news clipping dated 18 September 1931, both in Pletcher Family File, Biographical Files, GHS.

82. *Independent-Gazette,* 6 October 1905, p. 1; "Pletcher," undated death notice, Pletcher Family File, Biographical Files, GHS; Philadelphia Census Schedules (1900), E.D. 494, p. 4b.

83. "Henry W. Pletcher Dies Suddenly"; *The Parish of St. Vincent de Paul, 1851–1951: The Mother Parish of Germantown* (Philadelphia, [1951]), 33 (in PAHRC); *Beehive* 20 (October 1931): 15–16; *Independent-Gazette,* 6 October 1905, p. 1.

84. See, for example, John Bodnar's critical description of such views in Bodnar, *The Transplanted: A History of Immigrants in Urban America* (Bloomington, Ind., 1985), 118.

85. The Germantown YMCA did have fourteen female members on its 1900 membership roll, denoted "Miss" or "Mrs."

86. Hocker, *Germantown,* 304, 245, 247. Hugh McLeod notes that in the nineteenth century, churches counted among the few public arenas open to large-scale, female participation; McLeod, "Weibliche Frömmigkeit—männlicher Unglaube? Religion und Kirchen im bürgerlichen 19. Jahrhundert," in *Bürgerinnen und Bürger. Geschlechterverhältnisse im 19. Jahrhundert,* ed. Ute Frevert (Göttingen, 1988), 145.

87. Conzen, "Immigrant Neighborhoods," 614; Kathleen Neils Conzen, "Pat-

terns of German-American History," in *Germans in America: Retrospect and Prospect; Tricentennial Lectures Delivered at the German Society of Pennsylvania in 1983*, ed. Randall M. Miller (Philadelphia, 1984), 34.

88. "Henry W. Pletcher As I Knew Him."

CHAPTER THREE
THE GENDERED CRISIS OF THE *VEREINSWESEN*

1. Georg von Bosse, *Ein Kampf um Glauben und Volkstum. Das Streben während meines 25jährigen Amtslebens als deutsch-lutherischer Geistlicher in Amerika* (Stuttgart, 1920), 226. Internal evidence suggests von Bosse delivered this speech in the early 1910s, before the summer of 1914.

2. *Philadelphia Tageblatt*, 14 June 1914, p. 25 (quotation); 9 July 1914, p. 3; 26 July 1914, p. 25; 28 July 1914, p. 3 (quotation). The final quotation appears to be a reporter's paraphrase of the speaker's words.

3. James M. Bergquist, "German Communities in American Cities: An Interpretation of the Nineteenth-Century Experience," *Journal of American Ethnic History* 4 (Fall 1984): 17; Kathleen Neils Conzen, "Germans," in *Harvard Encyclopedia of American Ethnic Groups*, ed. Stephan Thernstrom (Cambridge, Mass., 1980), 410 (table 2), 413 (table 4), 406 (table 1).

4. Philip Gleason, *The Conservative Reformers: German-American Catholics and the Social Order* (Notre Dame, Ind., 1968), 46–47.

5. Karl J. R. Arndt and May E. Olson, *The German Language Press of the Americas*, vol. 1, *History and Bibliography 1732–1968: United States of America*, 3d ed. (Munich, 1976), 558, 576, 553, 558. The other three surviving newspapers were the *Morgen-Gazette*, the *Philadelphia Tageblatt*, and the *Philadelphia Abend-Post*; their circulation figures are given in ibid., 558, 575, 548.

6. Bergquist, "German Communities in American Cities," 17.

7. *Deutsch-Amerikanisches Vereins-Adressbuch für das Jahr 1911. German-American Directory 1911* (Milwaukee, Wis., 1911), passim.

8. "Deutsche Institute in Philadelphia," in *German Day 1892* (Philadelphia, n.d.), 42–43; *Vereins-Adressbuch 1911*, 59, 165–167, 176–178; *Official Souvenir Program, Twenty Third National Sängerfest of the Nord Oestliche Sängerbund of America, Philadelphia, June 29–July 4, 1912* ([Philadelphia], 1912), 101. One of the forty-one choirs listed in the Sängerfest program was located outside of Philadelphia. The United Singers' growth, of course, may have signified merely that the federation had incorporated a greater number of previously existing singing societies.

9. See chapter 2.

10. Christian Lang, "Der Sängerbund," *Mitteilungen des Deutschen Pionier-Vereins von Philadelphia* 17 (1910): 11–12, cited in Bergquist, "German Communities in American Cities," 20, 20n. The translation is Bergquist's.

11. "Dues, income & expenses (oversize), 1873–88," unpaginated, vol. 4, box 11, RTC; "Dues, 1898–1905," unpaginated, box 8, RTC; "Dues, 1906–1920," box 8, RTC. These membership figures represent adult male members in good standing as of January of each year.

12. These figures represent my calculations from "Ladies' Auxiliary: Dues & Membership Data, 1887–1917," unpaginated, vol. 1, box 11, RTC (the frontispiece of this volume reads: "Damen-Section des Germania Turnverein's v. Roxborough & Manayunk"). Annual figures cited are for the entire given year.

13. "Harugari," in Alexander J. Schem, *Deutsch-amerikanisches Conversations-Lexicon*, vol. 5 (New York, 1871), 191; *Verhandlungen der Ver. Staaten Groß-Loge des Deutschen Ordens der Harugari. In General Sitzung versammelt Am 7., 8. und 9. Sept. 1870, zu Reading, Penn'a* (Reading, Pa., 1870), 6–7; "Uebersicht des Standes und der Arbeiten des D.O.H. in den Vereinigten Staaten," in ibid., [unpaginated]; *Verhandlungen der Ver. Staaten Groß-Loge des Deutschen Ordens der Harugari. In General-Sitzung versammelt vom 3ten bis 5ten September 1890, zu St. Louis, Mo.* (St. Louis, n.d.), 50, 13, 4.

14. Philadelphia totals are my calculations, from *Verhandlungen der Ver. Staaten Groß Loge des Deutschen Ordens der Harugari. In General-Sitzung versammelt Am 6., 7., und 8. September, 1876, zu St. Louis, Mo.* (Reading, Pa., n.d.), 83–84; *Verhandlungen der V.S. Groß-Loge 1890*, 54–55; *Verhandlungen der Ver. Staaten Gross-Loge des Deutschen Ordens der Harugari. In General-Sitzung versammelt am 2. und 3. September 1908, zu Davenport, Iowa.* (Reading, Pa., 1908), 78–79.

15. Harry W. Pfund, *A History of the German Society of Pennsylvania* (Philadelphia, 1944), 15, 17–18, 23–26; Oswald Seidensticker and Max Heinrici, *Geschichte der Deutschen Gesellschaft von Pennsylvanien. 1764–1917*, 1. Teil, *Von der Gruendung im Jahre 1764 bis zur Jubelfeier der Republik 1876*, by Oswald Seidensticker; 2. Teil, *Von 1876 bis 1917*, by Max Heinrici (Philadelphia, 1917), 196–197 (hereafter Seidensticker, *Deutsche Gesellschaft*, I; Heinrici, *Deutsche Gesellschaft*, II); Lesley Ann Kawaguchi, "The Making of Philadelphia's German-America: Ethnic Group and Community Development, 1830–1883" (Ph.D. diss., University of California, Los Angeles, 1983), 313–314, 401.

16. Seidensticker, *Deutsche Gesellschaft*, I: 59, 62; Heinrici, *Deutsche Gesellschaft*, II: 255.

17. Heinrici, *Deutsche Gesellschaft*, II: 256; Harjes cited in ibid., 259.

18. Joseph L. J. Kirlin, *Catholicity in Philadelphia: From the Earliest Missionaries Down to the Present Time* (Philadelphia, 1909), 490–492, 494; Francis Xavier Roth, O.S.A., *History of St. Vincent's Orphan Asylum of Tacony, Philadelphia: A Memoir of Its Diamond Jubilee, 1855–1933.* (Philadelphia, 1934), 45. My counts of German parishes founded draw on a number of sources, including Kirlin, *Catholicity*; Roth, *History of St. Vincent's;* "Deutsche Institute," 38; and a list of German parishes printed in *Nord Amerika*, 15 September 1900, p. 5.

19. Roth, *History of St. Vincent's*, 77. Roth states here that St. Henry's was founded in 1915, but other sources give a date of 1916; see James F. Connelly, ed., *The History of the Archdiocese of Philadelphia* (Philadelphia, 1976), 324; *1916–1966: Golden Jubilee, St. Henry's Parish; Solemn Mass of Thanksgiving, Sunday, September 18, 1966* ([Philadelphia], [1966]), 11 (in Balch).

20. In 1900, the city's eleven German national parishes held a total of 23,395 men, women, and children; the corresponding figure for 1921, including the parishioners of St. Henry's, was 21,221. These figures are drawn from the *Archdiocese of Philadelphia, Annual Report* for each German national parish for 1900

and 1921. German parishes were identified in part through an undated list of "Foreign Churches," item 81.330, folder 81.330, Manuscript Collection 80, Dougherty Papers. Internal evidence suggests that this list was compiled between 1920 and 1928; the membership it provides for each German parish corresponds exactly to that given in the 1921 annual reports, with the exception of St. Henry's, whose annual report counts 100 more members. My thanks to the Archdiocese of Philadelphia for granting me permission to examine the Dougherty Papers.

An example of a post–Civil War German national parish that had become mixed by the early twentieth century, with a large Irish contingent, is St. Elizabeth's; see chap. 1, note 48.

21. The total 1920 communing membership was calculated from figures provided in "Philadelphia German Conference—Statistics for the Year Ending May 1, 1920," *Minutes of the Proceedings of the 173rd Annual Convention of the Evangelical Lutheran Ministerium of Pennsylvania and the Adjacent States . . . June 1 to 4, 1920* (Philadelphia, [1920]), 198–200. The Pennsylvania Ministerium counted nineteen German congregations in Philadelphia in 1900, with a total of 6,429 communing members. By 1920, the Ministerium's German Conference had lost one congregation—the Lutheran Orphans Home—but added two new, if small, congregations, Erloeser (Redeemer) and Martin Luther, in the city. In addition, St. Paul's Independent Evangelical Lutheran Church, which had existed since 1870, was listed on the conference's roll by 1920. Given the prior existence of St. Paul's Independent, the most accurate comparison of total conference communing membership would factor out that church's 400 members in 1920. The resulting figure of 6,645 for the German Conference's Philadelphia congregations in 1920 represents an increase of 216 (3 percent) in the Conference's communing city membership, compared to 1900. "Philadelphia German Conference—Statistics," *Proceedings of the Ministerium, 1920,* 198–200; "Parochial Statistics for the Year Ending Whit-Sunday, 1900," *Minutes of the 153d Annual Convention of the Evangelical Lutheran Ministerium of Pennsylvania and Adjacent States . . . 1900* (Philadelphia, n.d.), 84–119.

22. "Parochial Statistics"; "Philadelphia German Conference—Statistics," *Proceedings of the Ministerium, 1920,* 198–201; von Bosse, *Glauben und Volkstum,* 27.

23. Elsie Lillian Spalde Moore, "These Things I Remember," 1983, TMs [photocopy], Library, Balch, 1, 5, 8b; *The Bulletin Year Book and Citizens' Manual, 1925* (Philadelphia, 1925), 272. Quotations from "These Things I Remember," an unpublished memoir that Moore wrote for her family, are reproduced courtesy of Moore's daughter, Jean M. Husher.

24. Von Bosse, *Glauben und Volkstum,* 80.

25. Ibid., 201; Gleason, *Conservative Reformers,* 31.

26. See, e.g., von Bosse, *Glauben und Volkstum,* 19; *Lutherisches Kirchenblatt,* 17 March 1900, p. 85; 9 June 1900, p. 180; 20 October 1900, p. 332.

27. For uses of this term, see von Bosse, *Glauben und Volkstum,* 44, 133, 134, 141; and Harriet R. Spaeth, ed., *Life of Adolph Spaeth, D.D., LL.D: Told in his Own Reminiscences, His Letters and the Recollections of His Family and Friends* (Philadelphia, 1916), 277.

28. Von Bosse, *Glauben und Volkstum,* 41, 25, 28–29, 31–32; Heinrici,

Deutsche Gesellschaft, II: 265; *Souvenir of the Re-Opening of St. Peter's Church: 1842–1901* (Philadelphia, 1901); *Kalender, Philadelphia Tageblatt, 1899* (Philadelphia, n.d.), unpaginated [inside back cover]; *Kalender des Philadelphia Tageblatt für das Jahr 1902* (Philadelphia, n.d.), 78.

29. *Nord Amerika,* 8 September 1900, p. 4; *Philadelphia Sonntags-Journal,* 6 October 1901, p. 1.

30. On nineteenth-century female associations, see chapter 1.

31. This description draws primarily on the synthesis offered in Steven Mintz and Susan Kellogg, *Domestic Revolutions: A Social History of American Family Life* (New York, 1988), 43–65. The literature describing these changes is vast; among the more important works are Barbara Welter, "The Cult of True Womanhood, 1820–1860," *American Quarterly* 18 (1966): 131–175; Nancy F. Cott, *The Bonds of Womanhood: "Woman's Sphere" in New England, 1780–1835* (New Haven, Conn., 1977); Linda K. Kerber, *Women of the Republic: Intellect and Ideology in Revolutionary America* (Chapel Hill, N.C., 1980); and Mary P. Ryan, *Cradle of the Middle Class: The Family in Oneida County, New York, 1790–1865* (Cambridge, 1981). More recently, historians have questioned the extent to which the notion of nineteenth-century separate spheres either accorded with reality or was all that new; for important reconsiderations, see Nancy A. Hewitt, "Beyond the Search for Sisterhood: American Women's History in the 1980s," *Social History* 10 (October 1985): 299–321; and Linda K. Kerber, "Separate Spheres, Female Worlds, Woman's Place: The Rhetoric of Women's History," *Journal of American History* 75 (June 1988): 9–39. Kerber interprets the developments of the late eighteenth and early nineteenth centuries as undermining an older "variant of the separation of spheres." Ibid., 18–20, 21.

32. For an early reassessment of separate spheres as an ideology with a limited reach in class, racial, and immigrant ethnic terms, see Hewitt, "Beyond the Search for Sisterhood."

33. On "Yankees" as an ethnic group, see Oscar Handlin, "Yankees," in *Harvard Encyclopedia of American Ethnic Groups,* ed. Thernstrom, 1028–1030.

34. James J. Sheehan, *German History, 1770–1866* (Oxford, 1989), 25–26, 81–82; Ute Frevert, *Women in German History: From Bourgeois Emancipation to Sexual Liberation,* trans. Stuart McKinnon-Evans (Oxford, 1988), 24, 13; Yvonne Schütze, "Mutterliebe—Vaterliebe. Elternrollen in der bürgerlichen Familie des 19. Jahrhunderts," in *Bürgerinnen und Bürger. Geschlechterverhältnisse im 19. Jahrhundert,* ed. Ute Frevert (Göttingen, 1988), 120.

35. Frevert, *Women in German History,* 33, 15, 32, 14–19. See also Karin Hausen, "Family and Role-Division: The Polarisation of Sexual Stereotypes in the Nineteenth Century—An Aspect of the Dissociation of Work and Family Life," in *The German Family: Essays on the Social History of the Family in Nineteenth- and Twentieth-Century Germany,* ed. Richard J. Evans and W. R. Lee (London, 1981).

36. Schütze, "Mutterliebe—Vaterliebe," 123.

37. Frevert, *Women in German History,* 21, 84, 89–92, 97; Jon Gjerde, *The Minds of the West: Ethnocultural Evolution in the Rural Middle West, 1830–1917* (Chapel Hill, N.C., 1997), 14–16.

38. Gjerde, *Minds of the West,* 163, 165–167, 170–177.

39. Karin Hausen, "'. . . eine Ulme für das schwanke Efeu.' Ehepaare im deutschen Bildungsbürgertum. Ideale und Wirklichkeiten im späten 18. und 19. Jahrhundert," in *Bürgerinnen und Bürger,* ed. Frevert, 105, 112; Spaeth, ed. *Life of Adolph Spaeth,* 176, 357, 364.

40. Spaeth, ed., *Life of Adolph Spaeth,* 69, 122; David A. Gustafson, *Lutherans in Crisis: The Question of Identity in the American Republic* (Minneapolis, 1993), 117, 119; Spaeth, ed. *Life of Adolph Spaeth,* 359. That Adolph Spaeth spent a good deal of his day at home—and therefore could exercise such oversight—is also suggested by his wife's description of their last residence, where the pastor's study formed "the heart of the house"; ibid., 364–365.

41. Von Bosse, *Glauben und Volkstum,* 82–85, 135.

42. Esther Louise Little and William Joseph Henry Cotton, "Budgets of Families and Individuals of Kensington, Philadelphia" (Ph.D. diss., University of Pennsylvania, 1920), 28, 2, 35–36, 82–83, 87–88. The bulk of the research for this study was carried out in 1913 and 1914; ibid., 1.

43. Moore, "These Things I Remember," 4.

44. Ibid., 10. The two families in the Kensington budget study that had both daughters and German fathers sent at least some of those daughters out to work for wages; Little and Cotton, "Budgets of Families," 82–83, 87–88.

45. Kathleen Neils Conzen, "Ethnicity as Festive Culture: Nineteenth-Century German America on Parade," in *The Invention of Ethnicity,* ed. Werner Sollors (New York, 1989), 52–53; Kathy Peiss, *Cheap Amusements: Working Women and Leisure in Turn-of-the-Century New York* (Philadelphia, 1986), 20, 30.

46. *1846–1906: 60. Stiftungsfest des Philadelphia Schützen-Verein, abgehalten in den Tagen vom 19. bis 21. November 1906* (Philadelphia [1906]), 61, 63; Oswald Seidensticker, *Die Erste Deutsche Einwanderung in Amerika und die Gründung von Germantown, im Jahre 1683. Festschrift zum deutsch-amerikanischen Pionier-Jubiläum am 6. October 1883* (Philadelphia, 1883), 10.

47. On women as a source of morality and other tenets of domesticity shared by middle-class people in Germany and the United States, compare Welter, "Cult of True Womanhood," and Hausen, "Family and Role-Division." Kathleen Conzen sees nineteenth-century German Americans as supporting an "elaborate range of public familial celebration;" Conzen, "Ethnicity as Festive Culture," 53. Similarly, Kathy Peiss notes that compared to men of other ethnic groups, German men in New York City before the First World War took their leisure "most often with their families;" Peiss, *Cheap Amusements,* 30.

48. Von Bosse, *Glauben und Volkstum,* 135, 82; Donna Gabaccia, *From the Other Side: Women, Gender, and Immigrant Life in the U.S., 1820–1990* (Bloomington, Ind., 1994), 118; George J. Sánchez, *Becoming Mexican American: Ethnicity, Culture and Identity in Chicano Los Angeles, 1900–1945* (New York, 1993), 98. The final quotation is from the first volume of the Cincinnati historical journal, *Der Deutsche Pionier,* issued for the year 1869–1870, and is cited in John A. Hawgood, *The Tragedy of German-America: The Germans in the United States of America during the Nineteenth Century—and After* (New York, 1940), 278, 278n. The translation is Hawgood's.

49. Monika Blaschke, "Communicating the Old and the New: German Immigrant Women and Their Press in Comparative Perspective around 1900," in *Peo-*

ple in Transit: German Migrations in Comparative Perspective, 1820–1930, ed. Dirk Hoerder and Jörg Nagler (Cambridge, 1995), 314–317.

50. *Verhandlungen der V.S. Groß-Loge 1890,* 4, 10, 32, 45; *Verhandlungen der Ver. Staaten Gross-Loge D.O.H. In General-Sitzung versammelt vom 5. bis 8. September 1894, zu Denver, Colo.* (Reading, Pa., 1894), 18, 75; *Verhandlungen der V.S. Gross-Loge 1908,* 86–87, 78–79.

51. Seidensticker, *Deutsche Gesellschaft,* I: 58; Heinrici, *Deutsche Gesellschaft,* II: 296, 297n; *136. Jahres-Bericht der Deutschen Gesellschaft von Pennsylvanien für das Jahr 1900* (Philadelphia, 1901), 10. German Society *Jahres-Berichte* cited in the book are held at GSP and VPL.

52. *Constitution und Neben-Gesetze des Frauen-Hilfsverein der Deutschen Gesellschaft in Philadelphia* (Philadelphia, 1901), 3 (in GSP); *By-Laws and Rules of Procedure of the Women's Auxiliary of the German Society of Pennsylvania* ([Philadelphia], 1952), 8 (in GSP); *136. Jahres-Bericht der Deutschen Gesellschaft 1900,* 11; Heinrici, *Deutsche Gesellschaft,* II: 303–304, 276, 296; *137. Jahres-Bericht der Deutschen Gesellschaft von Pennsylvanien für das Jahr 1901* (Philadelphia, 1902), 43–44, 10; *139. Jahres-Bericht der Deutschen Gesellschaft von Pennsylvanien für das Jahr 1903* (Philadelphia, 1904), 43–44.

53. *139. Jahres-Bericht der Deutschen Gesellschaft 1903,* 42; *146. Jahres-Bericht der Deutschen Gesellschaft von Pennsylvanien für das Jahr 1910* (Philadelphia, 1911), 41; *151. Jahres-Bericht der Deutschen Gesellschaft von Pennsylvanien für das Jahr 1915* (Philadelphia, 1916), 6, 40. The comparison of male and female membership through 1930 draws on Heinrici, *Deutsche Gesellschaft,* II: 255, which provides male membership figures through 1916; available male and female membership figures from 1917 on are taken from the German Society's annual reports. The society ceased publishing an overall male membership figure in the report for 1918 and only resumed the practice in the late 1920s. I had available male membership totals for 1925 (which I calculated myself from a members' list), 1929, and 1930. Membership figures for the Frauen Hilfsverein throughout are taken from that association's annual reports, which were published as part of the society's annual reports.

54. J. B. Mayer to "Wertes Mitglied des Frauen Hilfs-Vereins," April 1917, "Frauenverein der D.G./The Women's Auxiliary" collection, GSP.

55. Mari Jo Buhle, *Women and American Socialism, 1870–1920* (Urbana, Ill., 1981), 125; *Tageblatt,* 28 May 1903, p. 2; 12 August 1903, p. 2; 18 March 1910, p. 3; 4 March 1910, p. 5.

56. Estelle Freedman, "Separatism as Strategy: Female Institution Building and American Feminism, 1870–1930," *Feminist Studies* 5 (Fall 1979): 512–529; Nancy F. Cott, *The Grounding of Modern Feminism* (New Haven, Conn., 1987), 18; Frevert, *Women in German History,* 113–118, 138–147. For a case study of this development among middle-class women in Germany, see Nancy R. Reagin, *A German Women's Movement: Class and Gender in Hannover, 1880–1933* (Chapel Hill, N.C., 1995).

57. Reagin, *German Women's Movement,* 25–26; Frevert, *Women in German History,* 125–130; Seth Koven and Sonya Michel, "Womanly Duties: Maternalist Politics and the Origins of Welfare States in France, Germany, Great Britain, and the United States, 1880–1920," *American Historical Review* 95 (October 1990): 1076–1108.

58. Buhle, *Women and American Socialism*, 105, 214–241; *Tageblatt*, 28 February 1910, p. 5.

59. Buhle, *Women and American Socialism*, 63; Clifton James Child, *The German-Americans in Politics, 1914–1917* (Madison, Wis., 1939), 12.

60. "Argument Delivered by Mrs. Fernande Richter, of St. Louis, at a Hearing before the Committee on the Judiciary, House of Representatives, U.S., March 2, 3, 4, 1904," *German American Annals*, n.s., 2 (March 1904): 199–205.

61. Ibid., 202–203.

CHAPTER FOUR
DESTINATIONS: THE AMBIGUOUS LURE OF MASS COMMERCIAL AND
CONSUMER CULTURE

1. Georg von Bosse, *Ein Kampf um Glauben und Volkstum: Das Streben während meines 25jährigen Amtslebens als deutsch-lutherischer Geistlicher in Amerika* (Stuttgart, 1920), 226.

2. Elsie Lillian Spalde Moore, "These Things I Remember," 1983, TMs [photocopy], Library, Balch, 1, 5, 4.

3. Examples of the extensive literature on mass culture's rise include Stuart Ewen, *Captains of Consciousness: Advertising and the Social Roots of the Consumer Culture* (New York, 1976); Roy Rosenzweig, *Eight Hours for What We Will: Workers and Leisure in an Industrial City, 1870–1920* (Cambridge, 1983); Kathy Peiss, *Cheap Amusements: Working Women and Leisure in Turn-of-the-Century New York* (Philadelphia, 1986); Lizabeth Cohen, *Making a New Deal: Industrial Workers in Chicago, 1919–1939* (Cambridge, 1990); and William Leach, *Land of Desire: Merchants, Power, and the Rise of a New American Culture* (New York, 1993).

4. Dorothy Gondos Beers, "The Centennial City, 1865–1876," in *Philadelphia: A 300-Year History*, ed. Russell F. Weigley (New York, 1982), 444; Nathaniel Burt and Wallace E. Davies, "The Iron Age, 1876–1905," in *Philadelphia*, ed. Weigley, 485–487; J. Thomas Jable, "Philadelphia's Sporting and Athletic Clubs in the Nineteenth Century," in *Invisible Philadelphia: Community through Voluntary Organizations*, ed. Jean Barth Toll and Mildred S. Gillam, (Philadelphia, 1995), 1139; Burt and Davies, "The Iron Age," 517–519, 484; Federal Writers' Project, Works Progress Administration, *WPA Guide to Philadelphia* (reprint, Philadelphia, 1988; originally published as *Philadelphia: A Guide to the Nation's Birthplace* [Philadelphia, 1937]), 660.

5. For examples, see *Philadelphia Tageblatt*, 4 June 1903, p. 2; 25 February 1910, p. 5; 28 February 1910, p. 5; 5 March 1910, p. 5; 26 March 1910, p. 5; 2 July 1914, p. 5; 3 July 1914, p. 5; 10 August 1914, p. 5.

6. Andrew R. Heinze, *Adapting to Abundance: Jewish Immigrants, Mass Consumption, and the Search for American Identity* (New York, 1990), 28–30; Esther Louise Little and William Joseph Henry Cotton, "Budgets of Families and Individuals of Kensington, Philadelphia" (Ph.D. diss., University of Pennsylvania, 1920), 83–85.

7. John Higham, "The Reorientation of American Culture in the 1890's," in

The Origins of Modern Consciousness, ed. John Weiss (Detroit, 1965), 28; Harriet R. Spaeth, ed., *Life of Adolph Spaeth, D.D., LL.D.: Told in His Own Reminiscences, His Letters and the Recollections of His Family and Friends* (Philadelphia, 1916), 368, 363.

8. *Tageblatt,* 29 May 1903, p. 2; 19 August 1914, p. 7.

9. Dorothee Schneider, "'For Whom Are All the Good Things in Life?' German-American Housewives Discuss Their Budgets," in *German Workers in Industrial Chicago, 1850–1910: A Comparative Perspective,* ed. Hartmut Keil and John B. Jentz (DeKalb, Ill., 1983), 156; Little and Cotton, "Budgets of Families," 21. Families were classified as German if the household head was a first- or second-generation German immigrant.

10. Spaeth, ed., *Life of Adolph Spaeth,* 361–364; Lucretia L. Blankenburg, *The Blankenburgs of Philadelphia: By One of Them* (Philadelphia, 1928), 164–165; Little and Cotton, "Budgets of Families," 90, 97, 65.

11. *Tageblatt,* 1 June 1903, p. 4; 12 April 1903, p. 3. On the opening of New Jersey shore resorts to immigrants of "ordinary means" by the 1890s, see Heinze, *Adapting to Abundance,* 131–132.

12. Little and Cotton, "Budgets of Families," 37–39; Lloyd M. Abernethy, "Progressivism, 1905–1919," in *Philadelphia,* ed. Weigley, 534; *Tageblatt,* 19 February 1910, p. 8; 24 February 1910, p. 8; 20 February 1910, p. 7; 22 February 1910, p. 5; 7 March 1910, p. 3.

13. For examples of Willow Grove Park notices, see *Tageblatt,* 4 July 1914, p. 8; 10 July 1914, p. 8; 27 July 1914, p. 8; 3 August 1914, p. 8.

14. Cohen, *Making a New Deal,* 106, 105, 123; *Tageblatt,* 19 February 1910, p. 8; 11 October 1914, p. 8. See also *Tageblatt,* 10 October 1914, p. 6.

15. On this point, see, e.g., Rosenzweig, *Eight Hours,* 182; Gerhard Wiesinger, *Die deutsche Einwandererkolonie von Holyoke, Massachusetts, 1865–1920* (Stuttgart, 1994), 304.

16. *Hundert jähriges Jubiläum, 1972: Cannstatter Volksfest Verein, Philadelphia, Pennsylvania* (Philadelphia, [1972]), unpaginated (in Balch); *Cannstatter Volksfest-Verein, Philadelphia: Geschichte des Vereins von der Gründung in 1873 bis zum Goldenen Jubiläum im September 1923* (Philadelphia, [1923]), 10; Lesley Ann Kawaguchi, "The Making of Philadelphia's German-America: Ethnic Group and Community Development, 1830–1883" (Ph.D. diss., University of California, Los Angeles, 1983), 308; David J. Roscoe, "Cannstatter Volksfest Verein," in *Invisible Philadelphia,* ed. Toll and Gillam, 89.

17. Kathleen Neils Conzen, "Ethnicity as Festive Culture: Nineteenth-Century German America on Parade," in *The Invention of Ethnicity,* ed. Werner Sollors (New York, 1989), 50–51; *Cannstatter Volksfest-Verein 1923,* 10, 11–33.

18. Meeting of 15 June 1900, Minutes of the Vergnügungs-Committee (1898–1924), folder 2, box 1, CVV; O. J. Stetser, Point Breeze Park Amusement Co., to C. J. Preisendanz, 24 March 1916, folder 2, box 4, CVV; *Cannstatter Volksfest-Verein 1923,* 11–33; A. R. Hofheinz, "Ein herzliches 'Grüss Gott' an alle Festteilnehmer," *1873–1949: Diamantenes Jubiläum, Cannstatter Volksfest-Verein* (Philadelphia, [1949]), unpaginated (in Balch); *Philadelphia Press,* 1 September 1907, p. 3; "Cannstatter Volks Feste," folder 1, box 4, CVV.

19. The *Tageblatt* noted in 1914 that "With the exception of the Cannstatter

Volksfest-Verein, there exists hardly a German association in Philadelphia today that can put on a halfway decently attended festival"; *Tageblatt,* 11 August 1914, p. 8.

20. *Cannstatter Volksfest-Verein 1923,* 11–33.

21. Bergquist, "German Communities in American Cities," 20; Oswald Seidensticker and Max Heinrici, *Geschichte der Deutschen Gesellschaft von Pennsylvanien. 1764–1917,* 1. Teil, *Von der Gruendung im Jahre 1764 bis zur Jubelfeier der Republik 1876,* by Oswald Seidensticker; 2. Teil, *Von 1876 bis 1917,* by Max Heinrici (Philadelphia, 1917), 258.

22. "Cannstatter Volks Feste," folder 1, box 4, CVV; *Press,* 1 September 1907, p. 3.

23. *Press,* 30 August 1905, p. 7; von Bosse, *Glauben und Volkstum,* 199, 200; *Press,* 1 September 1907, p. 3.

24. *Cannstatter Volksfest-Verein 1923,* 25; David Glassberg, "Public Ritual and Cultural Hierarchy: Philadelphia's Civic Celebrations at the Turn of the Twentieth Century," *Pennsylvania Magazine of History and Biography* 107 (July 1983): 421–431.

25. 19 August 1898, 8 July 1906, Minutes of the Vergnügungs-Committee (1898–1924), folder 2, box 1, CVV; Glassberg, "Public Ritual," 434–435.

26. 23 August 1901, 19 August 1898, 28 July 1899, 1 August 1902, 26 August 1898, Minutes of the Vergnügungs-Committee (1898–1924), folder 2, box 1, CVV.

27. Berndt Ostendorf, "'The Diluted Second Generation': German-Americans in Music, 1870 to 1920," in *German Workers' Culture in the United States, 1850 to 1920,* ed. Hartmut Keil (Washington, D.C., 1988), 261–266, 274–282, 265–266, 275; "Albert Von Tilzer, Composer of Many Song Hits, Dies at 78," United Press dispatch, 1 October 1956, and "Albert Von Tilzer, 78, Dies; Composed Popular Songs," Associated Press dispatch, 1 October 1956, news clippings in "Von Tilzer, Albert," Biographical Files, National Baseball Hall of Fame Library, Cooperstown, N.Y. (my thanks to Stan Green for locating these news clippings).

28. Conzen, "Ethnicity as Festive Culture," 73; *Cannstatter Volksfest-Verein 1923,* 15.

29. Peiss, *Cheap Amusements,* 16, 17, 21–26, 88–162, 137, 125, 128–129, 138; *Cannstatter Volksfest-Verein 1923,* 21, 47; photographs in ibid., 28, 44.

30. In this sense, the Volksfest-Verein may represent an example of what Peter Conolly-Smith calls "subversive [cultural] appropriation" and the "hybridization of cultural forms." That hybridization grew out of a struggle for control over turn-of-the-century popular culture waged by German Americans and other social groups. See Peter J. D. Conolly-Smith, "The Translated Community: New York City's German-Language Press as an Agent of Cultural Resistance and Integration, 1910–1918" (Ph.D. diss., Yale University, 1996), 6–13, 162–164.

31. Rosenzweig, *Eight Hours,* 182. On German Americans and baseball, see Conolly-Smith, "Translated Community," 148–151, 514–515.

32. Wiesinger, *Holyoke,* 325–326, 302–304; see also ibid., 286–302; Conolly-Smith, "Translated Community," 16–25, 478–480, 511–513, and passim. Roy Rosenzweig similarly argues that the amusement park helped to undercut ethnic working-class cultures; Rosenzweig, *Eight Hours,* 182.

33. Spaeth, ed., *Life of Adolph Spaeth*, 368; *Tageblatt*, 2 April 1900, p. 4; 20 June 1900, p. 4; 17 April 1903, p. 4; 12 August 1903, p. 4.

34. For examples, see *Tageblatt*, 3 July 1914, p. 8; 4 July 1914, p. 8; 10 July 1914, p. 8; 19 August 1914, p. 7.

35. *Tageblatt*, 27 July 1914, p. 8; 3 August 1914, p. 8; 10 August 1914, p. 8; 18 August 1914, p. 8; Conolly-Smith, "Translated Community," 149–150 and passim.

36. For one such appeal, see *Tageblatt*, 11 April 1903, p. 2. On married women's role as shoppers, see Heinze, *Adapting to Abundance*, 105–115.

37. Peiss, *Cheap Amusements*, 35, 41, 62.

38. Moore, "These Things I Remember," 2, 10–15. On the slit skirt, see Conolly-Smith, "Translated Community," 217–221.

39. Moore, "These Things I Remember," 13–14. The photographs are located in ibid., after pages 8, 9, and 11.

40. Ibid., 6, 2, 14–15, and photographs after 10, 13, and 9. The fox stole in fig. 4.2 is the same one Spalde described in her memoir, according to her daughter; Jean M. Husher to author, 16 March 2003 (my thanks to Jean Husher for locating and sharing this photograph of her mother).

41. Ibid., photograph after 10.

CHAPTER FIVE
DESTINATIONS: FRACTURED WHITENESS, "AMERICAN" IDENTITY, AND THE "OLD STOCK" OPENING

1. *Philadelphia Press*, 1 August 1905, p. 3.

2. Ibid.

3. Ibid. The *Press* put the Hanf residence at 417 North Eighth Street and identified Hattie Hanf as "the prettiest girl in the Tenderloin," a section that abutted Chinatown. On these neighborhoods, see Mark H. Haller, "Recurring Themes," in *The Peoples of Philadelphia: A History of Ethnic Groups and Lower-Class Life, 1790–1940*, ed. Allen F. Davis and Mark H. Haller (Philadelphia, 1973), 283.

4. Matthew Frye Jacobson, *Whiteness of a Different Color: European Immigrants and the Alchemy of Race* (Cambridge, Mass., 1998), 29, 42, 74; Reed Ueda, *Postwar Immigrant America: A Social History* (Boston, 1994), 52.

5. See, e.g., David R. Roediger, *The Wages of Whiteness: Race and the Making of the American Working Class* (London, 1991); David R. Roediger, "Whiteness and Ethnicity in the History of 'White Ethnics' in the United States," in *Towards the Abolition of Whiteness: Essays on Race, Politics, and Working Class History* (London, 1994); Noel Ignatiev, *How the Irish Became White* (New York, 1995).

6. Roediger, *Wages of Whiteness*, 134, 133, 144–150; Jacobson, *Whiteness of a Different Color*, 41–42, 14, 91–135, and passim.

7. Gary Gerstle, "The Working Class Goes to War," *Mid-America* 75 (October 1993): 313, 318; Arnold R. Hirsch, *Making the Second Ghetto: Race and Housing in Chicago, 1940–1960* (Cambridge, 1983), 80–81, 186–187; Russell A. Kazal, "Revisiting Assimilation: The Rise, Fall, and Reappraisal of a Concept in American Ethnic History," *American Historical Review* 100 (April 1995): 469–

470; Thomas J. Sugrue, *The Origins of the Urban Crisis: Race and Inequality in Postwar Detroit* (Princeton, N.J., 1996), chaps. 8–9; John T. McGreevy, *Parish Boundaries: The Catholic Encounter with Race in the Twentieth-Century Urban North* (Chicago, 1996), chaps. 2–4; James R. Barrett and David Roediger, "Inbetween Peoples: Race, Nationality, and the 'New Immigrant' Working Class," *Journal of American Ethnic History* 16 (Spring 1997): 3–44. The term "not-yet-white ethnics" is Barry Goldberg's, cited in ibid., 8.

For critical overviews of the literature on whiteness, see Peter Kolchin, "Whiteness Studies: The New History of Race in America," *Journal of American History* 89 (June 2002): 154–173; and Eric Arnesen, "Whiteness and the Historians' Imagination," *International Labor and Working-Class History,* no. 60 (Fall 2001): 3–32. Arnesen deems whiteness "a problematic category of historical analysis"; ibid., 23. Indeed, some works within the larger field of "whiteness studies" have at times generalized from too thin an evidentiary base or tended to slight other elements of subjects' identity. However, I agree with James Barrett in his response to Arnesen that a promising direction for research on whiteness lies in case studies of racial identity as it evolved "in particular places and situations," and I view this book in part as one such effort; James R. Barrett, "Whiteness Studies: Anything Here for Historians of the Working Class?" *International Labor and Working-Class History,* no. 60 (Fall 2001): 37.

8. Jacobson, *Whiteness of a Different Color,* 40; Lorenz Degenhard to his father and siblings, 1 October 1835, in *"Amerika ist ein freies Land . . ." Auswanderer schreiben nach Deutschland,* ed. Wolfgang Helbich (Darmstadt and Neuwied, 1985), 29, 162–163; Jacobson, *Whiteness of a Different Color,* 47; see also ibid., 46–48.

9. Peter Martin, *Schwarze Teufel, edle Mohren* (Hamburg, 1993), 16–18, 43–49, 113, 121–128.

10. Ibid., 33–37; Sander L. Gilman, *On Blackness without Blacks: Essays on the Image of the Black in Germany* (Boston, 1982), 57, 35–48, 61–75.

11. Martin, *Schwarze Teufel,* 101, 81–89, 273, 223–225; Gordon A. Craig, *Germany, 1866–1945* (New York, 1978), 116–124.

12. Werner Conze and Antje Sommer, "Rasse," in *Geschichtliche Grundbegriffe: Historisches Lexikon zur politisch-sozialen Sprache in Deutschland,* ed. Otto Brunner, Werner Conze and Reinhart Koselleck, vol. 5, *Pro–Soz* (Stuttgart, 1984), 142–150; Reginald Horsman, *Race and Manifest Destiny: The Origins of American Racial Anglo-Saxonism* (Cambridge, Mass., 1981), 47. See also Martin, *Schwarze Teufel,* chap. 4.

13. Horsman, *Race and Manifest Destiny,* 25–38, 43–44, 34; George L. Mosse, *The Crisis of German Ideology: Intellectual Origins of the Third Reich* (New York, 1964; reprint, New York, 1981), 89, vii, 4–5, 88–97; Conze and Sommer, "Rasse," 149, 156–159, 168–169.

14. *Philadelphia Sonntags-Journal,* 6 October 1901, p. 5.

15. For examples, see *Philadelphia Tageblatt,* 4 October 1901, p. 4; 6 October 1901, p. 8; 11 April 1903, p. 4; 12 August 1903, p. 4; 22 February 1910, p. 8; 24 February 1910, pp. 1, 5; 9 March 1910, p. 2; 2 July 1914, p. 7; 8 July 1914, p. 5; 6 August 1914, p. 8; and *Philadelphia Morgen-Gazette,* 5 March 1915, p. 2; 25 June 1915, pp. 2, 5; 29 October 1915, p. 2.

16. *Tageblatt,* 19 August 1914, p. 5.

17. *Lutherisches Kirchenblatt,* 3 February 1900, p. 37; *Nord Amerika,* 14 July 1900, p. 6.

18. On the impact and long career of blackface minstrelsy, see Roediger, *Wages of Whiteness,* 115–131; Eric Lott, *Love and Theft: Blackface Minstrelsy and the American Working Class* (New York, 1993); David Nasaw, *Going Out: The Rise and Fall of Public Amusements* (New York, 1993), chaps. 5, 12; and Michael Rogin, *Blackface, White Noise: Jewish Immigrants in the Hollywood Melting Pot* (Berkeley, Calif., 1996). On westerns, see Barrett and Roediger, "Inbetween Peoples," 14; and Richard Slotkin, *Gunfighter Nation: The Myth of the Frontier in Twentieth-Century America* (New York, 1992).

19. Elsie Lillian Spalde Moore, "These Things I Remember," 1983, TMs [photocopy], Library, Balch, 12; *Tageblatt,* 5 August 1914, p. 7; Berndt Ostendorf, "'The Diluted Second Generation': German-Americans in Music, 1870 to 1920," in *German Workers' Culture in the United States, 1850 to 1920,* ed. Hartmut Keil (Washington, D.C., 1988), 280–281; *Tageblatt,* 30 September 1901, p. 2. Turner clubs in Holyoke, Massachusetts, began offering minstrel shows at the turn of the century; Gerhard Wiesinger, *Die deutsche Einwandererkolonie von Holyoke, Massachusetts, 1865–1920* (Stuttgart, 1994), 302.

20. W.E.B. Du Bois, *The Philadelphia Negro: A Social Study* (Philadelphia, 1899; reprint, Philadelphia, 1996), 5, 11.

21. Ostendorf, "'Diluted Second Generation,'" 280–281. On blackface's "Americanizing" potential, see Rogin, *Blackface, White Noise.*

22. Toni Morrison, *Playing in the Dark: Whiteness and the Literary Imagination* (Cambridge, Mass., 1990), 47.

23. Gary Gerstle, *American Crucible: Race and Nation in the Twentieth Century* (Princeton, N.J., 2001), 4; Kathleen Neils Conzen, "German-Americans and the Invention of Ethnicity," in *America and the Germans: An Assessment of a Three-Hundred-Year History,* ed. Frank Trommler and Joseph McVeigh, vol. 1, *Immigration, Language, Ethnicity* (Philadelphia, 1985), 136–144. Lawrence H. Fuchs sees German Americans as providing the best early example of such "ethnic-Americanization"; Fuchs, *The American Kaleidoscope: Race, Ethnicity, and the Civic Culture* (Hanover, N.H., 1990), 19–30. On American civic nationalism, see also Hans Kohn, *American Nationalism: An Interpretative Essay* (New York, 1957); Philip Gleason, "American Identity and Americanization," in *Harvard Encyclopedia of American Ethnic Groups,* ed. Stephan Thernstrom (Cambridge, Mass., 1980), 31–58.

24. Gerstle, *American Crucible,* 4 and passim. For other recent works that address civic and racial nationalism, although using somewhat different terms, see Rogers M. Smith, *Civic Ideals: Conflicting Visions of Citizenship in U.S. History* (New Haven, Conn., 1997); and Eric Foner, *The Story of American Freedom* (New York, 1998).

25. Carol Poore, "Whose Celebration? The Centennial of 1876 and German-American Socialist Culture," in *America and the Germans,* ed. Trommler and McVeigh, 1:176–188; *Tageblatt,* 4 July 1914, p. 4.

26. *Tageblatt,* 3 June 1903, p. 1; 3 October 1901, p. 1; 27 May 1903, p. 1; Bruce C. Levine, "Free Soil, Free Labor, and *Freimänner:* German Chicago in the

Civil War Era," in *German Workers in Industrial Chicago,* ed. Keil and Jentz, 163–182; Maria Diedrich, *Love across Color Lines: Ottilie Assing and Frederick Douglass* (New York, 1999); Neil Foley, *The White Scourge: Mexicans, Blacks, and Poor Whites in Texas Cotton Culture* (Berkeley, Calif., 1997), 8.

27. Poore, "Whose Celebration?" 185; Oswald Seidensticker, *Die Erste Deutsche Einwanderung in Amerika und die Gründung von Germantown, im Jahre 1683. Festschrift zum deutsch-amerikanischen Pionier-Jubiläum am 6. October 1883* (Philadelphia, 1883), 80–84; *Mitteilungen des Deutschen Pionier-Vereins von Philadelphia* 12 (1909): 3. The protest was signed by Franz Daniel Pastorius and three other settlers and appears in Samuel Whitaker Pennypacker, *The Settlement of Germantown, Pennsylvania, and the Beginning of German Emigration to North America* (Philadelphia, 1899), 145–147.

28. Barrett and Roediger, "Inbetween Peoples," 28–33; Philip Scranton, *Figured Tapestry: Production, Markets, and Power in Philadelphia Textiles, 1885–1941* (Cambridge, 1989), 268–269; *Tageblatt,* 8 March 1910, p. 1; *Public Ledger,* 10 March 1910, p. 3, cited in Scranton, *Figured Tapestry,* 269n.

29. *Tageblatt,* 23 February 1910, p. 5; the chicken-stealing cartoon appeared in *Tageblatt,* 6 March 1910, p. 2. During this two-month period, the newspaper ran only two other such cartoons; they appeared side by side in *Tageblatt,* 4 February 1910, p. 3. For examples of the Sunday jokes page, see *Tageblatt,* 20 February 1910, p. 16; 6 March 1910, p. 16; 27 March, 1910, p. 16.

30. See, e.g., "Sambo" and other strips in the (unpaginated) comics section of the *Public Ledger,* 6 March 1910, 13 March 1910.

31. Walter Licht, *Getting Work: Philadelphia, 1840–1950* (Cambridge, Mass., 1992), 45–51. While whiteness thus might have seemed important to German workers in an economic sense, those in German-speaking union locals could exclude blacks from membership unthinkingly, on the same principle—language—that kept out all non-German workers. Interestingly, the Cigarmaker's Union, which had a German local in 1910, was one of the very few white unions in the city to have blacks on its rolls; ibid., 50; *Tageblatt,* 4 March 1910, p. 5.

32. Robert Gregg, *Sparks from the Anvil of Oppression: Philadelphia's African Methodists and Southern Migrants, 1890–1940* (Philadelphia, 1993), 25, 28. Proportions calculated from data in U.S. Census Bureau, *Thirteenth Census of the United States, Taken in the Year 1910,* vol. 3, *Population: Reports by States . . . Nebraska-Wyoming* (Washington, D.C., 1913), 605–608.

33. *Tageblatt,* 12 August 1903, pp. 1, 2.

34. Oswald Seidensticker and Max Heinrici, *Geschichte der Deutschen Gesellschaft von Pennsylvanien. 1764–1917,* 1. Teil, *Von der Gruendung im Jahre 1764 bis zur Jubelfeier der Republik 1876,* by Oswald Seidensticker; 2. Teil, *Von 1876 bis 1917,* by Max Heinrici (Philadelphia, 1917), 576, 627; *Opening of the Bechstein Germanic Library, Addresses, University of Pennsylvania, March 21, 1896* (Philadelphia, 1896), 20–21, E. F. Smith Collection, Special Collections, VPL. In current-day German, *Stamm* is translatable as "race," "stock," "tribe," or "breed"; Harold T. Betteridge et al., *Cassell's German-English, English-German Dictionary/Deutsch-Englisches, Englisch-Deutsches Wörterbuch,* rev. ed. (London and New York, 1978), s.v. "Stamm"; Gerhard Wahrig et al., *Deutsches Wörterbuch,* rev. ed. (N.p., 1980), s.v. "Stamm." Harriet Spaeth translated her husband's use of *Volksstamm* in a 1900 speech as "race"; *Sonntags-Journal,* 7 October 1900,

p. 1; Spaeth, ed., *Life of Adolph Spaeth*, 272. An 1897 reference work gave *Stamm* as one equivalent for the English word "stock"; *Meyers Konversations-Lexikon*, 5th ed., vol. 16 (Leipzig, 1897), s.v. "Stock."

35. *Opening of the Bechstein Germanic Library*, 21. This translation draws in part on that in Spaeth, ed., *Life of Adolph Spaeth*, 271.

36. *Sonntags-Journal*, 12 October 1902, p. 5. Hexamer delivered essentially the same passage in an English-language speech the following month, using the term "a great race" where in October he had spoken of a *Volk*; C. J. Hexamer, "German Achievement in America," *German American Annals*, n.s. vol. 1 (January 1903): 46.

37. For this use of "nationality" in 1900, see *Nord Amerika*, 7 April, p. 4; 12 May, p. 4; 8 September, p. 1; 29 September, pp. 4, 5, 8; 6 October, p. 4. The issues of the weekly examined ran from 6 January through 6 October, 1900.

38. *Nord Amerika*, 29 September 1900, p. 1; David Francis Sweeney, O.F.M., *The Life of John Lancaster Spalding, First Bishop of Peoria, 1840–1916*, with a foreword by John Tracy Ellis (New York, 1965), 12. On Irish-American usages of Irish or Celtic "race" in the nineteeth and early twentieth centuries, see Jacobson, *Whiteness of a Different Color*, 49–52; for contemporary Philadelphia examples, see *Catholic Standard and Times*, 6 January 1900, p. 1; 17 March 1900, p. 4; 6 October 1900, p. 8.

39. I examined issues of the *Tageblatt* for 14 June 1914, 2–5 July 1914, 7 July–21 August 1914, 10–11 October 1914, and 13 June–15 August 1916.

40. *Tageblatt*, 13 July 1914, p. 4; Melvin G. Holli, "Teuton vs. Slav: The Great War Sinks Chicago's German *Kultur*," *Ethnicity* 8 (December 1981): 411; *Tageblatt*, 9 August 1914, p. 4; 4 August 1914, p. 3; 8 October 1914, p. 4. A 1903 editorial did mention European races: it compared the relationship between Hungary and Croatia to that between England and Ireland, noting similar "antagonisms of race [*Rasse*] and religion;" *Tageblatt*, 28 May 1903, p. 2.

41. Craig, *Germany*, 145–150, 173–174.

42. Russell A. Kazal, "Irish 'Race' and German 'Nationality': Catholic Languages of Ethnic Difference in Turn-of-the-Century Philadelphia," in *Race and the Production of Modern American Nationalism*, ed. Reynolds J. Scott-Childress (New York, 1999), 161–162.

43. Horsman, *Race and Manifest Destiny*, 1–4, 9–12, 14–24.

44. Ibid., 32–36, 62–77, 158–186, 181; Stuart Anderson, *Race and Rapprochement: Anglo-Saxonism and Anglo-American Relations, 1895–1904* (East Brunswick, N.J., 1981), 37–45.

45. Barbara Miller Solomon, *Ancestors and Immigrants: A Changing New England Tradition* (Cambridge, Mass., 1956; reprint, Chicago, 1972), 70–79, 102, 111; Francis A. Walker, "Restriction of Immigration," *Atlantic Monthly* 77 (June 1896): 828–829; Anderson, *Race and Rapprochement*, 56; John Higham, *Strangers in the Land: Patterns of American Nativism, 1860–1925*, 2d rev. ed. (New York, 1981), 103.

46. Solomon, *Ancestors and Immigrants*, 111, 111n, 115–117, 158, 109, 109n. Richard Mayo Smith, later an IRL member, spelled out this Revolutionary War dividing line in an 1890 sociological study; ibid., 77–81, 104–105.

47. *Oxford English Dictionary*, 2d ed., on-line (http://oed.library, accessed 16 July 1997), s.v. "stock," A.I.1; A.I.2; A.I.3.a, c, d; A.I.4. Shakespeare, for exam-

ple, referred in *Cymbeline* (1611) to "Branches, which being dead many yeares, shall . . . bee ioynted to the old Stocke, and freshly grow"; ibid., s.v. "joint," 1.a.

48. Ibid., s.v. "aborigines," 1.b. (1655); see also ibid., s.v. "Parsee," 1, for a 1698 citation in this vein.

49. William Dwight Whitney, ed., *The Century Dictionary: An Encyclopedic Lexicon of the English Language*, vol. 7 (New York, 1895), s.v. "stock," Furness Collection, Special Collections, VPL.

50. John S. Farmer, ed., *Americanisms Old and New: A Dictionary of Words, Phrases and Colloquialisms Peculiar to the United States, British America, the West Indies, &c., &c.* . . . (London, 1889; reprint, Detroit, 1976), s.v. "old planters"; C. Merton Babcock, "The Social Significance of the Language of the American Frontier," *American Speech* 24 (December 1949): 257.

51. Solomon, *Ancestors and Immigrants*, 87, 87n.

52. Cited in Colman J. Barry, O.S.B., *The Catholic Church and German Americans* (Washington, D.C., 1953), 166, 166n.

53. Solomon, *Ancestors and Immigrants*, 123; *Germantown Independent-Gazette*, 30 October 1908, pp. 1, 4; 16 October 1908, p. 8.

54. Edward N. Saveth, *American Historians and European Immigrants, 1875–1925* (New York, 1948), 122–123, 122n; Frederick Jackson Turner, "The Significance of the Frontier in American History" [1893], in *The Frontier in American History* (New York, 1920), 22–23; Frederick Jackson Turner, "Middle Western Pioneer Democracy" [1918], in ibid., 349; Frederick Jackson Turner, "Pioneer Ideals and the State University" [1910], in ibid., 277–278. Turner elsewhere could still draw distinctions between "the old native democratic stock" and the nineteenth-century German and Scandinavian immigrants who had "been added" to it; Frederick Jackson Turner, "Contributions of the West to American Democracy" [1903], in ibid., 263; see also Frederick Jackson Turner, "Since the Foundation [of Clark University (1889)]" [1924], in *The Significance of Sections in American History*, with an introduction by Max Farrand (n.p., 1932; reprint, Gloucester, Mass., 1959), 211–212.

To some extent, Theodore Roosevelt's invocations of an "English-speaking race" or an "American 'race'" resembled Turner's frontier melting pot. Drawing heavily on Teutonist theory, Roosevelt in his *The Winning of the West* (New York, 1889–1896), 4 vols., depicted the frontier battles of the late eighteenth century as forging an "intensely American stock" out of settlers of Scotch-Irish, English, German, and other northwest European backgrounds. This process, moreover, "has gone on ever since," as later German and Irish immigrants arrived; Thomas G. Dyer, *Theodore Roosevelt and the Idea of Race* (Baton Rouge, La., 1980), 28–29, 142, 131, 65, 63; Gerstle, *American Crucible*, 21. Ultimately, however, Roosevelt was willing to open the crucible of his American race to southeastern European immigrants as well—although not to African Americans or others beyond the European circle; Gerstle, *American Crucible*, 22, 50–53.

55. Higham, *Strangers in the Land*, 131–157; Jacobson, *Whiteness of a Different Color*, 77–85; Madison Grant, *The Passing of the Great Race: or, The Racial Basis of European History*, 3d ed. (New York, 1920), 88–92, 27; Higham, *Strangers in the Land*, 173.

56. Solomon, *Ancestors and Immigrants*, 151, 151n; Higham, *Strangers in the Land*, 201. Some race thinkers questioned how Nordic the Germans might be.

The *Dictionary of Races or Peoples* prepared for the Dillingham Commission described Germany's Germans as racially heterogeneous, ranging from Nordics in the German north to Alpines in Bavaria; U.S. Immigration Commission, *Dictionary of Races or Peoples,* Reports of the Immigration Commission, vol. 5, prepared by Daniel Folkmar, assisted by Elnora C. Folkmar, 61st Cong., 3d sess., S. Doc. 662, serial 5867 (Washington, D.C., 1911), 64–66. Some American theorists embarrassed by World War I retreated on the topic; Grant, who first published *The Passing of the Great Race* in 1916, revised it in 1918 to declare that most present-day inhabitants of Germany were Alpines, not Nordics; Matthew Frye Jacobson, *Barbarian Virtues: The United States Encounters Foreign Peoples at Home and Abroad, 1876–1917* (New York, 2000), 162; Higham, *Strangers in the Land,* 201–202, 218. Yet the 1920 edition of Grant's book asserted that Irish and German newcomers of the mid-nineteenth century were "for the most part of the Nordic race"; Grant, *Passing of the Great Race,* 84, 87.

57. Desmond King, *Making Americans: Immigration, Race, and the Origins of the Diverse Democracy* (Cambridge, Mass., 2000), 79.

58. U.S. Immigration Commission, *Dictionary of Races or Peoples,* 32. On the *Dictionary*'s racial assumptions, see Jacobson, *Whiteness of a Different Color,* 78–80.

59. Nearing cited in Frederick Franklin Schrader, *"1683–1920": The Fourteen Points and What Became of Them—Foreign Propaganda in the Public Schools . . . and a Thousand Other Topics* (New York, 1920), 17–18; "Are We Still Anglo-Saxon?" *Literary Digest* 74 (September 9, 1922): 32, cited in Charles H. Anderson, *White Protestant Americans: From National Origins to Religious Group* (Englewood Cliffs, N.J., 1970), 108.

60. D. W. Brogan, *The American Character* (New York, 1944), 98 ("old stocks"); Max Lerner, "Is There an American Stock?" *Common Ground* 10 (Autumn 1949): 3–10, 8 ("west-European whites"); Cornelius Weygandt, *On the Edge of Evening: The Autobiography of a Teacher and Writer Who Holds to the Old Ways* (New York, 1946), 6, 58, 55.

61. For examples, see *Sonntags-Journal,* 6 October 1901, p. 1; *Tageblatt,* 20 June 1916, p. 5; Georg von Bosse, *Ein Kampf um Glauben und Volkstum. Das Streben während meines 25jährigen Amtslebens als deutsch-lutherischer Geistlicher in Amerika* (Stuttgart, 1920), 145; *Nord Amerika,* 3 April 1924, p. 1. Citations of *Nord Amerika* for 1924 are to Balch holdings. In current-day German, *Stock* is used as a prefix to describe a typical or true representative of a particular people or nationality; thus, a *Stockengländer* is a "true-blue or typical Englishman;" see Wahrig et al., *Deutsches Wörterbuch,* s.v. "Stock"; Betteridge et al., *Cassell's German-English, English-German Dictionary,* s.v. "Stockengländer." Whether this use of *Stock* predated the invention of *Stockamerikaner,* or was itself prompted by the English term "old-stock American," is difficult to say. However, in all uses I have seen where an individual is identified as a *Stockamerikaner,* that person bears an Anglo-American surname, and where that person's ethnic background is available, it is colonial English. Charles Hexamer, for example, referred to Marion Dexter Learned, a descendant of English colonial settlers, as "that most German of *Stockamerikaner*"; *Protokoll der Vierten Konvention des Deutsch-Amerikanischen National-Bundes der Ver. Staaten von Amerika. Abgehalten vom 4. bis 7. Oktober 1907 im Terrace Garden zu New York, N.Y. (N.p.,*

[1907]), 5; John J. Appel, "Marion Dexter Learned and the German American Historical Society," *Pennsylvania Magazine of History and Biography* 86 (July 1962): 297.

62. M. D. Lichliter, *History of the Junior Order United American Mechanics of the United States of North America* (Philadelphia, 1908), 14, xiv–xv; Higham, *Strangers in the Land,* 57, 173–174.

63. U.S. Immigration Commission, *Statements and Recommendations Submitted by Societies and Organizations Interested in the Subject of Immigration,* Reports of the Immigration Commission, vol. 41, 61st Cong., 3d sess., S. Doc. 764, serial 5881 (Washington, D.C., 1911), 16–18.

64. Ibid., 16; House Committee on Immigration and Naturalization, *Hearings Relative to the Further Restriction of Immigration,* 62nd Cong., 2nd sess., 2 February 1912 (Washington, D.C., 1912), 6, cited in Higham, *Strangers in the Land,* 174. Since Lichliter was born in 1849, a German grandfather could have arrived before 1800; Lichliter, *History of the Junior Order,* 791.

65. Ibid., 710, 775, 702–790, 723–724, 741.

66. U.S. Immigration Commission, *Statements and Recommendations Submitted by Societies,* 14–15, 28. Weitzel also introduced Lichliter at the 1912 hearing; House Committee on Immigration and Naturalization, *Hearings Relative to the Further Restriction of Immigration* (1912), 3–4. On Weitzel, see Lichliter, *History of the Junior Order,* 741–743.

67. *Trades Union News,* 16 June 1904, p. 4 (in UA).

68. *Germantown Telegraph,* 16 May 1902, p. 1; 22 May 1903, pp. 1, 5; Thomas E. Clemens, *The Mighty Works of Washington Council No. 1, Junior Order United American Mechanics of Germantown* (Germantown, Philadelphia, 1913), 74–75, 69, 79–80, 72; *Constitution, State Laws and Rules of Order of the State Council of Pennsylvania, and Divisions V and VI of the National Laws, Relating to Councils, Together with the Constitution, Rules of Order and By-laws of Washington Council No. 1, Jr. O.U.A.M., Located at Philadelphia, Pa.* (Pittsburgh, 1902), 3, "Secret Societies, Box 1," PBC; Clemens, *Mighty Works,* 70, 66, and passim; Emily Greene Balch, *Our Slavic Fellow Citizens* (New York, 1910; reprint, New York, 1969).

69. The Germantown hat store proprietor Frederick W. Kaplan and paperhanger John L. Zimmerman both ran advertisements identifying themselves as Washington Council members; *Federation News* 1 (June 1915): 3, 4 (in "Secret Societies, Box 1," PBC). Both men had German-born parents. On Kaplan, see chapter 2. On Zimmerman, see U.S. Department of Commerce, Bureau of the Census, Fourteenth Census of the United States (1920), Population Schedules for Philadelphia County, Microfilm, NAP, Enumeration District 582, p. 5b.

CHAPTER SIX
RESISTING ASSIMILATION: MIDDLE-CLASS AND
WORKING-CLASS APPROACHES

1. Clifton James Child, writing in 1939, called the alliance "the largest organization of any single racial group in American history;" Child, *The German-Americans in Politics, 1914–1917* (Madison, Wis., 1939), 4.

2. *Fest-Ausgabe und Programm der Elften Staats-Konvention des Deutsch-Amerikanischen Central-Bundes von Pennsylvanien, vom 17. bis 19. Juni, und des Fuenften Saengerfestes der Pennsylvanischen Saenger-Vereinigung, vom 19. bis 21. Juni, Reading, Pa., 1910* (Reading, Pa., [1910]), 33; Georg von Bosse, *Dr. C. J. Hexamer, Sein Leben und Wirken* (Philadelphia, 1922), 10–11; "Der Deutsch-Amerikanische National-Bund der Ver. Staaten von Amerika," in *Das Buch der Deutschen in Amerika,* ed. Max Heinrici (Philadelphia, 1909), 783; "Adolf Timm . . . ," in ibid., 807; *Philadelphia Sonntags-Journal,* 7 January 1900, p. 5; 24 June 1900, p. 8; Child, *German-Americans in Politics,* 4. On the origins of the alliance movement, see also John J. Appel, "Marion Dexter Learned and the German American Historical Society," *Pennsylvania Magazine of History and Biography* 86 (July 1962): 295.

3. "National-Bund," in *Buch der Deutschen,* ed. Heinrici, 784; Appel, "Marion Dexter Learned," 296; von Bosse, *C. J. Hexamer,* 11; Oswald Seidensticker and Max Heinrici, *Geschichte der Deutschen Gesellschaft von Pennsylvanien. 1764–1917,* 1. Teil, *Von der Gruendung im Jahre 1764 bis zur Jubelfeier der Republik 1876,* by Oswald Seidensticker; 2. Teil, *Von 1876 bis 1917,* by Max Heinrici (Philadelphia, 1917), 588, 581 (hereafter Seidensticker, *Deutsche Gesellschaft,* I; and Heinrici, *Deutsche Gesellschaft,* II); "Hans Weniger . . . ," in *Buch der Deutschen,* ed. Heinrici, 808–809; "Adolf Timm . . . ," in ibid., 807.

4. Appel, "Marion Dexter Learned," 296; "Dr. Hexamer's Vater, Ernst Hexamer," in *Buch der Deutschen,* ed. Heinrici, 802–803; von Bosse, *C. J. Hexamer,* 10–11.

5. "National-Bund," in *Buch der Deutschen,* ed. Heinrici, 781. The National Alliance's constitution, which repeats the Central Alliance's founding document almost word for word, is in "Principles of the National German American Alliance of the United States of America," *German American Annals,* n.s. 2 (September 1904): 582–584.

6. Child, *German-Americans in Politics,* 10, 14–16, 13; Frederick C. Luebke, *Bonds of Loyalty: German Americans and World War I* (DeKalb, Ill., 1974), 98–99.

7. *Protokoll der Fünften Konvention des Deutsch-Amerikanischen National-Bundes der Ver. Staaten von Amerika. Abgehalten vom 2. bis 6. Oktober 1909. In der Nord Cincinnati Turnhalle zu Cincinnati, Ohio* (N.p., [1909]), 4–5. For similar statements by Hexamer that used *Erhaltung* or the verb form *erhalten* (to preserve), see *Sonntags-Journal,* 6 October 1901, p. 1; *Protokoll der Dritten Konvention des Deutsch-Amerikanischen National-Bundes der Ver. Staaten von Amerika. Abgehalten vom 4. bis 7. Oktober 1905 im Deutschen Haus zu Indianapolis, Indiana* (N.p., [1905]), 2–3; *Protokoll der Vierten Konvention des Deutsch-Amerikanischen National-Bundes der Ver. Staaten von Amerika. Abgehalten vom 4. bis 7. Oktober 1907 im Terrace Garden zu New York, N.Y.* (N.p., [1907]), 3; *Protokoll des Sechsten Konvents des Deutschamerikanischen Nationalbundes der Ver. Staaten von Amerika. Abgehalten vom 6. bis 10. Oktober 1911 im Hotel New Willard zu Washington, District of Columbia* (N.p., [1911]), 9. See also the "Denkschrift" published by the National Alliance's executive committee, in *German American Annals,* n.s. 1 (September 1903): 503.

8. C. J. Hexamer, "Der erste 'Spatenstich' zum Bau des 'Deutschen Theaters' zu Philadelphia . . . ," *German American Annals,* n.s. 3 (June 1905): 203. Timm

likewise spoke of the need to forestall the "[f]urther crumbling-away of parts of German-Americandom"; Adolph Timm, "Der Nationalbund und die Deutsch Amerikaner," *German American Annals,* n.s. 1 (January 1903): 56.

9. Timm, "Der Nationalbund," 54.

10. "Vorwort," in *Buch der Deutschen,* ed. Heinrici, 4; H. M. Ferren, "Monolingualism the Bane of this Country," *German American Annals,* n.s. 1 (August 1903): 442; *Protokoll des DANB 1911,* 7; "Address of Dr. C. J. Hexamer. Laying of the Corner Stone of the German Theater, July 4, 1905," *German American Annals,* n.s. 3 (July 1905): 295; *Sonntags-Journal,* 6 October 1901, p. 1.

11. Kathleen Conzen, "German-Americans and the Invention of Ethnicity," in *America and the Germans: An Assessment of a Three-Hundred-Year History,* ed. Frank Trommler and Joseph McVeigh, vol. 1, *Immigration, Language, Ethnicity* (Philadelphia, 1985), 131–147.

12. *Protokoll des DANB 1907,* 6, 13.

13. Ibid., 6; *Protokoll des DANB 1911,* 9; *Protokoll des DANB 1907,* 6.

14. Child, *German-Americans in Politics,* 11n; "Address of Dr. C. J. Hexamer," 298–299. Luebke notes that for ethnic loyalists, the fight against prohibition amounted to a defense of "their life style and value system"; Luebke, *Bonds of Loyalty,* 99.

15. See, e.g., Adolph Timm, "Für persönliche Freiheit—gegen Prohibitions-Verschärfung," *German American Annals,* n.s. 1 (November 1903): 686.

16. "Denkschrift," 502–504; M. D. Learned, "German in the Public Schools," *German American Annals,* n.s. 11 (January–April 1913): 100–106; *Protokoll des DANB 1905,* 41–43.

17. *Protokoll der Zweiten Konvention des Deutsch-Amerikanischen National-Bundes der Ver. Staaten von Amerika, abgehalten vom 12. bis 15. September 1903, in der Halle des Turn-Vereins "Vorwärts," Baltimore, Md.* (N.p., [1903]), 22.

18. *Sonntags-Journal,* 6 October 1901, p. 1; "Principles of the National German American Alliance," 584.

19. *Protokoll des DANB 1907,* 146–150, 80. Hexamer cited Kern's words on history's role in retaining the next generation approvingly at the 1911 convention; *Protokoll des DANB 1911,* 5. For a similar statement by F. H. Harjes, the secretary of the German Society of Pennsylvania, see *Protokoll des DANB 1905,* 72–73.

20. "Principles of the National German American Alliance," 584; "National-Bund" in *Buch der Deutschen,* ed. Heinrici, 782; "The German American Historical Society," *Americana Germanica,* o.s. 4, no. 2 (1902): 207–208; Appel, "Marion Dexter Learned," 297, 299.

21. Appel, "Marion Dexter Learned," 300, 297. Learned had founded the journal in 1897 as *Americana Germanica;* it became the historical society's organ, and in 1903 changed its name to *German American Annals;* ibid., 299.

22. Ibid., 317n. Hexamer explicitly advocated using such national venues "to show the entire people what the Germans have accomplished in this country"; *Protokoll des DANB 1907,* 11.

23. "Der Deutsche Tag auf der Jamestowner Ausstellung," *Mitteilungen des Deutschen Pionier-Vereins von Philadelphia* 12 (1909): 1–11. The speech was

printed in English, as Hexamer gave it. For other examples of such English-language speeches by Hexamer, see "Address of Dr. C. J. Hexamer," 295–299; "German Achievements in America," *German American Annals,* n.s. 1 (January 1903): 46–53.

24. *Protokoll des DANB 1907,* 11.

25. *Protokoll des DANB 1911,* 187; *Sonntags-Journal,* 13 October 1901, p. 5; *Protokoll des DANB 1903,* 7–9; "Der Deutsche Tag," 6; *Protokoll des DANB 1911,* 2–3, 179; Heinrici, *Deutsche Gesellschaft,* II: 409–413.

26. "Kronik," *German American Annals,* n.s. 1 (April 1903): 235.

27. James M. Bergquist, "German Communities in American Cities: An Interpretation of the Nineteenth-Century Experience," *Journal of American Ethnic History* 4 (Fall 1984): 22n; G. Kellner, "Deutsch-Amerikanische Geschichts-Forschung und Dr. Oswald Seidensticker," in *130th Anniversary of the German Society Contributing for the Relief of Distressed Germans in the State of Pennsylvania, December 26, 1894* ([Philadelphia], [1894]), 73–88.

28. C. F. Huch, "Oswald Seidensticker," *Mitteilungen des Deutschen Pionier-Vereins von Philadelphia* 12 (1909): 18, 21–22; Kellner, "Dr. Oswald Seidensticker," 80, 86; C. F. Huch, "Der Deutsche Pionier-Verein von Philadelphia," *Mitteilungen des Deutschen Pionier-Vereins von Philadelphia* 10 (1909): 21.

29. C. F. Huch, "Die Entstehung des Deutschen Tages," *Mitteilungen des Deutschen Pionier-Vereins von Philadelphia* 7 (1908): 31; Lesley Ann Kawaguchi, "The Making of Philadelphia's German-America: Ethnic Group and Community Development, 1830–1883" (Ph.D. diss., University of California, Los Angeles, 1983), 309–312; C. F. Huch, "Das Zweihundertjährige Deutschamerikanische Pionier-Jubiläum," *Mitteilungen des Deutschen Pionier-Vereins von Philadelphia* 16 (1910): 1–18.

30. Oswald Seidensticker, *Die Erste Deutsche Einwanderung in Amerika und die Gründung von Germantown, im Jahre 1683. Festschrift zum deutsch-amerikanischen Pionier-Jubiläum am 6. October 1883* (Philadelphia, 1883); Samuel Whitaker Pennypacker, *The Settlement of Germantown, Pennsylvania, and the Beginning of German Emigration to North America* (Philadelphia, 1899); Marion Dexter Learned, *The Life of Francis Daniel Pastorius, the Founder of Germantown* (Philadelphia, 1908); Julius Friedrich Sachse, *The German Pietists of Provincial Pennsylvania: 1694–1708* (Philadelphia, 1895); Julius Friedrich Sachse, *Letters Relating to the Settlement of Germantown in Pennsylvania, 1683–4* (Philadelphia, 1903).

31. *Sonntags-Journal,* 13 October 1901, p. 5.

32. Ibid.; *Protokoll des DANB 1911,* 187.

33. *Sonntags-Journal,* 13 October 1901, p. 5; Heinrici, *Deutsche Gesellschaft,* II: 388; *Protokoll des DANB 1911,* 188. On Cronau's fund-raising difficulties, see ibid., 187–188; *Protokoll des DANB 1907,* 75; *Protokoll des DANB 1909,* 87–88.

34. *Protokoll des DANB 1907,* 72, 71.

35. Harry M. Tinkcom, Margaret B. Tinkcom, and Grant Miles Simon, *Historic Germantown: From the Founding to the Early Part of the Nineteenth Century; A Survey of the German Township* (Philadelphia, 1955), 3–6; Stephanie Grauman Wolf, *Urban Village: Population, Community, and Family Structure in*

Germantown, Pennsylvania, 1683–1800 (Princeton, N.J., 1976), 128. Pennypacker provides evidence that many in the 1683 party were from the Netherlands, without discussing the matter as such; Pennypacker, *Settlement of Germantown*, 16–19.

36. Harry M. Tinkcom, "The Revolutionary City, 1765–1783," in *Philadelphia: A 300-Year History*, ed. Russell F. Weigley (New York, 1982), 132–137; Edward W. Hocker, *Germantown, 1683–1933: The Record That a Pennsylvania Community Has Achieved in the Course of 250 Years; Being a History of the People of Germantown, Mount Airy, and Chestnut Hill* (Philadelphia, 1933), 269, 283.

37. Meeting of 9 October 1900, Board Minutes, SRS; Katherine Richardson Wireman, "A Sketch of the Germantown Historical Society," *Germantowne Crier* 1 (January 1949): 19. Quotations from the society's board minutes are reproduced courtesy of the Germantown Historical Society.

38. David R. Contosta, "Philadelphia's 'Miniature Williamsburg': The Colonial Revival and Germantown's Market Square," *Pennsylvania Magazine of History and Biography* 120 (October 1996): 283, 288–295; *Germantown Independent-Gazette*, 20 October 1905, p. 1; Contosta, "'Miniature Williamsburg,'" 289–290.

39. Contosta, "'Miniature Williamsburg,'" 289; Cornelius Weygandt, *On the Edge of Evening: The Autobiography of a Teacher and Writer Who Holds to the Old Ways* (New York, 1946), 58; Homer Tope Rosenberger, *The Pennsylvania Germans, 1891–1965* (Lancaster, Pa., 1966), 246–247. While the Keysers were an Amsterdam family, family tradition holds they had migrated several generations previously from Bavaria; "Descendants of Dirck Keyser, 1635–1714," *Dirck Keyser Newsletter* 1 (September 1988): 2; news clipping dated 1914, both in Keyser Family File, Biographical Files, GHS. See also *Independent-Gazette*, 19 January 1900, p. 5.

40. Rosenberger, *Pennsylvania Germans*, 246; news clipping dated 3 December 1908, JCS, vol. 7, 117.

41. Wireman, "Sketch," 19; "Charles Francis Jenkins, 1866–1951," *Germantowne Crier* 3 (September 1951): 6; Charles Francis Jenkins, "A Plea for the Preservation of Germantown's Historic Spots," in *Germantown History: Consisting of Papers Read Before the Site and Relic Society of Germantown* (Germantown, Philadelphia, 1915), 3 (in GHS).

42. Jenkins, "A Plea," 4. Jellett early called for a monument to honor Germantown's German founders; Edwin C. Jellett, "Germantown Neglectful of Her Rich Colonial Treasures," and "Germantown's Founders," *Independent-Gazette*, 30 January and 6 February 1903, in "Founders—Articles and Publications," box 1 "Germantown: Founders . . . ," PBC.

43. Jenkins, "A Plea," 3; President's Report, 24 October 1904, Board Minutes, SRS; *Independent-Gazette*, 27 October 1905, p. 1; "Historic Sights and Buildings in Germantown . . . ," undated news clipping, JCS, vol. 7, 51.

44. 25 October 1907, Board Minutes, SRS.

45. William W. Mátos, comp., *Official Historical Souvenir: Philadelphia: Its Founding and Development, 1683 to 1908 . . . Including the Complete Program of the Two Hundred and Twenty-fifth Anniversary Celebration of the Founding of the City Government, October Fourth to Tenth* (Philadelphia, 1908), 12, 17–31.

46. 28 February 1908, Board Minutes, SRS; meeting of 3 March 1908, "Meeting Minute book, 1906–1913," folder 103, box 8, BMAG-UA; news clipping, *Germantown Guide,* 28 March 1908, JCS, vol. 5, 129; 27 March 1908, Board Minutes, SRS.

47. *Independent-Gazette,* 26 June 1908, pp. 1, 4; 3 July 1908, p. 1; *Official Programme for Founders' Day in Germantown, Tuesday, October 6, 1908, 225th Anniversary of the First Permanent German Settlement in America by Francis Daniel Pastorius* ([Philadelphia], [1908]), JCS, vol. 7, 26. William H. Emhardt Jr. served as the secretary and Walter Williams as the treasurer of the Committee for the Celebration of Founders' Day; ibid. Jenkins and Emhardt were both officers of the Improvement Association; Emhardt and Williams belonged to the Business Men's Association. The Improvement Association's officers are listed in *Germanopolis: 225th Anniversary of the Settlement of Germantown by Francis Daniel Pastorius, the First Permanent German Settlement in America; Official Historical Souvenir Book of Germantown* (Philadelphia, 1908), unpaginated [43]. A 1907 Business Men's Association membership list is contained in the pamphlet, "Our Ladies' Night," "Germantown Businessmen's Association," Business Box 1, PBC.

48. *Official Programme for Founders' Day;* "J. F. Otterstetter," in *Buch der Deutschen,* ed. Heinrici, 924–926; "Founders' Day Plans," *Germantown News,* 30 April 1908, JCS, vol. 6, 27; *Independent-Gazette,* 24 July 1908, p. 1; 7 August 1908, p. 1.

49. *Independent-Gazette,* 24 July 1908, p. 1; 7 August 1908, p. 1; *Official Programme for Founders' Day; Germanopolis,* unpaginated [43, 45].

50. This description is based on *Independent-Gazette,* 9 October 1908, p. 1; "Founders' Day in Germantown," *Germantown Guide,* 10 October 1908, JCS, vol. 7, 42–44; *Official Programme for Founders' Day;* and "German Day of Founders' Week," *German American Annals,* n.s. 6 (November–December 1908): 341–342.

51. This description is drawn from "German Day of Founders' Week," 350, 352, 357; "Founders' Day in Germantown," 42–44; photographs of the monument appearing directly before the "Vorwort" in *Buch der Deutschen,* ed. Heinrici, unpaginated; and "Founder's Day Celebration Great Success," undated news clipping, JCS, vol. 7, 54.

52. Jane Campbell, "Chronicle of Germantown from January to October 1908," news clipping dated 5 November 1908, JCS, vol. 7, 67; *Official Historical Souvenir: Philadelphia,* 17.

53. *Independent-Gazette,* 9 October 1908, p. 8.

54. "Founders' Day in Germantown," 42–44; "Founder's Day Celebration Great Success," 7: 52–54; "Men and Things," [*Public Ledger,*] undated news clipping, JCS, vol. 7, 54.

55. *Independent-Gazette,* 25 September 1908, p. 4; meetings for 1908, Board Minutes, SRS; meetings for 1908, "Meeting Minute book, 1906–1913," folder 103, box 8, BMAG-UA; Jane Campbell, "Germantown Chronicle for October 1908," undated news clipping, JCS, vol. 7, 64.

56. This planning is reflected in the parade order published in the *Philadelphia Tageblatt,* which declared that the entire German Day celebration would occur "under the auspices of the National German-American Alliance"; *Tageblatt,* 4 October 1908, p. 2.

57. *Tageblatt,* 7 October 1908, p. 1; 5 October 1908, p. 4.

58. *Tageblatt,* 4 October 1908, p. 3; 6 October 1908, p. 4.

59. *Tageblatt,* 5 October 1908, pp. 2, 4.

60. *Tageblatt,* 24 February 1910, p. 3; "Adreß-Kalendar der Ver. Deutschen Gewerkschaften," in ibid., 4 March 1910, p. 5; Minna Werner, interview by author, 2 May 1995, Philadelphia.

61. Philip Scranton, *Figured Tapestry: Production, Markets, and Power in Philadelphia Textiles, 1885–1941* (Cambridge, 1989), 269–271; *Public Ledger,* 7 March 1910, p. 2; *Tageblatt,* 4 March 1910, p. 5.

62. *Tageblatt,* 5 March 1910, p. 4; 7 March 1910, p. 4; 9 March 1910, p. 4; 15 March 1910, p. 4.

63. Ken Fones-Wolf and Elliott Shore, "The German Press and Working-Class Politics in Gilded-Age Philadelphia," in *The German-American Radical Press: The Shaping of a Left Political Culture, 1850–1940,* ed. Elliott Shore, Ken Fones-Wolf, and James P. Danky (Urbana, Ill., 1992), 71–73; *Tageblatt,* 7 March 1910, pp. 2, 3; 6 March 1910, p. 2.

64. *Tageblatt,* 8 March 1910, p. 1. For other examples of the Kensington Labor Lyceum serving as a meeting place for non-German as well as German unions, see ibid., 7 March 1910, p. 2; 9 March 1910, p. 1; 18 March 1910, p. 5; *Public Ledger,* 10 March 1910, p. 3. For the Labor Lyceum, see *Public Ledger,* 10 March 1910, p. 1; Scranton, *Figured Tapestry,* 273.

65. Stefano Luconi, *From "Paesani" to White Ethnics: The Italian Experience in Philadelphia* (Albany, N.Y., 2001), 76; *Tageblatt,* 5 March 1910, p. 5; 8 March 1910, p. 1. On Italian and Russian niches in tailoring, see chapter 1.

66. *Tageblatt,* 8 March 1910, p. 1; 13 March 1910, p. 1; *Public Ledger,* 15 March 1910, p. 2. See also *Public Ledger,* 16 March 1910, p. 2. In late February, Local No. 6 had accepted an invitation to a ball given by Local No. 201; *Tageblatt,* 24 February 1910, p. 3.

67. *Tageblatt,* 28 March 1910, p. 4; 14 March 1910, p. 5; 4 March 1910, p. 5; *Public Ledger,* 7 March 1910, p. 2; *Tageblatt,* 26 March 1910, p. 4.

68. *Tageblatt,* 14 March 1910, p. 5; 28 March 1910, p. 4. The *Tageblatt* described the vote as an expulsion of the brewery workers; ibid., 14 March 1910, pp. 2, 5.

69. *Tageblatt,* 14 March 1910, p. 5. These were identified simply as local unions 1073 and 359. The former was a carpenters' union local; the latter may have been a unit of the Machine Hands Union; ibid., 9 March 1910, p. 8. Neither local appeared on the UGT's roster of affiliates, or "Adreß-Kalender," as it appeared in ibid., 4 March 1910, p. 5; 20 March 1910, p. 5.

70. *Tageblatt,* 27 July 1914, p. 3.

CHAPTER SEVEN
EUROPEAN WAR AND ETHNIC MOBILIZATION

1. *Public Ledger,* 4 August 1914, p. 12.

2. Clifton James Child, *The German-Americans in Politics, 1914–1917* (Madison, Wis., 1939), 42.

3. *Public Ledger,* 20 January 1916, p. 1.

4. *Public Ledger,* 1 August 1914, p. 5; William Bell Clark, "Philadelphia's War Chronology," in Philadelphia War History Committee, *Philadelphia in the World War, 1914–1919* (New York, 1922), 16; *Public Ledger,* 3 August 1914, p. 8; 5 August 1914, p. 7; 9 August 1914, sec. 1, p. 6; *Philadelphia Tageblatt,* 3 August 1914, p. 8.

5. *Public Ledger,* 3 August 1914, p. 6; *Evening Bulletin,* 3 August 1914, p. 10.

6. *Public Ledger,* 3 August 1914, p. 6; *Tageblatt,* 3 August 1914, p. 8; 18 August 1914, p. 8; War History Committee, *Philadelphia in the World War,* 570–571, 568.

7. George Wharton Pepper, *Philadelphia Lawyer: An Autobiography* (Philadelphia, 1944), 107.

8. Lloyd M. Abernethy, "Progressivism, 1905–1919," in *Philadelphia: A 300-Year History,* ed. Russell F. Weigley (New York, 1982), 557–558; *Public Ledger,* 9 August 1914, sec. 2, p. 6.

9. *Mitteilungen des Deutschamerikanischen Nationalbundes* 6 (September 1914): 1.

10. Child, *German-Americans in Politics,* 23–25, 24n; Frederick C. Luebke, *Bonds of Loyalty: German Americans and World War I* (DeKalb, Ill., 1974), 89.

11. *Mitteilungen* 6 (September 1914): 1; Child, *German-Americans in Politics,* 25.

12. *Public Ledger,* 6 August 1914, p. 8, 10 August 1914, p. 11; *Mitteilungen* 6 (September 1914): 25.

13. *Mitteilungen* 6 (September 1914): 25; *Tageblatt,* 18 August 1914, p. 3; *Evening Bulletin,* 21 August 1914, p. 8.

14. While only scattered issues of the city's middle-class German dailies survive from the 1910s, the *Public Ledger,* starting on August 9, reprinted translations of a number of editorials run by the middle-class *Morgen-Gazette.*

15. In *Public Ledger,* 9 August 1914, sec. 1, p. 6; and 10 August 1914, p. 5.

16. In *Public Ledger,* 12 August 1914, p. 5. On the *Morgen-Gazette*'s continuing tangles with English-language newspapers, see its editorials, reprinted in translation, in *Public Ledger,* 23 August 1914, sec. 1, p. 3; 27 August 1914, p. 5; 28 August 1914, p. 5.

17. James Weinstein, *The Decline of Socialism in America, 1912–1925* (New York, 1967), 119, 120.

18. The analysis here is that of Dieter Groh, *Negative Integration und revolutionärer Attentismus. Die deutsche Sozialdemokratie am Vorabend des Ersten Weltkrieges* (Frankfurt am Main, 1973), 660, 720–721, 723–726.

19. Luebke, *Bonds of Loyalty,* 101; *Tageblatt,* 10 August 1914, p. 5; see also *Tageblatt,* 2 August 1914, p. 8.

20. The newspaper editorialized on July 30, for example, that voting for the SP represented "the only reasonable political approach for the workers"; *Tageblatt,* 30 July 1914, p. 4.

21. *Tageblatt,* 3 August 1914, p. 7.

22. The SP's National Executive Committee denounced the war unequivocally in August 1914, and despite a vocal pro-Allied minority, most American socialists and almost all of the party's top leadership opposed the conflict; David A.

Shannon, *The Socialist Party of America: A History* (New York, 1955; reprint, Chicago, 1967), 82–85; Weinstein, *Decline of Socialism*, 120–133.

23. *Tageblatt*, 3 August 1914, p. 2; 4 August 1914, p. 4.

24. *Tageblatt*, 6 August 1914, p. 4.

25. *Tageblatt*, 14 August 1914, p. 4; 8 May 1915, p. 4; 11 May 1915, p. 4.

26. *Tageblatt*, 3 August 1914, p. 8; 4 August 1914, p. 8; 5 August 1914, p. 7; 10 August 1914, p. 8; 16 October 1916, p. 7.

27. *Tageblatt*, 10 August 1914, p. 8; Gordon A. Craig, *Germany, 1866–1945* (New York, 1978), 340.

28. *Tageblatt*, 18 August 1914, p. 5. Of the seven singing societies listed as the event's organizers, at least three were members of the city's middle-class federation of German choirs, the United Singers of Philadelphia, while at least one belonged to the United Workers' Singing Societies. See ibid.; the list of United Singers' member societies in *Official Souvenir Program, Twenty Third National Sängerfest of the Nord Oestliche Sängerbund of America, Philadelphia, June 29–July 4, 1912* ([Philadelphia], 1912), 101; and the list of United Workers' Singing Societies member groups in *Kalender [des] Philadelphia Tageblatt [für das Jahr] 1899* (Philadelphia, n.d.), 36.

29. *Mitteilungen* 6 (November 1914): 20.

30. Child, *German-Americans in Politics*, 43–50; *Mitteilungen* 7 (January 1915): 6–7; Shannon, *Socialist Party*, 88; Sally M. Miller, *Victor Berger and the Promise of Constructive Socialism, 1910–1920* (Westport, Conn., 1973), 119–121.

31. Clark, "War Chronology," 23; *Tageblatt*, 25 April 1916, p. 7.

32. *Public Ledger*, 30 April 1916, sec. 1, p. 5; 27 April 1916, p. 20; *Tageblatt*, 25 April 1916, pp. 1, 7; Oswald Seidensticker and Max Heinrici, *Geschichte der Deutschen Gesellschaft von Pennsylvanien. 1764–1917*, 1. Teil, *Von der Gruendung im Jahre 1764 bis zur Jubelfeier der Republik 1876*, by Oswald Seidensticker; 2. Teil, *Von 1876 bis 1917*, by Max Heinrici (Philadelphia, 1917), 456, 534 (hereafter Seidensticker, *Deutsche Gesellschaft*, I; and Heinrici, *Deutsche Gesellschaft*, II); *Tageblatt*, 23 April 1916, p. 17 (*Vereins-Reporter des Philadelphia Tageblatt*, p. 1).

33. *Public Ledger*, 30 April 1916, sec. 1, p. 5; *Tageblatt*, 30 April 1916, p. 7. For the *Tageblatt*'s extremely favorable coverage of the bazaar, see also *Tageblatt*, 24 April 1916, p. 7; 25 April 1916, pp. 1, 7; 26 April 1916, p. 7; 27 April 1916, p. 7.

34. *Tageblatt*, 25 April 1916, p. 1.

35. Ibid., pp. 1, 7.

36. Philip Gleason, *The Conservative Reformers: German-American Catholics and the Social Order* (Notre Dame, Ind., 1968), 154–158; Luebke, *Bonds of Loyalty*, 110.

37. *Tageblatt*, 27 April 1916, p. 7; 25 April 1916, p. 7; 30 April 1916, p. 7.

38. *Tageblatt*, 23 April 1916, p. 17 (*Vereins-Reporter des Philadelphia Tageblatt*, p. 1); *Public Ledger*, 26 April 1916, p. 3.

39. See, e.g., *Tageblatt*, 24 April 1916, p. 7.

40. *Tageblatt*, 18 August 1914, p. 5; *Public Ledger*, 28 April 1916, p. 8; *Tageblatt*, 23 April 1916, p. 17 (*Vereins-Reporter des Philadelphia Tageblatt*, p. 1).

41. *Tageblatt,* 25 April 1916, pp. 1, 7. The number of booths in the charge of women was calculated from the list of booths in *Tageblatt,* 25 April 1916, p. 7; and from descriptions of individual booths in ibid., 30 April 1916, p. 7.

42. *Public Ledger,* 5 August 1914, p. 7; *Mitteilungen* 7 (June 1915): 4; *Mitteilungen* 7 (May 1915): 5.

43. On Blankenburg's preparedness stance, see *Public Ledger,* 19 September 1915, sec. 1, p. 5; Lucretia L. Blankenburg, *The Blankenburgs of Philadelphia: By One of Them* (Philadelphia, 1928), 191.

44. Luebke, *Bonds of Loyalty,* 118–125; Child, *German-Americans in Politics,* 43–64; John M. Murrin, Paul E. Johnson, James M. McPherson, Gary Gerstle, Emily S. Rosenberg, and Norman L. Rosenberg, *Liberty, Equality, Power: A History of the American People* (Fort Worth, Tex., 1996), 725; Child, *German-Americans in Politics,* 89–90; Luebke, *Bonds of Loyalty,* 142–147, 160–169, 183–185.

45. *Mitteilungen* 7 (February 1915): 11–12, 25; Child, *German-Americans in Politics,* 52.

46. Child, *German-Americans in Politics,* 121–122, 124–126; Luebke, *Bonds of Loyalty,* 167.

47. Child, *German-Americans in Politics,* 6, 6n; *Tageblatt,* 21 August 1914, p. 3. The quotation from the resolutions is a translation from the *Tageblatt*'s German version.

48. Luebke, *Bonds of Loyalty,* 69–77; Robert L. Pitfield to the editor, *Public Ledger,* 13 August 1914, p. 12. See also Louis Edward Levy to the editor, *Public Ledger,* 12 August 1914, p. 12.

49. *Public Ledger,* 8 August 1914, p. 7. See also the editorial comments on the war's nature in ibid., 1 August 1914, p. 12; 9 August 1914, sec. 2, p. 6. The first *Morgen-Gazette* editorial ran in ibid., 9 August 1914, sec. 1, p. 6; for further examples, see notes 15 and 16.

50. *Public Ledger,* 7 August 1914, p. 14.

51. *Public Ledger,* 25 August 1914, p. 12; 30 August 1914, sec. 1, p. 10.

52. *Public Ledger,* 24 August 1914, p. 12; *Evening Bulletin,* 19 August 1914, p. 6.

53. J. Bancroft to the editor, *Public Ledger,* 28 August 1914, p. 12. See also W. C. Hall to the editor, *Public Ledger,* 13 August 1914, p. 12; A Native American of British Stock to the editor, *Public Ledger,* 27 August 1914, p. 12.

54. Luebke, *Bonds of Loyalty,* 122; Child, *German-Americans in Politics,* 52–54.

55. John Higham, *Strangers in the Land: Patterns of American Nativism, 1860–1925,* 2d rev. ed. (New York, 1981), 197; Luebke, *Bonds of Loyalty,* 122–123.

56. Clark, "War Chronology," 19; Arthur S. Link and William B. Catton, *American Epoch: A History of the United States since 1900,* vol. 1, *The Progressive Era and the First World War, 1900–1920,* 4th ed. (New York, 1973), 162, 164–165; Murrin et al., *Liberty, Equality, Power,* 725.

57. Higham, *Strangers in the Land,* 197. A review of sabotage allegations concludes that two massive explosions of stored munitions in New Jersey in 1916 and early 1917 were undoubtedly linked to agents of the Central Powers and that a

1915 blast at the Philadelphia Benzol Plant may have involved foul play as well; Philip Jenkins, "'Spy Mad'? Investigating Subversion in Pennsylvania, 1917–1918," *Pennsylvania History* 63 (Spring 1996): 212.

58. Luebke, *Bonds of Loyalty*, 91, 128, 139; *Mitteilungen* 6 (June 1915): 21.

59. *Public Ledger*, 8 May 1915, p. 12; 10 May 1915, pp. 6, 14; C. Pemberton Jr. to the editor, ibid., p. 14.

60. Higham, *Strangers in the Land*, 198, 199. The *Literary Digest* came up with the "Swat-the-Hyphen" moniker in October 1915; Child, *German-Americans in Politics*, 85n.

61. Wilson in *Public Ledger*, 11 May 1915, p. 2; cited in Luebke, *Bonds of Loyalty*, 142; ibid., 144.

62. Luebke, *Bonds of Loyalty*, 145–146; Child, *German-Americans in Politics*, 87–88; Higham, *Strangers in the Land*, 198.

63. Child, *German-Americans in Politics*, 88; *Public Ledger*, 21 December 1915, p. 2. For other examples of antihyphen sentiment in *Ledger* editorials, see *Public Ledger*, 13 December 1915, p. 14; 16 December 1915, p. 14; 19 December 1915, sec. 3, p. 4.

64. Higham, *Strangers in the Land*, 236–237, 240–241. On patriotic education aimed at immigrant children, see Cecilia Elizabeth O'Leary, *To Die For: The Paradox of American Patriotism* (Princeton, N.J., 1999), chap. 10.

65. Higham, *Strangers in the Land*, 242–243; Edward George Hartmann, *The Movement to Americanize the Immigrant* (New York, 1948), 111–112, 125–128, 134; Roosevelt in *Public Ledger*, 21 January 1916, p. 10.

66. Higham, *Strangers in the Land*, 199; Roosevelt in *Public Ledger*, 21 January 1916, p. 10.

67. *Public Ledger*, 20 December 1915, p. 13; 19 January 1916, p. 13. Edward T. Stotesbury headed Drexel & Company, "the leading investment banking house" in Philadelphia; see E. Digby Baltzell, *Philadelphia Gentlemen: The Making of a National Upper Class* (Glencoe, Ill., 1958; reprint, Chicago, 1971), 38, 91, 126–127; J. St. George Joyce, ed., *Story of Philadelphia* (N.p., 1919), 371.

68. Higham, *Strangers in the Land*, 199, 208; David M. Kennedy, *Over Here: The First World War and American Society* (Oxford, 1980), 31; *Evening Bulletin*, 23 July 1915, p. 2.

69. *Public Ledger*, 20 September 1915, p. 3; War History Committee, *Philadelphia in the World War*, 81; Clark, "War Chronology," 21; *Public Ledger*, 15 December 1915, pp. 1, 5. On Biddle, see Baltzell, *Philadelphia Gentlemen*, 253.

70. Luebke, *Bonds of Loyalty*, 121 (quotation). Luebke and Child make similar assessments of the deficiencies of the National Alliance's political style; ibid., 121–124; Child, *German-Americans in Politics*, 174–176.

71. *Mitteilungen* 7 (June 1915): 19. In the original: "Er [Hexamer] . . . erklärte, er würde, wenn er an [Secretary of State William Jennings] Bryans Stelle wäre, in zwei Wochen England auf die Knie zwingen."

72. Senate Committee on the Judiciary, *National German-American Alliance: Hearings before the Subcommittee of the Committee on the Judiciary . . . on S. 3529, a Bill to Repeal the Act Entitled "An Act to Incorporate the National German-American Alliance," Approved February 25, 1907*, 65th Cong., 2d sess.,

23 February–13 April 1918 (Washington, D.C., 1918), 25–27; cited, in part, in Luebke, *Bonds of Loyalty*, 100.

73. Luebke, *Bonds of Loyalty*, 100; Gustavus Ohlinger, *Their True Faith and Allegiance*, with a foreword by Owen Wister (New York, 1916), 67–70; Clark, "War Chronology," 21; Owen Wister, foreword to *Their True Faith and Allegiance*, by Ohlinger, xvi–xvii (quotation), and passim. On the book's influence, see Frank Trommler, "Inventing the Enemy: German-American Cultural Relations, 1900–1917," in *Confrontation and Cooperation: Germany and the United States in the Era of World War I, 1900–1924*, ed. Hans Jürgen Schröder (Providence, R.I., and Oxford, 1993), 111.

74. O'Leary, *To Die For*, 220.

75. *Public Ledger*, 27 April 1916, p. 4; 26 April 1916, p. 3; 25 April 1916, p. 3.

76. Heinrici, *Deutsche Gesellschaft*, II: 463, 451–452; Blankenburg, *Blankenburgs of Philadelphia*, 190–191 (quotation, my emphasis); Trommler, "Inventing the Enemy," 111.

77. Trommler, "Inventing the Enemy," 117–118.

78. Ohlinger, *Their True Faith and Allegiance*, 28–29, 41–43, 66, 121.

79. Ibid., 119–120.

80. *Public Ledger*, 30 April 1916, sec. 2, p. 4; Wister, foreword to *Their True Faith and Allegiance*, by Ohlinger, xxix.

CHAPTER EIGHT
INTERVENTION, THE ANTI-GERMAN PANIC, AND THE FALL
OF PUBLIC GERMANNESS

1. Report of W. S. Carman, "Re: Louis Schneider and Wife (Pro-German Matter)," 31 May 1918, "No. 3432—German Notes (1), Restricted Reps, 118-39-1" (hereafter folder 3432-1), box 39, PCF.

2. Frederick C. Luebke, *Bonds of Loyalty: German Americans and World War I* (DeKalb, Ill., 1974), 190–191, 199–201; Clifton James Child, *The German-Americans in Politics, 1914–1917* (Madison, Wis., 1939), 158.

3. William Bell Clark, "Philadelphia's War Chronology," in Philadelphia War History Committee, *Philadelphia in the World War, 1914–1919* (New York, 1922), 27; Casimir A. Sienkiewicz, "Foreign Language Division, Liberty Loan Committee," in War History Committee, *Philadelphia in the World War*, 488; *Public Ledger*, 4 April 1917, p. 5.

4. *Philadelphia Demokrat* and *Philadelphia Tageblatt* editorials cited in *Public Ledger*, 4 April 1917, p. 5; ibid.; James Weinstein, *The Decline of Socialism in America, 1912–1925* (New York, 1967), 125–127, 140.

5. Robert Morris to Francis Fisher Kane (hereafter FFK), 26 March 1917, "7, Exhibit Material," box 38, PCF; Clark, "War Chronology," 29; *Germantown Independent-Gazette*, 19 April 1917, p. 6.

6. Luebke, *Bonds of Loyalty*, 208; *Independent-Gazette*, 5 April 1917, p. 6; 19 April 1917, p. 1.

7. Luebke, *Bonds of Loyalty*, 234. On "100 Per Cent Americanism," see John

Higham, *Strangers in the Land: Patterns of American Nativism, 1860–1925*, 2d rev. ed. (New York, 1981), 204–212.

8. David M. Kennedy, *Over Here: The First World War and American Society* (Oxford, 1980), 14, 46 (quotation), 59, 61–62; Luebke, *Bonds of Loyalty*, 207, 212–213.

9. Jacob Warner Rhine, "Four-Minute Men," in War History Committee, *Philadelphia in the World War*, 492, 494; War History Committee, *Philadelphia in the World War*, 644; Logan M. Bullitt Jr., "Financing the War by the Liberty Loans," in ibid., 481; J. St. George Joyce, ed. *Story of Philadelphia* (N.p., 1919), 336.

10. Kennedy, *Over Here*, 61–62. The "Halt the Hun!" poster, printed for the Third Liberty Loan, is reproduced in Luebke, *Bonds of Loyalty*, 272. A photograph shows it on display at the West Philadelphia Station of the Pennsylvania Rail Road; War History Committee, *Philadelphia in the World War*, 496.

11. Luebke, *Bonds of Loyalty*, 208–209, 220; Paul L. Murphy, *World War I and the Origin of Civil Liberties in the United States* (New York, 1979), 79.

12. Murphy, *Origin of Civil Liberties*, 73–74, 79–84; Kennedy, *Over Here*, 80.

13. Murphy, *Origin of Civil Liberties*, 92–93; Kennedy, *Over Here*, 81, 82.

14. Philip Jenkins, "'Spy Mad'? Investigating Subversion in Pennsylvania, 1917–1918," *Pennsylvania History* 63 (Spring 1996): 216; Report of L. L. Ford, "Franz Meisel (Seditious and Pro-German Remarks)," 31 May 1918, folder 3432–1, box 39, PCF.

15. Kennedy, *Over Here*, 82; Higham, *Strangers in the Land*, 204–205, 208, 247; Murphy, *Origin of Civil Liberties*, 124; Luebke, *Bonds of Loyalty*, 215, 251, 216.

16. Luebke, *Bonds of Loyalty*, 235–237, 244, 247–248, 252–253, 279. On Prager's murder, see ibid., 3–24.

17. Luebke notes that anti-German violence was most common in Midwestern states; ibid., 279.

18. Ibid., 247; Edward W. Hocker, *Germantown, 1683–1933: The Record That a Pennsylvania Community Has Achieved in the Course of 250 Years; Being a History of the People of Germantown, Mount Airy, and Chestnut Hill* (Philadelphia, 1933), 299.

19. Jenkins, "'Spy Mad,'" 212; Joyce, ed., *Story of Philadelphia*, 325–326; *Public Ledger*, 1 September 1917, p. 20.

20. *North American*, 23 July 1917, news clipping in "2009, U.S. v. Werner [4]" (hereafter folder 4), box 7, PCF.

21. *Public Ledger*, 16 September 1917, p. 6.

22. Carl Wittke, *German-Americans and the World War (with Special Emphasis on Ohio's German-Language Press)* (Columbus, Ohio, 1936), 185; cited in Lloyd M. Abernethy, "Progressivism, 1905–1919," in *Philadelphia: A 300-Year History*, ed. Russell F. Weigley (New York, 1982), 560.

23. *Philadelphia Inquirer*, 14 May 1918, p. 10; 15 May 1918, pp. 1, 4, 10. The petition was brought by twenty-four groups—some of them separate chapters of the same patriotic order—and two individuals; see ibid., p. 4.

24. *Independent-Gazette*, 11 April 1918, p. 6; 26 December 1918, p. 1; Abernethy, "Progressivism," 560; *Inquirer*, 12 May 1918, p. 1.

25. The term is used by Murphy, *Origin of Civil Liberties,* 71.

26. War History Committee, *Philadelphia in the World War,* 192–194, 315–316, 426; Chief, Military Intelligence Section to J. W. Rawls, 21 December 1917, "J. G. Brill Co., Philadelphia, Pa.," box 6 "BO-BU," PPS.

27. See, e.g., Aide for Information, 4th Naval District, to FFK, 4 April 1918; Frank L. Garbarino (hereafter FLG) to FFK, 13 April 1918; and Aide for Information, 4th Naval District, to FFK, 13 April 1918; all in "6, #1752, Correspondence, 2/20/18–7/22/18, Letters from . . . [to] 7/24/18" (hereafter folder 6), box 38, PCF.

28. War History Committee, *Philadelphia in the World War,* 343–346; Jenkins, "'Spy Mad,'" 216–217.

29. Higham, *Strangers in the Land,* 210; Telegram, [U.S. Attorney General Thomas] Gregory to FFK, 18 September 1918, "118–39–3, Exhibit Materials, Socialist Activities," box 39, PCF; FFK to Attorney General, 10 April 1917, folder 5, box 38, PCF.

30. See, e.g., Report of Claude Shipe, "In Re: Frank Domeraski—#227 Fitzwater Street (Alleged German Alien enemy)," 19 November 1918, "No. 3432, Miscellaneous Reports—Restricted (2), 118–39–1, 1918" (hereafter folder 3432–2), box 39, PCF; and FFK to Attorney General, 19 September 1918, folder 6, box 38, PCF.

31. Higham, *Strangers in the Land,* 210; Luebke, *Bonds of Loyalty,* 255–256; Clark, "War Chronology," 35; Telegram, Gregory to FFK, 7 July 1917, and FFK to U.S. Commissioner of Immigration, 10 August 1917, "F4, Letters 'Rat,' July 5, 1917–Feb. 20, 19[1]8" (hereafter folder 4), box 38, PCF.

32. Child, *German-Americans in Politics,* 162–163, 166, 169, 171; Senate Committee on the Judiciary, *National German-American Alliance: Hearings before the Subcommittee of the Committee on the Judiciary . . . on S. 3529, a Bill to Repeal the Act Entitled "An Act to Incorporate the National German-American Alliance," Approved February 25, 1907,* 65th Cong., 2d sess., 23 February–13 April 1918 (Washington, D.C., 1918), 8–94, 11, 41, 52, 405.

33. Child, *German-Americans in Politics,* 171; Senate Judiciary Committee, *National German-American Alliance Hearings,* 405.

34. Child, *German-Americans in Politics,* 173; Georg von Bosse, *Dr. C. J. Hexamer: Sein Leben und Wirken* (Philadelphia, 1922), 113.

35. Child, *German-Americans in Politics,* 168; von Bosse, *Hexamer,* 111–112, 110, 13; Oswald Seidensticker and Max Heinrici, *Geschichte der Deutschen Gesellschaft von Pennsylvanien. 1764–1917,* 1. Teil, *Von der Gruendung im Jahre 1764 bis zur Jubelfeier der Republik 1876,* by Oswald Seidensticker; 2. Teil, *Von 1876 bis 1917,* by Max Heinrici (Philadelphia, 1917), 535 (hereafter Seidensticker, *Deutsche Gesellschaft,* I: and Heinrici, *Deutsche Gesellschaft,* II).

36. Report of J. F. McDevitt, "German American Alliance," 10 June 1918; and Report of J. F. McDevitt, "German-American Alliance (See previous report)," 10 June 1918, both in folder 3432–1, box 39, PCF; Senate Judiciary Committee, *National German-American Alliance Hearings,* 398.

37. Report of J. F. McDevitt, "German American Alliance," 10 June 1918; and Report of J. F. McDevitt, "German-American Alliance (See previous report)," 10 June 1918; FFK to Edward S. Buckley, 24 April 1918, folder 6, box 38, PCF. For

titles of German Society officials named in McDevitt's reports, see *153. Jahres-bericht der Deutschen Gesellschaft von Pennsylvanien für das Jahr 1917* (Phila-delphia, 1918).

38. Report of W. S. Carman, 21 May 1918, "Re: Gustav Peterson, alias Henry P. Schneider (Alleged former sailor from 'Prince Idel Frederick')," folder 3432–1, box 39, PCF; Frank Schmidt to Todd Daniel, June 1918, folder 6, box 38, PCF.

39. Report of W. H. Furrow, "Violations of Conscription Act, Section 12—Re: Inspection of German Clubs," 20 June 1918, folder 3432–2, box 39, PCF; S. McCauley Jr. to Colonel Van Deman, 18 December 1917, "Austrian Soc in Phila," box 2 "At-BA," PPS.

40. Documentation on these fifty-five cases is contained in boxes 38 and 39, PCF.

41. The Philadelphia police, for example, arrested a German named John Burg on August 31, 1917, for "denouncing the President, the war and American poli-cies generally" in German outside of City Hall. While the *Public Ledger* reported that Burg "was closely questioned by James J. McDevitt of the Department of Jus-tice," no record of Burg's case appears in Kane's files; *Public Ledger,* 1 September 1917, p. 3.

42. The Plant Protection Section's cases are scattered through the surviving Cor-respondence of the Philadelphia District Office, with some filed by name of sub-ject and others by the name of the plant where a given subject worked; PPS.

43. An American to FFK, 15 July 1918, folder 6, box 38, PCF; Report of De-tective Walter, "Carl Gebhart Bumcke, 4749 Penn Street—German Matter," 19 June 1918, folder 3432–1, box 39, PCF.

44. Report of Edward C. Burgess, "Barker, 2123 S. 64th Str. (Correct, Carl Bacher)," 17 May 1918, "Barker, Phila, Pa, Pa P B," box 3 "BA-BE," PPS.

45. Unsigned letter to FFK, received 12 March 1918; and FFK to FLG, 12 March 1918, folder 6, box 38, PCF.

46. Unsigned letter to FFK, 26 July 1918, and FFK to Todd Daniel, 27 July 1918, folder 6, box 38, PCF.

47. Form no. 2, undated, "American Asbestos Co., Norristown, Pa.," box 1 "AB-AN," PPS. The Plant Protection Section's no. 2 form required manufactur-ing companies with government contracts to provide a wealth of information to Military Intelligence, including steps taken to check on national loyalty and an ethnic breakdown of the workforce.

48. See, for example, Form no. 2, received 10 May 1918, "Electro Dental Mfg. Co., Philadelphia, 3/12/19"; Form no. 2, received 15 May 1918, "Emerson En-gineering Co., Philadelphia, Pa."; Form no. 2, received 13 May 1918, "Electric Tachometer Co."; all in box 12 "DY-FE," PPS.

49. Third Liberty Loan Committee pledge slips; Michael Banut to FFK, 18 April 1918; and FFK to Michael Banut, 20 April 1918; all in folder 6, box 38, PCF.

50. FFK to William F. Clark Jr., 1 October 1918, folder 6, box 38, PCF; Report of H. Ballenger, "N. Erbert 3108 N 25th St," 26 June [1918], "Erbert, N.," box 12 "DY-FE," PPS.

51. Report of W. S. Carman, "Re: Gottfred Wurz & George Wimmer (German Matter)," 8 October 1918, folder 3432–1, box 39, PCF; Form no. 2, received 10 May 1918, "Electro Dental Mfg. Co., Philadelphia, 3/12/19," box 12 "DY-FE," PPS.

52. War History Committee, *Philadelphia in the World War,* 428–429; Officer in Charge, Branch Naval Intelligence Office, Philadelphia, to Director of Naval Intelligence, Washington, 1 August 1918, "E. G. Budd Mfg. Co.," box 7 "BU-CA," PPS.

53. Report of H. N. Deats, "E. G. Budd Mfg. Co., Phila, Pa.: Defective Bombs," 9 July 1918, "E. G. Budd Mfg. Co.," box 7 "BU-CA," PPS.

54. Ibid.; Report of H. Ballenger, "Seditious Utterances—E. G. Budd Mfg. Company," 8 April 1918, "E. G. Budd Mfg. Co.," box 7: "BU-CA," PPS.

55. Report of W. J. Bourke, "Re—Mrs. Caroline Ring, 3221 Hurley Street (Alleged pro-German)," 11 December 1918, folder 3432–1, box 39, PCF; undated news clipping, received 30 August 1918, folder: "Chester, Pa.," box 8, PPS.

56. Clara Patton to FFK, 18 April 1918; and FFK to FLG, 19 April 1918, both in folder 6, box 38, PCF. See also Report of F. L. 14-4, "Mr. Marcus Lamb, and Wife, 903 W. Susquehanna Avenue," 11 November 1918, folder 3432–1, box 39, PCF.

57. Murphy, *Origin of Civil Liberties,* 236. These six cases were *Schaefer et al. v. United States* (the *Tageblatt* case), *Schenck v. United States, Frohwerk v. United States, Debs v. United States, Abrams et al. v. United States,* and *Pierce et al. v. United States;* Richard Polenberg, *Fighting Faiths: The Abrams Case, the Supreme Court, and Free Speech* (New York, 1987), 368. On the cases' significance, see ibid., chaps. 6–7 and epilogue.

58. "Hangen und Bangen," *Tageblatt,* 10 May 1917, reproduced in *United States v. Werner and Darkow, Indictment: Treason; Adhering to Enemy, Giving Aid and Comfort* (E.D. Pa, 1917), 16–17 (exhibit H). This indictment is referred to hereafter as *U.S. v. Werner,* Treason Indictment; a copy of it is located in "2009, U.S. v. Werner, et al. [5]" (hereafter folder 5), box 7, PCF.

59. "Washington am Berge," *Tageblatt,* 6 June 1917, in *U.S. v. Werner,* Treason Indictment, 22–23 (exhibit K); "Ein glänzender Erfolg deutscher Truppen," *Tageblatt,* 9 May 1917, in ibid., 14–15 (exhibit F); "Hat ihm schon," *Tageblatt,* 7 July 1917, in ibid., 46–47 (exhibit X). On the newspaper's disdain for the Allies, see *Tageblatt,* 22 June 1917, in ibid., 36–37 (exhibit P).

60. *North American,* 26 July 1917, p. 1; 30 July 1917; and 20 August 1917, news clippings in folder 4, box 7, PCF.

61. Ed J. Nocton to FFK, 25 August 1917; and FFK to Ed J. Nocton, 27 August 1917; both in folder 8, box 8, PCF. See also Lewis Lawrence Smith to FFK, 1 August 1917, in ibid.

62. FFK to Daniel Holsman, 18 July 1917, folder 4, box 38, PCF; FFK to Attorney General, 27 August 1917, folder 8, box 8, PCF. See also FFK to Lewis Lawrence Smith, 2 August 1917, folder 8, box 8, PCF.

63. FFK to Attorney General, 27 August 1917; and Samuel Rosenbaum to FFK, 29 August 1917; both in folder 8, box 8, PCF.

64. *Public Ledger,* 11 September 1917, p. 1; 15 September 1917, p. 1. A copy of the search warrant can be found in "2009 U.S. v. Werner, et al. [6]" (hereafter folder 6), box 8, PCF.

65. *United States v. Werner and Darkow. True Bill . . . Indictment: Making and Conveying False Reports, etc., to Promote the Success of the Enemies of the United States* (E.D. Pa. 1917), 9, 1–2, 8. A copy of this September 15 indictment is located in folder 5, box 7, PCF. The second, and superseding, Espionage Act in-

dictment was handed up on December 6, 1917; *United States v. Schaefer et al., Indictment: Making and Conveying False Reports to Promote Success of Enemy, etc. . . . ,* (E.D. Pa. 1917). This second indictment is referred to hereafter as *U.S. v. Schaefer,* Espionage Act Indictment; a copy is located in box 8, PCF.

66. FFK to Attorney General, 17 September 1917, folder 7, box 8, PCF.

67. FFK to Attorney General, 4 October 1917, folder 7; FFK to Attorney General, 27 March 1918, folder 8; *Inquirer,* 27 March 1918, news clipping in folder 6; all in box 8, PCF. A transcript of the treason trial is located in box 9, PCF.

68. Owen J. Roberts to Hon. Thomas W. Gregory, Attorney General of the United States, 28 September 1918, folder 1, box 7, PCF; *Inquirer,* 28 September 1918, p. 1; FFK to Attorney General, 19 December 1918, folder 1, box 7, PCF. For the specific counts charged against the defendants at this trial, see *U.S. v. Schaefer,* Espionage Act Indictment. A transcript of the trial is located in box 9, PCF.

69. *Schaefer v. United States,* 251 U.S. 482, 466, 474 (1920); Polenberg, *Fighting Faiths,* 213, 207; *Schaefer v. U.S.,* 483, 494–495.

70. William A. Gray to Hon. A. Mitchell Palmer, Attorney General, 7 April 1920; FFK to Hon. Charles D. McAvoy, United States Attorney, 15 April 1920; Telegram, [Attorney General] Palmer to [U.S. Attorney] McAvoy, 11 June 1920; all in folder 1, box 7, PCF.

71. *Public Ledger,* 12 September 1917, p. 3; 13 September 1917, p. 3; W. H. Lamar to FFK, 12 October 1917, folder 7, box 8, PCF. Werner stated that the revocation made circulating the newspaper outside the city "nearly impossible," so that "hundreds of its earlier subscribers in the country" could not receive it; see letter of L. Werner dated 26 February 1919, in *Tageblatt,* undated news clipping, in folder 6, box 8, PCF.

72. Murphy, *Origin of Civil Liberties,* 80–81; FFK to Attorney General, 23 May 1918, folder 2, box 7, PCF; FFK to Owen J. Roberts, 13 May 1918, folder 8, box 8, PCF.

73. Letter of L. Werner dated 26 February 1919, in *Tageblatt,* undated news clipping.

74. John P. Nicholson to FFK, 6 April 1918; FFK to John P. Nicholson, 9 April 1918; and FFK to John P. Nicholson, 17 May 1918; all in folder 6, box 38, PCF; Georg von Bosse, *Ein Kampf um Glauben und Volkstum: Das Streben während meines 25jährigen Amtslebens als deutsch-lutherischer Geistlicher in Amerika* (Stuttgart, 1920), 251.

75. *Inquirer,* 2 July 1918, p. 5; 5 July 1918, p. 1; *Tageblatt,* 27 June 1918, p. 8; 30 June 1918, p. 17 (*Vereins-Reporter des Philadelphia Tageblatt,* p. 1); 1 July 1918, p. 2.

76. *Tageblatt,* 30 June 1918, p. 17 (*Vereins-Reporter des Philadelphia Tageblatt,* p. 1); 1 July 1918, p. 2.

77. *Tageblatt,* 28 June 1918, p. 5; 30 June 1918, p. 17 (*Vereins-Reporter des Philadelphia Tageblatt,* p. 1).

78. Heinrici, *Deutsche Gesellschaft,* II: 399–404; *153. Jahresbericht der Deutschen Gesellschaft 1917,* 9, 21; *154. Jahresbericht der Deutschen Gesellschaft von Pennsylvanien für das Jahr 1918* (Philadelphia, 1919), 9.

79. *Cannstatter Volksfest-Verein, Philadelphia: Geschichte des Vereins von der Gründung in 1873 bis zum Goldenen Jubiläum im September 1923* (Philadelphia,

[1923]), 29–33; Richard F. Hamm, *Shaping the Eighteenth Amendment: Temperance Reform, Legal Culture, and the Polity, 1880–1920* (Chapel Hill, N.C., 1995), 240, 247, 251.

80. Minna Werner, interview by author, 2 May 1995, Philadelphia; Karl J. R. Arndt and May E. Olson, *The German Language Press of the Americas,* vol. 1, *History and Bibliography 1732–1968: United States of America,* 3d ed. (Munich, 1976), 553, 548–579; Gustav Mayer to FFK, 11 March 1919, folder 1, box 7, PCF. Werner in his February 1919 letter to the *Tageblatt* noted that it was "now the only exclusively German newspaper of this city"; letter of L. Werner dated 26 February 1919, *Tageblatt,* undated news clipping.

81. Esther Schuchard Browne, interview by author, 11 June 1996, Philadelphia; Report of W. S. Carman, "Re: August Henry Stone (German Matter)," 27 May 1918, folder 3432-1, box 39, PCF; Luebke, *Bonds of Loyalty,* 282.

82. Cecilia Elizabeth O'Leary, *To Die For: The Paradox of American Patriotism* (Princeton, N.J., 1999), 221; *Inquirer,* 2 July 1918, p. 5.

83. O'Leary, *To Die For,* 221, 242; Higham, *Strangers in the Land,* 218–222. See also William Preston Jr., *Aliens and Dissenters: Federal Suppression of Radicals, 1903–1933,* 2d ed. (Urbana, Ill., 1994).

84. Von Bosse, *Glauben und Volkstum,* 259.

CHAPTER NINE
AN ETHNICITY SUBDUED

1. Edward W. Hocker, *Germantown, 1683–1933: The Record That a Pennsylvania Community Has Achieved in the Course of 250 Years; Being a History of the People of Germantown, Mount Airy, and Chestnut Hill* (Philadelphia, 1933), 301; *Germantown Independent-Gazette,* 24 June 1920, p. 1; 1 May 1919, p. 1. See also ibid., 4 November 1920, p. 1.

2. *Independent-Gazette,* 13 September 1919, unpaginated news clipping, JCS, vol. 39, 95; Geo. Calvin Klein, Recording Secretary [Washington Council, No. 1, Jr. O.U.A.M.] to Honorable N. S. Baker, Secretary of War, 5 July 1919, letter located loose in "Secret Societies," box 1, PBC (quotation reproduced courtesy of the Germantown Historical Society).

3. *Independent-Gazette,* 28 October 1920, p. 1; Hocker, *Germantown,* 300–301; *Independent-Gazette,* 11 November 1920, p. 1.

4. *Independent-Gazette,* 11 November 1920, p. 1.

5. *Independent-Gazette,* 4 November 1920, p. 6.

6. *Lutherischer Herold,* 27 June 1929, p. 14. *Lutherischer Herold* citations are to holdings at LTSP.

7. Caroline Golab, *Immigrant Destinations* (Philadelphia, 1977), 168–169 (app. A); U.S. Department of Commerce, Bureau of the Census, *Fifteenth Census of the United States, 1930: Population,* vol. 3, part 2, *Montana–Wyoming* (Washington, D.C., 1932), 702; U.S. Department of Commerce, Bureau of the Census, *Sixteenth Census of the United States, 1940: Population and Housing: Statistics for Census Tracts, Philadelphia, Pa.* (Washington, D.C., 1942), 58; Sander A. Diamond, *The Nazi Movement in the United States, 1924–1941* (Ithaca, N.Y.,

1974), 357 (app. I); U.S. Census Bureau, *Fifteenth Census . . . 1930: Population,* vol. 2, *General Report, Statistics by Subjects* (Washington, D.C., 1933), 383.

8. *Deutsch-Amerikanisches Vereins-Adressbuch für das Jahr 1911. German-American Directory 1911* (Milwaukee, Wis., 1911), passim; *A City within a City* (Philadelphia, 1933), 9 (in Balch). The figures given here are for categories that seem most clearly comparable between the two lists.

9. *Elfte Staats-Konvention des Deutsch-Amerikanischen Zentral-Bundes von Pennsylvanien. Abgehalten am 18. und 19. Juni 1910. In der Männerchor Halle zu Reading, Penna.* (N.p., [1910]), 30; Fred Gartner, President [Deutsch-Amerikanischer Zentralbund von Pennsylvanien], to John Wanamaker [Inc.], Advertising Department, 31 May 1932, in Scrapbook [vol. 1], box 1, PGPC-Balch. These documents show that the Philadelphia branch gave a membership figure of 26,382 individuals—almost all of them belonging to member *Vereine*—in 1910, but claimed an individual membership of more than 35,000 in 1932. It is difficult to regard the latter figure as credible, given that the Philadelphia branch had lost nearly two-thirds of its constituent *Vereine* during the intervening years.

10. The 1925 total is my calculation from a membership list provided in *161. Jahresbericht der Deutschen Gesellschaft von Pennsylvanien für das Jahr 1925* (Philadelphia, 1926), 24–31. The figure of 640 is provided in *165. Jahresbericht der Deutschen Gesellschaft von Pennsylvanien für das Jahr 1929* (Philadelphia, 1930), 5.

11. Harry W. Pfund, *A History of the German Society of Pennsylvania* (Philadelphia, 1944), 21.

12. *151. Jahres-Bericht der Deutschen Gesellschaft von Pennsylvanien für das Jahr 1915* (Philadelphia, 1916), 40; *152. Jahresbericht der Deutschen Gesellschaft von Pennsylvanien für das Jahr 1916* (Philadelphia, 1917), 31; *153. Jahresbericht der Deutschen Gesellschaft von Pennsylvanien für das Jahr 1917* (Philadelphia, 1918), 31; *154. Jahresbericht der Deutschen Gesellschaft von Pennsylvanien für das Jahr 1918* (Philadelphia, 1919), 20; *161. Jahresbericht der Deutschen Gesellschaft 1925,* 33; *166. Jahresbericht der Deutschen Gesellschaft von Pennsylvanien für das Jahr 1930* (Philadelphia, 1931), 42.

13. *Cannstatter Volksfest-Verein, Philadelphia: Geschichte des Vereins von der Gründung in 1873 bis zum Goldenen Jubiläum im September 1923* (Philadelphia, [1923]), 57, 29, 33, 31; "Geschichte des Cannstatter Volksfest-Vereins," in *1873–1949: Diamantenes Jubiläum, Cannstatter Volksfest-Verein* (Philadelphia, [1949]), unpaginated; Otto Breuninger, "100 Jähriges Jubiläum," in *Hundert jähriges Jubiläum, 1972: Cannstatter Volksfest Verein* ([Philadelphia], [1972]), unpaginated.

14. Karl J. R. Arndt and May E. Olson, *The German Language Press of the Americas,* vol. 1, *History and Bibliography 1732–1968: United States of America,* 3d ed. (Munich, 1976), 558. In 1915, the *Morgen-Gazette*'s circulation stood at 35,000, while that of the *Demokrat* totaled 14,000; ibid., 558, 553.

15. Ibid., 558; *City within a City,* 17.

16. Rodman Bailey, Treasurer [John Wanamaker Philadelphia, Inc.] to Austro-American Society of Philadelphia, 24 May 1932, Scrapbook [vol. 2]; and "Letters from Philadelphia Gazette-Democrat Readers with Reference to Wanamaker's Advertisements," Scrapbook [vol. 1], both in box 1, PGPC-Balch. The thirty-four letters are located in Scrapbook [vol. 1], box 1, PGPC-Balch; at least

twenty-seven were signed by female writers, while another was signed by a husband and wife.

17. Two letters stated that their authors were "*langjährige*" readers (readers for a long stretch of years) of the newspaper. In another six letters, the authors declared that they had read the *Gazette-Democrat* for at least twenty years; in four of these cases, the writer had been taking the newspaper for at least thirty years; Scrapbook [vol. 1], box 1, PGPC-Balch.

18. Mrs. W. Dost to Dear Sir, 31 May 1932; and Mrs. A. Castor to Phila. Gazette-Democrat, 21 May 1932; both in Scrapbook [vol. 1], box 1, PGPC-Balch.

19. Castor to Gazette-Democrat, 21 May 1932.

20. Lizabeth Cohen, *Making a New Deal: Industrial Workers in Chicago, 1919–1939* (Cambridge, 1990), 123, 135; *Philadelphia Tageblatt*, 7 June 1924, p. 3; 2 July 1924, p. 4.

21. Cohen, *Making a New Deal*, 125–129, 143; *Philadelphia Gazette-Democrat*, 24 July 1928, pp. 2, 6; *Tageblatt*, 18 June 1924, p. 3. *Gazette-Democrat* citations are to microfilmed holdings in Balch. Philadelphia station WRAX, established in 1930, did offer foreign-language broadcasts for Germans, Italians, eastern European Jews, and Poles. The "lion's share" of this daytime station's programming, however, increasingly was devoted to Italian-language shows; Stefano Luconi, *From "Paesani" to White Ethnics: The Italian Experience in Philadelphia* (Albany, N.Y., 2001), 82.

22. *Gazette-Democrat*, 27 July 1928, p. 1; 26 July 1928, p. 2.

23. *Tageblatt*, 7 April 1924, p. 2. Mention was made of the Kensington Labor Lyceum in *Tageblatt*, 30 April 1924, p. 4, and the *Gazette-Democrat*, 26 July 1928, p. 9; and of the Southwark Labor Lyceum Association in *Tageblatt*, 3 May 1924, p. 8. The *Tageblatt* remained, as its banner proclaimed, the "Official Organ of the United German Trades"; see, e.g., *Tageblatt*, 21 April 1924, p. 1.

24. Arndt and Olson, *German Language Press,* 1: 575. During the immediate postwar period, Philadelphia saw a building-trades strike and a walkout of tugboat and coal handlers on Delaware River piers; Arthur P. Dudden, "The City Embraces 'Normalcy,' 1919–1929," in *Philadelphia: A 300-Year History*, ed. Russell F. Weigley (New York, 1982), 567.

25. *Tageblatt*, 27 May 1924, p. 4. The figures for union local losses derive from a comparison of 1899, 1910, and 1924 listings of constituent UGT unions; see "Deutsche Arbeiter-Organisationen in Philadelphia," *Kalender [des] Philadelphia Tageblatt [für das Jahr] 1899* (Philadelphia, [1899]), 35; and *Tageblatt*, 20 March 1910, p. 5; 7 April 1924, p. 2.

26. *Tageblatt*, 7 April 1924, p. 2; "Deutsche Arbeiter-Organisationen in Philadelphia," 35.

27. Richard F. Hamm, *Shaping the Eighteenth Amendment: Temperance Reform, Legal Culture, and the Polity, 1880–1920* (Chapel Hill, N.C., 1995), 252; Norman H. Clark, *Deliver Us from Evil: An Interpretation of American Prohibition* (New York, 1976), 130.

28. Rich Dochter and Rich Wagner, "Brewerytown, U.S.A.," *Pennsylvania Heritage* 17, no. 3 (1991): 29–30; "Half of One Per Cent Left of Brewerytown," *Evening Ledger*, 15 November 1926, cited in ibid., 30; George J. Beichl, interview by author, 18 March 1998, Philadelphia.

29. Dochter and Wagner, "Brewerytown," 31; Nuala McGann Drescher, "Labor and Prohibition: The Unappreciated Impact of the Eighteenth Amendment," in *Law, Alcohol, and Order: Perspectives on National Prohibition,* ed. David E. Kyvig (Westport, Conn., 1985), 48n, 45–47; *Tageblatt,* 8 April 1924, p. 8.

30. The Germania Turn Verein elected nine officers and four new directors for the year 1921 in December 1920. I was able to link six of these thirteen individuals to *Boyd's Combined City and Business Directory of Philadelphia, 1921* (Philadelphia, 1921). One officer was listed in the directory as an "artist," another as "USA" (presumably, a soldier in the U.S. Army), a third as a machinist, and a fourth as a textile worker. The directors included a machinist and a bartender. The names of the officers and directors appear in the minutes for 5 December 1920, "Protokoll Buch des Germania Turn Verein von Roxborough & Manayunk, Angefangen Oktober 1ten 1914 [Minutes 1914–1928]," 171, in box 9, RTC (referred to hereafter as GTV Minutes 1914–1928).

31. Minutes of 17 April 1921 and 6 June 1921, GTV Minutes 1914–1928, 179, 182.

32. "Dues, 1898–1905" [unpaginated], "Dues 1906–1920" [unpaginated], and, "Dues, 1929–1933," all in box 8, RTC. These membership figures represent adult male members in good standing as of January of each year; for January 1920, the dues roll shows eighty-three members. Membership rolls for the Turn Verein's female auxiliary are not available for the period after 1917.

33. The proportion for 1900 derives from my surname analysis of that year's dues list in "Dues, 1898–1905." I checked the surname of every male member in good standing as of January in each of the following: Elsdon C. Smith, *Dictionary of American Family Names* (New York, 1956); George F. Jones, *German-American Names* (Baltimore, 1990); Horst Naumann, ed., *Das große Buch der Familien Namen. Alter-Herkunft-Bedeutung* (Niedernhausen, Ts., 1994); Hans Bahlow, *Deutsches Namenlexikon* (Munich, 1967); Edward MacLysaght, *The Surnames of Ireland,* 3d ed. (Dublin, 1978); P. H. Reaney and R. M. Wilson, *A Dictionary of English Surnames,* 3d ed. (London, 1991).

34. These proportions stem from my surname analysis of the Turn Verein's membership rolls for 1920 and 1929. For each year, I checked every surname in at least two of the reference works listed in note 33. In 1920, of the club's eighty-three male members, 20 (24.1 percent) had clearly non-German surnames; "Dues 1906–1920." In 1929, twenty-four of the club's fifty-three male members (45.3 percent) had clearly non-German surnames; "Dues, 1929–1933."

35. In 1929, of the club's twenty-four non-German members, two had clearly Irish surnames, six had clearly British surnames, and fourteen had Irish or British surnames. This last category includes many names of English derivation that also came to be used in Ireland (as denoted in MacLysaght, *Surnames of Ireland*). One member had a possibly Italian surname (Massa), while another had a name of Slavic derivation. Significantly, this last name—that of Frank Benescheck—belonged to the Turn Verein's president in 1929; "Dues, 1929–1933."

36. Clark, *Deliver Us from Evil,* 132; minutes of 20 February, 11 July, 19 June, and 26 June, 1921, GTV Minutes 1914–1928, 176, 182–184.

37. Dudden, "City Embraces 'Normalcy,'" 578; Beichl interview; "Maenner-

chor's Beer Seized," news clipping dated 1928, in "Music (except Churches)," Subject Files, GHS.

38. John A. Eichman III, interview by author, 14 March 1998, Philadelphia; minutes of 1 August 1921, GTV Minutes 1914–1928, 186. Craighead is listed as a member in "Dues, 1906–1920."

39. Minutes of 2 May 1921, GTV Minutes 1914–1928, 180; minutes of 5 February 1928, "Minutes, 1928–1945," 3, in box 9, RTC (hereafter GTV Minutes 1928–1945). On the 1921 national Turnfest, see Henry Metzner, *History of the American Turners,* 3d rev. ed. (Rochester, N.Y., 1974), 29.

40. Eichman interview; minutes of 2 December 1928 and 6 January 1929, GTV Minutes 1928–1945, 11–12.

41. Wm. A. Nicolai, District President, to Officers and Board of Directors, Roxborough Germania Turners, 14 April 1942, letter located loose in GTV Minutes 1928–1945.

42. Beichl interview.

43. Oswald Seidensticker and Max Heinrici, *Geschichte der Deutschen Gesellschaft von Pennsylvanien. 1764–1917,* 1. Teil, *Von der Gruendung im Jahre 1764 bis zur Jubelfeier der Republik 1876,* by Oswald Seidensticker; 2. Teil, *Von 1876 bis 1917,* by Max Heinrici (Philadelphia, 1917), 58.

44. These figures derive from a surname analysis of membership lists provided in *Cannstatter Volksfest-Verein: Jahres-Berichte pro 1912* (Philadelphia, n.d.), 13–30 (in Balch); *Cannstatter Volksfest-Verein 1923,* 73–101.

45. William G. Moellhoff, "United Singers of Philadelphia," in *Invisible Philadelphia: Community through Voluntary Organizations,* ed. Jean Barth Toll and Mildred S. Gillam (Philadelphia, 1995), 88; *Catholic Standard and Times,* 14 January 1928, p. 2; 11 February 1928, p. 2.

46. *Nord Amerika,* 1 May 1924, p. 1.

47. Ibid.

48. *Nord Amerika,* 8 May 1924, p. 1. This article continues that of May 1, 1924.

49. Philip Gleason, *The Conservative Reformers: German-American Catholics and the Social Order* (Notre Dame, Ind., 1968), 176. The article was written by Rothensteiner for the Central-Verein's press service and presumably was picked up from that service by *Nord Amerika; Nord Amerika,* 1 May 1924, p. 1.

50. Francis Xavier Roth, O.S.A., *History of St. Vincent's Orphan Asylum of Tacony, Philadelphia: A Memoir of its Diamond Jubilee, 1855–1933* (Philadelphia, 1934), 77.

51. These figures represent my calcuations, drawn from the *Archdiocese of Philadelphia, Annual Report* for each German national parish for 1900, 1921, and 1930. German parishes were identified in part through an undated list of "Foreign Churches," item 81.330, folder 81.330, Manuscript Collection 80 (hereafter MSC 80), Dougherty Papers. On this list, see chapter 3, note 20.

52. Arndt and Olson, *German Language Press,* 1: 566.

53. Roth, *St. Vincent's,* 77.

54. Beichl interview.

55. Eichman interview.

56. Beichl interview.

57. Eichman interview.

58. See chapter 3, note 21.

59. Communing membership for 1930 was calculated from figures provided in "Parochial Report of the German Conference," *Minutes of the Proceedings of the 183rd Annual Convention of the Evangelical Lutheran Ministerium of Pennsylvania and the Adjacent States . . . June 2 to 5, 1930* ([Philadelphia], [1930]), 192.

60. *Lutherischer Herold,* 7 March 1929, p. 4. While the *Herold* was the German-language organ of the United Lutheran Church in America, of which the Pennsylvania Ministerium was only one synod, the newspaper was published in Philadelphia, and Kline's article elsewhere referred specifically to that city's German Lutheran congregations. The author may himself have been Otto Kleine, the pastor of Philadelphia's Christ German Lutheran Church; see "Parochial Report of the German Conference," 192.

61. *Lutherischer Herold,* 7 March 1929, p. 4.

62. Esther Schuchard Browne, interview by author, 11 June 1996, Philadelphia.

63. Alberta Schilling Brosz, interview by author, 28 May 1996, Philadelphia.

64. Browne interview.

65. *The Bulletin Year Book and Citizens' Manual, 1925* (Philadelphia, 1925), 272; *Minutes of the Proceedings of the 173rd Annual Convention of the Evangelical Lutheran Ministerium of Pennsylvania and the Adjacent States . . . June 1 to 4, 1920* (Philadelphia, [1920]), 194–196.

66. *Tageblatt,* 27 April 1924, p. 2; 25 May 1924, p. 6. The quotation appears in a *Tageblatt* story on the festival that bears all the marks of having been submitted to the newspaper by the Central Alliance's Philadelphia branch.

67. *Parish Calendar, St. Ignatius Church* 3 (November 1922): 1; *Tageblatt,* 9 April 1924, p. 7.

68. "Executive Committee for the Reception of the 'Bremen' Fliers," undated list, and C.P.B. to Geo. W. Elliott, 20 June 1928, both in "Philadelphia *Gazette-Democrat* papers, 1928," box "Correspondence, etc.: 1923–1930," PGPC-HSP; Pfund, *German Society,* 20.

69. Pfund, *German Society,* 19.

70. *St. Ignatius' Monthly Calendar* (April 1921): unpaginated [1]; "Owen Wister Raps Fund for Starving German Children," *Philadelphia Inquirer,* 22 February 1924, news clipping in "Wister, Owen—Novelist—Speeches & Comments," Bulletin Collection.

71. Margaret Zinser, interview by author, 31 March 1998, Philadelphia; *Beehive* 23 (April 1933): 14, 18; *Beehive* 23 (May–June 1933): 15; *Beehive* 23 (October 1933): 19.

CHAPTER TEN
CHANGING NEIGHBORHOODS

1. Caroline Golab, *Immigrant Destinations* (Philadelphia, 1977), 11, 173–175 (app. C), 172 (app. B), 19 (table 4).

2. Ibid., 174 (app. C), 12, 168–169 (app. A).

3. Robert Gregg, *Sparks from the Anvil of Oppression: Philadelphia's African*

Methodists and Southern Migrants, 1890–1940 (Philadelphia, 1993), 13, 24, 33, 14.

4. Lloyd M. Abernethy, "Progressivism, 1905–1919," in *Philadelphia: A 300-Year History,* ed. Russell F. Weigley (New York, 1982), 527–529; Maxwell Whiteman, "Philadelphia's Jewish Neighborhoods," in *The Peoples of Philadelphia: A History of Ethnic Groups and Lower-Class Life, 1790–1940,* ed. Allen F. Davis and Mark H. Haller (Philadelphia, 1973), 246–247, 250; Richard A. Varbero, "Philadelphia's South Italians in the 1920s," in *Peoples of Philadelphia,* ed. Davis and Haller, 269–270.

5. Gregg, *Sparks from the Anvil,* 25, 28.

6. Ibid., 27; Abernethy, "Progressivism, 1905–1919," 532.

7. George Morgan, *The City of Firsts: Being a Complete History of the City of Philadelphia from Its Founding, in 1682, to the Present Time* (Philadelphia, 1926), 305.

8. Proportions and rankings calculated from figures provided in U.S. Department of Commerce, Bureau of the Census, *Fourteenth Census of the United States, Taken in the Year 1920,* vol. 3, *Population, 1920: Composition and Characteristics of the Population by States* (Washington, D.C., 1922), 896–899. The published census for 1920 does not provide population figures for second-generation German immigrants at the ward level.

9. See, for example, *Philadelphia Morgen-Gazette,* 30 October 1915, p. 6.

10. These census tracts are Tracts 42-B and 42-Q in the Forty-second Ward, and 29-C in the Twenty-ninth Ward. I calculated percentages for them from an unpublished compilation of Census Bureau work sheets tabulating statistics for Philadelphia census tracts in 1930. A photostat of the compilation is located in box 1, "1930 Census: Census Tracts, Table 1," while photostats of the worksheets are located in box 2, "1930 Census: Census Tracts, Table 2," both boxes in possession of the Government Publications Department, FLP.

11. *1870–1940: Seventieth Anniversary, St. Paul's Evangelical Lutheran Congregation, Fifth Street and Nedro Avenue, Philadelphia, Pa.* (Philadelphia, 1940), 8 (in LACP).

12. *Philadelphia Inquirer,* 19 February 1995, p. L10; George J. Beichl, interview by author, 18 March 1998, Philadelphia; Kathleen Neils Conzen, "Immigrants, Immigrant Neighborhoods, and Ethnic Identity: Historical Issues," *Journal of American History* 66 (December 1979): 614.

13. These industrial uses are evident in ward-level maps; see George W. Bromley and Walter S. Bromley, *Atlas of the City of Philadelphia (Central): South Street to Lehigh Ave., Wards 5 to 20, 28, 29, 31, 32, 37 & 47; from Actual Surveys and Official Plans* (Philadelphia, 1922), plates 10, 11, 16, 17. A city planning commission study described Northern Liberties as undergoing "a boom in industrial construction and expansion . . . through the 1920s"; Mary L. Dankanis, "1920 and Beyond," in *Guide to Northern Liberties,* ed. Mary L. Dankanis, Thomas S. Mitros, Marjori Viguers, Robin Widing, and Thomas Widing (Philadelphia, 1982), 43.

14. Of the 1,412 working individuals in the 1920 Girard Avenue district sample, 1 percent (±0.6 percent) were employers, 9.8 percent (±3.5 percent) were self-employed—"working on own account," in the language of the census—and

89.2 percent (±3.8 percent) were wage or salary workers. Of the 3,890 working individuals in the 1920 Germantown sample, 5 percent (±1.2 percent) were employers, 9.3 percent (±1.4 percent) were self-employed, and 85.7 percent (±1.8 percent) were wage or salary workers. The figures in parentheses are 95 percent confidence intervals for each proportion, corresponding to the 0.05 level of significance (see appendix).

15. In 1900, the Sixteenth and Seventeenth wards had a combined population of 33,696. See U.S. Census Office, *Census Reports: Twelfth Census of the United States, Taken in the Year 1900,* vol. 1, *Population* (Washington, D.C., 1901–1902), 345; U.S. Census Bureau, *Fourteenth Census,* vol. 3, *Population, 1920,* 897.

16. *Archdiocese of Philadelphia, Annual Report of the Church of St. Peter's, Philadelphia; Religious and Financial Statistics, January 1, 1900, to January 1, 1901; Archdiocese of Philadelphia, Annual Report of the St. Peter's Church . . . Religious and Financial Statistics, January 1, 1921, to January 1, 1922.*

17. "Parochial Statistics for the Year Ending Whit-Sunday, 1900," *Minutes of the 153d Annual Convention of the Evangelical Lutheran Ministerium of Pennsylvania and Adjacent States . . . 1900* (Philadelphia, n.d.), 114; "Philadelphia German Conference—Statistics for the Year Ending May 1, 1920," *Minutes of the Proceedings of the 173rd Annual Convention of the Evangelical Lutheran Ministerium of Pennsylvania and the Adjacent States . . . June 1 to 4, 1920* (Philadelphia, [1920]), 200; "Parochial Report of the German Conference," *Minutes of the Proceedings of the 183rd Annual Convention of the Evangelical Lutheran Ministerium of Pennsylvania and the Adjacent States . . . June 2 to 5, 1930* ([Philadelphia], [1930]), 192. St. Paul's communing membership in 1900 stood at 500.

18. *Inner Missionary* 4 (April 1920): 2; *Inner Missionary* 9 (January–February 1926): 4; John T. McGreevy, *Parish Boundaries: The Catholic Encounter with Race in the Twentieth-Century Urban North* (Chicago, 1996), 18–20, 35. *Inner Missionary* citations are to holdings at LTSP.

19. Federal Writers' Project, Works Progress Administration, *WPA Guide to Philadelphia* (reprint, Philadelphia, 1988; originally published as *Philadelphia: A Guide to the Nation's Birthplace* [Philadelphia, 1937]), 102; Joseph Gruninger, interview by author, 12 June 1996, Philadelphia.

20. William B. Richter, *North of Society Hill, and Other Stories* (North Quincy, Mass., 1970), 119–120, 53, 30; Philadelphia Chamber of Commerce, Americanization Committee, *Aid for Foreign Born* ([Philadelphia], [1925]), 20. On the evolution of Marshall Street, see Elaine Krasnow Ellison and Elaine Mark Jaffe, eds., *Voices from Marshall Street: Jewish Life in a Philadelphia Neighborhood, 1920–1960* (Philadelphia, 1994).

21. Gruninger interview.

22. Form no. 2, "Ajax Metal Co., Phila., Pa," box 1 "AB-AN," PPS; Form no. 2, "Dornan Bros., Phila., Pa.," box 11 "DI-DU," PPS.

23. Gruninger interview.

24. This analysis compares surnames given in "Fall or Block Collection," *St. Michael's Kalendar* 4 (December 1901): 25–38, and in "Christmas, Monthly and Offertory Collections," *Parish Monthly Calendar, Church of St. Michael* 8 (Feb-

ruary 1933): 12–21. On the 1901 list, see chapter 2. Of the 1,102 donors on the 1933 list, 234 (21 percent) had clearly non-Irish surnames. This figure includes 111 donors with clearly German surnames, thirty-four individuals with clearly British (English, Scottish, or Welsh) surnames, and nineteen with last names clearly of either British or German derivation. Thirty individuals had surnames that were clearly non-Irish but could not otherwise be classified. In analyzing this list, I checked each name that appeared either questionably Irish or non-Irish in at least one of the following: Elsdon C. Smith, *Dictionary of American Family Names* (New York, 1956); Edward MacLysaght, *The Surnames of Ireland,* 3d ed. (Dublin, 1978); P. H. Reaney and R. M. Wilson, *A Dictionary of English Surnames,* 3d ed. (London, 1991); George F. Jones, *German-American Names* (Baltimore, 1990); Horst Naumann, ed., *Das große Buch der Familien Namen. Alter-Herkunft-Bedeutung* (Niedernhausen, Ts., 1994); Hans Bahlow, *Deutsches Namenlexikon* (Munich, 1967).

25. Gruninger interview.

26. These figures represent my analysis of "Christmas Collection, 1920," *Parish Messenger of St. Peter's Church* 10 (February 1921): 11–16. Of the 127 individuals on this collection list with clearly non-German surnames, thirty had names that were clearly Irish, twelve had names that were clearly British (English, Welsh, or Scottish), and twenty-five had names of either Irish or British derivation. Surnames among the forty clearly Slavic donors included Kleska, Krotak, Laskowski, Lobasuk, Mordavsky, Palecko, Pluchinski, Rusnak, Skorupka, Winiecki, and Zastko, among others. In analyzing the list, I checked each name that appeared either questionably German or non-German in at least one and usually two or more of the six surname dictionaries cited in note 24.

27. I derived these figures from a surname analysis of donors to the 1930 Christmas collection listed in "Christmas and School Collections," *Parish Monthly Calendar, St. Peter's Church* 6 (February 1931): 19–24. Individuals on the Christmas collection list with clearly or possibly German surnames numbered 621, or 80.5 percent of all donors. Of the 150 contributors with clearly non-German surnames, twenty-six had names that were clearly Irish, nineteen had names that were clearly British, thirty-two had names of either Irish or British derivation, and forty-six had clearly Slavic last names. Three individuals had Italian surnames. I checked every name that appeared either questionably German or non-German in at least one and usually two or more of the six surname dictionaries cited in note 24.

28. Compare, e.g., *St. Peter's Parish Messenger* 1 (April 1912), and *Parish Messenger of St. Peter's Church* 10 (February 1921).

29. *Parish Messenger of St. Peter's Church* 10 (February 1921), 7; Gruninger interview.

30. *Parish Messenger of St. Peter's Church* 10 (February 1921): 9; *Parish Monthly Calendar, St. Peter's Church* 4 (April 1927): 25–27; *Archdiocese of Philadelphia, Annual Report of the St. Peter's Church . . . Religious and Financial Statistics, January 1, 1930, to January 1, 1931.*

31. Helen U., interview by Robert Zecker, 18 July 1996, Philadelphia. I am grateful to Robert Zecker for making available to me transcribed excerpts from interviews he conducted with Slovak immigrants and their children for his doctoral dissertation, "'All Our Own Kind Here': The Creation of a Slovak-Ameri-

can Community in Philadelphia, 1890–1945" (Ph.D. diss., University of Pennsylvania, 1998). Following Zecker's agreement with his interviewees, I identify them by their first names and the initial letter of their last names.

32. *St. Peter's Parish Messenger* 1 (April 1912): 29–30; Helen U. interview.

33. *1904–1976: Diamond Jubilee, St. Peter the Apostle Church, Philadelphia, Pennsylvania* ([Philadelphia], [1976]), unpaginated (in PAHRC); Gruninger interview.

34. Gruninger interview; Helen U. interview; George N., interview by Robert Zecker, 14 May 1996, Lafayette Hill, Pa.

35. U.S. Department of Commerce, Bureau of the Census, *Thirteenth Census of the United States, Taken in the Year 1910*, vol. 3, *Population, 1910: Reports by States . . . Nebraska-Wyoming* (Washington, D.C., 1913), 549; U.S. Census Bureau, *Fourteenth Census*, vol. 3, *Population, 1920*, 897.

36. George W. Bromley and Walter S. Bromley, *Atlas of the City of Philadelphia, 22nd Ward: From Actual Surveys and Official Plans* (Philadelphia, 1923; corrected 1924, 1927, 1928), plates 2–6, 14, 9; E. Digby Baltzell, *Philadelphia Gentlemen: The Making of a National Upper Class* (Glencoe, Ill., 1958; reprint, Chicago, 1971), 197–198, 200–201.

37. Richard R. Wright Jr., *The Negro in Pennsylvania* (Philadelphia, 1912), 64–65, cited in Gregg, *Sparks from the Anvil*, 23, 21n; Armstrong Association of Philadelphia, *A Study of Living Conditions among Colored People in Towns in the Outer Part of Philadelphia and in Other Suburbs both in Pennsylvania and New Jersey* ([Philadelphia], 1915), 28–29, 6, item 364–21, folder 364–21, box 364–365, Pamphlet Collection, UA; *Official Catholic Directory, Anno Domini, 1930, of the Archdiocese of Philadelphia* (Philadelphia, [1930]), 51.

38. *Germantown Independent-Gazette*, 18 May 1900, p. 8; "Italian School to be Dedicated," news clipping dated 27 August 1914, in "Italians," Subject Files, GHS; *Independent-Gazette*, 22 July 1920, p. 1; typed transcription of news clipping, "Italians Now Have a Building and Loan Association," *Germantown Guide*, 18 March 1920, in "Italians," Subject Files, GHS; *Independent-Gazette*, 22 July 1920, p. 1.

39. "Maennerchor's Beer Seized," news clipping dated 1928, in "Music (except Churches)," Subject Files, GHS; "Philadelphia German Conference—Statistics," *Proceedings of the Ministerium, 1920*, 200; "Parochial Report of the German Conference," *Proceedings of the Ministerium, 1930*, 193; *1855–1925: Fest-Nummer des St. Thomas-Boten zur Feier des 70jaehrigen Bestehens und Wiederweihe der renovierten Ev.-Luth. St. Thomas-Kirche, Herman und Morton Strasse, Germantown, Phila.* (Philadelphia, 1925), 8, located loose in "Lutheran Church" box 1, PBC.

40. *Business Men's Association of Germantown: Directory of Membership Classified as Individuals and Business Organizations* ([Philadelphia], 1928), 1–8, located in folder 5, box 20, BMAG-UA.

41. Figures derived from my surname analysis of the donor list, "Easter Collection," *Parish Monthly Calendar, Church of St. Vincent De Paul* 5 (May 1930): 18–23.

42. Margaret Zinser, interview by author, 31 March 1998, Philadelphia.

43. *Federation News* 9 (June 1924): 4; *1877–1922: Thirty-fifth Anniversary of*

Winona Council, No. 63, Order Independent Americans . . . ([Philadelphia], [1922]); and *Local Laws of Washington Camp No. 345 Pa., Patriotic Order Sons of America . . . Germantown, Philadelphia* (Philadelphia, 1907); all located loose in "Secret Societies" box 1, PBC; *Proceedings of the Sixty-First Annual Session, Pennsylvania State Camp, P.O.S. of A., Held at Philadelphia, Pennsylvania, August 24, 25, 26, 1926* (Philadelphia, [1926]), 358; Edward W. Hocker, *Germantown, 1683–1933: The Record That a Pennsylvania Community Has Achieved in the Course of 250 Years; Being a History of the People of Germantown, Mount Airy, and Chestnut Hill* (Philadelphia, 1933), 218.

44. Philip Jenkins, *Hoods and Shirts: The Extreme Right in Pennsylvania, 1925–1950* (Chapel Hill, N.C., 1997), 67, 76, 72.

CHAPTER ELEVEN
MIDDLE-CLASS GERMANS: AMERICAN IDENTITY AND THE "STOCK" OF "OUR FOREFATHERS"

1. *Lutherischer Herold,* 11 April 1929, p. 15. On the final implementation in 1929 of the national origins system called for under the Johnson-Reed Act of 1924, see Robert A. Divine, *American Immigration Policy, 1924–1952* (New Haven, Conn., 1957), chap. 2.

2. *Proceedings of the Sixty-First Annual Session, Pennsylvania State Camp, P.O.S. of A., Held at Philadelphia, Pennsylvania, August 24, 25, 26, 1926* (Philadelphia, [1926]), 194; *Philadelphia Tageblatt,* 16 May 1924, p. 4. The second *Tageblatt* quotation is the newspaper's subjunctive paraphrase of Reed's statement.

3. Gary Gerstle, "Liberty, Coercion, and the Making of Americans," *Journal of American History* 84 (September 1997): 557; John Higham, *Strangers in the Land: Patterns of American Nativism, 1860–1925,* 2d rev. ed. (New York, 1981), 330.

4. John A. Eichman III, interview by author, 14 March 1998, Philadelphia; Esther Schuchard Browne, interview by author, 11 June 1996, Philadelphia; George J. Beichl, interview by author, 18 March 1998, Philadelphia.

5. Gary Gerstle, *American Crucible: Race and Nation in the Twentieth Century* (Princeton, N.J., 2001), 4 and passim. For a discussion of the recent literature on whiteness and American identity, see chapter 5.

6. Higham, *Strangers in the Land,* 313–315, 319–324; Matthew Frye Jacobson, *Whiteness of a Different Color: European Immigrants and the Alchemy of Race* (Cambridge, Mass., 1998), 83.

7. On this point, see Gerstle, *American Crucible,* 166–167.

8. Naaman H. Keyser, "Settlement of Germantown," *Beehive* 3 (October 1922): 6; *Tageblatt,* 20 May 1924, p. 4. A speaker at a German-American Central Alliance of Pennsylvania function in 1924 similarly declared that the "Nordic storm" roared in the German language; *Tageblatt,* 10 June 1924, p. 5.

9. "The Man on the Corner," *Germantown Independent-Gazette,* news clipping dated 1914; and "Seventieth Birthday of Junior Mechanics," news clipping dated 1923, both in folder "Secret Societies," "Secret Societies" box 2, PBC; *Fed-*

eration News 1 (June 1915): 1. Scattered issues of the *Federation News* are located loose in "Secret Societies" box 1, PBC.

10. *Federation News* 1 (June 1915): 2, 4; *Federation News* 9 (March 1924): 4; *Federation News* 9 (June 1924): 4.

11. *Federation News* 9 (June 1924): 4; *Federation News* 9 (March 1924): 4.

12. These were Bumm, Klein, and Beitenman; U.S. Department of Commerce, Bureau of the Census, Fourteenth Census of the United States (1920), Population Schedules for Philadelphia County, Microfilm, NAP, Enumeration District 1330, p. 7a (Bumm); E.D. 569, pp. 2a–2b (Klein); E.D. 569, p. 5a (Beitenman). Citations below to the 1920 manuscript census for Philadelphia are given as Philadelphia Census Schedules (1920).

13. Vogelsang was listed as a federation "brother" in *Federation News* 9 (June 1924): 3. He was born in Pennsylvania of a German-born mother and a German-speaking, Swiss-born father; Philadelphia Census Schedules (1920), E.D. 574, p. 11a. Zimmerman ran an advertisement identifying himself as a Washington Council member in *Federation News* 1 (June 1915): 4; both of his parents were German-born; Philadelphia Census Schedules (1920), E.D. 582, p. 5b. On Kaplan's background, see chapter 2.

14. *Federation News* 1 (June 1915): 3; *Beehive* 2 (June 1922): 10.

15. Kaplan was listed as chairman of the July Fourth committee in 1908, 1916, 1917, 1918, 1919, 1920, and 1922, and may have held the same post in other years. See *Independent-Gazette*, 5 June 1908, p. 1; "Committees for 1916" and "Committees for Year 1917," in folder 44, "Board of Directors, Committee Appointments, 1913–1929," box 4, URB47, BMAG-UA; *Songs Being Sung by the Germantown Center of the Liberty Sing Commission of the War Camp Community Service . . .* ([Philadelphia], [1918]), cover; Minutes of the Fourth of July Committee, 27 May 1919 and 14 June 1920, in folder 86, "Fourth of July Committee, 1919–1920," box 7, BMAG-UA; *Beehive* 2 (June 1922): 10.

16. Minutes of the Fourth of July Committee, 27 May 1919, folder 86, box 7, BMAG-UA; *Federation News* 1 (June 1915): 4, 3.

17. Higham, *Strangers in the Land,* 57–58; U.S. Immigration Commission, *Statements and Recommendations Submitted by Societies and Organizations Interested in the Subject of Immigration,* Reports of the Immigration Commission, vol. 41, 61st Cong., 3d sess., S. Doc. 764, serial 5881 (Washington, D.C., 1911), 15–30, 325.

18. *Camp News* 57 (March 1924): 2, 4; *Camp News* 57 (April 1924): 10, 1 (quotation); *Camp News* 57 (May 1924): 4, 15.

19. *Proceedings of the Fifty-Fifth Annual Sessions, Pennsylvania State Camp, P.O.S. of A., Held at Harrisburg, Pennsylvania, August 24, 25 and 26, 1920* (Johnstown, Pa., [1920]), 318–323. A complete list of recording secretaries in 1920 is given in the closing (unpaginated) pages of ibid. Names of recording secretaries are also listed in a directory in *Camp News* 57 (April 1924): 18–19. Camps were included at their own initiative and expense in the 1924 directory, which, therefore, likely did not name every Philadelphia camp that year.

20. Examples of such German-surnamed officers with native-born parents in 1924 include Charles B. Fritz, William W. Stanger, and Albert P. Zink; see Philadel-

phia Census Schedules (1920), E.D. 1572, p. 6a (Fritz); E.D. 1337, p. 1a (Stanger); E.D. 378, p. 6a (Zink).

21. Hammer and Schmidt are listed in *Camp News* 57 (April 1924): 18; Rasener and Baumert appear in the camp list in *Proceedings of the Pennsylvania State Camp, 1920*. For their parentage and occupations, see Philadelphia Census Schedules (1920), E.D. 1559, p. 13b (Hammer); E.D. 437, p. 7a (Schmidt); E.D. 1087, p. 38a (Rasener); E.D. 1499, p. 9a (Baumert).

22. *Camp News* 57 (April 1924): 4.

23. "Says Philadelphia Has 76,000 Illiterate Aliens," *Bulletin*, 21 May 1923, news clipping in "Americanization," Bulletin Collection; Americanization Committee, Philadelphia Chamber of Commerce, *Americanization in Philadelphia: A City-Wide Plan of Co-Ordinated Agencies . . . A Manual for Americanization Workers* (Philadelphia, 1923), passim, 8–9, 44; Board of Public Education, School District of Philadelphia, *Annual Report of the Superintendent of Public Schools of the City of Philadelphia, for the Year Ending June 30, 1922* (Philadelphia, 1922), table 41 (unpaginated).

24. Elizabeth Mellor, "The Woman's Club of Germantown: Its Organization and Activities," *Beehive* 9 (November 1925): 1–2. On the shift among white, middle-class club women from literary and charitable interests to politics, see Robyn Muncy, *Creating a Female Dominion in American Reform, 1890–1935* (New York, 1991), 10.

25. *The Woman's Club of Germantown: Year Book, 1919–1920* ([Philadelphia], [1920]), 10; *First Annual Report, 1918–1919: The Woman's Club of Germantown* (Philadelphia, [1919]), 10, 22, 3; *Woman's Club Year Book, 1919–1920*, 25. These Woman's Club annual reports and those cited below are located loose in "Women's Club" box, PBC. Quotations from them are reproduced courtesy of the Germantown Historical Society.

26. *Woman's Club Year Book, 1919–1920*, 25; "Women's Good Work in Americanization," *Independent-Gazette,* news clipping dated 1921, in "Community House," Subject Files, GHS; *Woman's Club of Germantown: Year Book, 1920–1921* ([Philadelphia], [1921]), 24.

27. George J. Sánchez, *Becoming Mexican American: Ethnicity, Culture and Identity in Chicano Los Angeles, 1900–1945* (New York, 1993), 97–106; *Report of the Americanization Committee of Germantown: From May, Nineteen Twenty-one to May, Nineteen Twenty-two* ([Philadelphia], [1922]), unpaginated [3–4], located loose in "Women's Club" box, PBC; *Woman's Club of Germantown: Year Book, 1922–1923* ([Philadelphia], 1923), 27; *Woman's Club of Germantown: Year Book, 1927–1928* ([Philadelphia], 1928), 30.

28. *Woman's Club Year Book, 1920–1921*, 24.

29. *Report of the Americanization Committee of Germantown, 1924–1925* ([Philadelphia], [1925]), unpaginated [3], item 19, folder "659–14 thru 659–22," box 659 "Miscellaneous," Pamphlet Collection, UA.

30. Ibid., unpaginated [6–7]; *Report of the Americanization Committee, 1920–1921,* unpaginated [2] (quotation reproduced courtesy of the Germantown Historical Society).

31. The committee's members are listed in *Report of the Americanization Com-*

mittee, 1924–1925, unpaginated [2]. Occupations of the husbands of nine members were found using *Boyd's Combined City and Business Directory of Philadelphia, 1921* (Philadelphia, 1921); and the 1920 manuscript census. On Kane's husband, Edward V. Kane, see Philadelphia Census Schedules (1920), E.D. 591, p. 9a.

32. Buehler, Bossert, and Ziegler were native whites of native parentage, as was Ida Kane. See, respectively, Philadelphia Census Schedules (1920), E.D. 619, p. 2a; E.D. 1580, p. 3a; E.D. 603, p. 8a; and E.D. 591, p. 9a.

33. Ibid., E.D. 618, p. 2a.

34. *Woman's Club Year Book, 1919–1920,* 6; *Woman's Club Year Book, 1920–1921,* 6. During the 1920s, the Woman's Club annual reports frequently listed only the officers of the Americanization Committee; see *Woman's Club of Germantown: Year Book, 1921–1922* ([Philadelphia], 1922), 6; *Woman's Club Year Book, 1922–1923,* 6; *Woman's Club of Germantown: Year Book, 1926–1927* ([Philadelphia], 1927), 7; *Woman's Club Year Book 1927–1928,* 8. Wallerstein was, however, included on a "List of Contributors to Americanization Work in Germantown, 1921–1922," in *Report of the Americanization Committee, 1921–1922,* unpaginated [6–7]. She was no longer a committee member by 1930, as her name does not appear on a full committee roster provided in the 1930 annual report; *Woman's Club of Germantown: Year Book 1930–1931* ([Philadelphia], 1930), 8.

35. Philadelphia Census Schedules (1920), E.D. 583, p. 4b. One should note that from 1919 to early 1920, the Americanization Committee, or the women that would come to form that group, did include a member with an Italian surname: Mrs. Aladino A. Autilio. Autilio's name did not, however, reappear on the committee's 1920–1921 roster or on that for 1924–1925, suggesting that the committee's self-understanding, as shaped by the rising rhetoric of restriction between 1921 and 1924, would not have had to account for her. See *Woman's Club Year Book 1919–1920,* 6; *Woman's Club Year Book, 1920–1921,* 6; *Report of the Americanization Committee, 1924–1925,* unpaginated [2].

36. *Minutes of the Proceedings of the 173rd Annual Convention of the Evangelical Lutheran Ministerium of Pennsylvania and the Adjacent States . . . June 1 to 4, 1920* (Philadelphia, [1920]), 109–110; Homer Tope Rosenberger, *The Pennsylvania Germans, 1891–1965* (Lancaster, Pa., 1966), 158–159, 491; John A. Kaufmann, ed., *Biographical Record of the Lutheran Theological Seminary at Philadelphia, 1864–1962* (Philadelphia, 1964), 23; *Minutes of the Second Biennial Convention of the United Lutheran Church in America, Washington, D.C., October 19–27, 1920* (N.p., [1920]), 7 (in LTSP).

37. *Lutheran,* 1 May 1924, p. 14, and 17 July 1924, p. 19; Committee on Congregational Interests, *Report of Survey of the Ministerium of Pennsylvania* (Philadelphia, 1927), 55 (in LTSP). *Lutheran* citations are to holdings at LTSP.

38. Margaret Zinser, interview by author, 31 March 1998, Philadelphia.

39. *The Lutheran Settlement Presents Its 40th Anniversary Celebration* ([Philadelphia], [1946]), unpaginated [3, 5] (in LTSP); "History of the Settlement," *Inner Missionary* 19 (January 1936): unpaginated [3]. On the modern Inner Mission movement, see E. Clifford Nelson, ed., *The Lutherans in North America* (Philadelphia, 1975), 197–198, 355–356.

40. *Inner Missionary* 2 (November and December 1916): 4; Richard Moll,

"Mission Efforts in the United Lutheran Church in America Among Italian Immigrants in America, c. 1900–1940," unpublished paper, Lutheran Theological Seminary at Philadelphia, [1991], 10, 10n, 2 (in LTSP); *Inner Missionary* 7 (March [1924]): 1; *Inner Missionary* 15 (August 1932): 3; Pamela Pittenger and Patricia Malinak, "Lutheran Social Mission Society," in *Invisible Philadelphia: Community through Voluntary Organizations,* ed. Jean Barth Toll and Mildred S. Gillam (Philadelphia, 1995), 455. The *Inner Missionary* stated in 1932, however, that the Neighborhood House had been started in 1908; *Inner Missionary* 15 (August 1932): 3.

41. *Inner Missionary* 1 (June 1915): 2; *Lutheran,* 3 July 1924, p. 27; Kaufmann, ed., *Biographical Record,* 41; Luther D. Reed, ed., *The Philadelphia Seminary Biographical Record, 1864–1923* (Mt. Airy, Philadelphia, 1923), 146.

42. *Inner Missionary* 1 (June 1915): 2; Philadelphia Census Schedules (1920), E.D. 682, p. 11a. Hofstetter served as treasurer from 1909 until 1929, although he remained on the society's board thereafter; *Inner Missionary* 11 (April 1929): 4–5.

43. Kaufmann, ed., *Biographical Record,* 90; *Inner Missionary* 14 (June 1931): 1; "History of the Settlement," unpaginated [3]; Philadelphia Census Schedules (1920), E.D. 1549, p. 10a (Bechtold); E.D. 215, p. 15a (Schantz); E.D. 1556, p. 6a (Hess).

44. *Inner Missionary* 4 (May 1920): 7–8; *Inner Missionary* 2 (September–October 1916): 2; *Inner Missionary* 15 (August 1932): 2; *Inner Missionary* 17 (March 1934): 3.

45. *Inner Missionary* 2 (November–December 1916): 4; *Inner Missionary* 2 (February 1917): 1; *Inner Missionary* 3 (March 1919): 3.

46. "History of the Settlement," unpaginated [3]; *Inner Missionary* 4 (October–November 1919): 3. From 1916 until 1922, the newsletter stated that "all communications" should be sent to the settlement's address; see, e.g., *Inner Missionary* 1 (January 1916): 2; *Inner Missionary* 6 (November 1921): 4. Schantz was listed as the publication's editor from 1923 through 1930; *Inner Missionary* 7 (January 1923): 3; *Inner Missionary* 13 (November 1930): unpaginated [5].

47. *Inner Missionary* 1 (March 1916): 3. See also *Inner Missionary* 3 (April 1919): 2.

48. *Inner Missionary* 4 (September 1919): 1–2. On Bechtold's views, see *Inner Missionary* 1 (May 1916): 2–3.

49. *Inner Missionary* 2 (July–August 1916): 3; *Inner Missionary* 5 (June 1920): 6. On the Lutheran Settlement's relations with German-stock residents, see, e.g., one contributor's description of visiting "a typical German family" in *Inner Missionary* 2 (September–October 1916): 4; and a report of assistance given to an elderly woman who was "formerly a member of the German Lutheran Church," in *Inner Missionary* 8 (January–February 1925): 3–4.

50. Bechtold was born in Philadelphia in 1882, while Schantz was born in rural Lehigh County in 1875; Reed, ed., *Biographical Record,* 220, 197; *Inner Missionary* 14 (June 1931): 1.

51. Anna P. Hess, "Fifteen Years at the Martin Luther Neighborhood House," *Inner Missionary* 7 (February 1923): 7. Lillian Cassaday's full name is given in Moll, "Mission Efforts," 2.

52. Browne interview.
53. Eichman interview.

CHAPTER TWELVE
WORKERS AND CATHOLICS: TOWARD THE "WHITE ETHNIC"

1. *St. Ignatius' Monthly Calendar* 2 (September 1921): unpaginated [3]; *Catholic Standard and Times,* 19 April 1924, p. 1.

2. Theodore Hammeke to Most Rev. Archbishop D.J. Dougherty, 1 October 1918, item 80.6036, folder 80.6036–80.6046, Manuscript Collection 80 (hereafter MSC 80), Dougherty Papers. Quotations from the Dougherty Papers are reproduced courtesy of the Philadelphia Archdiocesan Historical Research Center (PAHRC).

3. Joseph Gruninger, interview by author, 12 June 1996, Philadelphia; *Philadelphia Tageblatt,* 28 April 1924, pp. 3, 7.

4. *Tageblatt,* 16 April 1924, p. 4; 6 April 1924, p. 21.

5. Robert Gregg, *Sparks from the Anvil of Oppression: Philadelphia's African Methodists and Southern Migrants, 1890–1940* (Philadelphia, 1993), 25–28; Charles Ashley Hardy III, "Race and Opportunity: Black Philadelphia During the Era of the Great Migration, 1916–1930" (Ph.D. diss., Temple University, 1989), 170.

6. *Tageblatt,* 8 June 1918, p. 4; 28 June 1918, p. 4.

7. Gregg, *Sparks from the Anvil,* 27; Vincent P. Franklin, "The Philadelphia Race Riot of 1918," *Pennsylvania Magazine of History and Biography* 99 (July 1975): 339, 343; *Tageblatt,* 5 July 1917, p. 4; 29 July 1918, p. 8.

8. *Tageblatt,* 1 July 1923, p. 8; 29 June 1924, p. 15; 18 April 1924, p. 4.

9. *Inner Missionary* 3 (March 1919): 1–2; *Tageblatt,* 26 May 1924, p. 8; 25 April 1924, p. 3.

10. Hardy, "Race and Opportunity," 177–181.

11. Sadie Tanner Mossell, "The Standard of Living among One Hundred Negro Migrant Families in Philadelphia," *Annals of the American Academy of Political and Social Science* 98 (November 1921): 178. The census tracts referred to are Tracts 29-C and 29-D. These figures represent my calculations from an unpublished compilation of Census Bureau work sheets tabulating statistics for Philadelphia census tracts in 1930, and from the worksheets themselves; box 1 "1930 Census: Census Tracts, Table 1," and box 2 "1930 Census: Census Tracts, Table 2," both in possession of the Government Publications Department, FLP.

12. George J. Beichl, interview by author, 18 March 1998, Philadelphia.

13. "Henry W. Pletcher As I Knew Him," news clipping dated 18 September 1931, in Pletcher Family File, Biographical Files, GHS.

14. James F. Connelly, ed., *The History of the Archdiocese of Philadelphia* (Philadelphia, 1976), 339, 344, 412; *Standard and Times,* 12 April 1924, p. 1; 17 March 1928, p. 6.

15. Richard A. Varbero, "Philadelphia's South Italians in the 1920s," in *The Peoples of Philadelphia: A History of Ethnic Groups and Lower-Class Life,*

1790–1940, ed. Allen F. Davis and Mark H. Haller (Philadelphia, 1973), 270–271.

16. *Standard and Times,* 14 January 1928, p. 7; 28 January 1928, p. 4. For a Catholic Daughters of America branch with officers bearing Irish and Italian surnames, along with at least one German surname, see ibid., 11 February 1928, p. 2.

17. *Standard and Times,* 24 March 1928, p. 8. Similarly, the weekly listed one Albert J. Becker as a former chairman of the Philadelphia Chapter of the Knights of Columbus; ibid., 7 July 1928, p. 1.

18. These figures represent my calculations from "Foreign Churches," item 81.330, folder 81.330, MSC 80, Dougherty Papers. On this list, see chapter 3, note 20.

19. *Standard and Times,* 29 December 1928, p. 6.

20. Gregg, *Sparks from the Anvil,* 25; U.S. Department of Commerce, Bureau of the Census, *Thirteenth Census of the United States, Taken in the Year 1910,* vol. 3, *Population, 1910: Reports by States . . . Nebraska-Wyoming* (Washington, D.C., 1913), 607; U.S. Department of Commerce, Bureau of the Census, *Fourteenth Census of the United States, Taken in the Year 1920,* vol. 3, *Population, 1920: Composition and Characteristics of the Population by States* (Washington, D.C., 1922), 898; U.S. Department of Commerce, Bureau of the Census, *Fifteenth Census of the United States, 1930: Population,* vol. 3, part 2, *Reports by States . . . Montana-Wyoming* (Washington, 1932), 750. In 1920, the population of St. Ignatius' census tract (tract X-7 of Ward 24) was 29.8 percent black; W. Wallace Weaver, "West Philadelphia: A Study of Natural Social Areas" (Ph.D. diss., University of Pennsylvania, 1930), 154 (table XX).

21. Weaver, "West Philadelphia," 81; *Public Ledger,* 5 November 1914, p. 3. For other examples of such opposition during and after the Great Migration, see Gregg, *Sparks from the Anvil,* 27; and Hardy, "Race and Opportunity," 179–181.

22. Hammeke to Dougherty, 25 July 1920 and 27 July 1920, both in item 80.6039, folder 80.6036–80.6046, MSC 80, Dougherty Papers.

23. *Archdiocese of Philadelphia, Annual Report of the St. Ignatius Church . . . Religious and Financial Statistics, January 1, 1921, to January 1, 1922; Archdiocese of Philadelphia, Annual Report of the St. Ignatius' Church . . . Religious and Financial Statistics, January 1, 1927, to January 1, 1928;* Connelly, ed., *History of the Archdiocese,* 370. In the early 1920s, Dougherty had Dever conduct a census of black Catholics in the archdiocese, and he apparently sent the priest on a tour of the South to examine race relations among Catholics there; ibid., 368; V. A. Dever to D. Cardinal Dougherty, 29 April 1924; and Dever to Dougherty, 19 May 1923, both in item 80.4643, folder 80.4643, MSC 80, Dougherty Papers.

24. Connelly, ed., *History of the Archdiocese,* 370; Dever to Dougherty, 25 July 1928; and Dougherty to Dever, 27 July 1928 (quotation); both in item 80.4643, folder 80.4643, MSC 80, Dougherty Papers.

25. Hammeke to Dougherty, 27 July 1920.

26. These figures represent my analysis of the list provided in "Block Collection 1921," *St. Ignatius' Monthly Calendar* 2 (November 1921): unpaginated. I checked every name on the list that appeared either questionably German or non-German in at least one and usually two or more of the following: Elsdon C. Smith, *Dic-*

tionary of American Family Names (New York, 1956); George F. Jones, *German-American Names* (Baltimore, 1990); Horst Naumann, ed., *Das große Buch der Familien Namen. Alter-Herkunft-Bedeutung* (Niedernhausen, Ts., 1994); Hans Bahlow, *Deutsches Namenlexikon* (Munich, 1967); Edward MacLysaght, *The Surnames of Ireland,* 3d ed. (Dublin, 1978); P. H. Reaney and R. M. Wilson, *A Dictionary of English Surnames,* 3d ed. (London, 1991).

27. Hammeke to Dougherty, 27 July 1920; Dougherty to Hammeke, 2 August 1920, item 80.6039, folder 80.6036–80.6046, MSC 80, Dougherty Papers.

28. Hammeke to Dougherty, 27 July 1920, 25 July 1920.

29. *Standard and Times,* 19 April 1924, p. 1. For examples of relief work, see *St. Ignatius' Monthly Calendar* (May 1921): unpaginated [3]; *St. Ignatius' Monthly Calendar* 3 (November 1922): 3.

30. *St. Ignatius' Monthly Calendar* (April 1921): unpaginated [3]; *St. Ignatius' Monthly Calendar* (March 1921): unpaginated [7, 8]; *Standard and Times,* 19 April 1924, p. 1. For examples of the bulletin's generic nature after Regnery's arrival, see *St. Ignatius' Monthly Calendar* 5 (May 1924); *St. Ignatius' Monthly Calendar* 1 (November 1926); *Parish Monthly Calendar, St. Ignatius Church* 2 (September 1927).

31. See, e.g., *St. Ignatius' Monthly Calendar* 3 (August 1922): unpaginated [1]; *Parish Monthly Calendar, St. Ignatius Church* 2 (December 1927): 11.

32. *St. Ignatius' Monthly Calendar* 3 (March 1922): 7–9; *Standard and Times,* 4 February 1928, p. 4. For other examples of parish minstrel shows, see *Standard and Times,* 3 May 1924, p. 8.

33. On the Catholic Club as an association for young men, see "Our Club Shatters All Previous Records," *St. Ignatius' Monthly Calendar* 2 (December 1921): unpaginated, and the pastor's diary on the previous page.

34. *Parish Monthly Calendar, St. Ignatius Church* 3 (May 1928): 11.

35. John T. McGreevy, *Parish Boundaries: The Catholic Encounter with Race in the Twentieth-Century Urban North* (Chicago, 1996), 36.

36. Ibid., 34; Dever to Dougherty, 19 May 1923; Dever to Dougherty, 10 July 1930, item 80.4643, folder 80.4643, MSC 80, Dougherty Papers.

37. Peter Binzen, *Whitetown, U.S.A.* (New York, 1970), 122, 7, 110–111, 6.

38. For a recent overview, see Elliott Robert Barkan, *And Still They Come: Immigrants and American Society, 1920 to the 1990s* (Wheeling, Ill., 1996), 146–151. Michael Novak, *The Rise of the Unmeltable Ethnics: Politics and Culture in the Seventies* (New York, 1971), was the revival's most influential manifesto.

39. Scholars who see enduring aspects to the revival include Barkan, *And Still They Come,* 146–151; and Rudolph J. Vecoli, "Return to the Melting Pot: Ethnicity in the United States in the Eighties," *Journal of American Ethnic History* 5 (Fall 1985): 7–20. Skeptics include Stephen Steinberg, *The Ethnic Myth: Race, Ethnicity, and Class in America* (New York, 1981); Herbert J. Gans, "Symbolic Ethnicity: The Future of Ethnic Groups and Cultures in America," *Ethnic and Racial Studies* 2 (January 1979): 1–20; and Richard D. Alba, *Ethnic Identity: The Transformation of White America* (New Haven, Conn., 1990). See Barkan, *And Still They Come,* 239–242, for an overview of this debate.

40. McGreevy, *Parish Boundaries,* 232 (quotation); Barry Goldberg and Colin Greer, "American Visions, Ethnic Dreams: Public Ethnicity and the Sociological

Imagination," *Sage Race Relations Abstracts* 15 (1990): 30 (quotation); Barkan, *And Still They Come,* 148.

41. Arnold R. Hirsch, *Making the Second Ghetto: Race and Housing in Chicago, 1940–1960* (Cambridge, 1983; 2d ed., Chicago, 1998); Thomas J. Sugrue, *The Origins of the Urban Crisis: Race and Inequality in Postwar Detroit* (Princeton, N.J., 1996); McGreevy, *Parish Boundaries.*

42. Stefano Luconi, *From "Paesani" to White Ethnics: The Italian Experience in Philadelphia* (Albany, N.Y., 2001), 156, 127–128, 133–142; John F. Bauman, *Public Housing, Race, and Renewal: Urban Planning in Philadelphia, 1920–1974* (Philadelphia, 1987), 160–169.

CONCLUSION
PLURALISM, NATIONALISM, RACE, AND THE FATE OF GERMAN AMERICA

1. Erich Uhlenbrock, "Steuben Day Observance Association of Philadelphia and Vicinity," in *Invisible Philadelphia: Community through Voluntary Organizations,* ed. Jean Barth Toll and Mildred S. Gillam (Philadelphia, 1995), 1130; William G. Moellhoff, "United Singers of Philadelphia," in ibid., 89.

2. James M. Bergquist, "Three Centuries of German-American Organizational Life," in Toll and Gillam, eds., *Invisible Philadelphia,* 85–86; Karl J. R. Arndt and May E. Olson, *The German Language Press of the Americas,* vol. 1, *History and Bibliography 1732–1968: United States of America,* 3d ed. (Munich, 1976), 574–575; Eugene P. Willging and Herta Hatzfeld, *Catholic Serials of the Nineteenth Century in the United States: A Descriptive Bibliography and Union List,* 2d series, part 5, *Pennsylvania* (Washington, D.C., 1964), 69.

3. George J. Beichl, interview by author, 18 March 1998, Philadelphia; Joseph Gruninger, interview by author, 12 June 1996, Philadelphia; *1842–1992: Celebrating 150 Years: St. Peter the Apostle Parish, Philadelphia, Pennsylvania* ([Philadelphia], [1992]), unpaginated (in author's possession).

4. Richard D. Alba, *Ethnic Identity: The Transformation of White America* (New Haven, Conn., 1990), 30, 59.

5. Alberta Schilling Brosz, interview by author, 28 May 1996, Philadelphia; Beichl interview.

6. Philip Jenkins, *Hoods and Shirts: The Extreme Right in Pennsylvania, 1925–1950* (Chapel Hill, N.C., 1997), 137, 139, 145. Jenkins provides the best profile of the Philadelphia Bund, and my description relies heavily on his account.

7. Ibid., 157–164; Sander A. Diamond, *The Nazi Movement in the United States, 1924–1941* (Ithaca, N.Y., 1974), 328–332, 322.

8. Jenkins, *Hoods and Shirts,* 143n, 143.

9. Diamond, *Nazi Movement,* 147, 154, 156; Jenkins, *Hoods and Shirts,* 141, 150, 145, 143.

10. Jenkins, *Hoods and Shirts,* 149, 143; Fred Gartner, President [Deutsch-Amerikanischer Zentralbund von Pennsylvanien], to John Wanamaker [Inc.], Advertising Department, 31 May 1932, in Scrapbook [vol. 1], box 1, PGPC-Balch; Jenkins, *Hoods and Shirts,* 150–151, 77.

11. Jenkins, *Hoods and Shirts,* 150, 159–161.

12. Ibid., 163, 163n.

13. Frederick C. Luebke, *Bonds of Loyalty: German-Americans and World War I* (DeKalb, Ill., 1974), 330; Bergquist, "Three Centuries of German-American Organizational Life," 85; Jenkins, *Hoods and Shirts*, 146.

14. Gary Gerstle, *Working-Class Americanism: The Politics of Labor in a Textile City, 1914–1960* (Cambridge, 1989), 289–290; Esther Schuchard Browne, interview by author, 11 June 1996, Philadelphia; Brosz interview; Beichl interview; Gruninger interview.

15. Browne interview; Uhlenbrock, "Steuben Day Observance Association," 1130; Kathleen Neils Conzen, "Germans," in *Harvard Encyclopedia of American Ethnic Groups*, ed. Stephan Thernstrom (Cambridge, Mass., 1980), 425.

16. The exceptions include Andrew P. Yox, "Decline of the German-American Community in Buffalo, 1855–1925" (Ph.D. diss., University of Chicago, 1983); Don Heinrich Tolzmann, *The Cincinnati Germans after the Great War* (New York, 1987); Stephen J. Shaw, *The Catholic Parish as a Way-Station of Ethnicity and Americanization: Chicago's Germans and Italians, 1903–1939* (Brooklyn, N.Y., 1991); and Ronald H. Bayor, *Neighbors in Conflict: The Irish, Germans, Jews, and Italians of New York City, 1929–1941*, 2d ed. (Urbana, Ill., 1988).

17. My calculations, from figures given in U.S. Census Office, *Census Reports: Twelfth Census of the United States, Taken in the Year 1900*, vol. 1, *Population* (Washington, D.C., 1901–1902), lxix, 796–803.

18. Kathleen Neils Conzen, "Immigrants, Immigrant Neighborhoods, and Ethnic Identity: Historical Issues," *Journal of American History*, 66 (December 1979): 610–611.

19. Shaw, *Catholic Parish*, 66, 131; see also ibid., 68–70. On the Oktoberfest, see Tolzmann, *Cincinnati Germans*, 200, and www.oktoberfestzinzinnati.com (accessed 2 August 2001). On the German Fest, see www.officialmilwaukee.com (accessed 2 August 2001) and www.germanfest.com (accessed 2 August 2001).

20. Conzen, "Germans," 412 (table 3); Nathan Glazer and Daniel Patrick Moynihan, *Beyond the Melting Pot: The Negroes, Puerto Ricans, Jews, Italians, and Irish of New York City* (Cambridge, Mass., 1963), 311 (emphasis in original), 311–313.

21. James M. Bergquist, "German Communities in American Cities: An Interpretation of the Nineteenth-Century Experience," *Journal of American Ethnic History* 4 (Fall 1984): 17, 20–22; Audrey L. Olson, *St. Louis Germans, 1850–1920: The Nature of an Immigrant Community and Its Relation to the Assimilation Process* (New York, 1980), 234–238; Yox, "Decline," 214–215; Guido Andre Dobbert, *The Disintegration of an Immigrant Community: The Cincinnati Germans, 1870–1920* (New York, 1980), 310–311, 431.

22. Luebke, *Bonds of Loyalty*, 279. On the anti-German panic in various Midwestern cities, see Melvin G. Holli, "Teuton vs. Slav: The Great War Sinks Chicago's German *Kultur*," *Ethnicity* 8 (December 1981): 438–439, 444–445; Olson, *St. Louis Germans*, 202–211; Dobbert, *Disintegration*, 369–400; and Tolzmann, *Cincinnati Germans*, 14–17. On Buffalo, see Yox, "Decline," 317–324.

23. Tolzmann, *Cincinnati Germans*, 84, 198; Yox, "Decline," 352. For very dif-

ferent views on the degree of German visibility in Chicago after World War I, compare Holli, "Teuton vs. Slav," 446–447, and Shaw, *Catholic Parish,* 66, 68–70.

24. Hartmut Keil and Heinz Ickstadt, "Elements of German Working-Class Culture in Chicago, 1880 to 1890," in *German Workers' Culture in the United States, 1850 to 1920,* ed. Hartmut Keil (Washington, D.C., 1988), 85; Heinz Ickstadt, "A Tale of Two Cities: Culture and Its Social Function in Chicago during the Progressive Period," in *German Workers' Culture,* ed. Keil, 302, 304–306, 309. Unionized slaughterhouse workers temporarily achieved such common ground at the century's turn; see James R. Barrett, "Americanization from the Bottom Up: Immigration and the Remaking of the Working Class in the United States, 1880–1930," *Journal of American History* 79 (December 1992): 1010, 1010n.

25. Lizabeth Cohen, *Making a New Deal: Industrial Workers in Chicago, 1919–1939* (Cambridge, 1990), 40–46, 24–26, 357. On the "culture of unity" and the role of mass culture, see ibid., chap. 8 and passim.

26. Shaw, *Catholic Parish,* 16, 18, 46, 76–78, 80–81.

27. Ibid., 76–78, 20, 27; Cohen, *Making a New Deal,* 84–87, 90–94. On the weakening of ethnic divisions among white Catholics in Chicago and nationally during the 1940s and after, see John T. McGreevy, *Parish Boundaries: The Catholic Encounter with Race in the Twentieth-Century Urban North* (Chicago, 1996), 80–84.

28. McGreevy, *Parish Boundaries,* 78. Important recent work by Arnold Hirsch has pushed back to the interwar period the broad acceptance of a "white" identity by south and east European immigrants in Chicago. Hirsch here sees the 1920s as a key period, when such immigrants "picked up their 'whiteness' as both a shield" against racial denigration by nativists "and a club" against the city's growing African-American population; Arnold R. Hirsch, "E Pluribus Duo: Learning Race on the Local Level, Chicago, 1900–1930," unpublished manuscript (in author's possession), 33, 4, 22, and passim.

29. McGreevy, *Parish Boundaries,* 107; Arnold R. Hirsch, *Making the Second Ghetto: Race and Housing in Chicago, 1940–1960,* 2d ed. (Chicago, 1998), 197; James R. Barrett and David Roediger, "Inbetween Peoples: Race, Nationality, and the 'New Immigrant' Working Class," *Journal of American Ethnic History* 16 (Spring 1997): 31–32, 29; Thomas Lee Philpott, *The Slum and the Ghetto: Immigrants, Blacks, and Reformers in Chicago, 1880–1930* (New York, 1978; reprint, Belmont, Calif., 1991), 195–197. On the ethnic nature of mobs in the 1919 riot, compare William M. Tuttle, Jr., *Race Riot: Chicago in the Red Summer of 1919* (New York, 1970; reprint, Urbana, Ill., 1996), 266.

30. Hirsch, *Making the Second Ghetto,* 4, 1–39, 41, 53–59.

31. Ibid., 78–85, 187; McGreevy, *Parish Boundaries,* 94–96, 19, 105.

32. Hirsch, *Making the Second Ghetto,* 81; McGreevy, *Parish Boundaries,* 88; Thomas J. Sugrue, *The Origins of the Urban Crisis: Race and Inequality in Postwar Detroit* (Princeton, N.J., 1996), 257, 241, 211. Surnames cited by Sugrue in connection with these associations include the likely German names of Berge and Benzing, as well as names such as Fadanelli, Watson, Kopicko, Clanahan, Twomey, and Beardsley; ibid.

33. McGreevy, *Parish Boundaries,* 228–233; Stephen Steinberg, *The Ethnic*

Myth: Race, Ethnicity, and Class in America (New York, 1981), 51; Gary Gerstle, *American Crucible: Race and Nation in the Twentieth Century* (Princeton, N.J., 2001), 330–335.

34. An exception is Alan Graebner, *Uncertain Saints: The Laity in the Lutheran Church-Missouri Synod, 1900–1970* (Westport, Conn., 1975), which describes internal change in a synod with a strong presence in the urban Midwest.

35. Holli, "Teuton vs. Slav," 410–411; Philpott, *The Slum and the Ghetto,* 165–168, 191–201; Charles H. Anderson, *White Protestant Americans: From National Origins to Religious Group* (Englewood Cliffs, N.J., 1970), 86.

36. M. D. Lichliter, *History of the Junior Order United American Mechanics of the United States of North America* (Philadelphia, 1908), 743.

37. Caroline Golab, *Immigrant Destinations* (Philadelphia, 1977), 174–175.

38. Kathleen Neils Conzen, *Immigrant Milwaukee, 1836–1860: Accommodation and Community in a Frontier City* (Cambridge, Mass., 1976), 12; William Cronon, *Nature's Metropolis: Chicago and the Great West* (New York, 1991), 26. Cronon notes that the first non-Indian occupant of the land along the Chicago River was, in fact, a mulatto trader from Quebec, Jean Baptiste Point du Sable; ibid.

39. Kathleen Neils Conzen, "Mainstreams and Side Channels: The Localization of Immigrant Cultures," *Journal of American Ethnic History* 11 (Fall 1991): 13.

40. Mary C. Waters, *Ethnic Options: Choosing Identities in America* (Berkeley, Calif., 1990), 84–85.

41. Sucheng Chan, *Asian Americans: An Interpretive History* (Boston, 1991), 123–127; George J. Sánchez, *Becoming Mexican American: Ethnicity, Culture and Identity in Chicano Los Angeles, 1900–1945* (New York, 1993), 95; Eileen H. Tamura, *Americanization, Acculturation, and Ethnic Identity: The Nisei Generation in Hawaii* (Urbana, Ill., 1994), 56. For an overview of these exclusionary efforts, see Chan, *Asian Americans,* chaps. 3 and 5.

42. Matthew Frye Jacobson, *Special Sorrows: The Diasporic Imagination of Irish, Polish, and Jewish Immigrants in the United States* (Cambridge, Mass., 1995), 222–227; Stefano Luconi, *From "Paesani" to White Ethnics: The Italian Experience in Philadelphia* (Albany, N.Y., 2001), 39–94; Cohen, *Making a New Deal,* 29, 68–70, 146–147; John Higham, *Strangers in the Land: Patterns of American Nativism, 1860–1925,* 2d rev. ed. (New York, 1981), 215–217.

43. Jacobson, *Special Sorrows,* 223, 225–227; Thomas J. Rowland, "Irish-American Catholics and the Quest for Respectability in the Coming of the Great War, 1900–1917," *Journal of American Ethnic History* 15 (Winter 1996): 22–23, 27.

44. Kerby A. Miller, "Class, Culture, and Immigrant Group Identity in the United States: The Case of Irish-American Ethnicity," in *Immigration Reconsidered: History, Sociology, and Politics,* ed. Virginia Yans-McLaughlin (New York, 1990), 107, 118; Conzen, "Germans," 417–422.

45. For a similar argument, see Kathleen Neils Conzen, "Patterns of German-American History," in *Germans in America: Retrospect and Prospect. Tricentennial Lectures Delivered at the German Society of Pennsylvania in 1983,* ed. Randall M. Miller (Philadelphia, 1984), 32–34.

46. See, e.g., Kathy Peiss, *Cheap Amusements: Working Women and Leisure in Turn-of-the-Century New York* (Philadelphia, 1986); Andrew R. Heinze, *Adapting to Abundance: Jewish Immigrants, Mass Consumption, and the Search for American Identity* (New York, 1990); and Vicki Ruíz, "'Star Struck': Acculturation, Adolescence, and the Mexican American Woman, 1920–1950," in *Building with Our Hands: New Directions in Chicana Studies,* ed. Adela de la Torre and Beatríz M. Pesquera (Berkeley, Calif., 1993).

47. Higham, *Strangers in the Land,* 268, 267; Gerstle, *American Crucible,* 91–93.

48. Gerstle, *American Crucible,* 93–94; Gary Gerstle, "Liberty, Coercion, and the Making of Americans," *Journal of American History* 84 (September 1997): 557; Gerstle, *Working-Class Americanism,* 8. See also Cecilia Elizabeth O'Leary, *To Die For: The Paradox of American Patriotism* (Princeton, N.J., 1999), chap. 12. Jonathan Zimmerman has questioned the power of conformist nationalism; see Zimmerman, "'Each "Race" Could Have Its Heroes Sung': Ethnicity and the History Wars in the 1920s," *Journal of American History* 87 (June 2000): 92–111.

49. April R. Schultz, *Ethnicity on Parade: Inventing the Norwegian American through Celebration* (Amherst, Mass., 1994), 8–9, 51, 115, and passim.

50. Gerstle, *American Crucible,* chap. 8 and passim.

51. See, e.g., Gerstle, *Working-Class Americanism,* 43–47; John Bodnar, *Remaking America: Public Memory, Commemoration, and Patriotism in the Twentieth Century* (Princeton, N.J., 1992), 249.

52. Schultz, *Ethnicity on Parade,* 37–38; Rowland, "Quest for Respectability," 24.

53. Schultz did note that the organizers "successfully set Norwegian Americans apart from the 'unassimilable' southern and eastern Europeans," and that their Norwegian "romantic nationalism" was "not immune" to racism; Schultz, *Ethnicity on Parade,* 92, 101–102.

54. Ibid., 77. For similar language in connection with the centennial, see ibid., 60, 63, 79, 99, 101–102.

55. *Svenska Tribunen-Nyheter,* 6 June 1923, cited in Hirsch, "E Pluribus Duo," 22–23.

56. Gerstle, *American Crucible,* 170, 166, 168.

57. Michael Novak, *The Rise of the Unmeltable Ethnics: Politics and Culture in the Seventies* (New York, 1971), 85. Gerstle, *American Crucible,* chap. 8, offers a version of this reading, as did I in Russell A. Kazal, "Revisiting Assimilation: The Rise, Fall, and Reappraisal of a Concept in American Ethnic History," *American Historical Review* 100 (April 1995): 437–471.

58. Matthew Frye Jacobson, *Whiteness of a Different Color: European Immigrants and the Alchemy of Race* (Cambridge, Mass., 1998), 88, 91–96.

59. Alba, *Ethnic Identity,* 291, 11–14. The idea of a triple melting pot was proposed by Ruby Jo Reeves Kennedy and elaborated on by Will Herberg and Milton Gordon; Ruby Jo Reeves Kennedy, "Single or Triple Melting-Pot? Intermarriage Trends in New Haven, 1870–1940," *American Journal of Sociology* 49 (January 1944): 331–339; Will Herberg, *Protestant-Catholic-Jew: An Essay in*

American Religious Sociology (Garden City, N.Y., 1956); Milton M. Gordon, *Assimilation in American Life: The Role of Race, Religion, and National Origins* (New York, 1964).

60. Alba, *Ethnic Identity*, 321, 301, 305–306; Herbert J. Gans, "Symbolic Ethnicity: The Future of Ethnic Groups and Cultures in America," *Ethnic and Racial Studies* 2 (January 1979): 1–20.

61. Alba, *Ethnic Identity*, 308–309, 73, 70, 315.

62. Ibid., 312–318, 315, 313. Alba borrows the concept of a "group of unhyphenated whites" from Stanley Lieberson, "Unhyphenated Whites in the United States," *Ethnic and Racial Studies* 8 (January 1985): 159–180.

63. Alba, *Ethnic Identity*, 4, 9–10; Gerstle, *American Crucible*, 369–371.

64. Alba, *Ethnic Identity*, 314–318.

65. Ibid., 73, 315, 70–71.

66. The leading recent synthesis of immigration history, John Bodnar's *The Transplanted*, for example, integrates Germans into its analysis of nineteenth-century ethnic life, but makes little reference to them in the early twentieth century; Bodnar, *The Transplanted: A History of Immigrants in Urban America* (Bloomington, Ind., 1987).

67. Conzen, "Patterns," 15.

68. Gerstle, "Liberty, Coercion, and the Making of Americans," 539; Gans, "Symbolic Ethnicity," 15n.

69. Novak, *Rise of the Unmeltable Ethnics*, 55.

Appendix
The Neighborhood Census Samples

1. I thank Mark Stern and Michael Guilfoyle for their considerable assistance in designing, coding, and analyzing these samples, as well as Michael Katz for his advice and guidance. A number of other scholars generously offered advice on the sample design and analysis as it evolved, including Olivier Zunz, Michael White, Samuel Preston, Douglas Massey, Herbert Smith, Ram Cnaan, Steven Ruggles, and William Yancey.

2. Olivier Zunz, *The Changing Face of Inequality: Urbanization, Industrial Development, and Immigrants in Detroit, 1880–1920* (Chicago, 1982), 20–23, 407–419. See also Olivier Zunz, William A. Ericson, and Daniel J. Fox, "Sampling for a Study of the Population and Land Use of Detroit in 1880–1885," *Social Science History* 1 (Spring 1977): 307–332, and Olivier Zunz, "Detroit en 1880: Espace et Ségrégation," *Annales*, no. 1 (January–February 1977): 106–136. I found a useful introduction to sampling theory in Graham Kalton, *Introduction to Survey Sampling* (Beverly Hills, Calif., 1983).

3. More than thirty separate volumes of maps were used in this project. These included George W. Bromley and Walter S. Bromley, *Atlas of the City of Philadelphia* (Philadelphia, 1895; 1901); George W. Bromley and Walter S. Bromley, *Atlas of the City of Philadelphia, 22nd Ward* (Philadelphia, 1899; 1923, corrected to 1928); George W. Bromley and Walter S. Bromley, *Atlas of the City of Philadel-*

phia (Central): South Street to Lehigh Ave., Wards 5 to 20, 28, 29, 31, 32, 37 &
47 (Philadelphia, 1922); Ernest Hexamer, *Insurance Maps of the City of Philadel-*
phia (Philadelphia), vol. 4 (1873, corrected to 1901), vol. 8 (1879, corrected to
1906); Ernest Hexamer and Son, *Insurance Maps of the City of Philadelphia*
(Philadelphia), vol. 4 (1889, corrected to 1903; 1901, corrected to 1918; 1907,
corrected to 1920), vol. 8 (1879, corrected to 1895; 1906, corrected to 1916), vol.
16 (1890, corrected to 1896; 1908; 1908, corrected to 1918; 1908, corrected to
1922), vol. 21 (1893, corrected to 1895; 1893, corrected to 1919; 1916), vol. 28
(1896; 1896, corrected to 1919; 1914; 1914, corrected to 1922), vol. 29 (1896;
1896, corrected to 1914; 1896, corrected to 1919; 1896, corrected to 1922), vol.
33 (1898; 1898, corrected to 1919); Sanborn Map Company, *Insurance Maps of*
Philadelphia, Pennsylvania (New York), vol. 8 (1917), vol. 22 (1926), vol. 23
(1924). The Hexamer atlases are located in the Map Collection of the Social Science and History Department, FLP, and in the Geography and Map Division of
the Library of Congress, Washington, D.C. On Ernest Hexamer, see "Dr. Hexamer's Vater, Ernst Hexamer," in *Das Buch der Deutschen in Amerika,* ed. Max
Heinrici (Philadelphia, 1909), 802–803.

4. For the bevy of coders who helped me to complete the neighborhood samples, please see the acknowledgments.

5. The description of P^* in this and the preceding paragraph is taken from
Douglas S. Massey and Nancy A. Denton, "The Dimensions of Residential Segregation," *Social Forces* 67 (December 1988): 284, 287–289.

6. Zunz, *Changing Face of Inequality,* 421, 422n. Zunz here cites Stephan Thernstrom, *The Other Bostonians* (Cambridge, Mass., 1973), 290–292; Theodore
Hershberg and Robert Dockhorn, "Occupational Classification," *Historical Meth-*
ods Newsletter 9 (March–June 1976): 78–98; and Theodore Hershberg et al.,
"Occupation and Ethnicity in Five Nineteenth-Century Cities: A Collaborative In-
quiry," *Historical Methods Newsletter* 7 (June 1973): 174–216.

7. Zunz, *Changing Face of Inequality,* 424–429 (table A3.2). My thanks to
Walter Licht for making his occupational title lists available to me. The results of
his analysis appear in Walter Licht, *Getting Work: Philadelphia, 1840–1950* (Cambridge, Mass., 1992), 32–33 (table 2.4).

8. *1900. Boyd's Co-Partnership and Residence Business Directory of Philadel-*
phia City (Philadelphia, 1900); *Gopsill's Philadelphia City Directory for 1900*
(Philadelphia, 1900). Historical works consulted included Caroline Golab, *Im-*
migrant Destinations (Philadelphia, 1977); Philip Scranton, *Figured Tapestry:*
Production, Markets, and Power in Philadelphia Textiles, 1885–1941 (Cambridge, 1989); Licht, *Getting Work;* Dorothee Schneider, *Trade Unions and Com-*
munity: The German Working Class in New York City, 1870–1900 (Urbana, Ill.,
1994); and David Brody, *Steelworkers in America: The Nonunion Era* (Cambridge, Mass., 1960; reprint, New York, 1969).

9. Zunz, *Changing Face of Inequality,* 428–433.

10. Ibid., 410–411, 411n.

11. Ibid., 24–26, 410–411.

12. U.S. Census Office, *Census Reports: Twelfth Census of the United States,*
Taken in the Year 1900, vol. 1, *Population* (Washington, D.C., 1901–1902), 639;

U.S. Department of Commerce, Bureau of the Census, *Fourteenth Census of the United States, Taken in the Year 1920*, vol. 3, *Population, 1920: Composition and Characteristics of the Population by States* (Washington, D.C., 1922), 897.

13. Christopher Z. Mooney and Robert D. Duval, *Bootstrapping: A Nonparametric Approach to Statistical Inference* (Newbury Park, Calif., 1993), 1 and passim.

Index